The Clinical Assessment Workbook

Balancing Strengths and Differential Diagnosis

Elizabeth Pomeroy
University of Texas at Austin

Kathryn Wambach
Late of University of Texas at Austin

BROOKS/COLE
CENGAGE Learning™

Australia • Brazil • Japan • Korea • Mexico • Singapore • Spain • United Kingdom • United States

BROOKS/COLE
CENGAGE Learning™

The Clinical Assessment Workbook: Balancing Strengths and Differential Diagnosis
Elizabeth Pomeroy, Kathryn Wambach

Executive Editor: Lisa Gebo

Assistant Editor: Shelley Gesicki

Editorial Assistant: Sheila Walsh

Technology Project Manager: Barry Connolly

Marketing Manager: Caroline Concilla

Marketing Assistant: Mary Ho

Advertising Project Manager: Tami Strang

Signing Representative: Richard Colangelo

Project Manager, Editorial Production: Stephanie Zunich

Print /Media Buyer: Vena Dyer

Permissions Editor: Sue Ewing

Production Service: Gretchen Otto, G&S Typesetters, Inc.

Text Designer: Jeanne Calabrese

Copy Editor: Cynthia Lindlof

Cover Designer: Roger Knox

Compositor: G&S Typesetters, Inc.

For product information and technology assistance, contact us at
Cengage Learning Customer & Sales Support, 1-800-354-9706

For permission to use material from this text or product, submit all requests online at **cengage.com/permissions**
Further permissions questions can be emailed to **permissionrequest@cengage.com**

Library of Congress Control Number: 2002108816

ISBN-13: 978-0-534-57843-5

ISBN-10: 0-534-57843-8

Brooks/Cole
10 Davis Drive
Belmont, CA 94002-3098
USA

Cengage Learning is a leading provider of customized learning solutions with office locations around the globe, including Singapore, the United Kingdom, Australia, Mexico, Brazil, and Japan. Locate your local office at: **international. cengage.com/region**

Cengage Learning products are represented in Canada by Nelson Education, Ltd.

For your course and learning solutions, visit **academic.cengage.com**

Purchase any of our products at your local college store or at our preferred online store **www.ichapters.com**

Printed in the United States of America
11 12 13 14 15   17 16 15 14 13

In Loving Memory of Kate and Holly

Contents

Acknowledgments

As with any large project, the authors are indebted to a number of others for their assistance and support in the process. We are indebted to our colleague, Lori Holleran, for her assistance with material related to Substance-Related Disorders. Her clinical and pedagogical expertise in the area of chemical dependency contributed significantly to the text in this chapter. In addition, we thank her for her support through the final stages of the publishing process. Lisa Gebo, Executive Editor, was invaluable in helping us crystallize vague ideas into a meaningful project and in motivating us through the first draft.

In the home stretch, Shelley Gesicki, Assistant Editor, and Stephanie Zunich, Production Project Manager, shepherded the project through the final stages. A special thanks to Sue Ewing, Cynthia Lindlof, and Gretchen Otto for their assistance through the editing and formatting process. We extend our gratitude to the entire production staff of Brooks/Cole.

We would also like to thank Barbara White, dean of the University of Texas, School of Social Work, whose support through the completion of the first draft of this book and whose encouragement through the difficult issues we faced in the end was invaluable. We are fortunate to be a part of such a collegial faculty.

Authoring a book is a lengthy, time-consuming process and would not be possible without the sustenance that friends and family members provide. For their continuous, unconditional, enthusiastic support and ability to lend an ear when we needed one, we would like to provide a special thanks to Janet Boes, Charles and Loretta Prokop, and all our colleagues at the School of Social Work. Jasper, Oscar, Holly, Lucy, Joy, and Morgan were always by our sides.

We would like to thank the manuscript reviewers who offered helpful suggestions for improving the text: Scott Boyle, University of Utah; Diane Hodge, Radford University; Peter Manoleas, University of California at Berkeley; Kathleen Tunney, Southern Illinois University; and Vicki Vandover, Portland State University. We found their comments most thoughtful and instructive.

A SPECIAL TRIBUTE

The spirit of this book celebrates the life and scholarship of my co-author, Kate Wambach (1951–2001). Kate's unique character, bold irreverence, and ability to think clearly and critically shaped the framework of this text. Her excitement and enthusiasm about the subject matter was exemplified by her active contributions in the field of mental health and teaching. This book is a testament to her continuous, profound influence on all the lives she touched throughout her life.

About the Authors

Elizabeth C. Pomeroy, PhD LMSW-ACP, received her master's degree in social work from the University of North Carolina at Chapel Hill. She has over 18 years of clinical social work experience with children, adolescents, adults, and families in mental health and health settings. She received her PhD in social work from the University of Texas at Austin. She received the university's Outstanding Dissertation Award in social sciences for her research on families of people with HIV/AIDS. For the past 8 years, she has taught clinical assessment and diagnosis at the University of Central Florida and the University of Texas at Austin. Her research interests have focused on the effectiveness of mental health interventions for children, adults, and families, and interventions for individuals infected and affected by HIV/AIDS. She is currently an associate professor and the director of the Bachelor of Social Work program at the University of Texas at Austin.

Kathryn G. Wambach, PhD ACSW, received her master's degree in social work from Florida State University in 1980. She worked in publicly funded mental health and substance abuse treatment facilities for approximately 20 years, focusing primarily on crisis and emergency services. She received her PhD in social work in 1992 from Florida State University. After that time, she was on faculty at the University of Texas at Austin, teaching in both the undergraduate and graduate programs. She was the former director of the Bachelor of Social Work program. Her research interests were focused on the effectiveness of mental health and substance abuse interventions with high-risk populations, including juvenile offenders and persons with serious and persistent mental illnesses.

Introduction

1

CLASSIFICATION SYSTEMS

Along with the use of tools and development of language, classification systems are a distinctively human undertaking. One of the earliest classifications of mental disorders can be traced back to Hippocrates in ancient Greece. This system focused on characteristic symptoms associated with various imbalances in the four humors: phlegm (associated with indifference, loss of interest in usual activities, and sluggishness); blood (associated with rapid mood swings); black bile (connected to profound melancholia); and yellow bile (resulting in confusion, irritability, and aggressiveness).

Initially, researchers were motivated by the need to compile statistical or epidemiological information. The most universal of modern classification systems for mental disorders have been the various versions of the *Diagnostic and Statistical Manual of Mental Disorders* (DSM) produced by the American Psychiatric Association (APA). Although these systems grew to be widely accepted and were incorporated into the World Health Organization's *International Classification of Diseases* (ICD), controversies regarding the use of classification systems with mental disorders have been present throughout their use.

Some of this controversy has focused on the reliability of the diagnostic process. This issue has resulted in an increasing emphasis on descriptive (rather than etiological) diagnostic criteria for the various disorders. Another set of concerns has focused on the attribution of pathology to the individual. More specifically stated, environmental influences on the individual are ignored, thereby affixing exclusive "blame" on the individual even though the problem may well stem from or be exacerbated by people and situations in the individual's environment. This set of concerns led to the development of a multiaxial approach to diagnosis that includes consideration of medical and psychosocial situations that contribute to the disorder and/or will likely affect attempts to treat the disorder. However, it must be noted that many think that the multiaxial system in later versions of the DSM does not sufficiently address this concern.

Other controversies remain. Many fear that giving an individual a diagnosis inevitably results in certain negative "labeling" effects. For example, because mental illness is associated with a great deal of stigma, the individual may lose social support or be hindered in pursuing education or employment goals. Similarly, a diagnostic label may dramatically alter expectations and consequently encourage the individual to "live up to" (or down to) the label. Still another set of controversies has focused on the limited utility of diagnostic systems. From this viewpoint, any system that is not prescriptively linked to treatment protocols is insufficient.

Despite these concerns, the current version, DSM-IV-TR (APA, 2000), has become the primary "language" used by a variety of professionals to communicate about mental health and chemical dependency problems. Diagnostic labels serve as a shorthand for characterizing both the type and the severity of problems a client may be experiencing. In many instances, diagnoses are linked to eligibility for publicly funded treatment programs. For persons with private insurance policies, the diagnosis determines whether treatment will be covered as well as sets limits on the amount of service a client may receive in treating the specific disorder, particularly in managed-care arrangements. In short, familiarity with the DSM-IV-TR classification system is necessary in order to function appropriately in the multidisciplinary environments of both public and private mental health and chemical dependency treatment providers.

BALANCING THE PATHOLOGY PERSPECTIVE

Although knowledge of the current DSM may be essential to practitioners in the various helping professions, it should not be overlooked that in forming diagnoses, the DSM orients its focus toward an individual's deficits. In order to minimize the possibility of negative labeling effects and to maximize the basis for forming a therapeutic alliance with the client, it is essential that practitioners strive to achieve some balance to this inherent emphasis on pathology.

Similarly, a DSM diagnosis is clearly focused on an individual. However, all individuals exist in a complex environment, and components of that environment inevitably are involved in the individual's "problems." In order to understand someone's situation thoroughly, practitioners must examine interactions that precipitate or reinforce problematic behaviors. Also, a person's environment may include components that can assist directly or indirectly in resolving problematic behaviors. Ideally, practitioners will use information about an individual's environment in formulating and executing a plan to address the situation(s) described by their diagnosis.

Practitioners are encouraged to adopt principles of the strengths perspective in order to provide some balance in working with clients who have mental disorders. Simply stated, the strengths perspective is grounded in the beliefs that all persons have talents, goals, and confidence and that all environments contain resources, people, and opportunities. Bringing the strengths present in both the individual and his or her environment to bear in addressing problems is viewed as empowerment (see Rapp [1998] for an in-depth illustration of using the strengths perspective in practice).

Much of the support for a strengths perspective derives from the experiences in the mental health consumers' movement and its emphasis on recovery. Recovery does not imply that all symptoms are eliminated; instead, the emphasis in recovery is that one can lead a satisfying, hopeful, and contributing life even though symptoms exist (and may continue). A first step in recovery is acknowledging that one has a mental illness, a step made more accessible when individuals perceive the illness as only a part of themselves (rather than who they are). In addition, personal control, hope, purpose, and achievement are considered essential ingredients to recovery. Finally, membership in some community is necessary, it is important that one or more persons in the environment be able to attest to the aspects of the individual that are not related to the illness.

Social support and self-help opportunities are the building blocks of the strengths perspective. Consequently, in this workbook, informational and organizational resources will be suggested that may be useful in supporting clients and members of their social network. Although the Internet has brought a tremendous number of resources to consumers and their support systems, there is no systematic monitoring of Internet materials for quality or accuracy. Consequently, practitioners are cautioned to inspect suggested Web sites personally (and repeatedly) before offering sites as resources.

MULTIAXIAL CLASSIFICATION SYSTEM

The current version of the DSM, DSM-IV-TR (APA, 2000), is the sixth edition of the manual. In the initial two versions, the manual included a listing of mental disorders with some discussion regarding the likely etiology of each disorder. Beginning with the DSM-III (APA, 1980), several striking changes occurred. Most prominent, the emphasis in presenting disorders was moved from a more global focus on the broader disorder to a description of specific behavioral symptoms. The motivation for this change was primarily to increase the reliability of diagnoses. Secondarily, this new focus removed the intense disagreements regarding etiology related to various theoretical approaches from the DSM system. The more recent versions of the DSM have been intentionally atheoretical.

Along with this shift toward more specific behavioral descriptions, a multiaxial classification system was introduced. The intent of this change was to communicate relevant information regarding the client's medical condition, psychosocial issues, and overall functioning, thereby more clearly describing the person in his or her environment.

The first two axes in the five-axes classification system are used to present the clinical disorders actually listed in the manual. The majority of the mental disorders are listed on Axis I, whereas Axis II is reserved for persistent or chronic conditions, specifically Mental Retardation and Personality Disorders. The separation of these axes is intended to assure that more chronic conditions are not overlooked in the diagnostic process. If a client warrants multiple diagnoses on a single axis, the diagnoses are listed in order of their importance to the person's psychosocial functioning (i.e., "principal diagnosis") or in order of the focus of attention at a particular clinical interview (i.e., "reason for visit"). In instances when a client has at least one diagnosis on both Axes I and II, it is assumed that the first Axis I diagnosis is the principal diagnosis unless the first Axis II diagnosis is specifically labeled as such. The DSM also allows for communicating the level of uncertainty regarding a particular diagnosis (see "Provisional," "Not Otherwise Specified," and "Deferred" diagnoses in the DSM-IV-TR for more detail).

Axis III is designed to present general medical information. All medical conditions that may be important to understanding or treating the mental disorder(s) or that directly impact the likely prognosis of treatment should be listed on this axis. In general, this would include any medical problem related to the etiology of a mental disorder, any acute or chronic condition that impacts the client's psychosocial functioning, and any condition for which the client is taking routine medication (APA, 2000). Nonmedical practitioners should *not* diagnose general medical conditions on this axis. Instead, only conditions reported by the client, listed in a clinical record, or reported by a physician should be listed. It is strongly suggested that the source of the information about general medical conditions be included in the listing (e.g., diabetes [assumed due to client's use of insulin]; "bad blood" [per client self-report]; or concussion [per ER physician]). Similarly, nonmedical practitioners are not encouraged to utilize ICD diagnostic numbers on Axis III, an act akin to diagnosing.

Axis IV is designed to present specific information about the client's current psychosocial environment. Although only psychosocial problems that have occurred in the past year are usually listed, any psychosocial difficulty that is relevant to the client's current level of functioning may be reported. For example, childhood sexual abuse may lead to a variety of adult mental health problems and, consequently, should be included if clearly related to a disorder's etiology or if clearly pertinent in the client's perspective. A number of global categories of problem areas are suggested in the DSM text. Practitioners are encouraged to include specific information on Axis IV in addition to such global characterizations (e.g., occupational problems [recently fired from job]; problems with primary support group [3-week separation from husband]; or problems related to interaction with legal system [on probation with new charges for battery pending]) (APA, 2000).

In some instances, specific psychosocial problems are part of the diagnostic criteria for a disorder and consequently need not be repeated on Axis IV. A child with a diagnosis of Autism, for example, will clearly have problems in social relations. When such difficulties do not exceed the norm for diagnosis (for example, if the child is not forming friendships at school) they need not be listed on Axis IV. However, if that same child were being bullied on a daily basis, it would be appropriate to note that situation on Axis IV (APA, 2000).

Finally, a Global Assessment of Functioning (GAF) score is listed on Axis V. This 100-point scale is presented in the DSM. At a minimum, the client's current level of functioning is included. In some instances, additional GAF scores may be given (e.g., highest level of functioning in past year) (APA, 2000). Unfortunately, the GAF score was designed to address multiple aspects of functioning, including social relations, employment or school issues, and potential for danger to one's self or others. In some situations, an individual's functioning can be at very different levels depending on which aspect is emphasized. It is recommended that in those instances, the client's potential for danger to self or others should take precedence in determining the GAF score.

ASSESSMENT

While a DSM-IV-TR (APA, 2000) diagnosis is the shorthand description of a client's situation, assessment is a much broader term or process. Certainly, initial assessment leads to diagnosis. However, assessment ideally is a much more ongoing, collaborative, and detailed communication between a treatment provider and a client. In this broader sense, assessment informs monitoring and evaluative processes as well as diagnostic ones.

Many factors influence the breadth and depth of the assessment process. For example, if meeting the client for the first time in a hospital emergency room, it is likely that only the essential details of the presenting problem will be explored in any depth. Frequently, the amount of information a client is willing to divulge is limited, at least initially. As the rapport between practitioner and client is established over time, the client is apt to be more comfortable in sharing sensitive information or in discussing things that don't necessarily seem relevant at first. Typically, although there is pressure to move into treatment planning rapidly, initial assessment stretches over several interactions with the client.

It must also be noted that not all clients enter into a helping relationship on a completely voluntary basis. Some clients may be required through some legal system mechanism to receive treatment or at least be evaluated for their need for treatment. In many more instances, family, friends, or even employers pressure clients to obtain help for some specified concern. Regardless of the precise mechanism, engaging the involuntary client is more challenging. Generally, the practitioner must help the client find his or her own motivation or goals in order to secure any real cooperation.

Although the assessment process is obviously unique to the individual, there are some general principles that apply. Whenever possible, multiple sources of information are preferred over sole reliance on the client's perspective. Additional sources of assessment data include (but are not limited to) data from other professionals (e.g., medical, psychological, social, educational, spiritual, or legal), relevant family members, and other persons who provide social support. In any particular situation, there may well be others who could provide valuable data and/or perspectives.

Another guiding principle is that individual problems rarely occur in isolation. Consequently, both the history of the client and his or her current life context are essential in understanding the presenting problem. For example, although a person may present with a specific relationship problem, it would be important to review the person's prior successes and failures in the social realm. Similarly, it would be problematic to try to address this relationship problem without knowing basic information about the client's broader social and occupational functioning.

In a related issue, it is essential to view and process assessment data within the client's context. For example, thinking that is typical of young children might be viewed as quite pathological if held by an adult of normal intelligence. Beliefs that someone is trying to hurt the client may be viewed differently if the client is a member of an oppressed population. Practitioners must strive to become sensitive to the culture and/or circumstances that may impact the client's life and must consistently interpret assessment data through a culturally competent lens.

Assessment Interview

The most common approach to gathering assessment information is a semi-structured interview. The following outline delineates the range of data that is generally desirable, although certain areas of information may be more or less relevant in particular problem situations. The outline organizes the information into logical sections. However, in actually conducting an initial interview, practitioners seldom move through such an outline in a rigid, linear manner. Interviews tend to be more conversational. Consequently, this outline is intended to specify the breadth of information that is possible to obtain (rather than to supply an interview script).

I. Descriptive and Identifying Information
   A. Name
   B. Address
   C. Home phone number
   D. Work phone number
   E. Date of birth
   F. Occupation
   G. Income
   H. Gender
   I. Ethnicity
   J. Dress and appearance
   K. Personal hygiene
   L. Marital status
   M. Living arrangements (include names and relationship to client)
II. Description of Presenting Problem(s)
   A. How long has the problem existed?
   B. Has it occurred before?
   C. What attempts has the client made to resolve the problem? If it is a recurrent problem, what seemed to help resolve it in the past?
   D. What kinds of resources does the client have to help resolve the problem? Has he or she sought or received any treatment for this problem?
   E. Why did the client seek help now?
III. Developmental History [NOTE: For adult clients, little detail is usually sought in this section other than possibly asking if there was anything unusual about their early years. For children, the following information is usually gathered from their parent or primary caregiver.]
   A. Was the pregnancy planned?
   B. Were there any problems during the pregnancy?
   C. Were any medications or other substances used by the mother at any time during the pregnancy? If so, what and when?
   D. Were labor and delivery uneventful? If not, what happened?
   E. Was the child born with any unusual medical conditions or physical problems?
   F. Did the child have a consistent caregiver during the first two years? Who?
   G. Did the child crawl, walk, talk, and toilet train at the expected times? When?
   H. What opportunities did the child have to associate with same-age peers?
   I. Has the child incurred any significant problems or delays in school?
IV. Mental Status
   A. Cognitive functioning
      1. Does the client seem to be of normal intelligence?
      2. Is the client oriented to person, place, and time?
      3. Is there evidence of logical problem-solving thinking or capacities?
      4. Does the client seem preoccupied by anything?
      5. Is there evidence of delusional thinking? If so, are delusions bizarre?
      6. Is the client's thinking coherent and goal directed?

7. Does the client exhibit good judgment?
8. Does the client show any memory problems? If so, are they immediate, recent, or remote?
9. Does the client report hearing or seeing things that others don't seem to hear or see?
10. Is there anything unusual about the client's manner of speaking?

B. Emotional functioning
1. What emotions does the client describe in relation to the presenting problem?
2. Do the client's emotions appear to be congruent with the client's thoughts?
3. How has the client been feeling the majority of time over the past year?
4. Has the client's emotional state created difficulties for the client recently? Over the past year?
5. How stable are the client's emotions during the interview?
6. Does the client exhibit any blunting or flattening of affect?
7. Does the client seem unusually animated or expansive in his or her expression of emotions?

C. Physical functioning/Medical history
1. Does the client's level of energy or activity seem unusual (e.g., lethargy or hyperactivity)?
2. Does the client display any odd or peculiar motor behaviors (e.g., motor and/or vocal tics, mannerisms, or stereotypical movements)?
3. Does the client report any medical conditions or problems?
4. Has the client been examined by a physician during the past year? Results of exam?
5. Does the client take any prescription medications for current ailments?
6. Does the client take any over-the-counter medications on a regular basis?
7. Has the client ever had any psychological or mental health–related treatment in the past (including inpatient, outpatient, and/or psychotropic medications)? If so, describe in detail.
8. Does the client present with any disabilities?

D. Substance use
1. Does the client use alcohol? If so, what kind? How often?
2. Does the client use any other substances?
3. Has the client experienced any social, occupational, or legal problems associated with his or her use of alcohol and/or other drugs?
4. Has anyone ever encouraged the client to stop or cut back his or her use of substances?
5. Has the client ever been treated for a drug or alcohol problem?

V. Relational Functioning
A. Family
1. Does the client reside with other family members?
2. What is the client's relationship with other family members?
3. Does the client's presenting problem involve other family members?
4. Is there any history of family problems? Have any family members had problems similar to the client's current situation?
5. Would family members be willing to participate in treatment if necessary?

    B. Significant other
        1. Does the client have a relationship with a significant other?
        2. If so, what is the length of the relationship? The quality?
        3. Does the client's presenting problem involve the significant other?
        4. Would the significant other be willing to participate in treatment if necessary?
    C. Social support system
        1. Does the client have close friends and/or acquaintances?
        2. What is the quality of these relationships?
        3. Does the client feel that these are supportive relationships?
        4. Are any members of the client's social support system involved in the presenting problem?
VI. Occupational/School Functioning
    A. Employment
        1. Is the client employed? Underemployed? Unemployed?
        2. If so, where is the client employed? Full-time? Part-time?
        3. What is the client's occupation?
        4. If the client is not employed, is he or she retired?
        5. Does the client's presenting problem affect his or her job?
    B. School
        1. Is the client a student? Full-time? Part-time?
        2. What is the client studying?
        3. Does the client's presenting problem affect his or her studies?
VII. Legal Problems
    A. Does the client have current problems with the legal system?
    B. If so, what types of problems?
    C. Has the client had any history of problems with the legal system?
    D. If so, what types of problems?
    E. Has the client ever been convicted of a crime?
VIII. Diversity Issues
    A. What is the client's ethnicity?
    B. What is the client's nationality? If relevant, immigration status?
    C. How acculturated does the client appear to be?
    D. Is English the client's first language? Second? Third?
    E. What are some of the client's beliefs about mental health issues?
    F. Does the client engage in any religious or spiritual practices?
    G. Has the client discussed his or her sexual orientation?
    H. Does the client utilize any cultural resources?
    I. Does the client perceive barriers to accessing resources?
IX. Client's Strengths and Resources
    A. What do you perceive to be the client's strengths?
    B. How can these strengths be utilized to assist the client in resolving the current issues?
    C. What client resources could be utilized to enhance coping?
    D. What agency resources could be utilized to intervene with the client?

Assessment Review

In addition to the assessment interview, an assessment review can provide the practitioner with an overall understanding of the client's strengths and weaknesses in areas of psychosocial functioning (Pomeroy & Holleran, in press). The chart in Table 1 can be completed by the practitioner during or following an as-

Table 1 | Person in Environment (PIE) Assessment

Determine whether each category is a problem or a strength, then rate each 1–5 for intensity on the scale below. In some cells, notes will be more useful.

	Personal	Family	Friends	School/ Work	Community	Social Work Intervention
Appearance						
Biomedical/organic						
Developmental issues/Transitions						
Coping abilities						
Stressors						
Capacity for relationships						
Social functioning						
Behavioral functioning						
Sexual functioning						
Problem solving/ Coping skills						
Creativity						
Cognitive functioning						
Emotional functioning						
Self-Concept						
Motivation						
Ethnic identification						
Cultural barriers						
Role functioning						
Spirituality/Religion						
Other strengths						

C = concern
S = strength
N/A = not applicable
Scores for intensity of concern or strength:
  1 = minimal intensity
  2 = mild intensity
  3 = average intensity
  4 = above average intensity
  5 = significant intensity

sessment interview. It provides a brief and easy-to-use guideline for assessing clients in a variety of areas.

Structured Interviews

Although somewhat less commonly used in practice, a number of structured interview schedules exist that are designed for diagnostic purposes. These instruments may be particularly instructive for novice interviewers. Most frequently, these approaches are utilized in conjunction with research studies because they ensure that certain data about each client is obtained. Some agencies, as well, prefer their clinicians to use these structured approaches.

There are several instruments available for use with children, such as the Children's Interview for Psychiatric Syndromes (CHIPS) (see Weller, Weller, Fristad, Rooney, & Schecter [2000] for a review of its psychometric properties). This instrument package includes both child and parent versions and is written using simple language and short sentence structure to enhance comprehension and cooperation. It screens for roughly 20 Axis I disorders and includes attention to discerning psychosocial stressors. A second semistructured interview schedule, the Diagnostic Interview for Children and Adolescents (DICA) (see Reich [2000] for a review of its psychometric properties), is considered particularly useful for younger children.

The National Institute for Mental Health (NIMH) has supported the development of structured diagnostic interviews for some years. The most recent version for children and adolescents, NIMH Diagnostic Interview Schedule for Children—Version IV (NIMH DISC-IV) (see Shaffer, Fisher, Lucas, Dulcan, & Schwab-Stone [2000] for a review), is designed to assess more than 30 disorders. This instrument includes sections for the youth and his or her parents and is available in both Spanish and English. Additionally, an alternative version is under development to gather information from teachers.

For adults, the most commonly used semistructured diagnostic interview schedule is the Structured Clinical Interview for Axis I DSM-IV Disorders—Patient Edition (SCID-IP, ver. 2.0) (see First, Spitzer, Gibbon, & Williams, 1995), which is focused on Axis I disorders. This edition of the instrument comes in both "clinical" and "research" versions, with the latter covering more disorders, subtypes, and course specifiers and taking longer to complete. The clinical version has been targeted toward diagnostic categories typically encountered in clinical practice and can be further abbreviated on a module-by-module basis. There is also a separate version, SCID-II, ver. 2.0 (First, Spitzer, Gibbon, Williams, & Benjamin, 1994), which is focused on Axis II personality disorders.

Standardized Measures

A large number of standardized measures are also available for clinical use and typically rely on either client self-report or ratings by experts and/or trained observers. These instruments are usually narrowly focused to be relevant to a single diagnostic grouping or even to a single aspect of a diagnosis. To the extent that these instruments' psychometric properties (i.e., reliability and validity) are known, standardized instruments may offer a more "objective" approach than structured or unstructured interviews. When norms or "cutting scores" have been developed for standardized measures, practitioners can interpret a client's score with some comparative perspective.

Psychometric Considerations

In its most basic sense, reliability addresses whether applying a measure repeatedly with the same client would produce the same result each time. Consequently, a measure's reliability reflects the amount of random error that is likely clouding the accuracy of the results. Three different approaches to estimating an instrument's reliability are common. The first, interrater reliability, applies to measures that involve observers' ratings and is generally expressed by a correlation coefficient based on the agreement among various raters. It should be noted that interrater reliability is usually based on ratings from trained raters; therefore, to attain similar reliability in practice requires similar training and effort.

Two other approaches to estimate reliability are used with self-report measures. Test-retest reliability is based on administering the same measure to a group of people on two separate occasions and is expressed as a correlation coefficient based on the level of agreement between the occasions. Careful attention should be paid to the time element in interpreting test-retest reliability. The time period should be sufficiently long that respondents are not simply remembering what they answered previously. However, the time period should not be so long that the concept being measured is likely to have changed. Generally, a test-retest reliability coefficient should be at least above .80 and preferably above .90.

The final common approach to estimating reliability, internal consistency reliability, addresses the homogeneity of the measure (rather than its stability). Usually expressed as a "coefficient alpha" or "Cronbach's alpha," this approach is based on the average of all possible interitem correlations. For measures that address a number of distinct issues, estimates for both the subscales and the full scale are offered.

Assuming that a measure has reasonable reliability, its validity indicates whether it is measuring what we hope it is measuring. Consequently, a measure's validity reflects the amount of systematic error that is likely clouding the accuracy of the results. Two of the approaches to assessing an instrument's validity rely on experts' judgments. Face validity is based on assessments of experts about whether a scale seems to be measuring the concept it is intended to measure. Clearly, the validity of face validity rests heavily on the expertise of those rendering judgment. Similarly, content validity is focused on whether a scale adequately represents all relevant facets of a concept and again is judged by experts.

Two empirical approaches to validity are also used. In criterion-related validity, scores on the measure are correlated with some external criterion. For example, a new measure may be compared to an already-accepted measure of the same concept. Another common approach would be to test persons who are known to differ in respect to the variable being measured (e.g., people under treatment for depression and a community sample). The final approach to estimating validity is construct validation. In this approach, the measure's scores are examined to see if they relate to other variables in the expected ways.

Broad-Based Instruments

Several personality tests are designed to provide more broad-based assessment of an individual and, consequently, may be applicable to numerous diagnostic categories. The more commonplace of these instruments will be discussed here and mentioned briefly in other more focused chapters.

The Minnesota Multiphasic Personality Inventory-2 (MMPI-2) (Butcher & Williams, 2000) consists of 370 true-false items (an additional 183 items can generate additional subscales). The MMPI-2 generates a variety of validity and clinical scales; interpretation of the results includes both the numerous subscales and the pattern of subscale results. In the extended version of the MMPI-2, there are additional content scales that may be useful as well. Although the MMPI-2 is written at a sixth-grade reading level, it is generally recommended for use with persons 18 years and older. An adolescent version of the MMPI (MMPI-A) (Butcher & Williams, 2000) is also available. Administration and interpretation of both the MMPI-2 and MMPI-A are generally reserved for specially trained clinicians. Hundreds of studies have been conducted to support the reliability and validity of these instruments (see Butcher [2000] for reviews). The test and various scoring services are available through NCS Pearson Assessment (http://assessments.ncspearson.com).

Also available from NCS Pearson is the Symptom Checklist-90-Revised (SCL-90-R). This 90-item instrument generates nine primary symptom sub-scales and three global indices. It is used with individuals aged 13 and older and is commonly used as a screening and/or outcome measure. Again, hundreds of studies have demonstrated its reliability and validity (see Derogatis & Savitz [1999] for a recent review).

A final NCS Pearson product, the Millon Adolescent Clinical Inventory (MACI) (Millon & Davis, 1993), is designed for use with troubled youth ages 13–19. The 160-item instrument yields 12 personality pattern scales, 8 expressed concern scales, 7 clinical syndrome scales, and 4 additional scales that address reliability and validity issues. While the MACI is not as widely studied as the MMPI or SCL-90-R, a substantial amount of evidence supports its psychometric properties (see Davis, Woodward, Goncalves, Meagher, & Millon [1999] for a recent review).

Case Monitoring

As stated earlier, assessment in its broadest sense includes ongoing case-monitoring activities. While the routine interactions between practitioner and client provide a general sense of changes in the client's situation, it is preferable that case-monitoring materials be more concrete. It can be quite difficult for both practitioners and clients to see incremental change.

Although structured interviews and standardized instruments can be used in case monitoring, both approaches can become tedious, if not irritating, if repeated frequently. Further, these approaches may not be viewed as relevant by clients since they are based on professional judgment (directly or indirectly) rather than on the client's experience of his or her own situation.

The most common alternative approach to case monitoring is to engage the client in self-monitoring and recording. Examples of this approach include client logs, diaries, journals, and behavioral recordings. In all instances, clients can record things as they occur or summarize things at regular time intervals. For example, clients may be asked to stop and record everything they can remember about their thought processes each time they have a thought about death or suicide. In contrast, the same clients could record the number of times they thought about self-destruction or death each evening. These types of approaches are not only useful in case monitoring but can also help the practitioner and clients understand the target behavior, thought, or feeling better.

Another approach to case monitoring involves, in essence, construction of individualized "scales." In self-anchored scales, the client determines the specific dimensions of the problem that are particularly relevant. Then, for each dimension, the client sets anchors that represent different levels of the problem. Once the scale is completed, the client rates himself or herself at regular intervals. In this approach, the client is empowered through specifying what aspects of the situation are most critical and setting his or her own standards for what is to be considered "success."

Similarly, goal-attainment scaling involves a similar process. Early in treatment, the client sets his or her expectations regarding outcomes. Clients are encouraged to determine behavioral indicators that reflect different levels of improvement.

CONCLUSION

As should be evident, assessment is an extremely complex topic area. This workbook is structured around DSM-IV-TR (APA, 2000) sections or chapters. Within each section, targeted assessment information will be provided. However, the more primary focus of this workbook is diagnostic. The case materials provide an opportunity to hone diagnostic skills. The information provided regarding assessment and environmental resources, although useful, is supplemental.

 ### InfoTrac keywords

cultural sensitivity, DSM-IV, mental health assessment, mental health evaluation, social support

2 | Infant, Childhood, and Adolescent Disorders

INTRODUCTION

The section of the DSM-IV-TR (APA, 2000) "Disorders Usually First Diagnosed in Infancy, Childhood, or Adolescence," addresses a distinctively different grouping compared to those in other chapters. First, this category of the DSM-IV-TR includes those disorders that usually come to the attention of parents, caregivers, or health-care professionals before the child or adolescent has reached the age of 18. Second, these childhood and adolescent disorders cover a broad range of problems from chronic, long-term disorders (e.g., Mental Retardation or Autistic Disorder) to transient, developmental difficulties (e.g., some types of Tic Disorders or Elimination Disorders). Third, even though some disorders are frequently assessed and diagnosed in children or adolescents (e.g., Attention Deficit/Hyperactivity Disorder [ADHD]), other disorders are relatively uncommon and found in only a very small percentage of children (i.e., Rett's Disorder). Finally, many of these disorders can be assessed along a continuum from very mild to very severe.

Since this initial chapter of the DSM-IV-TR covers a broad spectrum of childhood and adolescent disorders, it is divided into 10 descriptive subcategories. All of the diagnoses, with the exception of Mental Retardation, are reported on Axis I as Clinical Disorders. Although these disorders begin before age 18, many have implications for the individual's adult functioning.

DISORDERS

Mental Retardation

Mental Retardation is diagnosed when the child has significantly below average intellectual functioning as measured by an individualized intelligence test (e.g., Wechsler Intelligence Scale for Children—Revised [WISC-R]) and has significant difficulties with adaptive functioning. A person with Mental Retardation can be classified as having Mild (IQ 50–55 to 70), Moderate (IQ 35–40 to 50–55), Severe (IQ 20–25 to 35–40), or Profound (IQ below 20–25) Mental Retardation. Mental Retardation is an Axis II diagnosis due to the chronic, long-term nature of the problem (APA, 2000).

Learning Disorders

Learning Disorders are distinguished by below average cognitive or academic functioning when compared to a person's intellectual capacity. These disorders are reflected in a child's or adolescent's underachievement for his or her age, educational level, or intelligence in reading, math, writing, or any other academic realm. The symptoms of these disorders are discerned by the use of achievement and intelligence testing where the child scores approximately two standard deviations lower on the achievement test than on the intelligence test. The child's academic difficulties may continue into adulthood although some children can learn to compensate for their learning deficits through the use of other learning strategies (APA, 2000).

Motor Skills Disorders

Motor Skills Disorders are distinguished by problems with physical or perceptual coordination. Developmental Coordination Disorder is diagnosed if the child has motor coordination deficits that significantly impair his or her ability to function in school or in daily living activities. This disorder is not diagnosed if the child's problems are due to a medical condition or are not significantly greater than those motor functioning problems normally found in children with Mental Retardation (APA, 2000).

Communication Disorders

Communication Disorders are distinguished by problems in the area of language or speech development. Five diagnoses are included in this general category: Expressive Language Disorder; Mixed Receptive–Expressive Language Disorder; Phonological Disorder; Stuttering; and Communication Disorder Not Otherwise Specified (NOS).

Stuttering is probably the best-known disorder in this category. Children who stutter have problems with the fluency and timing of speech patterns. Children with communication problems may have problems with psychosocial functioning, such as stigmatization, shame, lack of social support from peers, and familial pressures (APA, 2000).

Pervasive Developmental Disorders

Pervasive Developmental Disorders are distinguished by serious problems with an array of social and developmental delays and disabilities. Children with these disorders have severe impairments in social functioning and communication as well as severely restricted behaviors, interests, and activities. Autistic Disorder, Rett's Disorder, Childhood Disintegrative Disorder, Asperger's Disorder, and Pervasive Disorder NOS are included in this grouping. Neurological dysfunction is present in all of these disorders (APA, 2000).

The most common disorder in this category is Autistic Disorder. Children with Autistic Disorder display problems with language, social interaction, and imaginative play prior to age 3. In addition, two-thirds of autistic children also have some form of Mental Retardation.

Rett's Disorder and Childhood Disintegrative Disorder, although rare in occurrence, are particularly devastating to parents. In each of these disorders, there is a period of normal development followed by a loss of previously established functioning. Parents think they have a normal, healthy child only to discover that their child's developmental gains are only temporary and that the child will lose functional abilities rather than progress to a more advanced level.

Finally, Asperger's Disorder is distinguished from other disorders in this category in that there is no delay in cognitive or language skills. A child with this disorder experiences restrictive and repetitive behaviors, interests, and activities similar to those found in autistic children, as well as significant impairment in social skill development.

Attention Deficit and Disruptive Behavior Disorders

Attention Deficit and Disruptive Behavior Disorders are distinguished by problems with attention and behavioral conduct. These disorders are frequently diagnosed in school-age children. ADHD is composed of two major symptom categories: inattention and hyperactivity. A child may be diagnosed with either of these syndromes or with both of them. Children with ADHD begin to show symptoms of this disorder before the age of 7 (APA, 2000).

Symptoms associated with ADHD, Predominantly Inattentive Type include the following: inability to give tasks or schoolwork his or her attention; perseverating with tasks; problems with listening when spoken to; tendency to be easily distracted; problems with being forgetful; difficulty sustaining effort with a task; tendency to lose things easily; and difficulty following through with tasks. Children with this type of ADHD must display six of the above symptoms but not appear to be hyperactive.

A child with ADHD, Predominantly Hyperactive Type must display six or more of the following symptoms: fidgeting; inability to stay seated; running or climbing while talking; inability to play quietly; constant moving; talking continuously; problems taking turns; interrupting others; and answering questions before being asked. ADHD, Combined Type involves a combination of six inattentive and six hyperactive symptoms. ADHD NOS involves inattention, hyperactivity, or both but does not meet the criteria of the specific diagnoses. With all types of ADHD, the child must have displayed symptoms for at least 6 months.

A child with Oppositional Defiant Disorder (ODD) displays at least four disruptive, negative, and defiant behaviors for at least 6 months. The symptoms include the following: being argumentative; lack of compliance with authority figures' requests; annoying others deliberately; blaming others for his or her mistakes; anger, spitefulness, and irritability. The child with ODD, however, does not engage in unlawful behaviors (APA, 2000).

On the other hand, children or adolescents diagnosed with Conduct Disorder do participate in activities that violate social norms and may constitute illegal and criminal behaviors. The diagnosis of Conduct Disorder requires that the youth has engaged in three or more symptomatic behaviors or activities over a 12-month period. These behaviors are classified into four broad categories:

(1) aggression to people or animals; (2) destruction of property; (3) deceitfulness or theft; and (4) serious violations of rules. These behaviors are repetitive and form a pattern that significantly impairs social or academic functioning (APA, 2000).

If one or more symptoms are displayed before the age of 10, the child is diagnosed with Conduct Disorder, Childhood-Onset Type. If there is no evidence of these behaviors before the age of 10 and the pattern of behaviors is diagnosed after age 10, then the child would be diagnosed as having Conduct Disorder, Adolescent-Onset Type. Additional terms indicate the level of severity of the disorder: Mild, Moderate, or Severe. The practitioner considers the number of conduct problems and the degree of harm to others in assessing these levels of severity.

Feeding and Eating Disorders

Feeding and Eating Disorders are distinguished by problems with the process of eating and retaining food or eating inappropriate food. Children may be diagnosed with Pica (eating nonfood items such as paint chips, string, hair, or newspaper); Rumination Disorder (vomiting and re-eating food); or Feeding Disorder of Infancy or Early Childhood (failing to eat or gain weight over a period of at least one month). (See DSM-IV-TR for full description of these disorders.)

Elimination Disorders

Elimination Disorders are distinguished by problems with bowel and bladder control. Encopresis is diagnosed in children 4 years of age or older. It involves repeated bowel movements in inappropriate places. Encopresis can cause low self-esteem, shame, and embarrassment for a child in school and social situations.

Enuresis is marked by repeated urination in bed or clothing at least twice a week for at least 3 months. There are three types of enuretic conditions: (a) Enuresis-Nocturnal Only; (b) Enuresis-Diurnal Only; and (c) Nocturnal and Diurnal. The nocturnal subtype is diagnosed in children who urinate while sleeping in bed at night, and the diurnal subtype is diagnosed when the child urinates in inappropriate places only during the day (APA, 2000).

Tic Disorders

Tic Disorders are distinguished by irresistible movements and/or vocal sounds. According to DSM-IV-TR (APA, 2000), children may have simple tics that involve behaviors or incoherent vocalizations lasting a few seconds each. On the other hand, children and adolescents may experience complex tics that involve discernible speech patterns or complex movements. Tourette's Disorder is identified by having both motor and vocal tics. Other Tic Disorders described in the DSM IV-TR are related to the type and duration of the problematic symptoms.

Other Disorders

The Other Disorders of Infancy, Childhood, or Adolescence category is for disorders not classified in the other groupings. The specific diagnoses as described in the DSM-IV-TR (APA, 2000) include Separation Anxiety Disorder, Selective

Mutism, Reactive Attachment Disorder, Stereotypic Movement Disorder, and Disorder of Infancy, Childhood, and Adolescence NOS.

Separation Anxiety Disorder is experienced by the child as extreme anxiety and psychosomatic symptoms when separated from home or parents/caregivers. The child may fear that something "awful" will happen to loved ones if he or she is not present. The child may become so fearful that he or she cannot stay away from home (e.g., at school or camp) without being extremely upset.

The anxiety associated with being away from home is excessive for the developmental level of the child. Often, parents misinterpret this disorder as being fear associated with school when, in reality, it is a fear of leaving home or loved ones. Since children with this disorder often come from enmeshed families, it is often difficult for parents to "let go" and allow the child to experience the discomfort necessary in order to overcome this problem. Parents may also identify a physiological reason (e.g., stomachaches) rather than the psychological reason for the problems the child is experiencing. If the disorder occurs before the age of 6, the term "Early Onset" is used (APA, 2000).

Selective Mutism is diagnosed in a child who fails to speak in situations where speech is expected. Reactive Attachment Disorder is also a rare disorder but is commonly found in refugee populations where many children either have been abandoned or have lost their parents. Stereotypic Movement Disorder is another unusual disorder that may be diagnosed in combination with another childhood disorder (see DSM-IV-TR [APA, 2000] for a full description).

Children and adolescents are frequently diagnosed with many of the adult disorders, such as Bipolar Disorder, Major Depressive Disorder, Anorexia Nervosa, or Adjustment Disorder, in addition to the disorders in this chapter. There is some controversy concerning the appropriateness of diagnosing a child with certain adult disorders due to the developmental stages of childhood and the fact that children can "grow out of" certain transient problems that can occur prior to adulthood. Practitioners must be cautious when assessing and diagnosing a child or adolescent with an adult mental disorder.

On the other hand, certain problems that are initially diagnosed in childhood or adolescence are pervasive (such as Mental Retardation or the Pervasive Developmental Disorders) and will continue to merit attention and treatment into adulthood. When available, assessment instruments designed for use with children will be included in the assessment sections of the other chapters in this workbook.

ASSESSMENT

In working with children, practitioners usually gather information from a variety of sources. These may include the parents or caregivers, the child's physician, the child's teacher and/or school counselor, and any other adult professional who may play an important role in the child's life (e.g., a grandmother who cares for a child after school). In addition, the practitioner will spend at least one session with the child's parents to obtain a complete psychosocial history of the child. Clearly, obtaining extensive facts from a very young child is unfeasible; therefore, collaborative resources are needed in order to get a valid picture of the problems the child has been experiencing. On the other hand, older children and adolescents can provide very important information to the practitioner that can assist the counselor in understanding their strengths and weaknesses.

Because many of the infant, childhood, and adolescent disorders may have a predominant medical or neurological component, it is important that the caregivers seek medical advice and, at a minimum, a physical examination prior to beginning a psychological assessment. If the mental health practitioner is the first health professional to see the family, he or she should refer the family to a physician for a thorough examination prior to the start of therapy. Many times the pediatrician, neurologist, or family physician and the mental health practitioner work together as a team in order to provide the best treatment to the family. For example, a young child who presents with Encopresis may have a medical problem and should be thoroughly assessed by a physician before determining whether there is a psychological component to the problem.

Conversely, a child who has symptoms of Separation Anxiety Disorder may be referred to a mental health practitioner prior to being examined by the family's physician or pediatrician. Adolescents who have signs and symptoms of an Eating Disorder must work with a medical doctor and a mental health practitioner simultaneously in order to resolve the physical and nutritional issues as well as the psychological problems present with this disorder. Children with disorders such as Mental Retardation, Rett's Disorder, or Autistic Disorder should be referred to a specialist in retardation and disabilities, although the practitioner may be able to help the family cope with the reality of having a child with disabilities.

When a practitioner is assessing a child under the age of 13, play therapy techniques are most often employed to gather information about the child's feelings and behaviors. Play therapy consists of a set of professional techniques designed to elicit important psychological information from the child. For example, the practitioner may have the child draw a picture of his or her home, family composition, or favorite activity. The practitioner may also provide the child with play materials and play with the child in order to obtain information. For example, a family of dolls may be used to discover relationships within the family and feelings that the child may experience regarding other family members.

Older children, on the other hand, may be able and willing to have a conversation with the practitioner. Relevant topics might include why they think they were brought to see a mental health counselor, what they perceive to be the presenting problem, how they imagine resolving the problem, and what their view is regarding the history of the problem. Often, a combination of some activity along with conversation is a useful method of establishing rapport with older children and adolescents since their attention span may be of shorter duration than that of an adult.

Instruments

A broad range of assessment instruments can be utilized with infants, children, and adolescents to assess the client's psychosocial functioning and presenting problems. Although some of the scales may involve evoking responses from the child or adolescent, other scales depend on interviewer observation, assessment, and report. For most of the disorders found in the DSM-IV-TR (APA, 2000) related to infancy, childhood, and adolescence, there are assessment instruments that can be utilized to assess a specific problem.

For example, there are scales that are designed to be used specifically with children and adolescents to measure the degree of mental retardation, motor skills deficits, perceptual problems, attention deficit disorders, depression, and behavior problems. These scales are usually normed on a specific age range of children (e.g., ages 6 to 10; age 8 and older; age 12 and older) and should not be used with children younger than the given age range. The following section will provide examples of some of the more common assessment instruments utilized with children and adolescents. However, there are literally hundreds of scales that can be obtained that address specific issues relevant to this age group.

Scales for Infant Assessment   Two well-known scales that have been widely used to assess infants prior to acquiring language skills are the Bayley Scales of Infant Development—Second Edition (BSID-II) (Bayley, 1993) and the Wechsler Preschool and Primary Scales of Intelligence—Revised (WPPSI-R) (Wechsler, 1989). The BSID-II may be used for infants as young as 1–42 months old, the WPPSI-R can be used for children beginning at 4 years of age. The BSID-II is designed to assess an infant's level of engagement and performance with stimuli designed to be interactive for the infant. The scale can assist in the assessment of developmental delays. The subscales measure the motor performance, mental capacities, and behavioral development of very young children.

The WPPSI is a well-known scale of intelligence developed by David Wechsler and normed on over 1,700 children. Numerous studies attest to the reliability of this instrument with very young children. The scale provides a measure of intelligence including verbal capacities and performance abilities.

Advanced qualifications are required for the administration of the instruments of both of these scales. A Ph.D.-level psychologist would normally administer and interpret the findings from these scales.

Scales for Child and Adolescent Assessment   The Wechsler Intelligence Scale for Children—Third Edition (WISC-III) (Wechsler, 1991) is an intelligence test for children (ages 6–16) that is administered individually by a licensed psychologist. It is frequently used to test cognitive abilities as well as to assess ADHD and other learning disorders. The WISC-III is considered the "gold standard" for determining individual intelligence scores. Categories of the scale include a Verbal IQ score, a Performance IQ score, and a Full Scale IQ score. The verbal and performance sections consist of six subscales each. Time required for testing is 50–75 minutes.

The WISC-III was determined to have a test-retest reliability of .93 on the verbal; .90 on the performance subscales; and .95 on the full scale IQ (Canivez & Watkins, 1998). Studies have also shown that the WISC-R is highly correlated with other standard intelligence tests, attesting to its construct validity. Content validity of the test, however, is harder to prove, given the ongoing debate over the definition of "intelligence" and what the concept encompasses (Graham & Lilly, 1984).

The Vineland Adaptive Behavior Scale (VABS) (Sparrow, Balla, & Chicchetti, 1984) is a well-known developmental assessment instrument that examines the child's adaptive functioning abilities. The instrument is administered by interview to parents, caregivers, or teachers. Scales for the instrument range from birth to 19 years old. The VABS encompasses five behavioral categories, including the communication, daily living skills, socialization, motor skills, and maladaptive behavior domains (Sparrow, Balla, & Chicchetti). Raw scores for each domain are converted to standard scores, and a total composite score reflects the child's overall adaptive ability.

The VABS is frequently used to assess children with Mental Retardation and Pervasive Developmental Disorders to ascertain their daily living abilities rather than their cognitive or emotional abilities. One potential problem with this scale is that it may have an "inadequate floor," meaning that the scale may not score low enough to measure the skills of extremely low-functioning individuals (Gillham, Carter, Volkmar, & Sparrow, 2000).

The Child Behavior Checklist (CBCL) (Achenbach & Edelbrock, 1983) is a self-report instrument that is completed by parents reporting their observations of their child's behavior. It is appropriate for use with children ages 4 through 16. It contains 118 items that refer to specific behavioral and emotional issues as well as 2 open-ended items that can be used for describing other difficulties. In addition, the social competence scale contains up to 40 items measuring the degree or quality of the child's involvement with sports, family, organizations, school, and other extracurricular activities.

The scale is considered one of the best scales available due to its magnitude and diversity of items, standardization, and reliability and validity (Rubin & Babbie, 2001). The scale was normed on 2,368 children in the given age range. It has a 1-week test-retest reliability of .93 as well as interparent agreement of $r = .985$ for total behavioral problems and .978 for total social competencies. Studies indicate that the CBCL has internal consistency with an $r = .87$ (Walker, Garber, & Greene, 1993). There are profiles and specific forms of the scale for children by gender and for ages 4–5, 6–11, and 12–16 (Achenbach & Edelbrock, 1983). The CBCL/1–5 form is used for children under the age of 4. The forms can be hand scored or computer scored.

The Conners' Parent and Teacher Rating Scales (Conners, 1990) are designed to assess the problem behaviors of children ages 3–17. The Conners' Teacher Rating Scale (CTRS) is given to the child's teacher to fill out while observing the child in the classroom, and the Conners' Parent Rating Scale (CPRS) is given to the parents to report their child's behavior at home. The CTRS is available in 28- and 39-item forms, and the CPRS is available is 48- and 93-item forms (Conners).

While the Conners' Rating Scales can be used to assess a variety of emotional and behavioral problems in children, they are widely used to assess ADHD and the effects of medication on children. In studies, interrater reliability of the CTRS-39 has ranged from .39 to .94. The scale can be administered by any qualified professional to parents and teachers, and results can be scored by hand or by computer. Hundreds of studies using the Conners' Rating Scales attest to their validity as instruments for assessing emotional and behavioral problems in children.

Many times children who are being assessed by mental health practitioners are suffering from poor self-concept and low self-esteem in addition to other psychosocial problems. The Piers-Harris Children's Self-Concept Scale (Piers, 1984) measures the child's own perceptions of functioning in a variety of areas, such as appearance, popularity, intellectual and behavioral functioning, school functioning, and anxiety. It is an 80-item scale with declarative statements that the child marks "yes" or "no." The instrument can be used for children ages 8 to 18. It is designed for children with a third-grade reading level; however, for younger children in third to sixth grades, the administrator reads each statement out loud to the child, who then answers "yes" or "no" depending on whether the statement is applicable to him or her.

The instrument has been shown to have test-retest reliabilities of .62 to .96. The internal consistency of the scale is high, with alpha coefficients of .90–.91. Studies concerning the validity of the scale indicate positive correlations between the child's self-concept and school achievement and healthy peer relationships (Kanoy, Johnson, & Kanoy, 1980; Mannarino, 1978). The scale can be obtained from Western Psychological Services and can be computerized or hand scored.

For children and adolescents who present with more severe mental health problems, the Schedule for Affective Disorders and Schizophrenia for School-Age Children—Present and Lifetime Version (K-SADS-PL) (Ambrosini, 2000) is a semistructured interview tool that is compatible with DSM-IV criteria (Kaufman et al., 1997). The format of the tool does not have to be verbatim but is used to elicit information from the child and parents. Interviewers may substitute language that reflects the child's or parents' developmental level, if necessary.

The initial interview of the K-SADS-PL includes questions concerning demographic information, health information (including immunizations, the client's developmental history, history of abuse, and current risk for abuse), psychiatric treatment history, school adaptation and social relations, and the presenting problem (Kaufman et al., 1997). The "screen" portion of the interview assesses key symptoms in 20 different categories. The interviewer can skip sections of this portion of the interview that do not apply to the child. The scale has excellent validity and reliability (Ambrosini, 2000; Kaufman et al., 1997).

Emergency Considerations

There are instances in which children's or adolescents' problems are severe enough that the children or adolescents may be at risk of hurting themselves or others. Depression is a common problem among children and adolescents. Due to their wish to avoid such negative feelings and their lack of coping skills, they may either "act out" their feelings by harming themselves or others or "mask" their feelings with behaviors to keep adults from discovering their depressed affect.

Recent episodes of school violence are clear examples of the inability of some teens to control their anger and depression, with the end result being traumatic acting out at school and the attendant dire consequences for the adolescent involved. Other times, severely withdrawn behavior is a clear indication that the child or adolescent may be depressed and in need of short-term crisis intervention or inpatient treatment to stabilize his or her emotional state. It is important to be able to assess a child or adolescent for suicidal and/or homicidal ideation or behaviors. Many times a child or adolescent is making a "cry for help" by acting out with high-risk behaviors.

In other situations, the child or adolescent may pose more of a threat to others than to himself or herself. For example, the child with Conduct Disorder may be vandalizing the neighborhood and causing disruptions at school but may not be depressed. In these cases, it is important to get the child's behavior under control before someone gets seriously hurt because of the behavior. It is important for you to remember that as a practitioner working with children, you are joining an extended "family" in a team effort to assist the child. If there are indications that the child is at high risk for hurting himself or herself or others, it is of paramount importance to talk to the parents or caregivers of the child or teenager and to draw on additional resources as necessary.

A third situation that may constitute an emergency is the case of a child or adolescent in need of medical attention before any psychological assistance will be beneficial. For example, an anorectic child or teen who is severely underweight and at risk for serious metabolic or electrolyte imbalances must be seen immediately by a physician in order to stabilize the child's physical condition before counseling will be of value. In some instances, the family can be in denial concerning the seriousness of the problem, and the practitioner must convince the family of the need for medical intervention.

CULTURAL CONSIDERATIONS

The cultural background of the child and family must be taken into consideration in the assessment of the child's strengths and limitations. In some cultures, mental health issues are not discussed and are viewed as taboo. Children from these cultural backgrounds may present to a primary care physician with somatic complaints such as headaches, stomachaches, or other pain symptoms. The physician may refer the child for mental health treatment after examining the child and finding no medical reasons for the problems being experienced.

In other cultures, mental health symptoms may be viewed as significantly related to the family's religious beliefs. For example, psychotic symptoms may be viewed as a sign from God or the Devil. Parents from certain cultures may embrace "magic realism," in which there is a belief that some action on the part of the parent brought on the symptoms in the child. A mother might explain that because she dropped a knife on the floor, the child developed depressive symptoms.

In addition, it is important to keep in mind that the definition of age-appropriate behavior differs in different cultures. It is unremarkable to expect a 5-year-old child in England to be ready to go to boarding school, whereas in American culture, a child of this age would be considered too young to leave home for an extended period of time. Children who are attempting to bridge two different cultures may experience problems in understanding the different normative behaviors within the two cultures. Language difficulties may be a result of learning two languages at once rather than a psychological problem.

Cultural differences also exist in terms of gender roles for male and female children. For example, in Indian culture, females are expected to be dependent on the males in the family, whereas in Western European and American societies, independence is a valued attribute among males and females. In some Asian cultures, female children are taught to defer to males in making major decisions. In contrast, in American society, we teach children that there is equality between sexes in terms of power and authority within the family.

In addition, prevalence rates for various disorders differ between male and female children. For example, boys are more likely to be assessed with a Conduct Disorder, and girls are more frequently diagnosed with Separation Anxiety symptoms. Finally, children of color may experience discrimination, oppression, stigmatization, and ostracism in school situations and may display anxiety and depression related to these environmental and social factors. It is important to assess the child's entire psychosocial environment before attributing symptoms to intrapsychic factors.

SOCIAL SUPPORT SYSTEMS

A child's social support system is critical to his or her well-being. An assessment of a child must take into consideration the familial and other environmental support systems available to assist the child in the areas of growth and development. Children who have experienced familial disruptions may experience psychological stress related to these events. Children of divorce, children placed in foster care due to abusive family members, adopted children, and children who have highly dysfunctional parents may experience difficulties related to these events in their lives.

On the other hand, children may also display a high degree of resiliency that should be noted in the assessment. Some children develop coping strategies that may be highly beneficial to their psychological development. For example, a child may have a mentor outside the family system who serves as an important role model. Another child may develop an attachment to a relative outside the nuclear family in the absence of a parent, such as an aunt, uncle, or grandparent, who provides the child with nurturance and caregiving. Still other children live in an extended family situation, and the influence of other relatives in the children's lives should be considered.

In addition to family support, the influence of peers, especially for older children and teens, should be assessed. Peers can be a positive influence in a child's life, providing the child with socialization experiences that are imperative to the child's healthy development. However, peer groups can also have a detrimental influence on a child's behavior. Gangs, for example, can have a deleterious effect on the child's healthy functioning. Peers can be a powerful influence in a child's life depending on the child's or adolescent's stage of development. This influence must be fully examined when conducting a full psychosocial assessment.

A child who is experiencing psychological problems such as ADHD or Conduct Disorder can have an impact on his or her peer group. Children may not want to associate with a child whose behavior is inappropriate or uncomfortable for other children in the group. Children with disruptive behavior problems may find themselves ostracized by other children and unable to develop friendships due to their behavior problems. These children may develop secondary problems, such as depression or anxiety, due to their inability to "fit in" with the majority of children. These factors must also be taken into consideration when assessing a child's social environment.

Finally, the environment in which the child lives must be fully assessed by the practitioner. A child who resides in a very poor environment will be coping with the family's lack of resources and other stressors related to poverty. Children who live in very unstable environments (e.g., children of homeless parents or migrant workers) may experience a great deal of anxiety related to the lack of a place to call home. Other children may have highly stimulating environments with many resources at their disposal. Environmental factors have a powerful influence on the emotional development of children and should be taken into account in making an assessment.

The following resources may prove useful to families in which a child is experiencing a Mental Disorder.

www.thearc.org—The Association for Retarded Citizens, a national organization of and for people with Mental Retardation and related developmental disabilities and their families

www.autism-society.org—Information on Autistic Disorder and treatment

www.mhsource.com/disorders/tic.html—Information on Tic and Tourette's Syndromes

www.nimh.nih.gov/publicat/adhd.cfm—ADHD research and publications by the National Institute of Mental Health

www.mentalhealth.com/dis/p20-ch02.html—Diagnosis and treatment of Conduct Disorder

www.mentalhealth.com/dis/p20-ch03.html—Diagnosis and treatment of Separation Anxiety Disorder

www.kennedykrieger.org/familyreso/services/feeding.html—Feeding Disorders diagnosis and treatment

www.mentalhealth.com/dis/p20-ch07.html—Information on Asperger's Disorder

Case 2.1

Identifying Information

Client Name: Sarah Cisneros
Age: 7 years old
Ethnicity: Hispanic
Educational Level: Second grade
Parents: Regina and Don Cisneros

Background Information

Sarah Cisneros is a 7-year-old Hispanic female who has just started the second grade at Hutto Elementary School. She is a friendly and engaging child, although she has had numerous problems at school. Last year, the teacher reported that Sarah had difficulty following directions and staying in her seat and talked incessantly. She often got into disagreements with other children on the playground when she couldn't seem to follow the rules of a game they were playing. Her teacher also stated that she had difficulty learning the alphabet and writing letters and numbers. Sarah often reversed words, saying "tac" instead of "cat" and "kool" instead of "look." Although she had a difficult time in first grade, her teacher felt that Sarah was just an active child who would "settle down" when she entered second grade.

At the beginning of second grade, Sarah's parents separated. Sarah stayed with her mother, Regina, age 27. Regina moved back to Sarah's grandmother's home and went to work as an administrative assistant at a law firm in town. Sarah's father, Don, age 32, moved in with a girlfriend he had been seeing for several months prior to the separation. Don travels extensively in his job as an international computer sales representative. He is often out of the country for 3–4 weeks at a time. Sarah told her grandmother, "My heart won't hurt anymore when my daddy comes back to live with me." Regina and Don have told Sarah that they are just living in separate places for a little while.

When Regina discovered that Don was seeing another woman, she became very angry and depressed. She began working overtime, sometimes 12 hours a day, as a way of coping with the upheaval in her marriage. Sarah often sees her mother only early in the morning when Sarah is getting ready for school. Sarah's grandmother takes care of her after school. She complains to Regina that Sarah is "headstrong" and "can't seem to follow directions." She also tells Regina that if Sarah were given a good spanking she would "straighten up."

Regina just doesn't feel she has the energy to deal with Sarah's behavior and told her mother, "I just can't deal with everything, Mom. You need to help me with the discipline. I can't be mother and father, hold down a job, and deal with Don. It's just too much for me right now."

Regina's mother told Sarah that if she didn't follow directions, she would get a spanking. Sarah screamed, "If my Daddy was here, he'd give you a spanking," and ran to her room, slamming the door.

Regina decided to enroll Sarah in Brownie Scouts for one afternoon a week after school. The Brownie Scout leader is a friend of Regina's who lives down the street and said she'd bring Sarah home after the Scout meeting. Although Sarah was very excited about being a Brownie, she had difficulty getting along with the other girls. She couldn't sit quietly and work on projects; she often interrupted the leader with silly outbursts; she got bored easily and began running around the room; and she disrupted the meetings with her constant chatter.

After several weeks, the Brownie leader called Regina and told her that perhaps Sarah needs another year before she's mature enough to be in Brownie Scouts. Regina was so frustrated that when she got home from work, she screamed at Sarah, gave her a spanking, and sent her to her room. Sarah slammed her door and began throwing all her toys off the shelves. She screamed for 2 hours until she was so exhausted that she lay down on the floor and went to sleep.

After this incident, Regina, feeling very guilty, sought the advice of the counselor at school. The counselor suggested that Sarah may need an outlet for all her energy—something that involves physical activity. Regina decided to enroll Sarah in a ballet class on Saturday mornings at the local dance company. Once again, Sarah was very excited about being in the ballet class. She went shopping with Regina and bought a pink leotard with matching ballet slippers. Sarah danced around the house all day in her leotard in anticipation of the class.

Unfortunately, when Sarah began the dance lessons, the ballet teacher had the same complaints the Brownie leader had about Sarah's inability to follow directions and pay attention in the class. Regina felt at her wit's end about what to do next. She called Don and told him the problems she has been having with Sarah, and he told her, "You just let her get away with murder. When I was that age and I didn't obey my parents, I got a whipping and it never happened again. I'll take her for a weekend and teach her a lesson or two."

Regina angrily told him, "Don't bother," and hung up the phone.

Late one night shortly after this altercation with her husband, Regina was sitting by herself in the living room of the dark house watching the news on television. During a public announcement commercial for a Fun Run, she noticed that one of the sponsors was the Family Mental Health Center, a private nonprofit organization. Regina wrote down the phone number, and the next day at work, she made an appointment to go talk to a counselor about Sarah. The intake worker told Regina that the counselor would like to talk to Regina at the first appointment before she brought Sarah to the agency.

Initial Interview with Regina

The counselor introduces herself as Peggy Ross, a clinical social work practitioner who works with children and families. Peggy tells Regina about the agency and what her role as a counselor is. Regina tells Peggy about the problems she has been having with Sarah since her separation from her husband. She states that she just can't do anything with Sarah anymore and she just doesn't know what to do. She states that it is difficult living with her mother; however, her mother does provide child care so that Regina can work.

Peggy asks Regina whether the behaviors that Sarah has been displaying are new behaviors or ones that were present before the separation. "Come to think of it," says Regina, "Sarah has had trouble ever since she started school. Even in kindergarten, she didn't seem to listen to the teacher. She's not a dumb child. In fact, I think she's very smart, above average. But when it comes to completing her homework, she's a mess. She loses things she needs for assignments. She seems completely disorganized; she spreads all her stuff around and then can't find anything. She's always excited when she starts projects, but then it's like pulling teeth to get her to finish."

Peggy asks Regina about her and Don's childhood experiences. Although Regina doesn't know why that's important, she tells Peggy that she had no problems in school and, in fact, excelled in all her classes. "I was a classic good little girl. I knew if I wasn't, I'd get in big trouble at home," Regina told the counselor.

Peggy asked about Don's childhood experiences. Regina stated that Don's experience was very different. He was constantly getting into trouble and was very active as a little boy. He once told Regina that he was considered the "class clown" all through elementary school. Although he attempted a variety of sports, he was never very good at anything except soccer. He said he could run longer than most kids his age. He was a skinny, high-strung child. Regina tells the counselor that Don recently told her that he got whipped all the time for his bad behavior. She says that she doesn't really think spanking helps Sarah. She relates the incident of the night she spanked Sarah out of frustration and the tantrum that Sarah threw afterward.

After obtaining information about Regina, Don, and Sarah's present difficulties, Peggy suggests that Regina bring Sarah with her for the next interview. She states that she has some ideas about what is going on with Sarah but would like to talk with her before making any assessment. In the meantime, she gives Regina a form to fill out on Sarah's behavior as she observes it over the next week. She also asks her to sign a form giving Peggy permission to talk to Sarah's teacher at school. The following week, Regina brings Sarah to the agency to talk with Peggy.

Interview with Sarah

Peggy meets Sarah in the waiting room of the agency. She readily goes with Peggy to her office. Peggy gives Sarah a few choices of some things they can do together while they talk, including drawing, puppets, and a board game. Sarah has a hard time deciding what to do and after making a choice, she quickly grows bored with drawing a picture and wants to do something else.

When Peggy suggests they can do something else once they have finished their pictures, Sarah gets irritable and keeps jumping up from the table and wandering around the room. She says that she has lots of friends at school. She likes recreation time the best because she likes to jump rope. She also tells Peggy that she doesn't like her teacher, who is always mean to her. When Peggy asks her why she is mean, Sarah states, "She makes me sit in my chair and do my letters over and over again. It's boring."

While Sarah is easy to engage, she talks constantly and has difficulty focusing her attention on any one task. She wants to play with all the items on Peggy's desk, and when Peggy says she can't play with those things, Sarah stomps her feet and says, "If my daddy were here, he'd let me." Peggy feels very tired after 30 minutes with Sarah.

Peggy invites Don to come in for an interview, but Don states that he has to be out of town for a month and thinks that the problem is simply Regina's problem with lack of discipline with Sarah. Peggy tells Don that she'll call him when he returns from his trip.

After talking to Sarah's teacher at school and the school counselor, Peggy is ready to make an initial assessment of Sarah. She asks herself the following questions. How would you answer them?

2.1–1   How would you describe the presenting problem?

2.1–2   What resources might be available to help Sarah and her family?

2.1–3   Would you refer Sarah to any other professional while she is being seen by you?

2.1–4   What diagnosis would you give Sarah?
Axis I

Axis II

Axis III

Axis IV

Axis V

Case 2.2

Identifying Information
Client Name: Bobby Jones
Age: 9 years old
Ethnicity: African American
Educational Level: Fourth grade
Parent: Susan Jones

Background Information
Bobby, a 9-year-old African American boy, attends Lewistown Elementary School and is in the fourth grade. He is the third child in a family of six children ranging in ages from 3 to 12 years old. He has two older sisters, a younger sister, and two younger brothers. His mother, Susan, is 30 years old. She is a single mother and works as the activities director of a nursing home. She has a high school education and an associate's degree from a technical college. She has had two previous marriages, with three children by each husband. Bobby's alcoholic father has never worked or paid child support.

Bobby's teacher, Ms. Mathews, contacts you, the school counselor, about Bobby's behavior after the first 3 weeks of school. She states that Bobby has a very negative attitude about school, is disruptive, and never completes his work. She tells you that she has tried everything from rewards to "time out" in an attempt to change Bobby's negative behaviors. Ms. Mathews states that she doesn't know what goes on in Bobby's life outside school since he is rarely willing to share anything about his home life with her.

You ask Ms. Mathews if she can tell you more specifically what kinds of behaviors she has observed in Bobby.

"Well, ever since the first day of school, Bobby has been a major problem in class. He refuses to follow any of the rules, and when I confront him, he either stands there and just stares at me and won't say a word, or he says, 'Make me.' Several times when I have forced the issue, he has thrown a tantrum, pushing everything off his desk or knocking chairs over on his way to 'time out.' He never volunteers any information. I've tried talking to him one-on-one, and he refuses to talk to me. He won't tell me anything about how he's feeling or why he's angry. He just says, 'I don't know.' I am so frustrated I could scream. He disrupts the whole class. The other children don't want to be around him because he blames them when he breaks the rules. If he is on the playground with other children playing a game, he will begin fighting with them if he's not getting his own way. I just don't know what to do at this point. I've tried everything. Ms. Cameron, the third-grade teacher, told me Bobby was a handful, but I had no idea what a problem this child would be. Do you have any suggestions?"

You ask Ms. Mathews if Ms. Cameron, Bobby's third-grade teacher, had similar problems last year with Bobby. She indicates that Ms. Cameron was always talking about Bobby's bad behavior in the faculty lounge.

You state that you will try to talk to Bobby and also contact his mother. You feel that, perhaps, there are issues at home of which the school might be unaware. The following day, you talk with Bobby during lunch and free time at school.

Interview with Bobby
Bobby follows you down the hall to your office. Although you've asked him to come into your office and have a seat, he remains standing at the door looking as if he's trying to decide whether or not he will follow your directions. After some delay, he finally walks in and slouches down in a chair, crossing his arms in a defensive manner. When you ask him if he'd like to draw a picture, he tells you that he hates to draw. When you ask him what he would like to do, he points to the box of checkers.

While playing checkers, you ask him about his behavior in class. Bobby never makes eye contact and simply states "I don't know" to every question you ask. When you ask Bobby what he would like to talk about, he replies, "Nothing."

After three games of checkers, you tell Bobby it's time for him to go back to class. Bobby slams his fist on the table and turns the checkerboard upside down, sending checkers flying all over the room. You say, "You must really be angry about something." Bobby only shrugs his shoulders and begins walking to the door.

You tell Bobby that before he can go back to his classroom, he must help you pick up the checkers. Bobby says, "It's not my fault the stupid checkers fell on the floor." He quickly runs out of the room, slamming the door on his way out. You wait a minute or two and then go to his classroom to make sure he is there.

2.2–1   At this point, what symptoms have you noted?

2.2–2   Does Bobby display any strengths? If so, what are they?

2.2–3   Who are the other people involved with Bobby that you would like to interview in order to get more information?

Interview with Susan Jones

You call Susan at work and ask her if she can come in to the school to talk with you about Bobby. She states that she works until 4:30 every day but could come after she gets off work. You agree to see her at 5 P.M. Bobby attends the after-school program at the YMCA, which is open until 6:30 P.M.

Susan is a bubbly, enthusiastic woman who is neatly dressed in blue pants with a matching print blouse. She is petite with long brown hair tied back in a ponytail. She states that she has been having a very hard time dealing with Bobby at home and is glad someone is taking an interest in him at school.

You ask her what it's like at home with Bobby. She states that he argues with her about every little thing. She states that Bobby will be negative even about things she knows he would like to do. She explains, for example, "The other night I said, 'Bobby, do you want to go have pizza?' His response was, 'Can't we get it delivered?' When I finally convinced him that I was going out without him, he decided he'd go along. When we got to the restaurant, he argued about what kind of pizza to get, what kind of drink, and where to sit. I was so worn out by the time we got home, I just let him have his way. He wears me down. Every morning it's a tug-of-war getting him ready for school. He never wants to do as he's told."

You ask Susan about other negative behaviors like fighting with other kids or hurting animals. Susan tells you that he would never hurt an animal. She said they had a dog and a cat, and one thing Bobby does well is to take care of the pets. He likes to get the cat on his lap when he's watching TV, and he'll sit there petting him for hours. He also takes the dog out to play in the yard and seems to really care about the animals.

On the other hand, when it comes to following the rules, Bobby never complies. "He fights me over every little thing," Susan tells you. She rolls her eyes and rubs her forehead. "I just don't know what to do anymore. It's all I can do to get all the kids clothed and fed these days. My job doesn't pay much even though I got a college degree. It's hard to make ends meet with six kids."

"Does Bobby have any contact with his father?" you inquire.

Susan looks out the window and sighs. "Bobby's daddy never paid any attention to any of his kids. He's a drunk, and I think it's probably better that he never comes around. Bobby thinks his dad is superman, though. He has this fantasy that his daddy will come to the house one day and ask Bobby to come live with him. I've tried to explain to Bobby that his daddy has a drinking problem and can't hold a job and won't ever take care of him. That makes Bobby mad as can be when I tell him that. He doesn't want to believe his daddy doesn't want him. I think that's what's making Bobby so angry all the time."

"It sounds like it might have been hard being married to Bobby's father. How long were you married to him?" you ask empathically.

"Oh, I'd say too long," Susan says with a little laugh. "Actually it was about 6 years. Jerry was mean when he got drunk. He'd get so mad sometimes that he'd haul off and hit me and the kids and threaten to throw us out of the house with no place to go. I was going to school so I could get away from him. It took about 2 years but I finally got up the courage and left. It was the hardest thing I've ever done, but I knew I had to do it for the kids."

"Wow, that took a lot of courage," you respond. "How old was Bobby when you left?"

"He was almost 6 years old, I believe," Susan says. "He started being real disagreeable around that time, but he's never liked other people telling him what to do even when he was a toddler."

"When he gets so disagreeable, how do you usually handle that?" you ask.

"Sometimes I just try to ignore his bad behavior," Susan acknowledges. She frowns and begins tapping her foot on the floor. "Sometimes, when I just can't ignore it, I send him to his room. That doesn't always work, though, because he can throw a temper tantrum and tear up his room so it's almost destroyed by the time he gets through. Sometimes, I put him in the bathroom for 'time out.' I haven't really found anything that works very well."

"Okay, so perhaps one of the things we might work on is figuring out how to get Bobby to show more positive behaviors. What are some of the positive things you see in Bobby?" you ask.

"Well, like I said before, Bobby is real good with animals. He can talk to them and show them a lot of affection that he doesn't seem to be able to do with other people. Another thing is that there are times when I can just tell that Bobby really wants to be close to me, but he doesn't seem to know how to do it. It always makes me sad when he seems to want it so much, and then when I try to give it to him, he rejects me or gets angry and tells me to get away. I think he's crying for help."

"So there are times when you see some kindness and tenderness in Bobby that maybe other people don't get to see very often. Is that correct?" you suggest to Susan.

"Yes, that's absolutely right. I'm hoping this therapy will help Bobby and me to get closer and for Bobby to be able to get some control over all his anger," Susan says with a sigh.

"I think I can help you with both of those things, Susan. You are clearly very invested in helping your son, and that's a hopeful sign that we'll be able to help Bobby together. I'll need to be working closely with you in order to help Bobby since you are his mother. Okay?"

Susan sits back in her chair and looks relaxed for the first time in the session. "Okay, that sounds like a very good plan."

2.2–4   What strengths have you have assessed that Susan Jones possesses?

2.2–5   Who would you want to get permission to contact for additional information about Bobby's behavior?

2.2–6   What is your diagnosis for Bobby?
Axis I

Axis II

Axis III

Axis IV

Axis V

Case 2.3

Identifying Information
Client Name: Carlos Vasquez
Age: 4 years old
Ethnicity: Hispanic
Educational Level: Prekindergarten
Parents: Mona and Ricardo Vasquez

Background Information
You are a counselor/family therapist at University Hospital, a large Midwestern public teaching hospital, on the child psychiatric unit. A psychiatrist is the lead physician on the unit, which contains 16 beds for children between the ages of 5 and 12 who are experiencing psychiatric disturbances. There are two psychologists and two family therapists. Your primary role is working with the parents of the children who are hospitalized.

Intake Information
Mona and Ricardo Vasquez are referred to University Hospital by Carlos' pediatrician. The parents have had ongoing concerns about Carlos for the past 4 years. Upon admitting their son to the hospital, Mr. and Mrs. Vasquez tell the intake worker that they were initially concerned that Carlos had a hearing problem. Carlos appeared to be unresponsive and disengaged from Mona from birth. Mona reports that no matter how much she held and nurtured Carlos, he never seemed to respond to her.

When Carlos was 9 months old, his parents, fearful that he was deaf, took him to a hearing specialist. The specialist agreed with the parents that Carlos seemed unresponsive but said that his hearing was not damaged in any way. He urged the parents to give it some time and told them that, perhaps, Carlos was developing more slowly than other children.

At 14 months, Carlos made sounds with his voice, but he had not formed any intelligible words. He often seemed to be "in a world of his own" with little interest in interacting with other family members.

Mona spent hours trying to engage Carlos in play, to little avail. He often recoiled when Mona picked him up and screeched at the top of his lungs when Mona attempted to hug him. Carlos would sit for long stretches and rock back and forth without interruption. During this period of time, the pediatrician suggested that Carlos may have some "developmental delays" but rather than jump to any conclusions, he suggested that the parents needed to "give it some time." The parents stated that Carlos didn't start walking until he was 28 months old.

Ricardo states that his experience with Carlos was similar to Mona's experience. When he would come home from work, he would try to engage Carlos in play, with little success. Rather than show any interest in toys, Carlos would appear dazed, paying little attention to people or objects in the room. Ricardo states that Carlos did become very attached to a small rubber ball and would gaze at it for long periods of time. Ricardo states that, rather than play with the ball like most kids would, Carlos would place it on the floor and then flap his arms wildly.

The parents' concerns were heightened this year when they attempted to place Carlos in a prekindergarten class at East Brook Elementary School. They had hoped that Carlos would begin interacting with other children if placed in a structured environment with them. Carlos was in the class for less than a week when the teacher called Mona and expressed serious concerns about Carlos' readiness for the classroom environment. She stated that Carlos appeared to be extremely "out of step" with his peer group and that she recommended further testing before he continued in this class.

She stated that Carlos was spending most of the day rocking in a corner of the classroom with no interest in interacting with other children. When the teacher approached him and tried to engage him in activities, Carlos would refuse to make eye contact and would continue to rock back and forth endlessly. When the teacher attempted to physically move Carlos into a group activity with other children, he sat on the outer perimeter of the group, displaying no apparent interest in playing with other children. The teacher felt that Carlos was having some serious developmental difficulties and recommended further medical evaluation.

After talking with the preschool teacher, Mona and Ricardo contacted their pediatrician, who referred them to University Hospital for an extensive psychiatric evaluation. Mona and Ricardo are staying at the Ronald McDonald House while their son is hospitalized. After getting Carlos admitted to the hospital and talking with the intake worker, the parents make an appointment to see you the following day. During the interim period, Carlos will be observed closely and given a battery of psychological and developmental tests for children.

Observation of Carlos in the Playroom

Carlos is placed in the playroom at the hospital with an aide and two other children so that his behavior and social interaction can be observed. The room contains a variety of toys, stuffed animals, crayons and paper, a doll house, and other age-appropriate items of interest to most children. For the first 15 minutes, Carlos simply sits on the floor and rocks, despite efforts by the aide to engage him with a toy or stuffed animal. The other two children immediately begin playing with toys and displaying sharing behavior.

Carlos makes no eye contact with the aide. He moves to the corner of the room where he stands flapping his arms and twirling in a circle. He shows no interest in the other two children. Toward the end of the session, one child goes over to Carlos and offers him a toy, asking him if he wants to play. Carlos continues to twirl

and makes no response to the child's request. After a second attempt at trying to get Carlos' attention, the child gives up and goes back to playing with the other child in the room. Carlos sits down in the corner and begins rocking back and forth.

During the half-hour session, he displays poor social interaction skills. Developmentally, his play behavior is not age appropriate. He also displays disturbed behavior that appears to be neurological in origin.

Interview with Mona and Ricardo Vasquez

Mr. and Mrs. Vasquez are seated in the waiting room the following morning when you arrive for their appointment. They appear to be anxiously discussing a meeting they had with Carlos prior to your appointment with them. They both jump up to meet you and begin asking questions before they enter your office. You tell them that Carlos had a good night and slept well. The psychologist will be testing him during the day, and you tell them that you observed him in the playroom the day before.

Mona wants to know whether the doctor has seen Carlos and whether he has found any problems. You explain to her that Carlos received a physical exam when he was admitted but that the doctor will provide them with the information from that exam later in the day when he makes rounds. Mona states that she has been so anxious about her child that she didn't sleep all night. Ricardo nods his head in agreement. You reassure the parents that their child is being well taken care of and that they are going to receive help from the professionals at the hospital.

"You will be participating in the assessment we are doing with Carlos, and you will be kept informed of everything we are doing as we conduct the evaluation," you assure them.

Mona and Ricardo visibly relax and sit back in their chairs. You begin by explaining to them that you are going to need to gather some information about Carlos from the time he was born until the present. You will be asking them a lot of questions in order to understand Carlos and his strengths and weaknesses better. The parents nod their heads and say, "We'll tell you anything you want to know if it will help our son."

"Okay, let's start at the beginning. Why don't you tell me about how it was for you, Mona, during the time you were pregnant with Carlos," you begin.

"Well, it was really fine," Mona responds. "Nothing out of the ordinary. I was very happy to be pregnant. Ricardo and I had saved money to have a baby, and we had been married for 5 years before we planned for Carlos. I was having morning sickness for about the first 3 months, but after that time, I felt good."

"Besides morning sickness, did you get sick at all during your pregnancy?" you inquire.

"No, I took all these vitamins that my doctor gave me, and I didn't even have a cold for the 9 months," Mona responds.

"How was the delivery for you?" you ask. Mona laughs a little and turns to Ricardo.

"I think he was more nervous than I was," Mona states. "We took the Lamaze classes, and Ricardo was ready to call the ambulance when my water broke. I knew we had plenty of time to get to the hospital, so I was calming him down." Mona and Ricardo smile at each other.

"I think I was in labor about 18 hours, which they say isn't abnormal for your first child," Mona reflects. "Carlos arrived around 8 P.M. at night."

"Great. Were there any complications at birth?" you ask.

"No, the doctor said he was a normal, healthy baby boy," Mona replied. "We took him home 2 days later."

"And how about the first few months. How did Carlos seem during that period of time?" you ask.

Ricardo sits up in his chair and states, "I noticed something was different even at that early age. Carlos didn't seem to be developing that close attachment to us that you see with other babies. He didn't seem to like being held or picked up, and sometimes he seemed like a limp doll when I held him."

"When I looked into his eyes, he didn't always seem to be responding to me," Mona adds. "Sometimes, I would tell myself it was just my imagination, but I just sensed something was missing."

"Okay. What about later on when Carlos was 6 to 9 months old? How was Carlos during that period of time?" you ask.

"The thing that worried me the most," Mona says, "was that he never seemed to develop that smile that babies are supposed to have at that age. I would try to get him to smile at me or Ricardo, and he just didn't seem to respond to us. That really concerned me, but everyone told me that some children develop slower than others and not to get worried about it."

"I was concerned, too," Ricardo adds. "You expect to have a cute, little happy baby, and Carlos didn't seem happy. He just seemed to be sad even when he was a baby."

"How was Carlos doing when he was between 1 and 2 years old?" you question.

Mona sighs. "Well, again, we thought something must be wrong. He wasn't talking or walking, and he didn't seem to pay attention to us. So we got his hearing checked when he was about 2 years old, but the doctor said nothing was wrong with his hearing.

"He would just sit and rock in his crib for hours. He didn't seem interested in us or the toys. He was in a world of his own," Ricardo states.

"He finally started walking when he was 28 months old. We were so relieved and happy. We decided maybe he was just slow to develop and that he'd begin to catch up. He never tried to talk much to us, though. He just made sounds like a baby," Mona suggests.

Ricardo adds, "By the time he was 3 years old, we knew Carlos was different from most children. We didn't know what was wrong, and we couldn't get any answers. Everyone just told us that kids develop at different rates and Carlos would probably start talking in full sentences soon, but, as you can see, that hasn't happened."

"You've told me that sometimes Carlos would just sit and rock. What other kinds of behaviors did he show you?" you ask.

"Sometimes, he would just dance around in a circle like a top, but he wouldn't interact with us. He seemed like he wasn't interested in other human beings," Mona says.

"What about feeding? Have you had any difficulties getting Carlos to eat?" you inquire.

"He eats when he wants to, but you can't make him eat," Mona replies. "And he still doesn't use a fork or spoon. He just grabs food with his hand, and he likes to have a bottle of juice or milk. He will go lie down and rock back and forth with his bottle."

"How has toilet training gone for Carlos?" you inquire.

"Not well," Mona states. "Sometimes he'll sit on his potty chair and just rock back and forth for a long time. We started giving him a piece of candy when he used the toilet, but he still has accidents at night, and I still put a diaper on him at night. He doesn't seem to care."

"Okay, so it seems to both of you that Carlos is experiencing some delays in his development and in his social interactions with others. Is that correct?" you ask.

"Yes, definitely. We've really been worried about him lately. He just doesn't act normal like other children," Mona states.

"What do you see as some of Carlos' good qualities?" you ask.

"He's an adorable little boy whom we love with all our hearts," Ricardo tells you. "We just want to help him as much as we can."

"I know you love your son very much, and you're helping him a lot by bringing him here and getting him the help he needs," you reply.

2.3–1   What are some of the psychosocial issues facing Mona and Ricardo?

2.3–2   What are some of the strengths of this family?

2.3–3   What resources might be helpful to this family?

2.3–4   How do you envision your role as a mental health practitioner in helping this family?

2.3–5   How would you diagnose Carlos' problems?

Axis I

Axis II

Axis III

Axis IV

Axis V

_____

Case 2.4

Identifying Information
Client Name: Jamie Mason
Age: 10 years old
Ethnicity: Caucasian
Educational Level: Fifth grade
Parents: Joan and Sonny Mason

Intake Information

Joan Mason, age 36, called for an appointment with a mental health counselor at the Health Plus Center for her son, Jamie, age 10. She stated that Jamie is a fifth-grader at Rolling Elementary School and that the teacher has serious concerns about whether or not Jamie will be able to remain in her class due to his constantly disturbing other students.

Joan stated that Jamie has "severe compulsions" and that she has "tried everything but nothing seems to help." Joan told the intake worker that Jamie "loses control" frequently. During these times, he may run, clear his throat repeatedly, touch the doorknob twice before entering any room, tilt his head from side to side, rapidly blink his eyes, and suddenly touch the ground with his hands by flexing his whole body. According to the intake worker, Joan sounded quite frantic on the phone. She scheduled an appointment for you to see Jamie and Joan Mason the following day.

Initial Interview

You meet Joan Mason and her son, Jamie, in the waiting room at the scheduled time. They are seated in the corner of the waiting room looking at *Highlights for Children*. Jamie appears to be a cute, freckled-faced, redheaded little boy. The resemblance between mother and son is quite noticeable, as Joan also has a striking appearance—tall, thin, and red-haired like Jamie. After observing them for a moment, you notice that Jamie is frequently making gut-tural noises in his throat and odd gestures with his head.

You introduce yourself to Jamie and Joan and ask Joan if she would talk to you by herself in your office while Jamie remains in the waiting room. Joan tells Jamie that she won't be gone long and follows you back to your office. Jamie settles back in his chair, making some odd utterances as you and Joan walk out of the room.

After getting settled in your office and without any prompting, Joan asks you if you noticed Jamie's "noises." She states that he makes noises all day long without any provocation, and she is sure he can't help himself. She tells you that the problems began about 2 years ago but recently have gotten much worse. "Initially, Sonny and I would just tell him to stop making those noises in his throat, and he would tell us he couldn't help it. We didn't realize it was a problem for him and thought he was just trying to get all the attention or annoy us in some way. After we sent him to his room a couple of times for making those irritating noises, I began to realize Jamie really had no control over those noises, and then we just tried to get him to be quiet when he was losing control."

"Okay, so he makes noises in his throat like he's trying to clear it. Does he make any other noises?" you query.

"Well, after the throat clearing came these odd mannerisms," Joan tells you. "He will suddenly jerk his head from side to side for no reason at all. He also kicks his leg out to the side sometimes or suddenly jerks his body backward and then touches the floor. It looks very odd, and I've noticed it seems to actually get worse when we begin paying attention to it. If we just act like it's not an issue, it seems better after a while."

"He makes noises with his throat and jerks his head and body in odd ways and sometimes kicks his leg out to the side. Is there anything else?" you ask.

"Yes, all those things you just mentioned we could deal with more or less. When Jamie started school this year though, he began making the 'go to hell' sign with his middle finger and jumping around saying 'fuck you, fuck you, fuck you' right in the middle of class. His teacher was appalled, as you can imagine. The first time it happened, she screamed at Jamie to stop immediately and grabbed his arm and marched him down to the principal's office. It was pretty devastating to Jamie. When I got to school, he was crying hard and ran into my arms saying, 'Mom, I try to be good, but I can't stop it.' I felt terrible because I realized, maybe for the first time, that this problem really was out of Jamie's control. Sonny and I should have done something a long time ago, but we kept thinking he was just going through a stage and he'd grow out of it."

Joan continues by saying that right before this incident at school, she had seen a "talk show" program on television one morning where there were several children who had the same symptoms as Jamie had. For the first time, it dawned on her that Jamie's odd noises and compulsions could be a mental problem that Jamie might not grow out of. Since Jamie's outburst in class last week, he has not been back to school. The principal asked Sonny and Joan to have Jamie examined medically and suggested he could have a psychological problem.

"It really scared me when the principal said Jamie might have emotional problems. That's what those kids on TV had," Joan says. "I knew in the back of my mind he was right. I just didn't want to believe that Jamie might have that problem. I know he can't help it. Sonny and I have tried everything we know to get him to stop, but he can't. It's out of control."

"I think you're probably right, Joan," you suggest calmly. "These noises and movements probably are very difficult, if not impossible, for Jamie to control right now. What I would like to do is to get as much information as possible from you about Jamie's behavior so that we can help him in the best way possible."

"Okay, that sounds good. I'm relieved someone finally understands these problems we've been having," Joan responds.

"Are there any other habits or compulsions, as you put it, of which you are aware that Jamie exhibits?" you ask.

"Well, there's one other thing I haven't mentioned yet. You see, he has this thing about touching doorknobs. He seems to have this irresistible urge to touch doorknobs. It's as if he's obsessed with them. When I ask him about it, he says he's got to touch the doorknob and walk through the door in order to get rid of the thoughts. I'm not real sure what he's talking about, but it clearly gets him very upset when I ask too many questions about it. He just says, 'Mom, you don't understand; I've got to touch doorknobs twice to get rid of these thoughts in my head,' so I just don't push him any further about it."

"Does this seem to be all the time or just occasionally?" you ask.

"Oh, everywhere we go, all the time, no matter where we are, he's completely obsessed with doorknobs," Joan says with dismay.

"Can you think of anything else?" you ask.

"No, I think I've told you about everything," Joan says as she sinks lower in her chair. It appears that Joan is feeling discouraged after telling you about all of Jamie's issues.

"What do you see as Jamie's strengths?" you ask.

Joan brightens up and sits up straighter in her chair. "Well, he's a wonderful child. He's very bright and good-hearted. He loves animals, and he's not a mean child at all. He always thinks of others' feelings. Until he began having so much trouble at school, he was always a pretty happy child and got along well with other children."

"So, it sounds as if Jamie has some real strengths. What about his relationship with other people in the family?" you ask.

"Well, he gets along great with my husband, Sonny. They do a lot together, just the two of them. Sonny really loves Jamie and spends a good amount of time with him. And Jamie is our only child, so he's always been the focus of our attention, I guess."

"That's great," you respond. "It sounds like there are many really good qualities about Jamie and you have good relationships with each other as a family. Those are important factors in helping Jamie cope with the issues he's facing right now. Do you have any questions or other concerns before I talk with Jamie?"

"No, I think I've told you everything," Joan says as she stands up and walks with you to the waiting room.

2.4–1   What strengths did you notice in Jamie's family?

2.4–2   What impact would you imagine that these behaviors are having on Jamie's social development?

2.4–3   What resources would you recommend for Joan to access?

2.4–4   What other professionals would you plan to involve in this case?

2.4–5   What is your initial diagnosis for Jamie?
Axis I

Axis II

Axis III

Axis IV

Axis V

Case 2.5

Identifying Information
Client Name: Joey Brown
Age: 10 years old
Ethnicity: Caucasian
Educational Level: Fifth grade
Parents: Stella and Bill Gardner (stepfather)

Intake Information
Joey Brown, a 10-year-old, blue-eyed, blond-haired boy, has been scheduled for an appointment with you by the Family and Child Guidance Center intake worker. She wrote on the intake form that Stella Gardner, the mother, will be at the appointment also. Stella told the intake worker that Joey is a really lovable little boy; however, he is having a lot of problems with his schoolwork. The intake worker also noted that Mrs. Gardner is 32 years old, married to Joey's stepfather, Bill, and has another child, Jill Gardner, by him.

Initial Interview
You meet Stella and Joey in the waiting room. Joey is sitting quietly in the chair next to his mother, looking at a picture book of animals. Joey is pointing out different types of animals for his mother. You greet Stella and Joey and ask Joey if he has any pets at home. Joey says he has one dog, Gruffy, and three gerbils, Larry, Curly, and Moe. He tells you Gruffy can play catch with a ball when Joey throws it to him. When you ask Joey if he'd like to come to your office and talk for a little while, he readily agrees to go with you.

Joey talks about his gerbils on the way to your office. You suggest he might like to draw a picture of his family while the two of you talk.

Joey says, "Sure, I can draw with those marker pens on the table," which he noticed when he entered your office.

You ask Joey where he goes to school and what he likes best about it. He states that he goes to Foxtown Elementary and that he is in the fifth grade. He tells you he doesn't like much about school except recess. His least favorite subject is spelling and writing, and his most favorite subject is geography because of the maps.

Joey tells you he has two best friends, Jay and Charles, who like to play softball with him. He tells you he hates his reading teacher, Ms. Jones. "She's always telling me I'm not paying attention and I'm making mistakes, but I am paying attention. I just don't get what she's talking about." Joey tells you that Ms. Jones has put him in the dumbest reading group because she doesn't like him.

You ask him if he knows why Ms. Jones doesn't like him, and he says, "Because she thinks I'm really dumb." Joey also tells you that Mr. Mack, his math teacher, doesn't think he's dumb at all. He always makes good grades in Mr. Mack's class.

Overall, Joey appears to be a very affable boy with a sense of humor and pleasant personality. While in your office, he sits quietly drawing and is able to carry on a conversation with you easily. He appears to be focused on his drawing and the discussion you were having with him. His family drawing appears to be average for a 10-year-old and shows no indications of psychopathology.

After talking with Joey, you ask him to stay in the waiting room while you talk with his mother, Stella. Before seeing Stella, however, you write down some notes.

2.5–1   What are some of Joey's strengths?

2.5–2   What are some of Joey's weak areas?

Interview with Stella

Stella is 32 years old and works part-time as an administrative assistant at a local law firm. She states that she was married for 4 years to Joey's father and had Joey after 2 years of marriage. She states that Joey's father died in a motorcycle accident when Joey was 2 years old. She married her present husband, Bill, who works at the local hospital as a nurse anesthetist in the operating room, when Joey was 3 years old. She tells you that Joey doesn't remember his real father, and that Bill has always treated Joey as his son. Jill was born when Joey was 5 years old and has just started kindergarten.

Stella states that she is concerned about her son because "he just doesn't think much of himself." She states that she thinks Joey has low self-esteem due to problems he has in school. Stella quickly adds that she doesn't think Joey is dumb. "He just has trouble with reading and spelling, and his handwriting is atrocious," she exclaims.

"The teachers keep telling me that maybe he needs to be on that medicine they give kids these days, you know, Ritalin, but I thought that was for kids with behavior problems, and Joey is a nice child who hardly ever causes any problems. I took him to the doctor last year to see if he needed glasses, and the doctor said he had perfect eyesight, so I just don't know what to do. The teachers say that Joey always has the lowest grades on spelling tests, and he reads more like a third-grader."

Stella tells you that despite all of Joey's problems with reading and spelling, he is one of the top students in the class when it comes to math. "He even knows how to multiply double-digit numbers," she states.

Stella states that Joey is not a very rowdy child. He seems to be active like any child is, but he has no problem sitting still when told he needs to be quiet. He likes to play softball and basketball and has several friends in the neighborhood who come to the house and ask him to play on a daily basis. Joey gets along with his younger sister, although they sometimes bicker as any siblings would. He likes Bill and considers him to be his father.

You ask Stella if Joey has ever been kept back a year in school. She states that Joey is actually one of the oldest in his fifth-grade class because of his birthday. She didn't feel like pushing him into school early since he would have been the youngest in his class. She says that other than the problems with reading, writing, and spelling, Joey is a good, lovable child. "He has a great personality when you get to know him, and he really has been an easy child to manage."

2.5–3 What tentative diagnosis would you give Joey?

Axis I

Axis II

Axis III

Axis IV

Axis V

2.5–4 What would you recommend as the next step in getting help for Joey's problem?

Case 2.6

Identifying Information
Client Name: Michael Barron
Age: 12 years old
Ethnicity: Caucasian
Educational Level: Seventh grade
Parents: Mandy and Jerry Collins (stepfather)

Intake Information
Mike, a 12-year-old Caucasian male, was referred to the Children's Counseling Center by the school counselor at the middle school where he attends seventh grade. You are a practitioner at the Counseling Center and have had other referrals from this counselor. The referral resulted from an incident in which Mike and a friend were picked up by the police for skipping school. Mike and Bobby were hanging out near a local pool parlor when two patrol officers questioned why they weren't in school. Although Bobby gave the officers his correct name and address, Mike told the officers his name was "Barry Burrito" and he lived in Chihuahua on the border of Mexico.

When Mike and Bobby were taken to the local police station, Mike finally told the police his real name. He was given a citation, and his parents were called and interviewed at the station. Mandy works as a technician for a local computer corporation, and Jerry is a self-employed house painter and carpenter. At the request of the school counselor, Mandy made the initial appointment and arrived on time at 8 A.M. with Mike and her 2-year-old daughter, Elisa. Mandy is pregnant with her third child and is expecting to deliver in the next month.

Initial Interview
You greet the family in the waiting room and notice that Mike is sitting off in the corner looking very glum while Mandy is reading a book to Elisa. You suggest that a student intern can stay with Elisa in the playroom while you talk with Mike and Mandy. Mike makes no eye contact with you but gets up and follows his mother to your office. Mandy appears to be dressed for work in a tailored pantsuit, while Mike is wearing baggy blue jeans and an oversized T-shirt with a rock band logo on the back of it. Mandy apologizes for needing to bring Elisa with her, but she takes her to the child-care center at her job.

Mandy begins the session by stating that she feels as if she's losing control of Mike and is concerned about his risky behaviors and constant lying. "I just can't trust him anymore," she says.

The latest incident with the police is just one in a series of problems she has been having over the past year. She feels that Mike disregards any rules that are placed on his behavior. She states that on the day of the incident with the police she took Mike to school and told him to walk home afterward. She told him that she'd be home at 5 P.M. Mike and Bobby apparently decided to leave school during the midmorning break. They walked down to the local pool parlor where they were found panhandling to buy lottery tickets at the convenience store next door.

"I think Bobby is a bad influence on Mikey. Bobby is 16 years old and has been nothing but trouble since becoming friends with Mikey. That's when Mikey began sneaking out of the house at night, lying about his whereabouts, and drinking alcohol at Bobby's house when his parents weren't home." Mandy states that this is the first time the police have been involved and it's really scared her.

Interview with Mike
You decide to talk with Mike alone about the incident with the police and ask Mandy if she'd like a cup of coffee in the waiting room. Mike remains slouched in his chair, looking disinter-

ested and depressed. When his mother leaves the room, he states that she's always bugging him about school.

"She's always griping about my grades and how I'm never going to get into college if I don't make good grades. I don't even want to go to college. I'm never going to make A's in school. I'm just dumb, I guess."

"What grade are you in, Mike?" you query.

"Seventh grade, middle school," Mike replies.

You ask Mike if there's anything he likes about school, and he states that he likes to be with his friends and likes art class. "I don't like math; I hate language arts; science is okay, but I'm really not good at anything except art."

"What do you like to do in art?" you query. For the first time during the interview, Mike appears animated. "I like to draw, paint with watercolors or acrylics, and work with clay. One of my sculptures won a prize in the art contest last year." You note that Mike seems to feel good about this accomplishment.

You ask about any other activities Mike might enjoy. He states that he tried out for basketball but quit after being a substitute for part of the season. "It was so boring; I just sat on the bench the whole game."

"What about at home? How are things at home?"

Mike shrugged his shoulders and said, "Okay I guess."

"How do you get along with your stepfather, Jerry?"

Mike slumps back down in his chair and stares at the ceiling. "He's never home. He works all the time, and he's always telling me what to do. He's not my real father, and he doesn't care about me, just Elisa and the new baby."

"Do you ever get to see your real father?" you ask.

"He doesn't live here anymore and got married to someone else. I haven't seen him in about a year, and he never calls. My mom is always saying he never pays his child support. I don't really care about him. He and my mom got divorced when I was just 5 years old, and all I remember is that he was drunk all the time and used to yell at my mom and sometimes hit her."

You ask Mike if there's anything else he likes to do. He states that he likes to go to the mall with his friends; he likes to surf the Internet and play Nintendo. "My mom is a computer nerd. She knows everything about computers. I wish I had my own computer like hers."

"It sounds like you have some things you do very well and other things that you aren't so happy about. Maybe we can talk more about these things." Mike nods his head and plays with his belt buckle.

Mike appears to be getting noticeably more uncomfortable sitting still and talking. He taps his feet, fidgets with his fingers, and appears distracted by every sound in the hallway. You decide to stop the interview with Mike at this point and talk further with Mandy. You escort Mike back to the waiting room and give him some paper and colored pencils, asking him if he can draw a picture for you. He sits on the floor, using the child's table to spread out the paper and pencils, and seems occupied with the project. You tell him that you are going to talk to his mother about the family situation and his childhood. Mike shrugs his shoulders and says, "Okay."

Interview with Mandy

You ask Mandy if she would mind coming back to your office to talk about the family situation when Mike was younger. You start by explaining to Mandy that you'd like to get some information about the years when Mike was growing up and the family situation at the time.

"I'd like to start at the beginning and find out as much as I can about your experience with Mike as your son. So, I'd like to go back to the time before Mike was born and ask you about the pregnancy and birth and so forth," you begin.

Mandy nods and says, "Well, the pregnancy was fine. I had some morning sickness for about 3 months in the beginning, but it wasn't that bad and went away by about the fourth month of pregnancy." She goes on to tell you that she and her former husband, Tim, hadn't really planned on having a baby, but they were happy about her pregnancy. She states that nothing unusual occurred during the pregnancy and she had a normal birth without any complications.

Mandy goes on to say that shortly after Mike was born, she began having problems in her marriage due to Tim's drinking all the time. "He worked construction, and when he came home, he'd just sit in front of the TV and drink one beer after another. At first, he'd just fall asleep in front of the television, but then he began getting belligerent and would pick fights with me over little things."

Mandy describes a great deal of marital discord in the first 5 years of Mike's life. She finally decided to leave Tim and went to live with her mother for a couple of years while attending a community college to learn computer programming.

Mandy states that Mike seemed like a normal, happy, but very active little boy and didn't have any problems until he got to kindergarten. At that point, he began having trouble getting along with other kids in his class. He was so active that he would sometimes aggravate the other children, and the teacher called several times that year and said Mike just refused to follow the rules. It was apparent that Mandy was focused on her marital situation, as well as busy going to school, and had felt that he would just grow out of it.

In first grade, Mike had difficulties with his letters and numbers and seemed to be a little behind other kids his age. The teacher felt that he had a developmental problem and was maturing more slowly than other kids but didn't seem too concerned about it. In the second and third grades, it became apparent to Mandy that something more than just immaturity was going on, so she had him tested by the school psychologist, who told her Mike had ADHD and should be seen by a physician.

Mandy took him to a pediatrician who put him on Ritalin during the weekdays. He did not take Ritalin on the weekends. She said it helped his activity level, and he seemed better able to pay attention in class. His grades improved a little; he was making B's and C's instead of D's after he started taking the Ritalin. He still got into trouble for his conduct, especially on the playground. He couldn't seem to get along and never had many friends.

Mandy mentions an incident in sixth grade that really worries her. Apparently, Mike had walked into a neighbor's house through the back door and stolen some cookies that were sitting out on the counter, as well as a jar of loose change that was within eyesight. He had hidden the jar of change under his bed. Jerry walked into his room one night when he was sitting on his bed counting the money. Mandy was chagrined, and Jerry was livid. Jerry thought that Mike had stolen the money from his drawer in the bedroom, but Mike confessed he'd taken it from the neighbors' house. Jerry made Mike go over to the neighbors' and tell them he'd taken the money and apologize. Luckily, the neighbors didn't call the police or try to prosecute him.

Mandy relates another incident that occurred about 5 months ago. Mike had been to the swimming pool in the neighborhood one day during the summer and met another little boy over there who had some firecrackers from the Fourth of July. Mike and the other boy were found throwing the firecrackers at some cats who belonged to a neighbor who lived near the pool. The cats had been injured, and Mandy and Jerry made Mike work the rest of the summer to pay the vet fees for the injured cats. "The thing that bothered me the most," Mandy sighs, "was the fact that Mike didn't show any remorse about having hurt the animals. That really bothered me."

Mandy states that Jerry and Mike have never gotten along very well, and she's had to restrain Jerry on a couple of occasions when he wanted to whip Mike with a belt as punishment. "Jerry is very traditional. He thinks I've just been too lenient with Mike and all he needs is a good spanking. I really don't know what to do with Mike these days. He's getting bigger and older, and I'm afraid he's going to get into big trouble with the law if he doesn't learn how to follow the rules."

You tell Mandy that you feel you have an understanding of what some of the problems have been for Mike but that you would also like to know about some of his strengths.

Mandy tells you that Mike's biggest strength is his artistic abilities. "He is extremely artistic, which he probably gets from my father, who was an amateur artist. He can draw almost anything, and he paints and sculpts and can make beautiful pottery out of clay." Mandy states that he used to be helpful around the house, but recently, he won't do anything she asks. She states that she's concerned about the time she'll have to focus on the new baby when it arrives and how that will affect Mike.

2.6–1 What are some of the underlying issues that may be affecting Mike's behavior?

2.6–2 What are some of Mike's strengths?

2.6–3 What are some underlying fears that you imagine Mandy is having concerning her son?

2.6–4 Who would you like to get permission to talk with outside the family concerning Mike's behavior?

2.6 – 5   How would you initially diagnose Mike?

Axis I

Axis II

Axis III

Axis IV

Axis V

_____

Identifying Information
Client Name: Jason Jones
Age: 18 years old
Ethnicity: African American
Marital Status: Single, no children

Background Information
As a new caseworker at the State School for the Developmentally Disabled—Community Services Division, you have been given a client caseload of 30 developmentally disabled adults. These clients have been residents of the State School for at least 10 years and have been discharged to the Community Services Program where they participate in a companion-living program. In order to get to know your clients better, you decide to read the files from the previous caseworker. Jason Jones is one of your companion-living clients.

Social and Developmental History
Jason Jones was born to a 16-year-old, single, African American mother who received no prenatal care prior to giving birth. The mother gave birth with no medical assistance in the bathroom of a gas station. She had no permanent residence and after moving from one homeless shelter to another, she finally left the baby at Child Protective Services and gave up all parental rights. At that time, Jason became a ward of the state.

Jason lived with a foster family until he was 5 years old. At that time, the foster family stated they could no longer care for Jason because he was so "slow" and wasn't developing the way most children do. At 5 years old, he was speaking only in one-syllable words, was not toilet trained, and was becoming a behavior problem. Since the foster family had four other children to care for, they decided to return Jason to Child Protective Services. At that time, Jason was tested by a psychologist who determined he was developmentally delayed. He was placed at the State School for the Developmentally Disabled, where he has remained a client for the past 13 years.

From the ages of 5 to 18, Jason has made some achievements in his educational development. He is able to write the alphabet and his name. He can use a calculator to add and subtract. He knows the value of money and is able to discern the difference between lesser and greater amounts of money. He is able to understand time and is able to use a digital, electronic watch. He has also learned how to ride a bicycle.

At 15 years old, Jason was placed in the advanced residential unit to prepare him for community living. He was taught daily living skills that he would need in order to function in the community. He learned how to use the bus system, go grocery shopping, cook basic meals, perform basic housekeeping tasks (such as cleaning and laundering clothes), and manage basic hygiene. He was later placed in a job as a dishwasher at a local restaurant where he was teamed with a work coordinator who taught him the skills he would need to function adequately in that position. Jason has held the same job for the past 2 years and currently earns $10.50 an hour. His employer states that Jason is an excellent employee who rarely misses a day of work.

Currently, Jason lives in an apartment near the State School with a roommate who is also a client at the school. In order to stay in the apartment, he must remain employed. Jason rides his bike to his job each day. He has his own checking account although he needs assistance with writing checks and depositing his paycheck. Jason has bought his own microwave oven, television, VCR, and a CD player.

Jason pays half the monthly rent and utilities with his paycheck. He also buys his own groceries. Jason socializes with other State School clients living in the same apartment complex. He enjoys going to the mall and to the movies. He requires supervision with household management issues, such as cleaning and laundering his clothes. In the past year, Jason was tested by a State School psychologist and was assigned an IQ of 35–40.

Initial Meeting with Jason

You schedule a time to meet Jason at his apartment one afternoon after work. Jason is a tall and attractive African American man who does not give the appearance of being disabled. He greets you at the front door and shows you into his small apartment. He seems very excited and happy that you have come to see him.

When you begin conversing with him, you realize he has a serious stuttering problem that hinders his ability to communicate. He is often unable to pronounce words and becomes very anxious when he can't explain something adequately. You often have to ask him to repeat himself in order to understand what he is trying to say.

Jason asks you if you are his new caseworker and if you are a nice person. He seems eager to impress you with his apartment, opening all the cabinets and closets for you to examine. He states that he needs to go to the grocery store since he only has hot dog buns in the refrigerator. A strong odor of disinfectant throughout the rooms indicates that he attempted to clean the house before your arrival. Jason asks you if you're going to come check on him every week, and you tell him you'll come by to help him with his shopping and checkbook.

Jason pulls his checkbook from his back pocket and tells you that he needs to put his paycheck in the bank. He has his paycheck folded into the top flap of the checkbook. He tells you to look at it and says, "Isn't that good?"

You ask him if he knows how much money he made with this paycheck, and he says, "A hundred something dollars."

You explain to him that he's actually made $322 and that he can sign the check on the back to be deposited into his account. Together, you decide to take a trip to the bank to deposit his check.

On the way to the bank, Jason tells you about his job and his schedule. He gets up at 5 A.M. so that he can be at work by 6 A.M. He works through the lunch hour and gets home around 3 P.M. He tells you proudly that he has had the job for a long time. Jason appears to be a happy and gregarious fellow. You stop at the Dairy Queen on the way back to his apartment, and he gets a milkshake. The treat seems very satisfying to him.

Jason appears to function on a higher level than his IQ would indicate. He has some excellent daily living skills that have made it possible for him to live outside the State School. He is an engaging person who seems to enjoy his work and home.

He receives assistance and social support from the State School professionals and his friends who live in the apartment complex. Jason has some difficulties in getting along with his roommate, Lee, who is less industrious than Jason. Jason gets angry with Lee, who doesn't always follow through with his share of the housework. Overall, however, Jason is currently doing well in his independent living situation.

2.7–1   Write a paragraph describing Jason's strengths.

2.7–2   What are some areas with which you think Jason will need assistance?

2.7–3   What resources may be of benefit to Jason?

2.7–4   What is your diagnosis for Jason?
Axis I

Axis II

Axis III

Axis IV

Axis V

Case 2.8

Identifying Information
Client Name: Megan Coleman
Age: 6 years old
Ethnicity: Caucasian
Educational Level: First grade
Parents: Sue and Don Coleman

Background Information
You are a clinical social work practitioner for a children's mental health agency in a large metropolitan area in the Midwest. You have a meeting scheduled with Sue and Don regarding their 6-year-old daughter, Megan.

Intake Information
Sue, age 33, called to make the appointment due to her escalating concerns about Megan's inability to attend school because of constant headaches and stomachaches. She told the intake worker that the pediatrician had seen Megan on three occasions in the past 8 weeks and could find no evidence of illness. The physician had given her a referral to the Child Guidance Center. The intake worker suggested that, if possible, Megan's father, Don, should attend the initial interview along with Sue.

Initial Interview
You meet Sue and Don in the waiting room of the agency. Both look anxious and are sitting on the edges of their seats. When you introduce yourself, they both jump up immediately and hurriedly walk down the hall to your office with you. When they sit down in your office, they are still sitting on the edges of their seats, clutching the armrests of their chairs, and tapping their feet on the floor. You note their anxious expressions and behaviors as you begin the initial interview.

"I'm glad you could make the appointment today. You both look like you might have a lot on your minds, but before we begin, let me tell you a little bit about the agency and what I do here. The Child Guidance Center is a nonprofit, United Way agency that runs on a sliding-scale fee system, which means that the fee you pay for the services we provide here is based on your income. There is someone here who will talk to you more about that when we are finished here today. We have several programs at this agency, and I'm involved with the Counseling Program. We also have a Big Brothers/Big Sisters Program and a Domestic Violence Program. Do you have any questions so far?"

Both Sue and Don shake their heads indicating "no."

"Great. I want to find out what brought you to the agency today, but first I want to explain to you that everything we talk about here is confidential. I will not share any of the information we discuss today with anyone other than my supervisor, with two exceptions: If you tell me you are going to hurt yourself, I have to tell someone about that; or if you tell me you are going to hurt anyone else, I have to report that also. If I need to talk with anyone else, like a physician or the school, I will get your permission to do that before moving forward. Is all of this information clear to both of you?" you ask.

Sue and Don both say, "Yes."

"Good. I understand that you have some concerns about your 6-year-old daughter, Megan. Can you tell me what's been going on with her?"

Sue begins, "Well, Megan is a very sweet child. She has always been our angel and has never caused any problems out of the ordinary for us. She is really very bright and has already learned the alphabet and is beginning to read a little, like easy reading books. She also is mesmerized by the computer and has learned her numbers and beginning addition with the computer games. She loved kindergarten last year. We sent her to our church kindergarten, and she really seemed to enjoy being with the other kids and learning new things. But this year has been a completely different story."

"What's happened this year?" you ask. "She's started first grade, I assume."

"Oh yes, she started in August, so it's been about 3 months now, and she was doing fine the first week." Sue rolls her eyes and rubs her forehead.

"And then what happened?" you prompt.

"Well, on the Monday morning of the second week of school, she woke up and said her stomach hurt. I suggested maybe she was hungry and would feel better after breakfast. She got up and ate breakfast, and the minute she finished she said her stomach hurt even more. I suggested she go get dressed for school and see if she didn't feel better, and she burst into tears and said she had a stomachache and she felt terrible and she couldn't get dressed. She threw a regular tantrum, and so I decided she must really be sick and told her that maybe she needed to get back in bed and stay home that day. She immediately stopped crying and went to her bedroom and climbed into bed. Since this just isn't how she usually acts, I thought she must really not be feeling well.

"So, she stayed in bed all morning and watched TV, and by lunch time she was feeling much better. She got up and helped me around the house and played all afternoon. Then she ate a good dinner. And I thought everything was okay. But the next morning the same thing happened. She started complaining about her stomach hurting as soon as she got up and started screaming when I said I thought she'd be okay at school, although I told her if she wasn't, she could have the teacher call me."

"She stayed home the second day?" you ask.

"Yes, and the third day, and that's when I made an appointment at the doctor's office."

You ask Don what his thoughts and feelings were regarding Megan's stomachaches.

"Well, I didn't know what to think. Maybe she was really sick. Maybe she got food poisoning or something. I agreed with Sue that Megan needed to go to the doctor, but the doctor said he couldn't find anything wrong. The next day after seeing the doctor, we really pushed her to go to school. Sue was going to take her in the car, and Megan got as far as the front door of the school and began crying hysterically, saying she had a bad stomachache again. Sue didn't have much choice but to take her home. But now things are out of control. Megan has been home for 8 weeks and to the doctor three times, and he says there's nothing physically wrong with her. He says he thinks there is something psychological going on and we need to come here. I don't know; maybe we need to take her to a specialist," Don replies.

You ask Sue if she agrees with her husband's perspective on things.

"Yes, he's got it right except he's not home when she suddenly gets better every afternoon and is ready to go outside and play. I'm so frustrated and confused by all of this I don't know what to do anymore. And, in the meantime, she's missing all this school."

2.8–1   Write a short summary of the presenting problem.

You decide you need to gather more information about the family composition. You ask Sue and Don about any other children or relatives.

Sue responds, "We have a 2-year-old child, Donny. He's a handful. He keeps me busy 24 hours a day, 7 days a week. Little boys are so different from little girls. He is very active. I don't think he ever walked. He went from crawling to running. I have to keep my eye on him every minute."

Don chimes in, "My parents also live nearby. Sue's parents live in Florida, but my parents and my sister are right here. They sometimes take Donny and Megan for the evening or to spend the night so we can go out every once in a while. We all get along real well."

"How has it been for Megan when you leave her with your parents or a baby-sitter?" you ask.

"Well, we haven't been able to do that for the last couple of months because we've been too worried about her being sick," Sue responds. "So, actually, since all of this started with Megan, we haven't been out at all. One time Don's mother came over and watched the kids in the afternoon when I had a meeting to go to, but other than that, I haven't been away from them for the past couple of months."

"So, I assume, Sue, that you are a full-time mom and, Don, you work full-time. Is that correct?"

"Yes, I have a job with a computer company here in town, and sometimes I have to work from 7 A.M. until 7 P.M. and some Saturdays. I'm gone a lot, so I don't see everything that goes on at home the way Sue does," Don responds.

"Have you noticed anything else that has been different in your family over the past year or so or with Megan?" you inquire.

"Well, ever since the pediatrician told us we needed to come here, I've been thinking of every little thing that might've upset Megan," Sue responds. "We really are a very close-knit family and do everything with our kids, but I did think of one thing I've noticed over the past year that's been different with Megan. You see, she seems to have developed a little resentment toward Donny. It seems to me that it happened about the time Donny started to walk. Before that time, when he was just a baby, Megan used to be my big helper and liked to play with Donny and help me feed him and get him dressed and stuff like that. But, after he started walking, Megan seemed to resent him taking my attention away from her in a way."

"Then you've noticed that Megan gets angry when you're paying attention to Donny. What does she do when you notice she's feeling this way?"

"Well, for example, the other day I was playing with Donny on the floor while I was waiting for something to cook in the microwave. There were several cars and trucks on the floor, and Megan came in the room. I asked her if she wanted to play with us. Although she didn't look too happy, she sat down next to me and starting playing with some of the little cars. Then the microwave buzzed, and I went in the kitchen to fix dinner. When I came back just a few minutes later, Megan had taken all the little cars and hidden them behind the couch where Donny couldn't find them. When I asked her what happened to the toys, she just smiled and said, 'I don't know; I guess it's time to play with the dolls now, Mommy.' There have also been many times when I'm tending to Donny and she becomes very quiet and just goes off to a corner and sulks for a while."

"Sue, how long has this type of behavior been going on?" you ask.

"Well, probably for about 6 or 8 months now."

"And I've noticed that she seems to get mad more often and it always seems to be related to Donny somehow," Don offers. "I somehow thought that was just normal kid stuff though."

"Do you think it's possible that Megan might feel she might be missing something that's going on at home with Donny when she goes to school?" you ask.

Sue and Don agree that this might be a possibility. You explain to Sue and Don that you think you can help Megan with the problem she's having with school, but you will need their cooperation. First, you would like to have Megan come in for a half-hour session, followed by a half-hour session with Sue and Don. They agree to this arrangement and schedule another appointment when they can bring Megan to the agency.

2.8–2   What strengths do you assess this family to have?

Initial Interview with Megan

When Megan comes to the agency for an initial play therapy session, you observe that she is sitting very close to her mother in the waiting room on the couch. Sue is reading a book to her, and when you come into the room, Megan holds on to her mother's arm when you suggest she can come back to your office and play for a short time. You tell Megan that her mother will be right here in the waiting room and won't go anywhere while you and Megan are playing together. Sue encourages Megan to go with you, and Megan, somewhat shyly, agrees to go with you.

She tells you she likes to play dolls, and you give her the family of dolls (mother, father, girl, boy) and tell her she can make up a story for the dolls. In the first story, the little boy is bad and the little girl is good and the parents are mad at the little boy and punish him by making him sit in the corner. In the second story, the little girl goes to sleep, and the rest of the family goes away leaving the little girl alone. When you ask her about school, she says that she liked it at first and then she didn't like it at all. You ask Megan why she doesn't like school now, and she tells you that she doesn't know — it just makes her cry.

2.8–3   Based on this interview, what is your preliminary diagnosis for Megan?
Axis I

Axis II

Axis III

Axis IV

Axis V

2.8 – 4   What steps would you initially take to try to get Megan back into school?

DIFFERENTIAL DIAGNOSIS

Although many of the mental disorders of childhood and adolescence, such as Mental Retardation and Tourette's Disorder, have unique symptoms, other disorders are more difficult to differentiate. For example, Oppositional Defiant Disorder differs from Conduct Disorder in level of severity and harm to others. Conduct-disordered children also display a pattern of behavior that in the court system would be deemed delinquent.

2.DD–1   Describe the distinctions you saw between Cases 2.2 and 2.6.

Another issue that must be assessed carefully occurs in the case of a child diagnosed with ADHD. Frequently, these children appear to be "out of control" and defiant when, in fact, they are simply unable to focus their attention, stay in their seats, and/or remain calm. Children with severe cases of hyperactivity may appear initially as having problems with authority figures. These symptoms are similar to those of ODD. However, if the supposedly "defiant" behaviors occur only in conjunction with ADHD symptoms, the ODD diagnosis is not appropriate.

Furthermore, children with ADHD frequently have comorbid learning disabilities. In such cases, a dual diagnosis of a learning disability and ADHD should be diagnosed.

2.DD–2   What additional symptoms would Joey Brown have displayed in order to have a diagnosis of ODD?

2.DD–3   Which of the other cases in this chapter could have a second diagnosis?

2.DD–4   Based on this discussion, what diagnoses would you want to rule out for Case 2.1?

InfoTrac keywords

ADHD, child mental health assessment, Conduct Disorder, Learning Disabilities, Mental Retardation, Pervasive Developmental Disorders, Separation Anxiety Disorder, Tic Disorders

Cognitive Disorders and Neurological Disorders Due to a Medical Condition

3

DISORDERS

The mental disorders covered in these two sections of the DSM-IV-TR (APA, 2000) share etiology related to physiological processes. For most of these disorders, this physiological causal issue is a general medical condition. However, there are also some specific diagnoses in the first chapter that are related to the use of one or more substances or exposure to a toxic agent.

The hallmark of Delirium is a disturbance in consciousness (i.e., awareness of one's environment and/or the capacity to focus and direct one's attention). Other disturbances in cognitive functioning (e.g., language disturbance, disorientation, memory deficits) may be present as well. This condition develops over a relatively short period of time, and the intensity of symptoms fluctuates in the course of a day. Some of the most common risk factors for Delirium include use of a general anesthetic or multiple medications, a history of drug or alcohol abuse, sensory loss, social isolation, unfamiliar environments, sleep deprivation, central nervous system disorders, metabolic disorders, and cardiopulmonary disorders. The specific Delirium diagnoses are determined by the underlying cause (i.e., a medical condition, substance use, or an unknown etiology)(APA, 2000).

In contrast, the prominent symptoms for Dementia include memory impairment and other cognitive disturbances (particularly language disturbances, apraxia, agnosia, and/or disturbances in executive functioning). Most Dementias develop slowly and display a steadily deteriorating course. The exceptions to this pattern include Vascular Dementia and Dementia due to Head Trauma, in which symptoms appear rapidly after the damaging event. Symptoms are directly related to the portion of the brain that is being affected. For example, in Dementia of the Alzheimer's Type, impairment is focused in the parietal and temporal portions of the brain, which are central to memory functions. Some of the most common medical conditions related to Dementia are Alzheimer's disease, Pick's disease, HIV disease, Parkinson's disease, Huntington's disease, and brain traumas (including strokes). As it does for Delirium, the DSM-IV-TR

(APA, 2000) includes a series of Dementia diagnoses related to the underlying cause: Dementia due to a Specified General Medical Condition, Substance-Induced Persisting Dementia, Dementia due to Multiple Etiologies, or Dementia NOS (when the etiological basis is not known).

Amnestic Disorders are characterized by memory impairment in the relative absence of other cognitive problems. The most common medical conditions related to Amnestic Disorders are a variety of brain traumas or diseases that damage the midbrain structures of maxillary bodies, hippocampus, and fornix. Again, specific diagnostic options for Amnestic Disorders relate to the underlying cause: Amnestic Disorder due to a Specified General Medical Condition, Substance-Induced Persisting Amnestic Disorder, or Amnestic Disorder NOS (APA, 2000).

A diagnosis of Cognitive Disorder NOS completes this section. This category would be used for clients whose symptom display does not conform to any of those previously mentioned but seems to have a physiological basis (APA, 2000).

In the chapter "Mental Disorders due to a General Medical Condition," two specific disorders are specified. The first, Catatonic Disorder due to a Specified General Medical Condition, describes clients who show significant disruptions in motor activity, extreme negativism or mutism, oddities of voluntary movement, and/or "mirroring behaviors" (i.e., echolalia or echopraxia). A variety of neurological or metabolic disorders can result in catatonic behavior, but this diagnosis is not used if the symptoms occur only during an episode of Delirium (APA, 2000).

Similarly, the diagnosis of Personality Change due to a Specified General Medical Condition is used for clients who display negative and persistent changes to their previous personality pattern. These changes are usually associated with a variety of neurological, metabolic, or autoimmune disorders. Again, this diagnosis is not used if the symptoms occur only during an episode of Delirium (APA, 2000).

Finally, a broad diagnosis, Mental Disorder NOS due to a Specified General Medical Condition, may be used to describe any other patterns of maladaptive behavior that seem to be caused by physiological problems. In all of the above diagnoses, the general medical condition should be listed on Axis III (as well as mentioned in the specific diagnosis) (APA, 2000).

ASSESSMENT

When a practitioner conducts assessments related to these disorders, a crucial component is a thorough medical workup. Often, prognosis for these clients is determined by whether or not the underlying medical situation can be remedied. For nonmedical practitioners, the primary focus of assessment with these mental disorders is on cognitive functioning. Because deficits are, by definition, present, most standard assessment tools utilize ratings by clinical professionals rather than client self-reports.

The Memorial Delirium Assessment Scale (MDAS)(Breitbart et al., 1997) is the most commonly used rating scale for Delirium. The MDAS contains 10 items for which the clinician rates the severity of dysfunction, ranging from "none" to "severe." In addition to being a useful instrument, this scale gives a fairly clear understanding of the range of potential symptoms that can be classified as Delirium. Initial psychometric work has shown evidence of strong interrater reliability and concurrent validity with a variety of more burdensome measures (see Robertsson [1999] for a thorough overview of Delirium measures). The MDAS has been used as a monitoring tool as well.

Although a variety of ratings scales related to Dementia are available, the Clinical Dementia Rating scale (CDR) (Hughes, Berg, Danziger, Coben, & Martin, 1982) is recommended. The original CDR contains 6 areas for ratings and, similar to the MDAS, is instructive in clearly delineating the range of problems that may be present in clients with Dementia. The CDR has been updated (Morris, 1993) to include more emphasis on judgment and problem solving as they relate to financial management.

Another approach, the Mini-Mental Status Exam (MMSE) (Folstein, Folstein, & McHugh, 1975) has long been the primary monitoring tool used with people with cognitive problems. This scale specifies 11 tasks that range across various areas of cognitive functioning. For each, a scoring guide is provided and a cutoff score of 23 out of 30 possible points is considered diagnostically significant. Folstein (1998) has recently reviewed the use, limitations, and related ratings of the MMSE.

CULTURAL CONSIDERATIONS

Although not all persons with cognitive brain disorders are older individuals, a vast majority of persons with Dementia, Alzheimer's disease, and other chronic neurological problems (e.g., Parkinson's disease) are the elderly of our society. Regardless of age, most individuals with these disorders are in need of assistance and considerable caregiving. Research indicates that family members provide 80% of the informal care that older persons and individuals with chronic disabilities receive (Mangum, Garcia, Kosberg, Mullins, & Barresi, 1994). A spouse or adult child of the affected person is most likely to take the role of primary caregiver.

Informal caregiving can take many forms and ranges from an adult child dropping by once a week to check on a parent, to an older parent moving in with his or her adult children or a spouse caring for his or her partner 24 hours a day. Caring for a person with a cognitive disorder can be an exhausting activity, and there is ample evidence to suggest that cultural variations exist among different ethnic groups within our society in terms of the norms, values, and beliefs associated with caring for family members. Practitioners, who often provide additional support to families coping with the stress of caring for an individual with a cognitive disorder, should be aware of these cultural variations.

Informal caregiving activities are ubiquitous among all ethnic groups within our society. Although Caucasian families utilize formal support mechanisms more frequently than minority groups do, all families experience stresses and strains due to the necessity of caregiving. Traditionally, African American, Asian/ Pacific Islander, and Hispanic families have held strong beliefs about maintaining caregiving responsibilities within the family unit. Therefore, ethnic minority families are often seen as underutilizing resources available to them in the community.

Research also suggests that the predictors of caregiving burden differ among ethnic groups (Cox, 1995). One study suggests that African American caregivers felt that a lack of informal support (e.g., siblings not fulfilling their obligations to a disabled parent) and competence (e.g., not knowing what to do as the illness progressed) was extremely stressful. Caucasian caregivers, on the other hand, felt that the disability level of the care receiver was the most stressful aspect of the caregiving experience (Cox). In another study of 632 Alzheimer's caregivers, Lawton, Rajagopal, Broday, and Kleban (1992) found that African American caregivers overall had a more satisfying caregiving experience than Caucasian caregivers. They reported a greater sense of satisfaction, a stronger belief in caregiving as a part of life, and a lesser burden and sense of intrusiveness than did Caucasian caregivers. Thus, African American caregivers may not access services as frequently as Caucasian caregivers because they hold strong beliefs concerning the family-centered household taking care of the elderly or disabled members.

Likewise, Asian/Pacific Islander families, a culturally diverse group within itself, hold strong beliefs in the family caring for each other, particularly in respect to the older generation (Mangum et al., 1994). However, this tradition may vary among U.S. Asian ethnic groups because some groups, such as Japanese Americans, tend to have more established extended family units living in the United States while other groups, such as Chinese Americans, may have fewer family members living in the United States and, thus, are forced to seek formal supports as they develop disabling conditions (Mangum et al.).

Hispanic families who have immigrated to the United States have also maintained a traditional philosophy about family roles. The younger generation venerates the older generation and is expected to care for them when they become ill. Furthermore, unlike some of the Asian individuals who seek help if family members are not available, Hispanic older persons may "suffer in silence" rather than ask for outside assistance (Mangum et al., 1994). However, one study examining the development of support groups for Alzheimer's caregivers in the Hispanic and African American populations indicated that extensive personal contact with professionals who were culturally competent was conducive to good participation in culturally sensitive support groups. African American and Hispanic caregivers attended monthly support groups and benefited from the interaction with other group members when approached from an ethnically competent standpoint by group facilitators (Henderson, Gutierrez-Mayka, Garcia, & Boyd, 1993).

Therefore, it is important for practitioners working with cognitive-disordered clients and their families to be aware of culturally diverse philosophies of caregiving. Although all families may require support in coping with the stress of caregiving, the type and degree of support may vary across cultures. Being able to establish a culturally sensitive relationship with the client and family will more likely lead to a successful long-term outcome in caring for the individual with the disability.

SOCIAL SUPPORT SYSTEMS

Because most of the disorders in these sections of the DSM involve rather substantial problems in terms of cognitive functioning, it should be evident that clients with these disorders require assistance to maintain functioning. This dependency may become so pronounced that institutionalization becomes necessary.

Both the provision of assistance and the decision making about appropriate placement and care can cause substantial amounts of stress. Along with these demands, caregivers are typically grieving various losses associated with the client's deterioration. This accumulated physical, emotional, financial, and social stress is commonly referred to as caregiver burden (George & Gwyther, 1986; Rabins, Mace, & Lucas, 1982). Beeson, Horton-Deutsch, Farran, and Neundorfer (2000) found a significant relationship between loneliness, depression, and relational deprivation among Alzheimer's caregivers. Female caregivers experienced the greatest amount of loneliness and depression, with wives experiencing more loneliness than daughters. Husbands also experienced loneliness but at lower levels than those of the female caregivers. All of these negative outcomes of providing care for a loved one with Dementia suggest a need for interventions to help ameliorate some of the emotional consequences of caregiving.

As awareness of caregiver burden has grown, much of the attention in terms of resources has been focused on supporting caregivers. New services (e.g., respite care) and support groups have the dual objectives of reducing caregiver burden and reducing the likelihood of institutionalizing the client.

The following list includes some of the Internet resources available.

www.alzheimers.org/pubs/prog00.htm—Progress report on Alzheimer's Disease 2000 from the National Center on Aging

www.nih.gov/nia/—The National Institute on Aging site with links to research and publications regarding health issues and aging

www.ninds.nih.gov/—The National Institute of Neurological Disorders and Stroke for information on a variety of neurological and cognitive disorders and stroke

www.dementia.ion.ucl.ac.uk/pcped/—Personal Construct Theory and its application to persons with Dementia

www.neurologychannel.com/dementia/—Neurology channel for a description of a host of neurological disorders that can affect both young and old

www.caregiver.org/—Family Caregiver Alliance for information and resources concerning caregivers of persons with cognitive disorders

Case 3.1

Identifying Information
Name: Della Corbin
Age: 72 years old
Ethnicity: Caucasian
Marital Status: Widowed

Intake Information
You are a social worker at a hospital located in a small town in the mountains of Tennessee. The nurse on the medical floor has asked you to evaluate a woman who was admitted to the hospital for possible nursing home placement. The nurse stated that Della Corbin was admitted 2 days ago. Her husband died a year ago, and she has a son who lives out of state. Her daughter lives in Memphis—a 6-hour drive from her mother's home. Mrs. Corbin apparently has many friends from her church, and several of them have been inquiring about her health. One close friend told the nurse that Mrs. Corbin was in good health until she moved into an apartment house following her husband's death.

Initial Interview
As you enter Mrs. Corbin's room, you immediately observe a very petite, fragile woman lying in bed with a white sheet and two green blankets covering her bed. She appears to be enveloped in the bedding. Upon closer examination, you notice that Mrs. Corbin has been restrained in her bed. Her arms are loosely tied to the bed railings, which are fully extended on each side of the bed. Mrs. Corbin appears alert but very agitated. Misty Wells, the nursing assistant, is feeding her applesauce, and Mrs. Corbin is spitting and yelling obscenities at her. The situation is much more chaotic than you expected.

The nursing assistant is so intent on feeding Mrs. Corbin that she doesn't notice you entering the room. You quietly approach the bedside and ask the assistant why Mrs. Corbin is restrained. Misty jumps and appears surprised at your presence. She tells you that Mrs. Corbin has been "out of her head" since she was admitted to the hospital.

"I don't think she even knows where she's at," Misty tells you. "I think she believes she's at home. She's confused about who I am. Sometimes, she thinks I'm her daughter and that she's at home. This morning she was telling me to get her bathrobe out of the closet in the other bedroom, so I think she believes she's at her home."

"Okay. Is it all right if I try to talk with her for a few minutes?" you ask Misty.

"Oh yes, please do. She's not making much sense though," Misty replies.

You tell Mrs. Corbin your name and that you are the social worker at the hospital. She glares at you and asks you where her Coca-Cola is.

"Mrs. Corbin, I don't have your Coke. Would you like me to see if the nurse can get you a Coke?" you ask.

"Well, I wouldn't really need it if I had my bathrobe. Where the hell is my doctor? He needs to find my bathrobe. If I had that bathrobe, I could go and get those philodendron plants that I love. Then I could finish decorating the living room for the holidays. That angel up top of the tree looks like Barbra Streisand."

You repeat, "Would you still like me to get you a Coke?"

"I hate those goddamned commercials with the polar bears in 'em. Like that'll make someone want a soda, goddamn it! Those commercials just bug the crap out of me! I can't even believe you brought that up . . . look at my arms! Get these things off my arms! I'll call the cops if you don't get these damned things off my arms. And you keep asking about that soda? C'mere and I'll show you what I think of that Coke of yours." She bares her teeth and spit flies.

You back up a few feet since Mrs. Corbin is gnashing her teeth and spitting as she threatens you. You wonder what is wrong with this elderly woman. You have never observed this type of behavior in an older person even though you have worked with many dementia patients.

Mrs. Corbin has been writhing restlessly in bed and pulling at her blankets since you entered the room. Suddenly, she bolts upright and says that she is going home. You attempt to calm her down by going to her side, but she then tries to bite you. She struggles to free herself from the bed. And suddenly she bursts into tears, crying, "I'm so tired. Why don't they let me out of here?"

You explain to Mrs. Corbin that the doctors are trying to help her feel better and that you are going to help her find a good place to stay when she leaves. She looks wide-eyed and responds, "I can't move all my things. And what about my birds?"

"Right now, you just need to rest and get better. Don't worry about your birds. Your son told me that he was taking care of them," you attempt to reassure her.

Mrs. Corbin lies back in the bed and turns her head away from you. She mutters, "Well, I just don't care what happens. And what do you know anyway?"

You note the fact that Mrs. Corbin's emotions are erratic and extremely unstable at the moment. You decide to end the interview since it appears to be too difficult to establish rapport at this time.

You go out to the nursing station to Mrs. Corbin's chart and discover that while you were talking with this client, the doctor has noted the possibility of lead poisoning and has ordered blood tests.

3.1–1   Whom else would you like to talk to about Mrs. Corbin's situation?

3.1–2   Looking back on the interview, is there anything you would have done differently? If so, what and why?

3.1–3   What potential diagnoses would you rule out?

3.1–4   What is your preliminary diagnosis?
Axis I

Axis II

Axis III

Axis IV

Axis V

_____

Case 3.2

Identifying Information
Name: Olivia Joyner
Age: Unknown, but elderly
Ethnicity: African American
Marital Status: Widowed

Intake Information
You are the worker "on call" at the Goodheart Mental Health Center, which is located in a Southern town. You receive a call from local law enforcement that they are bringing an elderly African American female in for evaluation. They had been contacted by personnel from the Greyhound bus station after they became concerned about her apparent confusion and continued presence for the past 36 hours.

Initial Contact
The client appears quite elderly and frail. She is dressed neatly in a checked dress with comfortable shoes. She seems rather alarmed and confused. She is clutching a small handbag.

"Good morning, ma'am. What can I call you?" you begin.

"My name is Olivia Joyner," she responds.

"I work here at the clinic and hope I can help you out today," you say.

"That's okay, honey. I just can't find the el. These police are scaring me some," she whispers. "You can't be too careful, you know. White people can be real mean."

"I don't think he needs to stay if he's bothering you. Do you think I could look in your purse before he goes?" you ask.

"What purse?" she responds, but she allows you to take her bag and hand it over to the officer.

The officer finds an identification card in her purse indicating that she is 93 years old and resides in Gary, Indiana. The officer tells you he will try to get more information about her and leaves.

"Well, Mrs. Joyner, would you tell me what you've been doing at the Greyhound station the last few days?"

"Just call me Olivia, sweetie. Where's the el?" she responds. "I been wanting to do some real important shopping but then there's the weather. Can't fight city hall, you know."

You recognize that the "el" is a mass transit system in Chicago (not far from Gary, Indiana). "Okay, Olivia, where are you trying to get to?"

The client seems to have lost track of the conversation and is looking anxiously around the interview room. "Have you seen my bag?" she asks. "I got to keep my things together. People can take advantage of you when you get old. Do you know what time it is?"

When you return her handbag, she empties it and begins looking through its contents.

"Olivia, have you eaten recently? Can I get you something to eat or drink?" you ask.

She looks at you expectantly and then returns to her inspection of her handbag. "Strawberry shortcake is the best, don't you think?"

3.2–1 What diagnoses are you considering at this point?

While you are getting Mrs. Joyner a sandwich and a glass of water, you pick up a message from the police officer who brought her in. He has contacted the Indiana State Patrol and confirmed that she was reported missing 6 days ago. He is attempting to contact relatives in that area.

When you return to the client, she thanks you enthusiastically for the snack. "I just love lunch meats. When I was little, you know, we didn't have things like this. You have so many stores now. You can buy anything you want. And go to the bathroom wherever you want. Things sure are different these days."

"Mrs. Joyner, I mean Olivia, can you tell me how old you are?" you ask.

"I'm not sure I know anymore. What year is this?" she responds. "I can't even keep track of the schedule anymore."

"Ma'am, do you know where you are?"

She laughs softly. "I guess not since I can't find that station. I've been coming here most of my life, but everything just looks strange to me now."

"You're in Quitman, Georgia, at a clinic. Do you know how you got here?" you ask.

The client looks somewhat alarmed and begins to cry. "I thought that bus ride was too long. I just want to get my baby a present. Did anyone feed my cat?"

"Don't worry now. We'll make sure you get back home. Can you tell me how to contact a friend or a relative in Indiana?" you ask.

The client stops crying and says, "Carter'll come get me. Can you call Carter?"

"I'd be happy to call. Can you give me his number?" you ask.

"It's 459. But I haven't got a present yet. It's his birthday tomorrow, you know."

You excuse yourself again to see if law enforcement has gotten any more information.

3.2–2   What diagnosis would you give Olivia Joyner at this point?
Axis I

Axis II

Axis III

Axis IV

Axis V

3.2-3   Other than contacting a family member, are there any other resources you would want to involve at this point?

Collateral Information

About an hour later, the police officer calls with a telephone number in Gary. He has contacted a Mrs. Carter Joyner, the client's daughter-in-law. You immediately call this relative.

"Mrs. Joyner, I'm calling from Quitman about your mother-in-law, Olivia Joyner," you begin.

"Thank God. We've been so worried. She's been missing for a week now. Is she all right? Can I talk to her?" she asks.

"She seems to be all right physically. I'll be happy to let you speak with her in a few minutes, but I need a little information first if you don't mind." With her agreement, you continue. "Your mother-in-law seems a bit confused and disoriented. For example, she thought she was lost in Chicago, at least initially. Has she had problems with that kind of confusion before?"

"Well, no. Olivia's as sharp as a nail. She takes Greyhounds into the city and then goes all over on the el. She handles her own money and everything. Most of the time, she has it better together than me. Do you think something's happened to her?" she asks.

"I don't think she's been injured or anything. She may not have eaten or slept right for quite a while since we don't know what was going on with her for most of this week. Would you have any objections to me taking her to a medical doctor to have her checked?" you ask.

"Not at all. I've called my husband, Carter, and he's on his way home from work. We'll be flying down just as soon as we figure out the details. Olivia should have her Medicare card with her. Will that be enough for someone there to see her?"

"That should do it. I'll make arrangements to have her examined immediately. I'll call again in an hour or two so we can coordinate getting you all and Olivia back together."

3.2-4   Based on this interaction, would you change your diagnosis for Olivia Joyner? If so, what would be your new diagnosis?

Emergency Room Contact

After some calls, it seems clear that the most expedient way to get a medical examination of Olivia Joyner is to take her to the local hospital's emergency room. After you have waited roughly 30 minutes, an ER nurse comes out to speak with you.

"We're going to be admitting Olivia to the hospital, so I need more information about contacting her relatives."

"Sure, I'd be happy to relay information as well. I last spoke with her daughter-in-law about an hour ago. She and Olivia's son planned on coming as soon as they could. Can you tell me what's going on with her?"

"Well, at this point, it looks like she's had some sort of a brain bleed. I'm not sure whether it could technically be considered a stroke, but right now we're just trying to get her blood pressure back under control. Do you know whether she was taking antihypertensive medications?" she inquired.

"All I can tell you is that she didn't have any medicines in her handbag. I'm afraid I didn't think to ask her daughter-in-law specifically, although she indicated that Mrs. Joyner was 'healthy,'" you reply.

"Well, we'll call her family now and take it from there."

"Great. Please let them know that they can contact me at the clinic if I can help them make arrangements," you conclude.

3.2–5   What will be your "final" diagnosis for Olivia Joyner?

Axis I

Axis II

Axis III

Axis IV

Axis V

Case 3.3

Identifying Information
Name: Mildred Perkins
Age: 75 years old
Ethnicity: Caucasian
Marital Status: Married
Occupation: Retired

Background Information
You work as a hospital social worker. As part of your job, you visit patients when referred by their doctors in order to help them and/or their families with resources and discharge planning.

Referral Information
Mildred Perkins is a 75-year-old woman recently hospitalized due to her newly diagnosed diabetic condition. Her daughter, Janet Fletcher, is a 44-year-old single mother of two children ages 15 and 17. Janet is a human resources administrator for the Parks and Recreation Department of a small city in the Midwest. She enjoys her job and gets along well with her children.

Janet's parents, Mildred and Ray, lived in Pennsylvania most of their lives. They moved to the Midwest to be close to Janet when they were in their late 60s and after Janet had divorced her former husband. Mildred and Ray have remained very active in their retirement years. They own a recreational vehicle and have traveled extensively throughout the United States. Janet, an only child, has spent many hours at the hospital with her mother and 80-year-old father.

While spending time with her mother at the hospital, Janet noticed that her mother was becoming increasingly forgetful. On one occasion when Janet arrived at her mother's room, Mildred asked Janet if she was a new nurse on the unit. This comment was very disturbing to Janet. She told her mother, "I'm not a nurse, Mother, I'm your daughter."

"Oh, of course you are," her mother replied. "I just didn't have my glasses on and couldn't see you clearly." Janet then asked her mother's doctor about the problem. He referred the family to you for an initial screening.

3.3–1 What diagnoses are you considering before you visit with Mildred?

Collateral Information
Before visiting the family, you stop in to see the nurse who is giving care to Mildred. She tells you that she has noticed that Mildred appears to be becoming increasingly disoriented. For example, it seems that Mildred sometimes forgets that she is in the hospital. On two occasions, the nurse walked into the room and found Mildred getting dressed. When the nurse asked her what she was doing, Mildred replied that she was going downstairs to have dinner.

On another occasion, the nurse found Mildred attempting to use her toothbrush to cut her meat on her dinner tray. She seemed confused when the nurse suggested she use the knife instead of the toothbrush. The nurse also suggests that Mildred seems to get "agitated and edgy" for no apparent reason.

You find a chart note from the morning nurse indicating that Mildred is making good progress on her recovery from her diabetic episode but that she rang her bell frequently all morning and was asking the same questions over and over again. The nurse found herself having to repeat things to Mildred that she had just told her a few minutes earlier. She was very concerned about sending Mildred home because Mildred was having a great deal of difficulty remembering the instructions the nurse had given her regarding the need to check her glucose levels at regular intervals. The morning nurse has been attempting to explain the process to Mildred for several days, but Mildred is unable to recall what the nurse has told her to do. The nurse also felt that, due to Ray's advanced age, he might not be able to help Mildred with the type of assistance that she would require at home.

When you go to visit Mildred, she is not in her room but is wandering down the hall, apparently looking for someone. When you approach her and tell her your name, she states that she is looking for her room. You guide her back to her room and suggest the two of you talk about how she's been feeling and about going home.

Mildred says that she's ready to go home. "I have been in this hospital for weeks and they won't let me out of here," she states. When you ask her if she knows exactly how long she's been in the hospital, Mildred replies, "Since about June, I guess."

"And what month is it now?" you question.

"I believe it's November, and I have to get the house ready for Christmas," Mildred replies.

"Actually, Mrs. Perkins, it is September and, from your records, it looks as if you've been in the hospital for about a week now," you explain to her in a gentle and nonthreatening manner. "Do you know what year it is?" you query.

Mildred replies, "I believe it's 1995, isn't it?"

"Well, actually, this is the year 2000, Mrs. Perkins," you respond.

"Oh yes, I couldn't quite remember. You know it's harder to remember these things when you get older like me," Mildred suggests.

"What about children, Mrs. Perkins. Do you have any children?" you ask.

"Yes, my daughter, Janet, works for the Parks and Recreation Department. She is very good at her job."

"And has Janet come by to see you in the hospital?" you inquire.

"I don't think she's had the time. You know she has children of her own that take up a lot of her time," Mildred replies.

"What about your husband? Has he come to see you while you've been in the hospital?" you ask.

"Yes, I believe he came to see me yesterday," Mildred responds.

"Do you know who the president of the United States is this year, Mrs. Perkins?" you inquire.

Mildred stares at her hands, and after a long pause she suggests that it must be President Reagan. She again states that she really needs to get home since Christmas is right around the corner. Mildred then gets up and begins taking her belongings out of the drawers and placing them on the bed. She takes the trash can and begins placing all her things in the trash.

When you ask her what she is doing, she states that she's packing to go home. Mildred looks rather perplexed about the trash can but continues to pile her clothing in the bin. She then appears to realize that her clothes don't belong in the trash can and begins taking them out. She states that all her clothes won't fit in that small suitcase and that she needs her larger suitcase so everything will fit.

You suggest that it might be a good idea to wait until the doctor has seen her before she begins to pack her suitcase. Mildred looks astonished and asks why she needs to see a doctor. You tell her that she's in the hospital and that she's there in order to get her diabetes under control. Mildred looks confused and sits down on the bed again.

"I just don't know what's happening to me these days. I think I'm losing track of things," Mildred states.

You suggest that perhaps a doctor can help her sort things out so she will feel better. You tell her that you'll come back to see her again and that maybe she'd like to rest for a while.

With your encouragement, Mildred lies back down on the bed and states that she is feeling very tired.

3.3–2   What other information would you like to have? Whom else would you like to interview? Are there any other consultations you'd like to arrange?

3.3–3   What would be your preliminary diagnosis?
Axis I

Axis II

Axis III

Axis IV

Axis V

Follow-Up Information

Based on your report, Mildred's primary physician calls in a neurologist for consultation. While waiting for Mildred's evaluation, her daughter and husband ask to meet with you to plan for the future.

3.3–4   How will you assess the strengths of the family?

3.3–5   What questions are important for the family to consider in making discharge plans for Mildred?

DIFFERENTIAL DIAGNOSIS

Perhaps one of the most frequently encountered issues in making a diagnosis of Dementia in older people is that memory impairment is often a normal aspect of aging and not necessarily a symptom of a mental disorder. Determining what is normal aging and what constitutes Dementia is related to a variety of factors, including level of severity, patterns of behavior, length of problem, and other medical conditions.

In addition, persons with Dementia and persons with Delirium may have problems with memory. What distinguishes Delirium from Dementia is the symptom of reduced consciousness and the fluctuating nature of symptoms.

3.DD–1   What are some differences between Della Corbin and Mildred Perkins?

3.DD–2   Write a case scenario in which the individual has normal problems with aging but would need further evaluation or testing to "rule out" dementia or Alzheimer's disease.

3.DD–3   When Della Corbin becomes coherent, what additional questions would you want to ask her to rule out other cognitive disorders?

InfoTrac keywords

Alzheimer's disease, Cognitive Disorders, cognitive functioning scales, Delirium, Dementia

4 | Alcohol and Drug-Related Disorders

DISORDERS

When assessing adults, it is important to consider the possibility of substance-related disorders. The DSM-IV-TR (APA, 2000) offers a detailed way to diagnose problematic involvement with a range of substances.

The fundamental features of substance-related disorders include (1) the taking of a drug, medication, drink, or substance in order to experience an altered state; and (2) a cluster of cognitive, behavioral, and physiological symptoms when the substance use is continued despite problems associated with the use. Substance-related disorders are divided into two primary groupings: substance-use disorders (primarily dependence and abuse) and substance-induced disorders (i.e., intoxication, withdrawal, and mental health consequences of abuse).

There are 11 classes of substances mentioned specifically in the DSM-IV-TR (APA, 2000): alcohol, amphetamines, caffeine, cannabis, cocaine, hallucinogens, inhalants, nicotine, opioids, phencyclidine, and sedatives/hypnotics/anxiolytics. Polysubstance use is defined as the use of three or more of these substances. Also, diagnoses for other substances not listed in the 11 classes and an "Unknown" category (when substance is not known, as may be the case in an accidental overdose or reaction to toxins) are included. The DSM-IV-TR (APA) provides the criteria for those diagnoses appropriate for each of the 11 classes of substances.

Four primary clinical syndromes are described in this section of the DSM-IV-TR. Additional substance-related diagnoses are listed in the other relevant sections (e.g., Substance-Related Persisting Dementia, Substance-Induced Mood Disorder).

The first and arguably most serious of the clinical syndromes, substance dependence, describes a maladaptive pattern of substance use that has led to clinically significant impairment or distress. The diagnosis is based on having at least three symptoms occurring at any time during the same 12-month period. The first two symptoms, tolerance and withdrawal, are primarily physiological in nature.

Tolerance is defined as a need for increased amounts of the substance to achieve the desired effect or a diminished effect with continued use of the same amount of the substance. Withdrawal is a substance-specific syndrome experienced when the substance is discontinued or dramatically reduced. Avoiding withdrawal by ingestion of a similar substance is also considered a symptom (APA, 2000).

The remaining symptom possibilities are more psychologically oriented. Loss of control is evidenced by a person taking the substance in larger amounts or over a longer period than was intended. Cravings are persistent desires or unsuccessful efforts to cut down or control substance use. Spending a great deal of time in activities necessary to obtain the substance, use the substance, or recover from its effects can be considered a symptom, as can preoccupation with the substance to the extent that important social, occupational, or recreational activities are given up or reduced because of substance use. Finally, continuation of the substance use despite the individual's being aware of physical and/or psychological problems that are likely associated with the substance is also a symptom (APA, 2000).

The second clinical syndrome, substance abuse, describes a somewhat less problematic use of a particular substance. Once again, the diagnosis is based on a pattern of behavior that has manifested within a 12-month period and includes at least one of the following symptoms. The first is failure to fulfill major role obligations because of recurrent use of a substance. Recurrent use of the substance in situations in which use is physically hazardous or repeated substance-related legal problems also are symptoms. The final symptom is persistence in using the substance despite social or relational problems generated by its use (APA, 2000).

The third clinical syndrome is intoxication. This describes a reversible, substance-specific set of symptoms related to using a particular substance. For a diagnosis to be made, the person must display clinically significant maladaptive behaviors or personality changes. Intoxication is not diagnosed when someone simply ingests a substance that has the desired effect and no undesired side effects (APA, 2000).

The final clinical syndrome is withdrawal. As indicated previously, this also is a substance-specific set of symptoms. Withdrawal generally occurs when use of the substance has been prolonged or heavy. Also, the symptoms must be severe enough to cause clinical levels of distress and/or impaired psychosocial functioning (APA, 2000). It should be noted that withdrawal from central nervous system depressants is a potentially fatal process.

One of the most common substance-related disorders that a clinician will encounter is alcohol abuse or dependence. Most American adults have tried alcohol at some time in their lives, and approximately two-thirds of men and one-third of women have experienced adverse experiences related to alcohol. Statistics show that 1 in 5 men and 1 in 10 women who visit their doctor meet the criteria for at-risk drinking, problem drinking, or alcohol dependence (Manwell, Fleming, Johnson, & Barry, 1998). Alcoholism has been recognized for many years as a chronic, progressive, and often-fatal disease.

Although problems related to other substances may be less common, there is no less a possibility of devastating effects, both for the client and, potentially, for anyone associated with him or her. Clinicians are urged to familiarize themselves with the characteristic effects of all the substances listed in the DSM-IV-TR (APA, 2000). Unrecognized substance-related problems contribute dramatically to treatment "failure" among people with a variety of other Mental Disorders.

ASSESSMENT

The major complicating factor in diagnosing substance problems is the tendency for the user to minimize and deny the problems. Chemically dependent individuals are often aware that their use and subsequent behaviors are socially unacceptable. Therefore, they may become adept at hiding their use and at manipulating and lying to cover up their actions. They also may try to minimize consequences and find ways to deceive others, especially the people who care about them, who, in turn, "enable" or perpetuate the problem through caretaking.

Assessment Instruments

The best evaluative tool for withdrawal symptoms is the Clinical Institute Withdrawal Assessment for Alcohol/Drugs (CIWA-AD) (Sullivan, Sykora, Schneiderman, Naranjo, & Sellers, 1989). The CIWA-AD is an eight-item scale for clinical quantification of the severity of Withdrawal Syndrome. It is a reliable, brief, uncomplicated, and clinically useful scale that can also be used to monitor response to treatment.

There are a variety of assessment instruments that can be used to determine the presence and nature of potential substance abuse or dependence problems. The following are among the most commonly utilized and widely accepted assessment tools.

The CAGE (Mayfield, McLeod, & Hall, 1994) is a brief screening approach developed by John Ewing, founding director of the Bowles Center for Alcohol Studies, University of North Carolina at Chapel Hill. It is an internationally used screening instrument for identifying alcoholics and other substance abusers. It is particularly popular with primary caregivers. CAGE has been translated into several languages. The patient is asked four questions [emphasis added]: (1) Have you ever felt you ought to *Cut* down your drinking (or drug use)? (2) Have people *Annoyed* you by criticizing your drinking (or drug use)? (3) Have you ever felt bad or *Guilty* about your drinking (or drug use)? (4) Have you had a drink (or used drugs) first thing in the morning (*Eye opener*) to steady your nerves or get rid of a hangover? Affirmative answers to two or more questions constitute a positive screen and should prompt further history.

The Michigan Alcoholism Screening Test (MAST) (Selzer, 1971) is a self-report screening instrument that may be given to a patient initially or in follow-up to another screening test. Its brevity makes it useful as an outpatient tool. The questions in the 24-item scale address a variety of behaviors and feelings and can be answered with a simple "yes" or "no." The MAST has shown excellent internal consistency (Cronbach's alpha = .95) and known-groups validity (Fischer & Corcoran, 1994). The MAST has been modified for drug abuse. The Drug Abuse Screening Test (DAST) has also demonstrated good psychometric properties (Skinner, 1982).

Another set of self-report instruments, the Substance Abuse Subtle Screening Inventory (SASSI), includes versions for adults (SASSI-3) (SASSI Institute, 1997) and for teenagers (SASSI-A2) (SASSI Institute, 2001). These instruments are touted as being able to diagnose substance-abuse problems through examining patterns of "subtle" indicators (e.g., defensiveness) even when the respondent lies about his or her use of substances. The SASSI was developed 25 years ago and since has been empirically validated by numerous research studies attesting to its effectiveness as an assessment instrument to diagnose substance-abuse disorders. For example, the SASSI-3 reportedly is accurate in its assessment of substance-dependent people in approximately 95% of all cases (Lazowski, Miller, Boye, & Miller, 1998).

The general approach to assessment with a client contemplating or entering treatment is broadly focused (because substance-related problems impact most psychosocial areas) and based on semistructured interviews. The most commonly used of these semistructured interviews was developed under the auspices of the National Institute on Alcohol Abuse and Alcoholism and the National Institute on Drug Abuse. The adult version, the Addiction Severity Index (ASI-5) (McLellan et al., 1992) is in the public domain and can be administered as a self-report scale as well as a semistructured interview. It consists of approximately 200 items divided into seven potential problem areas and generally takes 50 to 60 minutes for administration. The instrument has been the subject of many psychometric studies and has proven reliable and valid (see, for example, Hodgins & El, 1992). The ASI has also been used as an outcome measure in clinical research.

Also in the public domain, the Teen Addiction Severity Index (T-ASI) (Kaminer, Bukstein, & Tarter, 1991) is recommended only as a semistructured interview. Based on 133 items divided into seven subscales, the T-ASI generally takes between 20 and 45 minutes to administer. Because it is a more recently developed instrument, far fewer studies have demonstrated its psychometric properties, but initial work suggests it is both reliable and valid (Kaminer et al., 1991; Kaminer, Wagner, Plummer, & Seifer, 1993).

Emergency Considerations

Once substance dependence is suspected, a practitioner must assess a client for those physical withdrawal symptoms that can be life-threatening. Many practitioners are surprised to learn that alcohol withdrawal is one of the most potentially fatal detoxifications, while cocaine withdrawal (although very uncomfortable) is virtually harmless.

Substance abuse also causes a wide variety of medical symptoms and diseases. Common medical symptoms of substance abuse include vitamin deficiency, malnutrition, dyspepsia, upper gastrointestinal problems, peptic ulcer, hepatitis, pancreatitis, hypertension, new-onset arrhythmia, cardiomyopathy, seizures, peripheral neuropathy, and AIDS. From this list, it should be obvious that prompt medical referrals should be made even when no immediate withdrawal risks are present.

Substance abuse can also be associated with the following behavioral, emotional, and cognitive problems: stress, insomnia, anxiety, depression, acute psychotic states, impaired cognition, and violent behavior. Further, substance abuse can generate myriad associated social problems. Substance abusers are at high risk for marital and family problems, legal difficulties, loss of employment, and financial deterioration. Clearly, broad-ranged assessment to screen for comorbid mental disorders and/or impending psychosocial problems that could greatly complicate recovery is warranted.

Finally, suicide risk is frequently present in substance-abusing clients, particularly as health and psychosocial deterioration is present. Even with clients who do not really warrant a substance-related diagnosis, intoxication can enhance risk. Careful screening for self-destructive thoughts and/or impulses is imperative with this population.

CULTURAL CONSIDERATIONS

Roughly 3.1 million Americans (approximately 1.4% of the population 12 years of age and older) receive treatment for alcoholism and alcohol-related problems in any given year; treatment peaked among people between the ages 26–34 (Substance Abuse and Mental Health Services Administration, 2000). Almost 3 times as many men (9.8 million) as women (3.9 million) are problem drinkers, and prevalence is highest for both sexes in the 18–29-year-old age group (Grant et al., 1994). Despite these statistics, practitioners are cautioned to screen both sexes carefully for substance-related problems. The assumption that women are less prone to such difficulties can inhibit diagnosis and treatment.

Although a significant body of research exists noting the varied levels of drug involvement by ethnic group, the literature is flawed in that it often fails to consider contextual variables such as poverty, gender, and acculturation. The stressors of poverty, joblessness, homelessness, and mental illness often contribute to substance-abuse disorders regardless of racial or ethnic identity. It is important to note that many myths exist with regard to ethnicity and alcohol/drug abuse.

Nonetheless, research shows that youth of varied ethnic groups maintain a spectrum of attitudes and behaviors with regard to drugs and alcohol. For example, research has found that Caucasian adolescents report the least perceived amount of risk in drug use (Wallace & Bachman, 1993) and they are more likely to be "sensation seekers" (Kaetner, Rosen, & Appel, 1977) with significant peer models for use of hard liquor (Newcomb & Bentler, 1986). African Americans report the highest levels of perceived risk regarding drug use (Wallace & Bachman) and have primary peer models for beer and wine use (Newcomb & Bentler, 1986). Latino/Latina adolescents fall between Caucasians and African Americans in degree of perceived risk of drug use (Wallace & Bachman) and have more peer models than other ethnic groups for using pills (Newcomb & Bentler).

Further, there may well be different rates of exposure (or, more precisely, marketing strategies) for the various ethnic subgroups. For example, in the study by Hecht, Trost, Bator, and MacKinnon (1997), Latinos/Latinas reported receiving drug offers at a significantly higher rate than either Caucasians or African Americans. Latinas (females), in particular, were significantly more likely to be offered drugs in general than other females.

Again, practitioners are cautioned against using these statistical trends to determine who will be screened for substance-related problems. Screening should be conducted routinely in both medical and mental health settings. Even though early detection is no guarantee of eventual treatment success, there is a general trend for persons whose substance use has not damaged their psychosocial functioning severely to have better treatment outcomes.

SOCIAL SUPPORT SYSTEMS

The potential for devastating effects associated with substance-related problems to the client should be evident from the previous discussion; the potential for harm to members of the client's social support system is also high. Along with the anguish that may be associated with seeing a loved one self-destruct, there are many direct effects associated with proximity to someone with these problems.

For example, being in an intimate relationship with someone with substance-abuse problems carries a number of risks. The client's deteriorating vocational functioning may directly impact his or her partner. The partner may also be financially responsible for damages caused by the client's behavior. Certainly, the relationship itself may be subjected to incredible strains. The focus on "enabling" in the substance-abuse literature should be understood within this context. Although a partner who calls a client in sick when the client is in fact intoxicated or withdrawing may be "enabling" the substance abuse, he or she may also be protecting the primary source of the couple's income. As can be seen, feeling "trapped" and seeing no "good solutions" may characterize many behaviors better than "enabling."

Not surprisingly, more than 50% of today's alcoholics are the children of alcoholics (National Association for Children of Alcoholics, 2001). There is a preponderance of references to the "dysfunctional" family systems of the addict/alcoholic, but it may be more accurate to view these families as "hyperfunctional" in their creative adaptations to the disruption of the family homeostasis. Due to the addicted parent being "out of control," the family develops a variety of reactive tactics to survive. As characterized by the classic work of Wegscheider (1981), children of addicted parents tend to "overfunction" or "underfunction," filling the roles of "hero," "scapegoat," "mascot," or "lost and forgotten" child.

All of these behaviors are attempts to deny and contain the addiction and to keep the family stabilized as symptoms escalate. Both family and friends often feel betrayed, confused, guilty, and defensive. They sometimes blame each other as well as themselves and the addicted person for their difficulties. Practitioners are urged to avoid labeling, which can be hurtful, and to strive to help friends and families to view their own behaviors within their environmental contexts. At the same time, practitioners can provide a realistic perspective regarding how much one person can influence another person's behavior.

Self-Help Groups

Despite the social stigma associated with substance abuse, or perhaps because of it, more self-help resources have been developed in this area of mental health than in any other (McCrady & Miller, 1993). Alcoholics Anonymous (AA) is an international program (referred to as a "fellowship") of men and women who have had a drinking problem. It is nonprofessional, self-supporting, nondenominational, multiracial, apolitical, and available almost everywhere. There are no requirements; membership is open to anyone who wants to do something about his or her drinking problem. AA members share their experience with anyone seeking help with a drinking problem; they give person-to-person service or "sponsorship" to any alcoholic coming to AA. The AA program as set forth in AA's Twelve Steps offers the alcoholic a way to develop a satisfying life without alcohol. This program is discussed at AA group meetings.

Open speaker meetings are open to both alcoholics and nonalcoholics. At open speaker meetings, AA members "tell their stories." They describe what their experiences have been with alcohol, how they came to AA, and how their lives have changed as a result of AA. In open discussion meetings, one member speaks briefly about his or her drinking experience and then leads a discussion on AA recovery or a drinking-related problem.

Closed meetings are for AA members or anyone else who may have a drinking problem. Step meetings (usually closed) are discussions of one of the Twelve Steps. AA members take service responsibilities very seriously in order to "give back what was given to them."

Many formal rehabilitation programs are built on the foundation of the AA Twelve-Step model. AA has a long history of cooperating but not affiliating with outside organizations and being available to provide AA meetings or information about AA upon request. For professionals working with people who have special needs, AA materials and literature are available through the AA Web site (see end of this section), in Braille, in American Sign Language videos, on audiotapes, and in easy-to-read pamphlets.

The Twelve-Step model has become the foundation of a number of mutual-aid support group settings for a variety of issues and illnesses: Narcotics Anonymous (NA); Gamblers Anonymous (GA); Overeaters Anonymous (OA); and Cocaine Anonymous (CA). These resources are generally not as widely available as AA, but at least some AA groups accept people who are primarily drug rather than alcohol abusers.

Family groups have also emerged, including Alanon (for families of alcoholics), Naranon (for families of drug addicts), Oanon (for families of compulsive overeaters and eating-disordered individuals), and several programs for children of addicts/alcoholics (ACoA, Alateen, Alatot). These family-oriented programs may be particularly useful in recovery because they allow the support systems to learn the same "language of recovery" that the client may begin to use.

In addition, the following Web sites may be useful to both clients and other affected parties.

www.niaaa.nih.gov/publications/assinstr.htm—The National Institute on Alcohol Abuse and Alcoholism (NIAAA) site; particularly useful for clinicians; includes an extensive list of assessment tools specifically for alcohol problems

www.alcoholics-anonymous.org/—Site maintained by Alcoholics Anonymous World Services; includes a comprehensive compilation of AA facts, brochures, and information for alcoholics, recovering individuals, and community professionals who need to know about this Twelve-Step program of recovery

www.nacoa.net/—National Association for Children of Alcoholics Web site; includes useful resources for children and families affected by alcohol and drug dependencies

www.samhsa.gov/—Substance Abuse and Mental Health Services Administration site with links to the National Clearinghouse for Alcohol and Drug Information, grant opportunities, and other drug and alcohol treatment and prevention information

www.jifoundation.org/index.html—Johnson Institute Web site with resources and information for the purpose of "improving the public's understanding of addiction as a treatable illness, and promoting the power and possibility of recovery from alcoholism and other drug addiction"

Case 4.1

Identifying Information
Client Name: Jason Marshall
Age: 35 years old
Ethnicity: Caucasian
Marital Status: Single

Intake Information
Jason Marshall is a 35-year-old single man who sporadically works in construction and owns his own drywall business. At present, he is living with and says that he is caring for his "elderly" (his term) mother. His mother brought him to the Behavioral Health Center (after insisting he call the 1-800 number after seeing a commercial) and is waiting in the lobby.

Jason reports to the assessment worker that he feels lethargic and unmotivated by his life and that the only time he enjoys himself is when he is "kicking back" and "partying." He states openly, "Yeah, I use pot, but only the good stuff that I grow myself. It's how I deal with the stress of taking care of my mom." Upon further questioning, Jason admits that his mother keeps nagging about his marijuana smoking and that "she doesn't understand how mind expanding it can be."

Initial Interview
Jason arrives at the Behavioral Health Center in a T-shirt, high-top Converse sneakers, and blue jeans. Though he is 35, he carries himself much more like a boy than a man. He walks slumped over and with his hands in his pockets. He plays with a cigarette immediately upon sitting down with you.

He doesn't wait for a question. He asks, "So what kind of treatment center has a 1-800 number anyway? You're not going to bilk my mom out of a whole bunch of money just to tell me that I'm depressed, are you?"

"So you're depressed?" you ask.

"Well, business hasn't been good and my mom needs a lot from me and my girlfriend just left me. So, yeah, I guess you could say that." He rolls the cigarette back and forth between his fingers. "How long is this going to take, anyway?"

"Less than an hour. Is there somewhere you need to go after this?" you ask.

"Nope."

"Tell me more about work, your mom, your girlfriend . . ." you prompt.

"I have my own business. Drywall. I have two guys that work for me, but they're not too reliable, so a lot of times they don't show and I'm left with the jobs. Jobs take longer than I estimated, and my customers get pissed. So sometimes I have to work construction again for extra money. That's why my girlfriend left me. She didn't like that I was low on money. My mom asked me to move in with her, so I did."

"How do you take care of your mom?" you ask.

"She's been lonely since Dad died so I keep her company," he replies.

"Oh?" You await elaboration, but Jason sits silently for a long while and plays with his cigarette. Thinking that the action of rolling the cigarette reminds you of someone rolling a marijuana joint, you ask, "So what do you do to feel better when you feel depressed?"

Suspiciously, he replies, "What do you mean?"

"Are there things you do that make you feel less depressed?"

"Well, after work, I like to come home and relax. Watch TV. Play my guitar."

"You said in your initial intake that you, hmmm, well let me read your words. 'Yeah, I use pot, but only the good stuff that I grow myself. It's how I deal with the stress.' You called marijuana 'mind expanding,'" you say.

"Well, it is. My pot smoking doesn't hurt anyone. It hasn't caused me any trouble."

"What does your mom think about it?" you ask.

"You can ask her, but she doesn't know anything about drugs. She's from the generation where anyone that used drugs or alcohol was considered a loser. I'm not like that. I could stop anytime I want. And why would I?" he responds.

"I might be wrong, but some people who smoke pot regularly find that it takes their motivation away and that other things in life get put on hold . . ." you prod gently.

Jason interrupts with more emotion than previously witnessed, "Look, lady, I'm a decent guy who's had some business problems because my mom needs me."

"I'd like to bring your mom in to get her opinion if that's okay with you," you counter.

"Sure."

Jason's mom comes in. It's evident that she's been crying. She is a vibrant 55-year-old woman dressed in a tailored casual dress.

"Ms. Marshall, Jason has shared his stressors with me, and it seems that you disagree on the cause of the difficulties with motivation, work, and relationships," you begin.

Talking in a pleading tone to her son, "Jason, did you tell her the truth? Did you tell her that the only reason you're living with me is that you couldn't make it on your own because of your damned pot smoking? Did you tell her that Susan left you because she felt that your marijuana was more important than she was?"

"Mom, you're so dramatic. I still have the business, and I can do construction whenever I want. I could live on my own if I didn't worry about you so much since Dad died. Why do you have to be so extreme when it comes to a little recreational drug use?" he replies.

His mother responds angrily. "Recreational? The whole house stinks of the stuff all the time. Do you think that I can't smell it when you close the bathroom door and crack the window? Maybe when you were 15, I was naive, but I've had YEARS of this with you, Jason." She sighs defeatedly and repeats, "Years."

"I'd like to do a standard screening test to assess the issue of your drug use. Would that be all right with you, Jason?" you ask.

"Go ahead. You'll see. I smoke some pot and use the laced stuff every once in a while. But other than that, I don't do anything. It relaxes me and helps me deal with stress. So? Oh yeah, and it helps me sleep. I could be taking sleeping pills, but I don't. I know people that are addicts. They are wild and out of control. I keep to myself. I'm laid back. Easygoing."

The clinician takes out the measurement instrument. After administering the DAST (the drug version of the MAST), the client scores in the problematic area, indicating a "probable drug problem."

4.1–1   What clues do you have that Jason may be minimizing his marijuana problem?

4.1–2   Is there additional collateral information you would like to obtain? If so, from whom?

4.1–3 Do you feel that Jason has other emotional issues? Which might you consider ruling out?

4.1–4 What is your initial diagnosis?
Axis I

Axis II

Axis III

Axis IV

Axis V

Case 4.2

Identifying Information
Client Name: Maria Quantas
Age: 47 years old
Ethnicity: Mexican American
Marital Status: Married

Intake Information
Maria Quantas, a 47-year-old Chicana, comes to the intake at the insistence of her 28-year-old son, Angel. She seems weak and has a visible tremor. Her son reports that she has recently demonstrated slow thinking and slurred speech and had noticeable bruises on her extremities. She has had cycles of sleeping excessively and then being up all night for several nights in a row.

Maria admits that she has felt restless lately. She reports that she recently went to her medical doctor, who prescribed some sleeping medications. She also says she has a chronic problem with migraine headaches, which has worsened recently. One week prior to this appointment, she had a seizure. The etiology remains a mystery, but the doctor at the hospital recommended an assessment with your office.

Initial Interview
After introduction to the caseworker, Angel addresses his mother. "I don't understand it, Mom. You have been doing so well for so long, and now everything seems to be falling apart."

Maria turns to you and says, "He is very protective. I used to have a pill addiction, but I stopped. I took everything back then . . . blues, rainbows, yellow jackets, reds."

Her son starts crying. "Mom, you're using them again, aren't you?"

"No, Angel. I'm fine! I only take what doctors prescribe now. I'm just having health problems. My migraines are horrible, and my med-ications hardly touch the pain. Other than that and sleep problems, I'm just fine. I don't know what everyone is so worried about. The doctors think the seizure was an isolated thing, and they've done tests and it doesn't seem to be anything serious."

She addresses you, "Did I tell you I have migraines?"

Angel interjects to you, "I know my mom. This isn't how she usually is. She's sharp. Smart, you know? Lately, she's so out of it. She asks the same questions several times. She bumps into things. She seems spaced out."

You ask, "Do you agree, Maria?"

"Well, I haven't slept that well, so I probably am not as sharp as I usually am because I'm tired. And I don't feel well physically. I think it's because I don't sleep well."

"Why do you think you're having trouble sleeping, Maria?" you inquire.

She pauses. "Sometimes, I can't stop my thoughts from racing in my head at night. I worry about my boys. I have two others, and all three are trying to figure out their lives and relationships. I work as a legal assistant, and I'm having trouble keeping up with the cases and so sometimes I try to review the day and figure everything out at night."

You wonder what her son thinks and decide to ask him, "What do you attribute your mother's changes to, Angel?"

"Well, I think she's under a great deal of stress with my dad. He's hardly ever home, and when he is, he yells a lot."

You realize that the drug issue hasn't been explored and suggest, "Let's get back to the issue of medications."

Maria defensively responds, "Look. I made a promise to God and my family that I wouldn't mess with drugs anymore, and it's been over a year since that mess. I only take what the doctor orders."

You follow up, "Do your doctors know about your history with drugs?"

"They don't know everything, but enough. They prescribe what I need."

You realize that she used the plural form just as you had and ask, "So you have more than one doctor prescribing medications?"

Appearing "caught," Maria says flatly, "Yes." She pauses and opens her mouth to explain and then says nothing.

"What's the deal, Mom?"

You decide that Maria's son's presence and consideration of his feelings are making it more difficult for her to speak openly. You ask, "Angel, can you step out while your mother and I talk?"

"Whatever." He gets up abruptly to go and mumbles, "For God's sake, Mom."

Maria says, "Look. I know I'm sick. I just know that if I get some sleep and some relief from the pain, I can get back on track. I haven't taken more than prescribed. You have to believe me. Why does everyone want to believe the worst of me?"

"Do your doctors know about the others?" you ask.

"I don't know," she replies.

You are not sure whether she will tell you the truth, but you decide to ask, "Maria, exactly what are you taking and in what amounts?"

"I'm taking Tylenol with codeine and another that I forget the name of, Propoxedrine or something. I don't know the amounts. I just take two of each every day. I take Klonopin (about 25 mg per day) and Restoril (I think I'm taking about 50 mg at night or something). Sometimes I take some Xanax, too, because my doctor says I can take it at my discretion when I'm particularly anxious. I hardly ever take that one."

You realize that she is probably not the best historian about her medications, so you ask her to sign a release to talk with her physicians and explain the danger of having a variety of medications from different doctors. She says that she'll think about it. You let her know that you cannot help her if she doesn't accurately describe her problems and treatments. She hesitantly agrees to sign the releases.

You do not want to allow much time to go by before engaging her again. You are aware of the possible dangers of overdose and/or detoxification (which you suspect has already resulted in a seizure), and you encourage Maria to stay in the hospital for observation overnight. She refuses vehemently, and you schedule an appointment for 2 days later, which is the soonest she will agree to.

4.2–1   What information would you like to obtain before you see Maria again?

4.2–2   What do you consider Maria's strengths?

4.2–3   What would you suggest to her son in terms of referrals? How would you respond if he asked you how he could help his mother?

4.2–4   Do you think Maria's ethnic background might have any impact on her assessment and potential treatment? How would you explore this with her?

4.2–5   What is your initial diagnosis?
Axis I

Axis II

Axis III

Axis IV

Axis V

Case 4.3

Identifying Information
Client Name: Stephanie Sellers
Age: 30 years old
Ethnicity: Caucasian
Marital Status: Divorced

Intake Information
Stephanie is a 30-year-old Caucasian woman referred by the Nursing Board. She is recently divorced (6 months ago), and she has no children. She has been described as an excellent nurse, but recently her performance evaluations have plummeted. She also has been moody and reactive. Her colleagues have complained to her supervisor that she's like Dr. Jekyll and Mr. Hyde. Her supervisor smelled alcohol on her breath in a team meeting and referred her to the "Can Do" program for nurses with alcohol problems.

Stephanie totally denies any problem with alcohol. She says that she had gone to a party the night before the team meeting and that the alcohol simply hadn't left her system by the time she came to work. She has been referred to you by the Nursing Board, and her job maintenance is contingent upon your assessment of her commitment to treatment and recovery.

Notes from Initial Session
Behavior: Stephanie comes to the session early, making sure that the receptionist alerted you of her arrival. She is dressed in her nursing garb. Her hair is neatly pulled away from her face. Though she has meticulously put on her makeup, it is apparent that she has been crying. She appears exhausted, with black circles under her eyes. She has deep worry lines on her brow. She is pleasant and greets you warmly. Her handshake is weak, and her hands cold and sweaty. She states, "I will do whatever I have to do to keep my job, but I also want to clear my name and my reputation. I will prove to you and everyone else that I am no alcoholic."

Intervention: You explain the Intensive Outpatient Program (IOP) in which Stephanie will be required to participate. It consists of 3-hour group meetings three evenings a week as well as assignments and Alcoholics Anonymous (AA) attendance three times per week. She is made aware that if she has no problem with alcohol, the program should be relatively easy. You administer the MAST, and the client scores 4 (answered "yes" to not remembering part of an evening that involved alcohol; guilt about her drinking at times; going to therapy to get help for an alcohol-related problem; and work problems connected to alcohol). She admits some black-out drinking in her life, but denies any recently.

Response: This client is reportedly "emotionally raw" from the experience of being "accused" of alcohol abuse and referred for treatment. She states, "After my miscarriage and my husband's leaving me, I thought things would get easier with time. But now this." She is angry about the time commitment required for the IOP program and especially indignant about attending AA, where she will be surrounded by "those people." She is, however, willing to follow all treatment recommendations in order to keep her job and nursing license.

Plan: Stephanie Sellers will attend IOP three times per week from 6:00 to 9:00 P.M. She will do all group assignments (e.g., First Step Inventory, Goodbye Letter to alcohol, and Relapse Prevention Plan), get a sponsor within a week of treatment onset, and attend at least three AA meetings per week. She will also attend the "Can Do" nurse's support group. She will be given sporadic Breathalyzer tests.

4.3–1   How do you think the involuntary nature of this referral will impact Stephanie's treatment experience?

4.3–2   What strengths can you see in her situation?

4.3–3   Along with the required "Can Do" program, are there other resources that you feel would be beneficial to the client?

4.3–4   What is your initial diagnosis?
Axis I

Axis II

Axis III

Axis IV

Axis V

Case 4.4

Identifying Information
Client Name: Rocky Littlebear
Age: 16 years old
Ethnicity: Pima (American Indian)
Educational Level: Ninth grade

Intake Information

You are an intake worker at an alcohol and drug treatment facility. You work primarily with adolescents and their families. Rocky was brought to you by his family after being referred from the emergency room at a local hospital. He reportedly was found "looking dead" in his backyard hammock. The ER report recommended drug/alcohol evaluation due to the apparent neurological symptomatology presented by the client. Specifically, he is lethargic, slurs words, is unresponsive, and displays poor motor coordination.

Initial Interview

You meet Rocky and his family in the waiting room. Rocky is slumped on the couch with his mother on one side and his father on the other. His eyes look glazed and unfocused. He is drooling. You smell an unusual odor that reminds you of turpentine.

You ask them into your office, and the parents respond by helping Rocky to his feet. He appears somewhat disoriented and stumbles several times on the way to your office. His parents state, "We don't know what's wrong with him."

Once in your office, you ask Rocky if he knows where he is.

He answers, "Sure."

You ask him to be more specific, and he responds, "Sure."

His mother chimes in, "You're in the rehab, Rocky."

He answers, "Sure." His head bobs as he looks around the office. He says, "I was at the hospital."

You think that his presentation reminds you of a mentally retarded individual that you worked with in another agency. You decide to proceed with a Mini-Mental Status Exam (MMSE). "Rocky, do you know what day it is today?"

He says, "Sure." Silence.

You ask again, and he says to his mother, "Are we done yet?"

"Rocky, will you repeat the following three items? Pencil, tree, carrot."

He answers, "Why?" You explain that it will help you with your assessment, and he says, "Whatever."

"Let's try again. Repeat these three words after me: pencil, tree, carrot."

Rocky replies, "Pencil, carrot, and . . . I forget."

You continue through the MMSE and from that assessment, Rocky appears to be experiencing cognitive impairment and significant disorientation. From this evaluation, you decide to discuss the problem with Rocky's parents.

4.4–1   What diagnoses are you considering at this point?

4.4–2 What collateral information/records would you like to obtain?

"Mr. and Mrs. Littlebear, what do you think is causing Rocky's problems?" you ask.

Mr. Littlebear responds, "He's skipping school and hanging out with bad kids. I think they drink liquor and smoke cigarettes. He's hardly ever home anymore. Sometimes others from the tribe carry him home to sleep, after finding him passed out in different places on our reservation."

Mrs. Littlebear adds with tears in her eyes, "We've never seen him like this. It's almost like he's not really here."

You ask, "How long has this been going on?"

"For almost a year now," she replies.

"Are you aware of any other drugs besides alcohol and cigarettes?" you inquire.

"Not that we know of," says Mrs. Littlebear.

"Are there any unusual behaviors or events that have happened lately that concern you?" you ask.

They sit quietly for a moment and think. Rocky's father notes that he found an empty spray paint bottle in his son's room, and he assumed that his son has been spraying graffiti on the reservation (a problem that the tribal council, of which he is a part, has been discussing).

"Rocky, have you been doing anything besides alcohol and cigarettes?" you ask.

Rocky laughs in surprise and then says, "Look, I'm not doing anything illegal. What are you trying to get at?"

You answer, "I'm concerned that you may be huffing something and that can be pretty serious and even life threatening."

"I don't take pills or shoot up. I don't do coke or anything. I don't even smoke pot," he responds sullenly.

"Okay, but how often are you huffing?" you persist.

"Whenever we have it."

"How often do you have it?" you ask.

"Mom, can we go now? This lady doesn't know anything. We just do this for fun. You know there's nothing else to do."

Mrs. Littlebear looks at you pleadingly and shakes her head. "My son is a good boy. He may have trouble in school, but he has always been a good boy. Haven't you, Rocky? What do you mean by 'huffing?'"

You explain that putting a substance such as paint or glue in a bag and breathing the fumes is a common practice among adolescents as a way of getting high. "This can be very dangerous and result in asphyxiation or seizures and, often, permanent brain damage. The symptoms usually include confusion, belligerence, assaultiveness, apathy, impaired judgment, and impaired social functioning (such as dropping out of school or truancy)," you continue.

Mrs. Littlebear turns to her husband and states, "He has been confused and fighting lately and hasn't wanted to do nothin'."

You suggest a 3-day stay at your facility to do a complete physical workup and further evaluate his substance use.

4.4–3   What information about the culture would you want to obtain before you continue working with this family?

4.4–4   If you were to conduct an interview with the parents privately, what further information would you want to obtain?

4.4–5   What initial diagnosis would you give Rocky?
Axis I

Axis II

Axis III

Axis IV

Axis V

Case 4.5

Identifying Information
Client Name: Rachel Steffenbaum
Age: 29 years old
Ethnicity: Caucasian
Educational Level: Some college

Background Information
You are an outreach caseworker for the HIV Services Department of the local health clinic. Your job involves making contact with high-risk individuals in a large metropolitan area who may be involved with drugs, alcohol, and/or sex-related activities. You distribute educational material and condoms, conduct blood pressure checks, and make referrals when indicated.

Initial Contact
You encounter Rachel while she is smoking a cigarette outside a local nightclub in a dilapidated part of town. She is frighteningly thin and dressed in a tight black leather skirt, a yellow halter top, spiked-heel shoes, and fishnet stockings. You can tell that her bleached-blond hair is actually a wig. Her makeup is thick and dramatic, but you can tell that her eyes are tired and bloodshot.

You ask her for a light and she obliges. She immediately complains about how "men are disgusting scum." You probe and find out that she has been working as an exotic dancer at the club for the past year. In her spare time, she often earns money as a prostitute, noting that there is no other profession where you can make almost a thousand dollars per evening. Your attention is drawn by her long, bright red nails to her fingers, which have needle marks between them.

"Would you like to have your blood pressure checked, Rachel?" you ask.

"That would be great . . . I haven't seen a doctor since I was a kid," she laughs. "I'm a little afraid that you'll find out I'm actually dead."

You muster a giggle and reply, "I'm an outreach worker from the health department . . ."

Rachel interrupts, "You're not going to report me to the cops or something, are you?"

"No. I just want to be helpful however I can," and you take out the blood pressure cuff and put it on her arm. In the process, you notice small scabs and more needle marks.

Rachel starts to ramble on (talkatively, almost frantically) about the men at the club, and you ask her to be quiet while you check her blood pressure. She laughs nervously. She picks at one of the scabs on her arms.

"Your blood pressure is a little high. Are you using any drugs or medication?"

Rachel stomps out her cigarette and blows smoke in your face saying, "What do you think? Are you new to your job or something? I've gotta get back in there, but thanks for the blood pressure thing." She starts to go inside.

"Wait just a minute. How long have you been using?" you ask.

"Since I graduated high school. Why?"

"I'd like to give you some information that might help you if you ever need it," you respond.

"Whatever floats your boat. I'm so exhausted right now. I think I could sleep for a week if I had the chance. I can't though because I already missed a week a few days ago because I just couldn't get out of bed." Her eyes dart about rapidly as if she's looking for someone.

"Is it cocaine or heroin you use?" you ask.

"Whatever I can get my hands on. Speedballs are what I need. You must know a lot of dealers around here, right?" She paces back and forth and appears to be waiting for someone.

"How long have you been high today?" you ask.

"Since first thing this morning, or actually last night I'd say. It's about time for me to crash. I'll have to get some more if I'm gonna finish my shift. Seriously, do you know who could score me some?"

You notice that Rachel is starting to nod off while she is standing up. Her eyes seem to roll back, and she struggles to keep them wide open. "What time do you get off tonight?"

"In about half an hour. Why?"

"You look so tired. Thought you might want to consider a hot meal and a cot at ARC. That's the detox. I could get you a bed there for the night to rest, and you could talk to some people that know a lot about your type of situation," you say.

Rachel looks at you wearily. "My boyfriend will get really pissed if I don't show up. I'm scared he's got a job for me tonight, and I just don't think I can do this anymore."

Rachel opens the door to go in and says, "Look, you're real nice and all, but you have no idea how complicated this thing is. I'll keep your number and call you."

You write down her name and location in your log and hand her your card and brochures along with a bag of free items, including condoms, alcohol swabs, and a bleach kit. You try one more time and ask her just to finish her shift and join you for a cup of coffee down the street in half an hour.

Rachel smirks and says, "Maybe some other time."

4.5–1   What other information would you like to have about Rachel?

4.5–2   What strengths do you see in her situation?

4.5–3   Are there non-substance-related diagnoses you might want to rule out if you get a chance to work more with Rachel?

4.5–4   What risks to Rachel would you consider most critical in addressing her problems? What resources would you try to find for her?

4.5–5   What is your initial diagnosis?

Axis I

Axis II

Axis III

Axis IV

Axis V

_____

Identifying Information
Client Name: Roy Bass
Age: 49 years old
Ethnicity: Caucasian
Educational Level: Some high school
Marital Status: Widower

Intake Information

You are a social worker at a community health clinic where you see clients who are unable to access the resources they need for everyday living. The community clinic is a nonprofit, city-funded agency.

You have noticed Mr. Bass around the clinic for several months on an almost weekly basis. He appears to have multiple physical complaints and at times seems to be agitated and in need of services. You ask the intake worker for additional information about Mr. Bass.

The intake worker informs you that Roy Bass has been seen at the clinic for the past 6 months. He often has hygiene problems and smells of alcohol. While at times he is lucid and personable, at other times he seems to go off on a tangent, talking about odd and eccentric issues from his past, such as his experiences in Vietnam and his loss of family and wife.

Initial Interview

You meet Roy at the waiting room and find that he is asleep, lying across two chairs with his head hanging off the side of one of them. You gently nudge Roy, saying, "Mr. Bass? I'm ready to see you now."

He jumps up, as if at attention, and salutes. He blurts out loudly, "Roy Bass, reporting for duty, sir!" You attempt to calm Roy by explaining to him that he is at the community health clinic and you are a practitioner who would like to assist him in any way that you can. He seems irritated at this and quizzically asks, "Sir, have I done something wrong, sir?"

In order to attempt to orient Roy to time, place, and person, you reiterate, "Mr. Bass, may I call you Roy?" (He nods.) You tell him your name and say, "I'm here to talk with you. Would you like to come to my office?"

He answers, "Okay, but I have to be back to the barracks by 1900 hours."

You usher Roy back to your office and notice that he is weaving through the hallway. He sits down in the chair next to your desk and leans his head back so that he is staring at the ceiling. "Star light, star bright; I think I see a star tonight. Stars are sure bright tonight, aren't they?" he asks.

"Mr. Bass, do you see stars in my office?" In a moment of lucidity, he gazes around your office and responds, "No, madam, I was just thinkin' about where I'm going to sleep tonight. It's been pretty cold out these days."

You ask, "Where did you sleep last night, Roy?"

"Well, down behind Sixth Street in the alley, next to Jake's Restaurant. It sure warms up when they run those dryers for those table linens."

"Okay, so you're living on the streets right now?"

"Yup. Haven't slept in a bed for weeks because the shelter's full. Sure miss a bed."

"Can I help you find a place to sleep, Roy?"

"That would be great. What did you say your name was?"

You give him your name again. "Can I ask you some other questions about your health?"

"Shoot. I don't mind tellin' you my health ain't good. I've got this rheumatoid condition. Joints hurt all the time. Only thing that helps is them pain pills the doctor give me. But I'm runnin' out of them, too. Do you think you could talk to that doctor and get me some more of them pain pills? I'd be forever grateful."

"Before talking to the doctor, I'd like to get a better picture of how you're doing. Are you eating every day?"

"Most days, I eat. Jake throws out a lot of really good food. It's a fancy place, and those fancy people don't eat much."

"Can you tell me what you had yesterday to eat, Roy?"

"Well, let's see. I had a biscuit, some meat, and bread, too. Got anything here to eat? This talk of food is makin' me hungry."

"Let's see to that after our discussion. Besides the food you ate yesterday, did you have anything to drink?"

"Well, I have a part-time job at the restaurant."

"Oh, really? What do you do?"

"Jake's cook hires me to put the trash he hands me in the dumpster."

"How much do you get paid?"

"Well, it's really an arrangement, you see. I take out the trash, and he lets me polish off the leftover bottles."

"Bottles?"

"Wine."

"So about how much do you drink per day?"

"Honey, it depends on how much trash they have. Mostly, I get about a bottle a day, give or take a few."

"Do you have any family that you stay in touch with?"

"Just my wife."

"How old is she?"

"Oh, she's dead."

"Dead?"

"Yup, she died in 1991. But I must say, she's a lot nicer these days than those days she was alive. Much better company."

"Roy, um, what exactly do you mean?"

"Well, when she died I thought that would be the last I saw of her. But surprise, surprise, one night, she just shows up and every night since."

"Now, Roy. Do you mean she shows up in real life or spirit?"

"She's real all right. In fact, she still pulls my ear when I curse and sets me upright when I'm drunk."

"But I thought you said she was dead?"

"Dead as a doornail."

"Do you see or hear other things that other people don't?"

"Sometimes Nell, my wife, talks to me through the radio."

"What does she say to you?"

"Sometimes she just says, 'Roy Bass, you need a bath.' And then other times, she directs me."

"Directs you?"

"Yup. Tells me where to go, what to do, and who to talk to. A real good help, I must say."

"Do you sometimes have trouble knowing where to go or what to do?"

"Almost always."

At this point, you realize that Roy is going to require extensive services, from a physical, mental, and environmental standpoint. You suggest to Roy that he wait for you in the waiting room while you talk to the physician on call and your supervisor. You believe that you will need to develop a plan of intervention in order to assist Roy.

4.6–1   As the social worker in this case, what do you think is the first action you would want to take on Roy's behalf?

4.6–2   List the emotional issues you perceive confronting Roy.

4.6–3   What are some resources that would be helpful to Roy?

4.6–4   Find a journal article on homelessness, and summarize the characteristics of this population and any related interventions cited.

4.6–5   What are the potential structural barriers to Roy's recovery?

4.6–6   What are some of Roy's strengths?

4.6–7   How would you diagnose Roy Bass?
Axis I

Axis II

Axis III

Axis IV

Axis V

_____

DIFFERENTIAL DIAGNOSIS

Undoubtedly, the greatest challenge in making substance-related diagnoses is the willingness to address the issue with clients. This difficulty is likely related to the traditional separation of mental health and substance-related services. Frequently, when the presenting problem is not focused on substances, practitioners feel free to ignore issues even when they are aware the person is using substances. Ideally, mental health practitioners should become more comfortable in assessing alcohol or other drug use. At a minimum, referral to appropriate professionals to screen for these problems is warranted when problematic use is apparent.

It is important to note that other conditions may disguise themselves as intoxication, drug-related behaviors, and substance abuse. For example, a person could present slurring words, walking with an unstable gait, and having glazed eyes. While this may appear to be alcohol intoxication, it might in fact be a diabetic reaction. Along with involving medical personnel for drug screenings and the like, observing the client's behavior over time is instructive in separating substance-related and other problems.

Even when substances are clearly part of the presentation, further investigation is needed to determine whether there is a pattern of use or abuse, or whether the client is showing the effects of withdrawal. For example, a college student could present at the emergency room "falling down drunk"; this incident might be the first occurrence, or it could be due to a long history of alcohol dependence. At the same time, practitioners must recognize that clients may actively minimize or even hide substance usage because of the associated stigma.

4.DD–1   In the case of Stephanie (Case 4.3), what questions would you ask to determine whether she was presenting with alcohol abuse rather than dependence?

4.DD–2   In the case of Maria (Case 4.2), what other symptoms would she have to display to warrant a diagnosis of Substance Withdrawal?

 InfoTrac keywords

alcohol disorders, amphetamine disorders, cocaine-related disorders, drug abuse, heroin abuse, substance abuse

5 | Schizophrenia and Other Psychoses

DISORDERS

The disorders in this section of the DSM-IV-TR (APA, 2000) are arguably the most serious and debilitating of the mental disorders. Generally, these disorders involve distortions in the perception of reality; impairments in the capacity to reason, speak, and behave rationally; and/or impairments in affect and motivation. In short, these disorders directly or indirectly disrupt all aspects of a client's life.

Generally, the symptoms of Schizophrenia include severe disruptions in thinking. The result may be gross disorganization in thoughts or may involve delusions (i.e., systems of false beliefs that vary in elaborateness but are not open to reason or appeal). The client may experience severe perceptual disturbances, such as hallucinations (i.e., sensory experiences in the absence of sensory input). The most common hallucinatory experiences are auditory, in which the client hears one or more voices in much the same manner as he or she would hear someone else talking. The remaining symptoms are sometimes labeled "negative" in that they represent the relative absence of things like affect, motivation, and/or interaction. Not surprisingly, an individual with such symptoms experiences significant psychosocial impairment and/or distress. For a diagnosis of Schizophrenia, the symptoms must have begun at least 6 months earlier (APA, 2000). With modern treatment, it is unlikely that a single episode would encompass this entire time frame.

The subtypes of Schizophrenia are determined by the predominant symptoms. When delusions and hallucinations are elaborate and encompassing, the client is considered a Paranoid Type. Although there can be significant disorganization in thoughts in this subtype, negative symptoms are not usually present. Indeed, the agitation often involved in Schizophrenia of the Paranoid Type may be misunderstood as affect. The Catatonic Type is the most rare, and the symptom display was explained in some detail in chapter 3. Clients diagnosed as Disorganized Type may also display some catatonic behaviors, but disorganized speech and negative symptoms are the prominent features. When negative symptoms alone are prominent, the designation is a Residual Type. Probably the most frequently diagnosed subtype is the Undifferentiated Type. In this instance no particular features are prominent. Stated differently, the person does not meet criteria for another specific subtype (APA, 2000).

If a client is displaying the symptoms characteristic of Schizophrenia and the time frame since initial display of symptoms is between 1 and 6 months, the appropriate diagnosis is Schizophreniform Disorder (APA, 2000). To a large extent, this particular diagnosis exists to ensure that the label of Schizophrenia is not used too quickly. Because the psychosocial impairment associated with Schizophrenia develops and usually intensifies over time, clients with Schizophreniform Disorder may not evidence marked psychosocial problems.

The diagnosis of Brief Psychotic Disorder describes situations in which there is a sudden onset of positive symptoms that last more than 1 day but remit within 30 days. Because the criteria include a return to the premorbid level of functioning, this diagnosis can only be made in retrospect. While the symptoms are present, the diagnosis of Brief Psychotic Disorder should be provisional. With this diagnosis, a specifier is used to indicate whether there is a discernible stressor that has triggered the episode. When a marked stressor is present, it is less likely that the client will develop a full-blown Schizophrenic Disorder (APA, 2000).

The diagnosis of Schizoaffective Disorder includes the same symptom display as Schizophrenia. However, in addition to having these symptoms, the client simultaneously has symptoms that constitute one of the episodes of a Mood Disorder (see chapter 6 for more detail). While this diagnosis requires the schizophrenic and mood symptoms to co-occur, there will also be periods when only the schizophrenic symptoms are evident. This disorder is usually diagnosed after examination of a rather extensive history of severe symptoms. The agitation associated with some delusional content may be difficult to distinguish from a Mood Disorder episode (APA, 2000).

Delusional Disorder differs in both symptoms and impairment from Schizophrenia. Disorganization and negative symptoms are not present. While some problems in social and/or vocational functioning are present, they are not severe. Further, the content of delusional material in people with this diagnosis is not considered bizarre. Briefly, the distinction between bizarre and nonbizarre delusions is focused on whether the delusional situation *could* occur in real life. Although this sounds clear-cut, the distinction can be difficult in practice (APA, 2000).

In Shared Psychotic Disorder, a person who is closely associated with someone else with some Psychotic Disorder "buys into" the delusional system. Although this diagnosis is rarely made, it apparently is more likely when the individual with the original delusions exercises substantial power over the other person. For example, children growing up with a parent who is delusional may well "buy into" that worldview, at least during their younger years (APA, 2000).

To complete this section, a series of diagnoses exists for describing psychotic symptoms that are known to be caused by a general medical condition or that are substance induced. A final designation, Psychotic Disorder NOS, is included to be used when more specific diagnoses are not possible (APA, 2000).

ASSESSMENT

As in the assessment of Dementia, Delirium, and Amnestic and Other Cognitive Disorders, the thought disorders common to clients with diagnoses in this section have constrained the development of self-report instruments. Broadly based approaches, like the MMPI-2 and MMPI-A (see chapter 1 for detail) offer self-report approaches to diagnosing these disorders. Frequently, however, clients with these disorders do not yield valid results for interpretation.

Most commonly, assessment with these clients is accomplished through structured interviews. Generally referred to as Mental Status Examinations, these approaches are designed to accrue information about the quality of the client's mental processes. From this general approach, a number of structured or semistructured clinical interviews have been developed (see chapter 1) and are used with this population.

In addition, several clinical rating scales are commonly used with clients diagnosed with Schizophrenia or Other Psychotic Disorders. The oldest and still most commonly utilized of these approaches is the Brief Psychiatric Rating Scale (BPRS) (Overall & Gorham, 1962). This instrument addresses 16 symptom dimensions that were empirically derived from data from the 1950s. The BPRS has been widely used to monitor clients, particularly in case-management settings.

A more recent instrument was developed to focus on the distinction between negative and positive symptoms. While the debate continues regarding this approach to understanding schizophrenic symptoms (see, for example, Lancon, Auquier, Nayt, & Reine, 2000), the Positive and Negative Syndrome Scale (PANSS) (Kay, Fiszbein, & Opler, 1987) has become a common instrument in drug trials and clinical research. Its 30 items are rated based on interviews with the client as well as available clinical records. Clinicians are provided with definitions and anchoring criteria for rating of psychiatric symptoms and functioning on a 7-point scale.

Emergency Considerations

Dangerous behavior (directed at either oneself or others) may occur in the course of a psychotic episode. Despite social stigma, people with Psychotic Disorders are not as "dangerous" as the general public in this regard. Further, when people with Psychotic Disorders become violent, the behavior is much more frequently aimed at themselves than at others. Studies indicate that 60 to 80% of schizophrenic clients experience suicidal ideation and that 10 to 15% of schizophrenic clients complete suicide (Black, Warrack, & Winokur, 1985; Roy, Mazonson, & Pickar, 1984). Furthermore, research has shown that up to 50% of persons with Schizophrenia make suicidal attempts (Caldwell & Gottsman, 1990). One study of 223 schizophrenic clients indicates that depression, life stressors, and age are factors that contribute to suicide risk among schizophrenic clients. Age was found to be inversely related to suicide risk; younger clients were more likely to attempt suicide than older clients (Schwartz & Cohen, 2001). Another study found that there is a positive correlation between the frequency and prevalence of positive symptoms (hallucinations and delusions) and the likelihood of suicidal thoughts and actions (Kaplan & Harrow, 1996, 1999). Nonetheless, the inherent unpredictability of psychotic behavior makes screening for potential for danger to oneself and others an important part of assessment with this population. Throughout the United States, potential for danger as a result of mental illness is grounds for involuntary psychiatric hospitalization.

Further, people having psychotic behaviors may be substantially less able to care for themselves and/or utilize judgment in their own behalf. Practitioners must peruse the legal statutes in their states to determine whether this type of debilitation constitutes grounds for involuntary hospitalization. In any event, practitioners should familiarize themselves with local resources and procedures for involuntary hospitalization.

CULTURAL CONSIDERATIONS

Schizophrenia has been found throughout the world in a multitude of cultures. However, a disproportionately high number of cases of Schizophrenia are found among disadvantaged ethnic cultures. In one study, the prevalence of Schizophrenia was found to be greater in those groups with high ethnic discrimination, low educational attainment, and low occupational status (Dohrenwend et al., 1992). The theory proposed for this phenomenon is known as social selection theory. It suggests that cultures that are oppressed and unable to attain a high socioeconomic status (SES) have a greater number of individuals with disabilities and poor health. Experts theorize that the higher incidence of mental illness among certain ethnicities and cultures is a result of their oppressed status over the centuries and subsequent genetic predisposition rather than their ethnic background per se (Dohrenwend et al.). Therefore, we find a greater number of individuals with Schizophrenia among oppressed minority populations than in populations who have attained higher SES and, therefore, healthier lifestyles.

In addition, cultural factors may play a role in the course of the illness. Sartorius et al. (1986), in a 2-year study of more than 1,000 patients, found that the prognosis for individuals diagnosed with Schizophrenia was more favorable in the developing countries of Nigeria, India, and Colombia than in nine industrialized countries (including the United Kingdom, the United States, and the former Soviet Union). Furthermore, expressed emotion (EE) (of the family over involvement with the patient and his or her treatment, and hostility and criticism of the patient with Schizophrenia) has been studied cross-culturally. Studies indicate that certain cultural factors, not merely high EE, may be detrimental to the schizophrenic family member. For example, one study of Chinese families coping with a schizophrenic relative found no significant difference between the impact that families that displayed high EE and those families that had low EE in terms of the impact on the patient (Phillips & Xiong, 1995). By the same token, a study of Japanese families found that high EE families within Japanese culture had a more detrimental influence on the schizophrenic family member than did low EE families (Mino et al., 1995). These studies suggest that cultural norms may play a role in the impact of the family on the person with severe mental illness. In the United States, many studies have examined the impact of EE on schizophrenic family members. Evidence has indicated that high EE within a U.S. family can have a negative impact on the person coping with Schizophrenia (Hogarty et al., 1988, 1991). Psychoeducational support for high EE families has been effective in reducing the relapse and rehospitalization of schizophrenic family members.

Social skills training has been an effective intervention with Caucasian individuals and families coping with Schizophrenia (Liberman et al., 2001). On the other hand, studies have shown that with Latinos who have Schizophrenia, social skills training must take the values of the culture into consideration if the intervention is to be useful for implementation with this ethnic population (Kopelowicz, 1998). For example, while Anglo American culture values autonomy of the individual and gears intervention toward independence from family for the schizophrenic member, as many as 90% of Latinos with Schizophrenia live with family members who act as caregivers for the individual. Social skills training, therefore, may be more effective with severely mentally ill Latinos if delivered to both the affected individuals and the family members with whom they reside.

SOCIAL SUPPORT SYSTEMS

The disorders in this section of the DSM-IV-TR (APA, 2000) typically have devastating consequences to the clients' psychosocial functioning. The social networks of people with Schizophrenia are markedly smaller, denser, and more dependent than those in the general population (Froland, Brodsky, Olson, & Stewart, 2000). Further, network members are primarily biological relatives and mental health service providers. The constrained networks tend to shrink over time, particularly in conjunction with extended hospitalizations. On the occupational side, people with Schizophrenia have unemployment rates greater than 80% (Cook & Razzano, 2000). Typically, this diagnosis foreshadows a lifetime of marginal economic and social status.

Although these facts certainly are partially explained by the debilitating symptoms of the illness, the social stigma attached to Psychotic Disorders contributes significantly to the lack of social support as well. Most people assume that these clients are unable to fulfill appropriately any kind of role expectations and, in fact, regard them somewhat fearfully. As a result of such negative expectations, psychosocial success becomes even more elusive. Schizophrenic males with unpredictable behavioral characteristics and a lack of family ties tend to evoke the strongest negative attitudes toward this population (Phelan, Bromet, & Link, 1998).

This social stigma of Schizophrenia adds to the burden often experienced by family members across many cultures. For example, family members in India report feelings of depression, sorrow, fear of rejection by neighbors, and desire to hide the diagnosis (Thata & Srinivasan, 2000). These findings are similar to reports from caregivers of schizophrenic clients in the United States (Phelan, Bromet, & Link, 1998). In addition to experiencing potential financial strain and social isolation, these families are usually ill-equipped to understand and manage their loved one's symptoms. Mental health providers have only recently understood the need to educate and support such families. Indeed, caregivers and relatives often are the only supports that stand between the client and complete social breakdown (e.g., homelessness or institutionalization). A number of professional-led and self-help groups have evolved in recent years to provide support and/or education to families of persons with mental illness. These approaches are referred to as *psychoeducation*.

Also in recent years, much more attention has been given to quality-of-life issues among those diagnosed with Psychotic Disorders. The consumer rights and psychiatric survivors movements have generated self-help and/or consumer-driven treatment options that are more focused on recovery than simple symptom control.

The following list includes some of the Internet resources available to these clients and their loved ones.

www.medscape.com/Medscape/psychiatry/ClinicalMgmt/CM.v05/public/index-CM.v05.html—Medscape article providing information on the history of Schizophrenia in an online course format (user must register by completing a brief application in order to access this information; registration free to students)

www.schizophrenia.com/research/research.html—Research on Schizophrenia and studies concerning families of people with Schizophrenia

www.mentalhealth.com/book/p40-sc01.html—An online handbook for family members of a person with Schizophrenia

www.mhsource.com/narsad/—Web site for the National Alliance for Research on Schizophrenia and Depression

psychiatry.medscape.com/govmt/NIMH/SchizophreniaBulletin/public/journal.SB.html—The *Schizophrenia Bulletin*, a journal devoted to research on Schizophrenia; site includes back issues of the journal

www.mentalwellness.com/—Information for consumers on mental illness and resources

Identifying Information
Name: Constance Pryor
Age: 19 years old
Ethnicity: African American
Marital Status: Single
Occupation: Student

Intake Information
The intake appointment was made by the client's mother, Betty Pryor. She indicated that her daughter, Constance, had been having "problems" at college and had been acting "strangely" since she had left school and returned home. Mrs. Pryor also indicated that Constance was not "very pleased" about coming to the mental health center for the appointment.

Initial Interview
When you go to the lobby to meet Constance, she is initially unwilling to come to your office. After some persuasion from her mother, she agrees only if her mother accompanies her.

Constance appears uncomfortable once you have all settled down in your office. She is dressed in jeans and an old T-shirt. She is wearing no makeup, and her hair is rather disheveled. In contrast, her mother is attractively, although casually, dressed.

"What can I do to help you?" you begin.

After an uncomfortable pause, with Constance looking at the floor, her mother replies. "This appointment was really my idea. Constance started classes at the university in the fall. Things seemed to be going well at first, but by October she was asking to come home. At first, I just thought she was having some roommate problems."

Constance interrupts her mother at this point. "It wasn't just Clara! Everyone on the floor of the dorm was in on it! Probably more than that!"

"Constance, can you tell me more about what was going on?" you ask.

Once again after a long pause, Mrs. Pryor continues. "Well, then she stopped calling, and we thought things might be getting better. But she didn't call at all, and when we'd try to call her, she was never in. I was really worried but my husband, Eddie, told me we had to let her find her own way. She did come home for Thanksgiving but hardly talked with us at all. Then, the semester was over, and she failed almost all her classes. When we tried to talk with her about it, she'd just get angry." Mrs. Pryor becomes tearful at this point.

Constance sighs deeply and turns away from both you and her mother. You again try to engage her. "Constance, would you like to tell me what happened with your classes?"

"Education isn't the point, you know. My room was the center, but everyone was involved. They tried to confuse me in those classes. It wasn't safe. I had to just stop going," she says.

"We didn't know any of this. She wouldn't tell us anything. Eddie and I finally thought she was embarrassed and just needed another chance. He had trouble his first semester in college, too. So we just told her we loved her and sent her back to school for spring semester. In less than a week, we got a call from the resident assistant in her dorm. She said she thought Constance was having a problem with drugs."

"That's not true!" Constance interrupts again. "They were trying to discredit me because I was starting to understand what they were all up to."

"Constance, will you tell me what they were up to?" you ask.

"They set up a communication system in my room. They had cameras everywhere. I mean everywhere. I couldn't do anything without them watching. Then they got the voice machine going!" Constance is shaking her head and speaking in a monotone.

"Did you hear voices, Constance?" you inquire.

"Yes, from the machine. All these different voices saying stupid things and mean things. I couldn't keep anything straight anymore. I couldn't pay attention to anything. Finally, I couldn't do anything anymore. I just stayed in my room . . . just let them look. Then I came home," she says.

"Have things gotten better since you came home?" you ask.

5.1–1   What diagnoses are you considering at this point?

5.1–2   What strengths have you noticed in Constance's situation?

"Okay, Constance. It sounds like you've been having some really frightening experiences. I want to try to help you, but I need to ask you a lot of questions so I can figure out the best way to help. Is that going to be all right with you?" you ask.

"I guess so. I don't know what to do," she responds.

"Let's start with what your mother said about drugs. Did you take any drugs while you were away at school?" you inquire.

"No, I didn't even drink beer or anything. They just told my mother that to try to get her on their side."

"Okay, do you have any idea why these people would do these things to you?"

"No, not really. It was better for a few days, but then they started setting up the network at my parents' house."

Constance starts holding herself and rocking quietly. Mrs. Pryor is looking more and more alarmed. You decide that you can talk with them separately now that Constance is interacting with you.

"Mrs. Pryor, I'd like to talk more to Constance alone. Would you mind waiting in the lobby for a while? I'll talk with you when we're through."

"Okay," she responds and leaves the room.

"I've thought about it a lot, you know. I think they want to be like me. I've always done really well in school. They wanted to understand how I did that and duplicate it. I would have told them. They didn't need to say bad things about me." She begins to rock gently again.

"Constance, did anything like this ever happen to you before you went to the university?" you ask.

"What do you mean?"

"Things like hearing voices, or having people working against you?" you clarify.

"No. And it didn't start until maybe October or November, 4, maybe 5, months ago," she answers.

"Okay, Constance, just one more question for right now. Did you see any doctors or counselors while you were at school?" you ask.

"No."

"Would you be willing to talk with a doctor if I could arrange it?"

• "I guess so if it's okay with my mother," she responds.

"Great, Constance. Why don't you stay here while I check in with your mother and try to set up an appointment with our doctor? Is that okay with you?"

"I guess so."

5.1–3   Do you have concerns for Constance's safety at this point?

5.1–4   What is your initial diagnosis?

Axis I

Axis II

Axis III

Axis IV

Axis V

5.1–5   What will you say to Mrs. Pryor about what's going on with her daughter?

5.1–6   Is there any other information you want to get before you finish with Constance today?

Case 5.2

Identifying Information
Name: Herschel Jarboe
Age: 31 years old
Ethnicity: Caucasian
Marital Status: Never married

Background Information
As the counselor "on call" at the public mental health center, you receive a call from law enforcement. They have taken into custody a Caucasian male who appears to be in his late 20s or early 30s. A motorist had summoned police when the client blocked traffic on the highway near the local airport. When the officers approached the young man, he explained his behavior as "protecting everyone from the Airstreams hovering over the city dropping hot water and chickens." He then fled when officers attempted to take him into custody. Six officers and 45 minutes were required to apprehend and subdue the client. During the "chase," he showed no awareness of potential dangers, darting into traffic several times. The police indicate that he is still quite agitated, and they want to know how to proceed to get a psychiatric screening for him.

You advise the police to take him to the local hospital. You will advise ER personnel of the situation, and you will speak with him after they do an initial medical screening. You tell police that if the client remains agitated and uncooperative, they will likely have to have at least one officer remain at the hospital until a disposition is decided.

Initial Interview
When you arrive at the hospital, you learn that the ER personnel have not found any indications of medical problems in a routine examination. The doctor has already drawn blood to screen for drugs. You go into an examination room and find the client in 5-point leather restraints on a gurney with two officers still present. He is dressed in shabby jeans and a tank top and has moderate body odor. He does not appear to have shaved for a day or two.

After greeting the officers, you introduce yourself to the client. He stares fixedly at you but does not respond. "I've been asked to see if you might be having some mental health problems. Will you speak with me?" you ask.

"Not with them here!" he whispers.

You ask the officers to wait outside the examination room. As soon as they leave, the client asks you to remove the restraints.

"I'm not authorized to do that. I think it's up to the ER doctor at this point. Let's try to sort this out, and then we'll see about the restraints. Will you tell me your name?" you ask.

"I'm Agent 1447," he replies.

"That's your title, perhaps, but I need to know your name, like what appears on your driver's license," you persist.

"Herschel, Herschel Jarboe, Agent 1447," he replies.

"Okay, Mr. Jarboe. The officers indicated that they were called because you were trying to stop traffic on the highway by the airport. Can you tell me what was going on?"

"The Airstreams are quite dangerous, but *you* already know that, don't you?" he replies.

"Do you mean Airstream trailers, Mr. Jarboe?" you ask.

The client has moved his attention from you for the first time since you spoke with him. He is now staring fixedly at the ceiling over his left shoulder and does not respond.

"Mr. Jarboe, I need to understand what was going on when the officers approached you. Will you tell me that?" you ask.

He looks at you again. "We understand each other. They're right outside the door, so I know we can't use the codes. Can you contact Agent 007?"

"I'm afraid I don't know any agents, Mr. Jarboe. The officers said you told them the Airstreams were dropping hot water and chickens. Is that right?" you ask.

"Of course, they're trying to weaken us. This might be more subtle than what happened on my mission to Panama, but it's all the same. You know very well how urgent this is. They must be stopped!" he says with growing agitation.

"Okay. I need to ask you some routine questions. Have you ever seen things or heard things that other people didn't?"

"Of course. I'm a highly trained professional," he responds.

"Can you tell me what day it is today?" you ask.

"Why do you need to know that? Are you trying to trick me or something? It's Thursday; this is a hospital; Bush is the president. Anything else?" he asks.

"I guess you've been asked questions like this before. Have you ever been treated by a psychiatrist or been in a psychiatric hospital?" you ask.

"Hound dog, hound dog. Over and out!" The client refocuses his gaze on the ceiling.

"Have you been having any thoughts about hurting yourself or anyone else?" you inquire.

"Can you tell me anything else about the Airstreams?" you ask after a long pause. The client does not return his attention to you or respond to other questions for approximately 5 minutes, so you decide to take a break.

5.2–1   What diagnoses are you considering at this time?

5.2–2   What collateral information do you need?

Collateral Information from Police

After leaving the client with one officer to observe him, you speak with the other officer. "Do you have any other information about this guy?" you ask.

"Not much, I'm afraid. We've searched his pockets and backpack. His name is Herschel Jarboe. He has an expired New York driver's license. I guess the most interesting things are these." He offers you two pieces of paper.

The first is another identification card. This one identifies Herschel as a resident of a state psychiatric hospital in North Carolina. Another letter-sized sheet of paper provides directions to a mental health center in Wilmington, North Carolina. The listed appointment was for 10 days ago.

"Well, this certainly answers the question about whether he has a psychiatric history. Have you been able to reach anyone at the state hospital?" you inquire.

"Dispatch got some night staff. They recognized the name and said he'd been there at least a half-dozen times in the past. They said this last stay was for almost 5 months. That's all we can get until the morning," the officer informs you. "Oh, yeah. While you were talking to him, the nurse said the drug screen is negative."

5.2-3   In what ways, if any, do you think this client poses a risk to himself or others?

5.2-4   Do you see any strengths in this situation?

5.2-5   What is your initial diagnosis for this client?
Axis I

Axis II

Axis III

Axis IV

Axis V

Case 5.3

Identifying Information
Name: Charlene Johnson
Age: 28 years old
Ethnicity: African American
Marital Status: Divorced
Occupation: Grocery store cashier
Children: Charlie, age 6; Tenny, age 3 (recently deceased)

Background Information
The client is a 28-year-old, divorced African American female brought into the emergency room at Cliffside General Hospital for evaluation by her live-in boyfriend, Greg.

Greg reported that 9 days ago Charlene witnessed their 3-year-old son's death. He stated that Charlene had just gotten off work on a Wednesday night and was walking to her car when her ex-husband drove through the grocery store parking lot at a high rate of speed and flung Tenny, her son, out of the driver's side window. Tenny hit a light pole in the parking lot, which fractured his skull. Charlene was about 20 feet from the speeding car when she saw her son fly out of the window. She screamed frantically as she ran toward her son, and when she saw the traumatic injuries to his head, she fainted in the parking lot.

Emergency Medical Services personnel attempted to revive Tenny, but he was pronounced dead at the scene and taken by ambulance to the hospital. The police arrested Charlene's ex-husband approximately 4 hours later, and he is being held without bail in the county jail facility on charges of first-degree murder.

Greg stated that Charlene has been "out of her mind" ever since the tragic incident occurred. He told the triage nurse that Charlene keeps calling for Tenny and searching the house and the neighborhood for him. During the child's funeral, she alternately shouted that the corpse was not her child and attempted to remove the corpse from the coffin. He also stated that she hasn't slept or eaten much since the tragedy occurred. According to Greg, Charlene has no history of mental problems and, in fact, has always seemed well adjusted and happy. He stated that they were planning on getting married around the holidays.

The emergency room personnel found no gross medical problems in their examination of Charlene. They then called you from the psychiatric unit for a screening interview. The emergency room physician briefly relayed the information to you and directed you to an examination room.

Interview with Charlene
When you walk into the room, Greg is sitting with Charlene and holding her hand. She appears very disheveled and scared. You explain to Charlene that you are a counselor and want to help her feel better. You start by asking Charlene if she knows what day of the week it is.

"I think it's Saturday, but I don't really know. I'm worried about Tenny," Charlene tells you. She looks over to Greg, who has moved to another chair to allow you to sit beside Charlene.

"I know you've been very upset about Tenny," you suggest, "but, right now, I'm concerned about how you are feeling. Do you know where you are, right now?" you ask.

"I guess I'm at the doctor's office," Charlene says after a long pause. "Do you think I'm sick? I really have to get home and find Tenny."

"Charlene, you're at the emergency room at the hospital," you tell her. "Greg brought you here because he's very concerned that you've been so upset about your son."

Charlene doesn't respond and seems to be having a hard time comprehending what you're saying. She begins humming what sounds like a child's lullaby.

"How are you feeling right now, Charlene?" you query.

Charlene doesn't respond directly to your question. Suddenly, she jumps up and starts putting on her sweater. "I've got to get home now; come on, Greg, we got to find Tenny. He's lost, and we've got to find him." She appears very agitated and worried.

Greg looks sadly at you and tells you that Charlene has been this way ever since Tenny died. "I don't know what to do. She doesn't seem to hear me when I tell her Tenny died," Greg says. "It's like she just went over the edge when Tenny was killed."

You gently persuade Charlene to sit down again. "Charlene, can we talk about what happened to Tenny?" you ask.

Charlene stares at the door and finally nods her head. "Okay, I guess," she says.

"Charlene, you are at the emergency room because you've been through a very difficult time lately concerning your son, Tenny. Can you tell me about what happened?" you ask gently.

After a long delay, Charlene begins humming again. She looks at you blankly and finally says that she's not feeling very well and needs to lie down. "I'm very, very tired. I think I better get the children and go on home now. Greg, can you take me home now?"

It is apparent to you that Charlene is not ready or able to discuss the tragic death of her son. After helping Charlene lie down on the bed, you ask Greg to talk with you for a few minutes in your office. A nursing assistant stays with Charlene, and you take Greg to your office.

5.3–1 What diagnoses are you considering at this time?

5.3–2 What kind of additional information would you like to have about Charlene?

Interview with Greg

You ask Greg if Charlene has shown any acknowledgment of Tenny's death. He says that she has been in a "state" ever since she saw Tenny die in the parking lot. "She hasn't talked about it at all. It seems like she doesn't believe it really happened. She hasn't cried about it and keeps trying to find him in the house or outside. She'll stand at the door calling for him to come home, and I can't persuade her that he's gone. It's like she's blanked out the whole incident."

"Has she talked about 'seeing' Tenny?" you ask. "Or has she talked about seeing things that aren't there?"

"I don't think so," Greg says, "but she seems to be hearing things that aren't real. Like she'll tell me that she just heard Tenny come in the door, or she'll hear Tenny calling her outside."

"Okay, and she hasn't been sleeping or eating very well?" you ask.

"Right," Greg tells you, "she's hardly eaten a bite since the funeral, and she's up pacing the floor in the living room at all hours of the night singing that lullaby. It's really scary to watch her, and she gets really irritated with me if I try to get her to calm down."

"Has she said anything about hurting herself?" you ask.

"No, I don't think so," Greg states. "She seems too 'out of it' to think about anything like that."

"I need to talk to the doctor, Greg, and Charlene may need to spend the night here so we can help her feel better. Does that make sense to you?"

"Yes, I just want her back to her old self," Greg says. "This has been a nightmare of a week, I can tell you that. We need to get her some help so we don't lose her, too. Her other son needs her right now."

"Where is Charlie staying right now?" you ask.

"With Charlene's mother, but he wants to come home. I just don't think it's good for him to see Charlene in this state. I've just told her mother she's got to wait until Charlene is doing better before she lets Charlie come home."

"Well, we're going to do everything we can to help her feel better soon. I'm going to talk to the doctor and see where we go from here," you tell Greg.

You take Greg back to Charlene's room and then talk to the doctor about your assessment of Charlene and her situation.

5.3–3   What strengths are there in this situation?

5.3–4   What is your initial diagnosis?
Axis I

Axis II

Axis III

Axis IV

Axis V

5.3–5   What other Axis I diagnoses will you try to rule out over time?

Case 5.4

Identifying Information
Name: Raul Perez
Age: 40 years old
Ethnicity: Hispanic
Marital Status: Never married

Background Information
You are a case manager at the local mental health center. You receive a call from Ruth Perez, Raul's mother. She asks if you have time to see him if she can bring him into the Center today. "He's really not acting right for about a week. He's kinda scaring me. I think he needs to see the doctor," she explains.

You agree to see him in about an hour. When you pull Raul's file, you remember some more information about him. Although he's been on your caseload for nearly a year, you've only seen him a few times in conjunction with routine visits (like his psychiatric appointments). He has a long history of hospitalizations dating back to when he was 16 years old. Now 40, he resides with his mother, attends day treatment on occasion, and has never worked as far as you know. His current medications, according to his chart, include Haldol, Cogentin, and insulin.

Interview with Client's Mother
When the Perez family arrives at the Center, Mrs. Perez asks to speak with you first.

"I know something's bad wrong here. He's almost always lived with me, and I know his ways. He's not sleeping right; I hear him pacing at all hours. He's not taking care of himself. He's talking to himself some. I'm sure he's stopped taking his meds. You gotta do something before he goes off in a big way," she explains hurriedly.

"Mrs. Perez, has he threatened you in some way?" you ask.

"No, he won't hurt me. Really, he don't hurt anybody; he just gets himself hurt. Next thing you know, he'll start going to the clubs talking crazy and make somebody really mad. Then he'll comes home in pieces, lose all his money. One of these days he'll get himself killed this way," she replies.

"What do you think needs to happen today?" you inquire.

"He needs to see the doctor at least. I hate to see him go back to the hospital, but that's better than him getting himself hurt."

Interview with Client
You return to the waiting room and bring Raul to your office. He is dressed in a ragged overcoat, bedroom slippers, and a baseball cap. His hair isn't very clean, and he has a noticeable body odor.

"Raul, do you remember me?" you begin.

"I sure do. You're the pretty new caseworker. Wanna get some lunch?" he smiles.

"No thanks, Raul. Did you know your mother is worried about you?" you ask.

"That's because she feeds me dog shit for lunch every day!" The client smiles broadly with this statement. "She's just worried the neighbors will find out how bad she is."

"Raul, you want me to tell your mother that?" you laugh as well.

"No."

"Well, Raul, what have you been doing with yourself lately?" you ask.

"Eating wires and lighting fires. Come on baby, light my fire," he sings.

Despite the playfulness of his speech, you notice that he's displaying very little affect. He is speaking in a monotone, and his laughter doesn't seem to "spread" to the rest of his face.

"How have you been feeling, Raul?" you continue.

"I need sex. Been under a hex. Eaten by a T-rex," he replies, again without any real affect.

"Raul, have you been taking your medicine?"

The client does not respond and slumps down in his chair, fixing his gaze on his bedroom slippers.

"Do you know what day it is today?" you ask.

"Don't know. Don't care. You got on any underwear?" he replies.

"Raul, I'm going to see if the doctor can see you. Is that okay?" you inquire.

"Is the pretty lady doctor here today?" he replies.

5.4–1   How would you assess Raul's mother's concern that he may pose a danger to himself?

5.4–2   What are the strengths in this situation?

5.4–3   What is your preliminary diagnosis?
Axis I

Axis II

Axis III

Axis IV

Axis V

5.4 – 4   Is there any other collateral information you would want before seeing the doctor?

_____

DIFFERENTIAL DIAGNOSIS

Psychotic symptoms may occur within the context of a number of mental disorders that are not a part of this section of the DSM-IV-TR (APA, 2000). Consequently, the primary focus of differential diagnosis will be on ruling out the other possibilities.

People suffering from any of the Deliriums or Dementias may present with symptoms so severe that they seem functionally psychotic. In those instances, there should be ample evidence from history and/or medical assessment to discriminate these from the Schizophrenic Disorders. When collateral information is not available, the diagnosis of Psychotic Disorder NOS is appropriate until such data are developed.

5.DD–1   For each of the cases in chapter 3, list the situational cues that would help you rule out a Schizophrenic Disorder.

Quite similarly, people who have Substance-Related Disorders may present with grossly disorganized behavior that may well appear psychotic. Again, history or medical assessments can help differentiate these diagnoses. Also, the passage of time (in which the effects of the substance wear off or withdrawal is concluded) can help in making a final diagnosis. It must be noted that substantial numbers of people diagnosed with Schizophrenia may have comorbid Substance-Related Disorders. In these instances, dual diagnoses are appropriate.

5.DD–2   What factors help you rule out a psychotic disorder with Rocky Littlebear (chapter 4, Case 4.4)?

Another differential diagnosis that is largely determined by having a thorough history on the client involves the Pervasive Developmental Disorders. Childhood onset of Schizophrenia is rare in general but is never seen in children under the age of 6. When children present with markedly disorganized behaviors and/or speech, practitioners must also carefully take into account the differences in fantasy life between adults and children. Taken literally, things like imaginary playmates can inappropriately be construed as delusional.

Perhaps the most difficult differentiation is among the various subtypes of Schizophrenia. Subtype assignment is defined by the predominant symptoms at the time of evaluation, leaving the clear possibility of someone being diagnosed with different subtypes at different times in the typical cycle of symptoms. However, subtypes have shown little value in studies examining treatment response, prognosis, and so forth.

InfoTrac keywords

hallucinations, paranoid schizophrenia, psychosis, Schizophrenia, severe mental illness

Disorders Related to Emotional State or Mood

DISORDERS

The diagnoses in the Mood Disorders section of the DSM-IV-TR (APA, 2000) are characterized by changes in a person's emotional state that are sufficiently severe to cause significant clinical distress and/or disruption in psychosocial functioning. The term *mood* refers to an internally experienced emotional state that influences an individual's thinking and behavior. A related term, *affect,* refers more specifically to the external demonstration of one's mood or emotions. This distinction is important because affect and mood may differ; that is, people do not always display accurately in their affect what their mood actually is.

This section of the DSM-IV-TR is generally organized around four different types of episodes that, in turn, serve as building blocks for determining specific diagnoses. An episode is a period of time during which a client evidences a particular set of symptoms and as a result, experiences a pronounced alteration in mood and/or a change in his or her social, vocational, and recreational functioning. Specifically, the four episodic states are major depressive, manic, hypomanic, and mixed (APA, 2000).

Two of the diagnoses in this section are determined by the etiological factors relevant to the mood disorder. Specifically, Mood Disorder due to a General Medical Condition is used when a mood episode is directly related to a diagnosable organic problem. Similarly, Substance-Induced Mood Disorder is used when the problematic mood episode is directly related to the use of a recreational drug, prescribed medication, or a toxin (e.g., lead, carbon monoxide) (APA, 2000).

The most disruptive disorders in this chapter include Major Depressive, Bipolar I, and Bipolar II Disorders. Each is diagnosed based on the number and pattern of episodes the individual has experienced in his or her lifetime. In the coding of each disorder, attention is given to the severity of symptoms, the overall number of episodes (in the case of Major Depressive Disorder), and specific characteristics of the most recent episode (in the case of Bipolar Disorder) (APA, 2000).

Two diagnoses represent more chronic conditions that are generally less disruptive to the individual's functioning. By definition, a set of symptoms severe enough to meet criteria for one of the four major episodes is not present. In Dysthymic Disorder, the individual's symptoms are similar to, but not as severe as, a major depressive episode. In Cyclothymic Disorder, an alternating pattern of mood states is present, although not severe enough to constitute any of the four mood episodes (APA, 2000).

Finally, a category of NOS diagnoses is included for both major disorders (i.e., Major Depressive and Bipolar Disorders), as well as a more general Mood Disorder NOS. These designations are used when an individual's symptoms fail to fit any of the more specific diagnoses but clearly are related to disruptions in mood (APA, 2000).

The Mood Disorder section in the DSM-IV-TR includes a comparatively large number of specifiers, including some that are reflected in the fourth and fifth digit of the numeric coding. A full description of each specifier is located at the end of the Mood Disorder section. Although a listing of the relevant specifiers is included in each disorder's diagnostic criteria, it can be confusing to try to determine which apply. Practitioners are encouraged to use the Classification Listing section in the DSM to help them determine which set of specifiers is used with each diagnosis.

People experiencing the symptoms of any of the depressive disorders are likely to seek treatment. However, many people will approach general medical practitioners rather than those who specialize in treating mental disorders. Seeking medical treatment for a depressive disorder can represent confusion about the problem and/or reflect the stigma often associated with mental health treatment. Individuals experiencing psychotic symptoms of either Depression or Mania will likely not seek treatment independently. However, their behavior may well result in others arranging involuntary mental health treatment on their behalf.

ASSESSMENT

When assessing someone who you suspect may have a mood disorder, particular attention will be focused on the person's emotional functioning. Although a thorough history of the presenting problem is required to make a diagnosis of a mood disorder, it may be difficult for the client to present detailed and accurate information. People who are severely depressed can be virtually mute, or those experiencing manic mood states may be unable to express themselves coherently. Clearly, the reliability of self-report is very uncertain if someone is experiencing psychotic symptoms. Someone with a history of psychiatric treatment may fear rehospitalization and deliberately minimize symptoms. Consequently, it is often helpful to gather data from collateral sources such as close friends or relatives, employers, or other professionals to specify both the timing and severity of symptoms.

Assessment Instruments

Depression   The most widely known and extensively utilized assessment instrument for ascertaining depressive symptomatology in adults is the Beck Depression Inventory II (BDI-II) (Beck, Steer, & Brown, 1996). The instrument consists of 21 items presented in a multiple-choice format that attempt to measure both the presence and degree of Depression in adolescents and adults. The self-administered instrument takes between 5 and 10 minutes to complete. It has excellent reliability with test-retest coefficients above .90; internal consistency studies have demonstrated coefficients of .86 or higher. Numerous research studies have been conducted using the BDI over the past 40 years attesting to its concurrent and criterion validity. A 13-item short form of the BDI (Reynolds & Gould, 1981) has also demonstrated strong correlations with the longer, original version.

Because the BDI-II was designed for use with clinical populations, some practitioners may be uncomfortable administering it to someone who may not, in fact, suffer from Depression. Another commonly used instrument to assess Depression is the Center for Epidemiologic Studies-Depression Scale (CES-D) (Radloff, 1977). This self-report scale consists of 20 items that measure the frequency and duration of cognitive, affective, behavioral, and somatic symptoms of Depression in the previous week. The CES-D has been found to be highly reliable and valid as a screening instrument with populations of varying ages, ethnicities, and cultures (Beals, Manson, Keane, & Dick, 1995).

For those instances in which an adult is unable or unwilling to take a self-report instrument, the Hamilton Rating Scale for Depression (Hamilton, 1967) is an assessment instrument completed by the interviewer. It is normally used when the interviewer has some knowledge of the client's affective status and strong evidence of symptoms of depressive disorder. The scale has 18 items measured on a 5-point Likert scale. It addresses the issues of depressed mood, suicide, anxiety, general somatic symptoms, and loss of interest in work and recreational pursuits.

When older adults are being assessed, the presentation of depressive symptoms may vary somewhat from those of other adults. The Geriatric Depression Scale (GDS) (Brink et al., 1982) is a well-known instrument designed to assess depressive symptoms in older adults. It is available in 30-item, 15-item, 10-item, 4-item, or 1-item versions. With the exception of the 1-item version of the GDS, all of the shorter versions are highly correlated with the original 30-item version (D'Ath, Katona, Mullan, Evans, & Katona, 1994). The GDS has high internal consistency and has been validated in a large number of studies. The scale is in the public domain.

For younger children, the Hopelessness Scale for Children (HSC) (see Kazdin, French, Unis, Esveldt-Dawson, & Sherick, 1983) is designed to measure thoughts concerning hopelessness, depression, and suicidal ideation (Fischer & Corcoran, 1994). Seventeen true-false statements assess the child's level of depression as well as his or her self-esteem. It can be used with children who are 7 years old and older. Although reliability coefficient alphas of .70 and .71 are considered only fair, they are within the acceptable range for children's instruments. Studies have indicated that the scale can discriminate between suicidal and nonsuicidal children.

Mania   In order to assess manic symptoms in adults, two self-report instruments have been shown to have excellent reliability and validity. The Internal State Scale (ISS) (Bauer, Crits-Cristoph, & Ball, 1991) is a 15-item instrument in which clients indicate the intensity of their mood by marking a line denoting the level of severity of symptoms. The scale has four subscales, including well-being, perceived conflict, depression, and activation. Mania is assessed by a well-being score equal to or higher than 125 and an activation score equal to or greater than 200. Each item is "biphasic." For example, on the items indicating well-being, clients who mark the lower end of the line (scale) are assessed to have depressive symptoms, whereas clients who mark the upper end of the line are assessed to have manic symptoms.

The Self-Report Manic Inventory (SRMI) (Shugar, Schertzer, Toner, & di Gasbarro, 1992) is a 47-item scale that includes statements that clients mark "true" or "false" depending on the presence or absence of symptoms during the prior month. The instrument has been validated as a screening tool for the severity of manic symptoms in adults. The scale has a maximum score of 47.

For Bipolar clients who are unable to complete a self-report instrument, the Young Mania Rating Scale (YMRS) (Young, Biggs, & Myers, 1978) can be completed by a skilled practitioner. The scale contains 11 items measuring internal mood states and behaviors experienced by the client and reported to the practitioner. Scores may range between 0 and 60.

Emergency Considerations

In some situations, people experiencing the more severe mood disorders may constitute a danger to themselves or others. Thoughts about self-destruction are among the criteria for determining the presence of a major depressive episode and are not at all uncommon. An assessment of suicide risk is of paramount importance in these cases, both at the time of initial contact and on a consistent, ongoing basis throughout treatment. Practitioners must develop skills in this area or utilize emergency assessment resources that are available in any community (e.g., local community mental health services, emergency rooms).

In some major depressive episodes and in most manic episodes, some degree of psychosis is present. In these situations, practitioners must attend to issues about the client's safety and secure whatever level of supervision and treatment is necessary. Again, familiarity with local resources for managing psychiatric emergencies is essential to ensuring safety. In such cases, the practitioner may not be able to complete a more broad-based, psychosocial assessment; the appropriate focus is on resolving the crisis and ensuring safety.

CULTURAL CONSIDERATIONS

The practitioner should be aware of common variations in the diagnosis and presentation of mood disorders based on diversity. For example, women are roughly twice as likely men to be diagnosed with a depressive disorder. In the United States, men have been raised to minimize emotional expression regardless of their internal state. On the other hand, women have been taught to use emotional expression as a tool for getting their needs met. Clearly, these gender differences concerning emotional expressiveness can influence the practitioner's perception and diagnosis of the client. Generally, practitioners should be careful to avoid overdiagnosing women with Depression, as well as underdiagnosing men.

Similarly, some cultures are more likely to express emotional states in somatic terms. This may be related to a fear that emotions like depression or anxiety will be interpreted as weak or "crazy." Therefore, in some cultures it is more acceptable to complain of a variety of physical symptoms rather than to acknowledge negative moods. For example, complaints of "nerves" or "headaches" may relate to negative moods among Latino clients. In addition, bilingual clients may appear to have more or less symptomatology depending on the language spoken during the interview, as well as the primary language of the practitioner (Malgady & Zayas, 2001). Practitioners should be aware that such variations may occur based on region or family background as well. Generalizations regarding this issue can lead to misunderstanding and misdiagnosis.

Another caution about misdiagnosis relates to the tendency for minority group members to receive more serious or more stigmatized psychiatric labels. For example, there is some evidence that Caucasians are more likely to be diagnosed with Bipolar I Disorder, while minority clients with the same symptom presentation are diagnosed with Schizophrenic Disorders. According to the National Comorbidity Survey, Hispanic clients had surprisingly high prevalence rates of all affective disorders compared to the rates in non-Hispanic white persons and African Americans (Kessler et al., 1994). While these higher rates may be due in part to the stress of acculturation and low SES, the higher reported incidence of affective disorders among Hispanic clients may be a result of communication barriers between client and practitioner. Cultural sensitivity education and training for English-speaking practitioners are important aspects of competent mental health practice.

SOCIAL SUPPORT SYSTEMS

Major Depressive Disorder and Bipolar I and Bipolar II Disorders are considered severe mental illnesses. Symptoms associated with these disorders cause severe impairment in the client's social and occupational functioning. Family members and close friends of a person with an affective disorder can feel confused, frustrated, fearful, or angry about the person's dramatic change in mood and inability to cope with daily life events. Families and friends may not understand the problem and why the client can't just "snap out of it."

Conflicts between family, friends, and the person with the disorder can arise due to disruptive thoughts and behaviors and extreme mood swings on the part of the symptomatic individual. In addition to an assessment of the symptomatic individual, an assessment of the person's family or friends is important for the practitioner to obtain to get a clear picture of the support available to the person coping with the illness. Family members and friends need to have accurate information about the disorder, as well as about how to cope with a loved one's symptoms and where to obtain help in a crisis situation. Families and friends can be a valuable source of fiscal and emotional support while the individual's mood is stabilized through medication and psychological treatment.

A psychoeducational group for individuals with similar problems may be an additional source of support for the person suffering from a Mood Disorder. For example, there are support groups for persons suffering from Bipolar Disorders as well as groups for persons affected by Depression. These groups provide individuals with a sense of belonging, education concerning the illness, and mutual support. Mental health practitioners conduct some groups; other groups are organized and run by persons who have previous experience with the disorder (either clients themselves or family members of clients). With the recent increases in knowledge concerning depression and bipolar moods, there has been a corresponding increase in the numbers of organizations and agencies providing specialized support for individuals with these disorders.

For many people with affective disorders, joining a group may be problematic because of the person's symptoms and/or because of group availability. Similar constraints may also apply to members of the person's social support system. The Internet contains a wealth of information, including organizations specializing in the support and treatment of persons with mood disorders, online chat rooms and bulletin boards, and current reports and articles related to particular disorders. The following list includes some useful Internet resources.

www.mentalhealth.com/fr20.html—Provides information on all mood disorders, including overview and treatment issues; contains a link to the Surgeon General's report on Depression in Adolescents and Children

www.mentalhelp.net/—Contains a variety of information on Depression and Mania resources, books, and scales

www.healthcme.com/dep1/sec1.shtml—Presents a case history and assessment of a woman suffering from Depression

www.depression.org—Provides an overview of depressive disorder and treatment resources

Case 6.1

Identifying Information
Client Name: Helen Stonewall
Age: 32 years old
Ethnicity: African American
Marital Status: Married
Children: Sonya, age 5

Background Information
You are a caseworker in the emergency room of a large urban hospital. You work the day shift from 8 A.M. to 5 P.M. Several hours before you came to work, the police brought the client to the emergency room in restraints. The following information was gathered from the police at intake.

Intake Information
The police state that Helen Stonewall, a 32-year-old African American woman was found dancing half naked in the middle of a busy intersection in the center of the city at approximately 2 A.M. She appeared to be high on drugs when the police approached her. She told the police that she hadn't taken any drugs and that she was "just high on life." She said she wasn't doing anything wrong, just "having a party." Witnesses stated that Helen had started the evening at a local restaurant and bar. She had been with a couple of gentlemen who seemed to know her. She began telling jokes and buying everyone at the bar drinks.

At first, she seemed like a person just having fun, but she kept getting louder and more rowdy as the night progressed. The two men left, but she stayed at the restaurant telling them loudly, "I'm just getting warmed up here." She sang and danced and finally ended up shoving all the glasses onto the floor and standing on the bar talking as fast as she could. Customers got irritated, and the bartender asked her to leave. She ignored his request and started singing at the top of her lungs. Finally, the bartender had to force her off the bar and push her out the door. At that point, she began dancing and singing in the street. The bartender told police that she had no more than two drinks throughout the evening. When the police attempted to get Helen out of the road, she became belligerent and began swearing at the officers. They had to take her out of the middle of the intersection by force and handcuff her to get her into the police car.

Lab tests indicated no evidence of excessive alcohol or other drugs. The physician on duty had prescribed a sedative, and Helen went to sleep at approximately 5 A.M.

6.1–1 Based on the intake information alone, which psychiatric disorders seem most likely? What type(s) of information will you be interested in during the initial interview to help you "narrow down" the choices of diagnoses?

Initial Interview
You go to see Helen at 9:30 A.M. She is lying in bed quietly staring at the ceiling. She seems very subdued in comparison to the description of the previous night. Helen glances at you as you enter the room but makes no attempt to sit up. You tell her who you are and your reasons for wanting to talk to her. Helen makes no re-

sponse to your introduction. You ask Helen if she has any relatives you could call for her. Helen looks over at you and says, "I just want to die. If it weren't for my baby, I'd've been dead a long time ago."

"What's your baby's name?" you ask.

"Sonya," Helen replies. "I'm such a lousy mother lying here like this. I should be home taking care of her."

"Where is Sonya now?" you ask.

"She's with my sister. She stayed with my sister last night," Helen responds. "I knew I was racing so I took her over to my sister's house."

"You were racing?" you query.

"Yeah, you know, I start racing sometimes, feeling real good and full of energy like nothing can stop me," Helen says. "But not now; I feel lousy now, like I just want to be left alone to die."

"Can you tell me what happened last night?" you ask.

"It's like living on a roller coaster," Helen tells you. "One minute you're way up there, and the next minute you're in the blackest hole you can imagine."

"And last night, you were way up there?" you query.

"Yeah, I was just feeling good and having a good time. It's like you're racing and you can't slow down. Like you're high or something, but I didn't take any drugs. I don't do drugs. This just comes over me sometimes, and I feel like I could take on the world."

"Have you ever felt this way before?" you ask.

"Oh yeah, up and down, that's how I am," Helen says.

"So, sometimes you feel really good and up, and then, sometimes you feel really down. Is that right?" you ask.

"Yeah, I'm scared I'm beginning to crash now. It's bad when you come down. It feels real bad," Helen says. "It lasts for weeks and weeks . . . just down all the time."

"How often does this happen, going from one extreme to another?" you ask. "Once a day or once a week or once a month?"

"See, for a few weeks I feel great. I can do anything—stay up all night having a good time. I don't sleep or eat or slow down. I just keep on going for a week, maybe two. Then, I begin to crash."

"Do you hear voices or see things when you're feeling high?" you ask.

"No, except for my own voice. I can't stop talking either. Gets me into trouble, sometimes," Helen admits.

"What else happens when you're feeling high?" you ask.

"I want to party. I can party all night when I'm high. I'm the life of the party," Helen says glumly.

"Have you ever gotten in trouble before, like you did last night?" you ask.

"Oh yeah," Helen agrees. "I've gotten thrown out of places lots of times, but I usually just move on down the street."

"Are you employed?" you ask Helen.

"I've tried to keep a job. Just can't seem to stick with it," Helen replies.

"How are you feeling right now?" you query.

"Feel like hell," Helen tells you. "This is a rotten way to live, I'm telling you."

"How long does the crashing last?" you ask Helen.

"Sometimes a few days, sometimes a few weeks," Helen says bleakly.

"Describe for me what these down times are like for you," you ask.

"It's like I'm a balloon and someone stuck a needle in me. I'm so sad that nothing looks good. It's hard to get out of bed and face the world . . . I sleep and sleep and sleep. When I do get up, I'm so tired that it feels like I'm carrying around invisible weights."

"What kinds of things go through your mind when you feel like this?"

"I can't think of anything I want to do," Helen tells you. "I can't seem to make myself think anything all the way through. Like making a decision about something no matter how trivial is just impossible. Sometimes, I just wish I were dead."

"Are you wishing you would die now?" you ask.

"Not yet . . . but it usually does get to that point when I crash."

"Have you ever seen a doctor for these changes in your mood?" you ask.

"One doctor told me it was just a female thing," Helen states.

"Maybe it's more than a female thing," you suggest. "Maybe there's some medication that could help even out your moods. Would you be willing to talk to a doctor about how you've been feeling?" you ask.

"Okay. I guess it wouldn't hurt," Helen says.

6.1–2   To what extent do you think Helen may be a danger to herself? What other information would be useful in determining her risk?

6.1–3   What would you like to know about Helen's social support system? Are there any steps you would take (given the client's permission) to assure that her support system stays intact?

6.1–4   What internal and external strengths do you see in Helen's case?

6.1–5   What is your initial diagnosis?
Axis I

Axis II

Axis III

Axis IV

Axis V

Case 6.2

Identifying Information
Client Name: Connie Kellogg
Age: 36 years old
Ethnicity: Caucasian
Marital Status: Married
Occupation: Homemaker
Children: Three children; currently pregnant with her fourth child

Intake Information

Little information was obtained from a phone call interview with Mrs. Kellogg by the intake worker. She stated that her psychiatrist in Massachusetts had referred her to Dr. Browning in Southfork, Oklahoma, for prescription monitoring. Dr. Browning has referred her to the Southfork Counseling Center to see a therapist. She requested an appointment with a therapist and said only that she had been hospitalized recently in Massachusetts before moving with her husband and children to Oklahoma. She stated that it was very important that she begin therapy immediately but did not want to discuss any details of the problems she has been experiencing lately. The intake worker scheduled her for the first available appointment with you later in the week.

Initial Interview

Connie Kellogg is an attractive, 36-year-old woman whose warm and effervescent personality is apparent from the first meeting. You notice that Connie is several months pregnant. Connie appears eager to get to your office and asks you how long you have lived in Southfork. You explain to her that you moved to Southfork after completing your master's degree 2 years ago.

"When did you move to Southfork?" you ask.

Connie wriggles in her chair and enthusiastically begins talking about her husband being relocated to Oklahoma to accept a new position with his company, which develops software for computer companies. She states that she's never lived in the Midwest, having grown up in Boston. She moved to another town in Massachusetts when she got married 10 years ago.

"We've been in Southfork for 3 months, and I feel like a fish out of water," Connie tells you. "I've got most of the responsibility for taking care of my three children and as you can see, I'm about to have another one. Bob, my husband, travels 3 or 4 days a week with his job, so I'm stuck at home with my children most of the time . . . not that I'm complaining. Bob has a good job and he has to travel, but it's a lot of work for me, and I haven't made a lot of friends yet. When I lived in Revere, Massachusetts, I had a lot of neighbors who were young mothers like me with kids, and we'd get together and baby-sit for each other and take our children to different activities. It was nice until I got sick."

"What happened when you got sick?" you ask Connie.

"Well, I've always been a pretty optimistic, upbeat type person with a lot of energy. Then, suddenly, I had no energy. I was drained. I was so tired I couldn't move and just got completely depressed. I was suicidal and felt hopeless about everything. I thought here I am with three little children and I can't get off the couch to take care of them. I felt like a complete failure as a mother, just completely worthless. I didn't want to do anything except sleep and block out the entire world. I wasn't interested in sex with my husband. I didn't care if I lived or died. It just got so bad that the psychiatrist I was seeing put me in the hospital." Connie slinks down in her chair and sighs deeply.

She takes a deep breath and then begins talking again. "Everything just looked so black. I couldn't imagine feeling any worse . . . and my poor kids. All I could think about was that I would die and they would be motherless. And then I began to feel better. I mean like overnight I felt a whole lot better. I had plenty of energy, and thoughts and ideas just flew through my head and I was on top of the world again. I told the doctor I was just fine and he should let me go home."

"How long had you been in the hospital when you began feeling so much better?" you inquire.

"About 4 weeks," Connie sighs. "Then I was okay—or so I thought."

"So initially, you were really depressed when you went into the hospital, and then you began to feel much better. Were you taking any medication?" you ask.

"Well, that's the really scary part about this problem I have. You see, the feeling of being on top of the world didn't last very long. Pretty soon, I was in the depths of despair again, and the medicine I was on wasn't working. So, the doctor said I really needed to be on Lithium. I didn't want to take anything because by then, I knew I was pregnant again. But I was so depressed I didn't know what else to do. I'm so worried about the medicine affecting the baby. The doctor has put me on a low dosage until the baby is born. I'm just keeping my fingers crossed the baby will be okay. Do you think that makes me a bad mother?"

"It sounds as if the psychiatrist thinks you really need to be taking Lithium right now," you respond. "You're trying to take care of yourself."

"He told me it was absolutely necessary if I wanted to stay out of the hospital," Connie replies. "I never want to go through that experience again. And I'm not sure it's really helping. I have to go get my blood tested every 2 weeks, and I'm not sure I've got enough of the medication in me to do me any good. I have days when I feel like I can function pretty well, and then there are other days when I feel like I'm sliding into a black hole and can't get out of it. It's an awful feeling."

6.2–1 At this point in the interview, what diagnoses are you considering? What information do you feel you need to complete your initial assessment?

"These feeling of depression just started about a year ago? Is that correct?" you inquire.

"Yes, I never felt down in the dumps and completely hopeless like I have this year. You know, I remember as a child, my father would have periods of deep depression. He was like Dr. Jekyll and Mr. Hyde. Some days he'd be great to be around and he'd play with us and laugh. Other times, he was really scary. He'd sit in a dark room and stare out the window for hours, and if any of us kids did anything that perturbed him, he'd get so angry that he'd take us behind the house and give us all a whipping with his belt. You could never tell what kind of mood he'd be in. I was scared of him my whole childhood. I sure hope I'm not turning into someone like him."

"Did your father ever see a doctor about his moods?" you ask.

"No, he thinks only crazy people see psychiatrists. I told Bob not to tell my parents I was in the hospital. They would have disowned me.

They are strict, conservative Catholics, and be-lieve me, they wouldn't ever understand. They'd tell me I'd be okay if I went to confession."

It seems to you that Connie identifies with her father's mood swings to some degree, and you decide to get more information about Connie's family of origin at this time. "Tell me what it was like for you growing up in Boston," you say.

Connie sits back in her chair and looks out the window. "Well, it was your typical Catholic family growing up in the sixties and seventies, I guess. I have five siblings—two older broth-ers, an older sister, and two younger sisters. My parents were strict and fairly religious. We went to confession on Saturdays and Mass on Sundays every week without fail. My mother cared for us while my father worked. We were a middle-class family, I guess. We never had a lot of money, but we weren't starving to death either. My parents sent us all to a Catholic school that cost more than public school but wasn't like a private school. I think I bought into all the Catholic guilt thing and have a real problem with feeling guilty about everything. My father reinforced that feeling of guilt all the time. He was very distant and authoritarian. We got punished a lot as children, and although I don't think I really thought so at the time, it

was pretty harsh punishment by today's stan-dards. And it seemed like I was always in the way when my father got mad, and I got pun-ished more than my sisters and brothers."

"How do you feel about that time growing up?" you inquire.

"I guess I consider it a pretty normal child-hood," Connie suggests. "All the kids in the Catholic school I attended grew up much the same way as I did. I think my mother saved us all from my father's wrath on many occasions. She had a way of diverting his attention away from us when we were in the line of fire."

"And what is your relationship like now, with your parents?" you ask.

"Since I've been in the hospital, I've discov-ered I have all this anger toward my father," Connie states. "I've been scared of him my whole life, and I'm tired of feeling that way and I hate how he made me feel. I've never really had any self-esteem and have always felt like I'm cowering in the corner afraid of my own shadow because of what he did to me."

"And your mother? How do you get along with her?" you ask.

"We get along well. We always have. I think we have a lot in common and she's had to put up with a lot, too," Connie says with a smile.

6.2–2 Discuss how much support Connie is likely to receive from her family of origin. Prelim-inarily, do you have any thoughts about how that support could be maximized?

"Do you feel that the way you were raised has something to do with the depression you've been experiencing, or do you think it's unre-lated to your childhood experiences?" you ask.

"I don't really know," Connie states. "It's something I want to figure out. The doctor told me some of this could be a neurochemical prob-

lem. Sometimes, I feel great and full of energy. In fact, it's hard to slow down. I become really talkative and friendly. It's like everything speeds up. Thoughts run through my head really fast, and I can't even sleep when I feel that good. It's like being high."

"How often does that happen?" you ask.

"It seems to happen about once a month after I've been really depressed," Connie states. "But it doesn't last as long as the depressed periods."

"Do you ever feel that you place yourself in high-risk or dangerous situations when you have a 'high' feeling?" you query.

"No, I don't think so," Connie reflects. "I have some pretty fantastic thoughts, but I don't actually do anything. I've got to think about my children and the one on the way."

"Okay, so you feel depressed a lot of the time, and sometimes, about once a month, you feel pretty good and full of energy. How long do you usually have that 'high' feeling?" you ask.

"It can last from 3 or 4 days up to a week before I begin sliding downward again," says Connie. "I always hope it will last longer, but it never does."

"So, it sounds like one of your goals is to learn how to cope with some of these ups and downs you've been experiencing?" you ask.

Connie says enthusiastically, "Yes, exactly, I need some help with the best way of coping with these moods, especially during this pregnancy."

"Would it be all right with you if I talked to the psychiatrist who is prescribing the medication for you?" you inquire. "I'll need you to sign a consent form."

"Absolutely. I'll give you his phone number," Connie asserts.

"And would you like to make an appointment on a weekly basis?" you ask.

Connie nods her head vigorously and says, "I'm so glad I've found someone I can talk to who doesn't look at me as if I'm crazy. I definitely want to come once a week to talk to you."

"Okay. We'll schedule an appointment for next week," you reply.

Connie leaves your office with a little bounce in her step and talks about going to shop for the new baby as you walk her to the reception area.

6.2–3   From this preliminary interview, it would seem that Connie may not have much social support in Southfork. How would you go about exploring that issue? How important do you think securing local support would be?

6.2–4   What is your initial diagnosis?
Axis I

Axis II

Axis III

Axis IV

Axis V

Case 6.3

Identifying Information
Client Name: Kathy Claybourne
Age: 45 years old
Ethnicity: Caucasian
Educational Level: B.S. degree in nursing
Marital Status: Divorced
Children: Tommy, age 14; Betty, age 12

Intake Information
Kathy Claybourne is a 45-year-old single mother who contacted the Family Counseling Center concerning counseling for herself and perhaps, later, for her two children. She stated that she feels "very alone right now" and needs someone to talk to about "how my life is going." She didn't want to go into the reason for an appointment with a counselor over the telephone. The intake worker scheduled an appointment for her with you, her counselor, for the following week. Kathy arrived on time for her appointment with you.

Intake Interview
Kathy presents as a polite, well-groomed, middle-aged woman who smiles and shakes hands with you in the waiting room. She says that she is very glad to have someone to discuss things with after spending much of her time talking to her children. Kathy indicates that she has been divorced for the past 3 years. She works as a nurse for four nephrologists in town who also have a kidney dialysis center connected to their practice. She has been a nurse for the past 20 years and loves her profession but lately has been feeling "burned out" on the job and has had difficulty concentrating on her work.

She feels that since her divorce, her life has been going downhill. A year after her divorce, her mother died of liver cancer, and several months later, her father was diagnosed with prostate cancer. She took care of her mother during her illness and is currently caring for her father. Over the past 2 years, she has felt increasingly despondent, isolated, and "blue" most of the time. She states that many of her "so-called friends" rejected her following the divorce because they were also friends with her ex-husband. She also feels that she hasn't had much time for a social life since her part-time job became full-time following the divorce.

When you ask her about her mood, she tells you it's generally been "blue." "I don't seem to have any energy some days. It's just hard to get up and face the day." Kathy states that she feels lethargic most of the time and has difficulty doing everyday tasks that she once found easy to accomplish.

"How has your sleeping been over the past year?" you ask. Kathy states that she has had difficulty falling asleep. She wakes up very early in the morning hours and is unable to get back to sleep.

Approximately 6 months ago, Kathy reports "feeling so bad that I went to my physician to see if anything was really wrong with me." She states that he found nothing physically wrong and recommended she get some exercise. At that time, she joined a health club and began working out. "I think I felt better for a while when I was going to the club, but after about 2 months, it became too much of an effort to get myself there to exercise." She rubs her forehead and states that she probably should go back but doesn't feel she has the energy.

She also tells you that her biggest worry is that she's not really "present" for her children. She has a hard time focusing on her children's activities and has lost interest in what they are doing. "I just feel bored with everything—my children, my job, my life. I'm too tired to cook when I get home from work so I often stop at McDonald's and get them hamburgers, which they're happy with, but I don't even feel like eating. I've lost about 20 pounds in the last year without even trying."

When you ask for background information, Kathy states that the problems she has been experiencing began shortly after her divorce from her husband approximately 2½ years ago. However, she suggests that she often struggled with feeling down and despondent throughout her 30s, prior to her divorce. She attributes those feelings to communication problems with her husband and states that she just couldn't "give in to them because of the children."

"I got married right after I finished nursing school at the age of 21 and moved from my parents' home to my husband's home. He was 10 years older than I was and already had established business and social relationships that I was invited to participate in. At the time, it seemed great to me, and I thought the world revolved around him since he seemed older and wiser and could take care of me. I worked part-time as a nurse, not because I had to, but because I wanted to have a profession. Gradually, I began feeling like our relationship was falling apart. He began traveling a lot on business, and I was home with the children. He didn't seem interested in anything but work. We socialized with friends that he knew because of his business, and I felt that he just wanted me around to make him look good. This didn't all happen overnight, you understand, but by my mid-30s I was having periods of utter despair over the kind of distant relationship I had with my husband and the total responsibility for my kids. His only goal in life was to make money, and he didn't care about anything or anyone else."

Kathy states that from the age of 32 onward, she can't really remember a time when she felt like her old self. "When I was a teenager, I was happy, outgoing, and enthusiastic about life. When I got into my 30s, everything seemed dreary most of the time."

Kathy states that she never was unable to function at her job or as a mother, but always felt sad and negative about the future. Kathy also tells you that she thinks her mother suffered from the same type of problem when Kathy was growing up. "If my mother could find a negative way to view a situation, she would find it." She remembers her mother would often tell her and her sister that they had to go outside to play because her mother had to take a nap. "I always thought it was strange that she was sleeping in the middle of the day, but for my mother, it was normal for her to always be tired." Despite the problems her mother may have had, Kathy states that she had a good childhood and often felt happy and full of life. "It seems like adulthood has ruined my mood," Kathy says glumly.

During your interview, Kathy often looks out the window, rather wistfully, when recalling the happier days of her childhood. She seems overwhelmed and obviously has difficulty coping with her feelings.

She summarizes that she is requesting help with her overall mood and that she is able to function adequately but not up to the level that she has in the past. She seems concerned about not being an adequate mother for her children and the activities in which they are engaged.

She spends most of the interview twisting the straps on her purse and only makes eye contact a few times throughout the session. She has apparently been experiencing these feelings for an extended length of time and is seeking help at this point because she worries about her job and her children. She doesn't see the future as being very bright at the present time.

You schedule another appointment for her in a week. She states as she leaves your office, "I'm so glad I finally made the decision to get some help. That was the hardest thing to do."

6.3–1   What are some of Kathy's strengths?

6.3–2   What diagnoses would you want to rule out in this case?

6.3–3   What resources might be valuable to utilize in this case?

6.3–4   Do you think Kathy should be referred to other professionals for further evaluation? If so, to whom would you make a referral?

6.3–5   What is your preliminary diagnosis for Kathy Claybourne?
Axis I

Axis II

Axis III

Axis IV

Axis V

_____

Case 6.4

Identifying Information
Client Name: Maggie Weinzapfel
Age: 26 years old
Ethnicity: Caucasian
Marital Status: Single

Intake Information

Maggie, a 26-year-old Caucasian female, contacted the Family Guidance Center after breaking up with her fiancé, whom she had been dating for the last 4 years. Maggie is a mechanical engineer at a fiber optics corporation in a small Southern town. She makes a good salary, owns her home, and recently bought a new car. Maggie moved from the large, metropolitan area in the Northeast where she had met her boyfriend to this rather small Southern town approximately 1 year ago when she procured her present job. Her parents and siblings also live in the Northeast. Maggie has two sisters, both in their 20s, and two teenage brothers who still live with their parents.

When Maggie called the clinic, she stated that she desperately needed to talk with someone as soon as possible. The intake worker wrote in her notes that the client "sounded panicky" when making an appointment to see a counselor. You are scheduled to see Maggie the day after she called.

Intake Interview

You meet Maggie in the waiting room at the agency. Maggie appears very disheveled. Her baggy pants and sweatshirt are wrinkled, and it looks as if she forgot to brush her long, wavy hair. She is pacing slowly back and forth and appears to be staring at her feet. She runs her hands through her hair continuously and looks generally distressed. Every now and then, she sighs deeply and shakes her head as if responding to some internal dialogue. You greet Maggie in the waiting room by introducing yourself and shaking her hand, which feels sweaty and limp. As you and Maggie walk down the hall to your office, Maggie bursts into tears and says, "Oh, I'm so embarrassed; I don't know what I'm doing here." As you and Maggie enter your office, you reassure Maggie that it's safe for her to express her feelings with you, offer her a chair, and provide her with a box of tissues.

You begin by gently asking Maggie where she would like to start. Maggie states that she broke off her engagement with her boyfriend, Leonardo, approximately 6 weeks ago. She says they had been arguing constantly for the past 6 months about where they were going to live. She wanted to keep her job and live in a small town, but he wanted to live in a large city and didn't want to leave his family in the North. He told her that Italian families are very close: "We stick together and want to see each other. I grew up in this city; I've been to the same church my whole life; and I intend to die in this city. If you're going to be my wife, you have to be willing to join my family because I'm not leaving."

Maggie tells you that she chose her current job partly because the insurance company that Leonardo worked for had offices in this town and he could transfer to the South and keep his job. Maggie says, "During the past year, I've been going up there to see Leonardo at least once a month for a weekend. I only had 2 days with him, and we spent all day Sunday at his mother and father's house. His mother treats him like a baby and does everything for him. I think she resents me for taking away her little boy. She's friendly enough, but there's tension between us. Lately, his parents have been talking a lot about us getting a house down the street from them. I just couldn't stand that!" Maggie states that she began feeling like an outsider and an intruder. "Leonardo was unhappy unless I agreed to everything he wanted," Maggie says glumly.

Maggie states that since the breakup she has had great difficulty sleeping. She often sleeps only 2 or 3 hours a night. She states that she has also lost her appetite and has dropped 15 pounds in the past month. In a very shaky voice, she tells you, "I've been having so much trouble with my job lately. I can't focus on what I'm doing for more than 3 minutes before I'm off thinking about Leonardo. It's so hard it makes me want to cry." She says she's missed work completely on four occasions during the last month when she just stayed in bed all day and watched soap operas on TV. Since the breakup with Leonardo, she says she feels ugly, unlovable, and hopeless about ever getting married.

6.4–1   At this point in the conversation, what things would you like more information about concerning Maggie?

You decide to find out more about Maggie's difficulties over the past month. You ask her if there are any other ways in which the breakup with her boyfriend has affected her. She tells you that she is normally a very avid reader of mystery books and lately hasn't been able to get past the first chapter. She also likes to go to community events on the weekends with friends, but since she has lived in this town, she has been so consumed with her work and her relationship with Leonardo that she hasn't made any good friends. "Oh, you know, I've gotten acquainted with some people, but I don't know them very well and it just seems so hard to pick up the phone and call them. I doubt if they'd want to do anything with me anyway. I think I'm just a loser all the way around."

You ask her if she really thinks it's over with Leonardo. She states that the last time he called, they just got into a shouting match. "By the end of the conversation I decided I just had to end this relationship and get on with my life," Maggie says despondently. "I really believe that, too. I just don't know where I'm going to find the energy to do it. When I do sleep, I have nightmares about fights with Leonardo. It's begun to take its toll on me, I think."

You say, "Maggie, you've mentioned having problems sleeping, and I was wondering whether you were having trouble going to sleep or problems waking up in the middle of the night and not being able to get back to sleep." Maggie states that her biggest problem is her inability to sleep through the night. She says she wakes up around 2 A.M. and often cannot get back to sleep until it's almost time to get up. "Then I feel groggy and unable to function very well the rest of the day," she hesitantly tells you in a quiet voice.

You also ask her if she's had any suicidal thoughts or had any plans for hurting herself due to this upsetting situation. Maggie responds that she has thought about just wanting to end all this pain, especially at night when she is alone. You ask her if she has taken those thoughts any further and considered how she might "end it all." She tells you that she doesn't think she could ever actually hurt herself since it is against her religion and she believes it would be wrong to commit suicide. You explain to Maggie that if she ever begins having thoughts of how she might hurt herself that it would be important for her to talk with you about those thoughts and feelings. Maggie agrees that she will discuss those issues with you should they arise.

When you ask Maggie about her family of origin, she states that she's always gotten along well with everyone in her family except her mother. She says that ever since she was little, her mother has wanted her to always act like the oldest. "She always tells me that I have to be the responsible one because I'm the oldest, and I don't think she really cares about whether I'm happy or not." When Maggie told her mother that the relationship with Leonardo had ended, her mother just told her to grow up and get over it. Maggie says she's never been able to go to her mother with a problem. "I'm not sure my mother is a very happy person. She's more concerned about what the neighbors will think than whether or not we are content with our lives. Ever since I was little, my mother would get in one of her moods and close herself in the bedroom and not come out for days." Maggie states that she has a much closer relationship with her father, who has called several times to see if she's okay.

Before leaving your office, Maggie tells you she's really glad she came to talk today. She says, "It's taken a big load off my shoulders." Maggie states that this is the first time in several weeks that she can remember not having a headache. She agrees to come back and see you at the same time next week.

6.4–2   What behaviors would you have Maggie track during the week?

6.4–3   What do you see as some of Maggie's strengths?

6.4–4   Describe two or three approaches Maggie might use to develop a local social support system.

6.4–5   What diagnosis would you give Maggie after this initial interview?
Axis I

Axis II

Axis III

Axis IV

Axis V

Case 6.5

Identifying Information
Name: Lucy Johnson
Age: 15 years old
Ethnicity: Caucasian
Educational Level: 10th grade

Referral Information
The 10th-grade high school science and home-room teacher has referred Lucy Johnson to you due to frequent school absenteeism, falling grades, and withdrawn behavior. Lucy is 15 years old and usually an A student. After several attempts to reach her mother by phone, you decide to make a home visit.

Home Visit
Lucy lives in a rural area approximately 10 miles outside a small town in Virginia. Her mother, Judy, works a rotating shift at a hosiery factory in town. Judy is a single mother with three daughters ages 12, 15, and 17. When you arrive in the vicinity of her house, you discover she lives in a run-down trailer park without numbers to identify the residences. You stop at the first trailer and ask where Ms. Johnson lives. The woman tells you the trailer is at the end of the road. As you drive up to the Johnson trailer, you see Lucy sitting on the steps with her head in her hands.

She looks up and waves when you get out of the car. She seems surprised to see you there. She walks over to your car and asks you why you're at her house. "You've missed a lot of school lately, and Ms. James has been worried about you," you reply. "Can we talk somewhere?"

"My mother is busy inside right now, but we can walk down the road if you like," Lucy suggests. She begins walking down the road, and you follow her.

"Why have you missed so much school?" you ask her.

Lucy tells you that her mother's car has been in the shop and she didn't want to take the bus with the little kids. Her boyfriend, Joe, has been taking her to school on days when he doesn't have to be at work early. Lucy looks very unhappy and tired.

You ask her if there are other things going on that she'd like to talk about. She shakes her head and says she'll be at school the next day.

You tell Lucy that she can come by your office anytime if she wants to talk. She glances at you and says, "All right, just not now."

You ask her if you can visit with her mother now, and Lucy quickly and emphatically tells you that her mother really can't be disturbed. "Please don't go into the trailer right now. I'll tell her you came by and give her your phone number. Okay?"

"Are you sure everything is all right, Lucy?" you implore.

"Yes, everything is fine. My mother just can't be disturbed right now. She'll call you," Lucy says with a look of determination in her eyes.

Because Lucy seems so concerned about you intruding, you agree to leave and talk to her mother later.

The following day, you check and find Lucy is at school as she said she would be. You try calling her mother at home, and once again, there is no answer. At lunch, Ms. James tells you that Lucy seems somewhat despondent but has made it to all her classes that morning.

Interview with Lucy
About a week later, as you're getting ready to leave for the day, you notice Lucy standing in the hallway outside your office. You ask her if she'd like to come in for a few minutes and talk.

Lucy walks into your office, and as you close the door, she bursts into tears. You guide her to a chair where she slumps down and continues to sob. You sit down opposite her and give her some time to calm down.

After crying hard for a few minutes, Lucy looks at you and says she doesn't know why she's so upset. "I'm just so very sad these days. I don't feel like doing anything except sleeping or crying. I've been crying for 3 days and can't seem to stop." She looks around the room for a tissue as she continues to apologize for getting upset.

"What do you think all those tears are about?" you ask.

"I'm really not sure. It seems ridiculous to me, but I just can't stop," Lucy sobs.

"Maybe you could tell me a little about what's been going on with you lately, and we can figure it out together," you suggest.

Lucy begins talking very rapidly as though she has been waiting for someone to help her for a long time. "You see, I live with my mother and sisters in the trailer, only they aren't ever home. My mother works a lot of hours, and when she gets home she's always tired. My father lives in Florida somewhere, but we don't ever see him. He was in jail for a while because someone pressed charges against him for child molestation. Terry, my older sister, dropped out of school and lives with her boyfriend most of the time. She got shot in the head and has a plate in her head now. She doesn't care about school or anything. Just her boyfriend. My younger sister, Sally, stays over at her friend's house a lot. So, it's just me at home and my mom. She has a lot of boyfriends who come over and spend the night. It just bothers me that they are always there. I just try to stay outside down by the river."

"And you mentioned you had a boyfriend, too, I believe. Does he come over to see you?" you ask.

"Well, on the weekends, when he's not working. Joe is 19 and works at the hosiery mill where my mom works. That's how I met him," she says.

"How long have you been seeing Joe?" you ask Lucy.

She tells you that she's been dating Joe for the past 3 months. After some hesitation, she tells you that Joe smokes a lot of pot and that they often go down to the river so that he can smoke.

"Do you smoke pot with him, Lucy?" you ask.

"Sometimes I have. It seems to make me feel weird and upset though. I always end up feeling down after I've smoked pot," she explains.

"Have you been smoking any pot lately?" you ask.

"A little, but please don't tell my mom. She'd kill me. I think it's why I'm in this state right now. I just feel like I'm losing control of myself. I don't think this relationship with Joe is good for me, but he's the only one who pays any attention to me. I just don't want to end up like my sister has. Dropping out of school and everything."

"Tell me what you mean by feeling like you're 'losing control' of yourself," you query.

"I just feel like I'm not myself sometimes. I'm usually a happy kind of person, and I really like to come to school. Lately, I just haven't been able to keep my mind on what's going on here. I'm worried about my mother and her finances. She's always scared she's going to lose her job if she doesn't work overtime, and she's always tired. And I'm worried about my sister, Terry. Her boyfriend isn't a very nice person, and he can be really mean to her. And I'm worried about my little sister, too. She's been getting into trouble lately because she never comes home when she's supposed to and my mom gets worried. I feel like I have to be there to take care of everyone. Sort of like a mother."

"Is there any other family around who could give you some help?" you ask.

"There's my aunt. She lives in town, though, and she works at the taxi company as a dispatcher. She has a daughter my age, and we get along real well. I really wish we could live in town like my aunt. I can talk to my aunt better than I can talk to my mother," she confides.

"So, you're feeling very responsible for your whole family, like you have to take care of them. Is that correct?"

"Yes, I feel that way most of the time," she says.

"Do you ever get to do anything for fun?" you ask.

"I like to read and walk in the woods," Lucy tells you. "But I haven't felt like doing anything lately except sleeping."

"How would you describe yourself, Lucy, when you're feeling okay?" you ask.

"I think I'm a fairly happy person most of the time. I like doing things outdoors, and I'm pretty outgoing. I like having friends, and I'm sort of a tomboy. I like to swim and run and hike in the woods and ride bikes. I used to play touch football with the neighbors and go on camping trips with my friends' families, but I haven't done anything like that lately. I also like school. I'm really good at math, foreign language, and literature. I read all the time when I'm feeling good. I think most people like me," Lucy says with a little smile.

This description makes you think that under normal circumstances, Lucy has good self-esteem and is intelligent and insightful. "Why do you think you've been so sad lately?" you continue.

"I think it's because of where we're living and my mother's boyfriends and Joe. I sometimes think I would be better off living with my aunt in town. I think I'd be happier and not so bored all the time. I'll tell you something else if you promise not to tell anyone," Lucy implores.

"Lucy, I have to explain to you that if you tell me anything that makes me think you might harm yourself or someone else, then I have to tell someone else. Also, if you tell me someone is hurting you, then I might have to tell someone else. Do you understand that?" you ask.

"No, this isn't about anyone getting hurt," Lucy exclaims. "It's just about the day you came to the trailer. You know, the reason that you couldn't see my mother was that she was in the bedroom with one of her boyfriends. I always have to go outside when she's with her boyfriends. It really gets to me sometimes. That's why I'd like to go live with my aunt," Lucy reflects.

"I see. So it bothers you when your mother has her boyfriends over at the trailer. Is that right?" you say.

"Yes, it really brings me down, like my mother doesn't care about me or how I feel," Lucy remarks.

"Have you ever talked to your mother about this issue?" you ask.

"Yes, and she just tells me she's got to have a life, too," Lucy replies.

"Maybe she doesn't know how upset you feel about her activities with her boyfriends," you suggest.

"Maybe," Lucy replies. "I think she's just caught up in her own world and doesn't really care about anyone else that much. She's not like my aunt at all."

"Do you think your mother or your aunt would be willing to come talk to me about this situation?" you query.

Lucy thinks about this question for a moment and then says she'll ask her mother, but she doesn't think it will do any good.

At this point, you ask Lucy how she's feeling now. She tells you she's relieved someone else knows what is happening in her life. She adds that she doesn't mind if you talk to her mother or aunt, but it's going to be hard to get in touch with them. They both work long hours. You ask her if you could contact them at work to set up an appointment. Lucy tells you that her aunt can be reached at her office, but her mother can't take calls at the hosiery mill.

6.5–1   What other information would you like to obtain from Lucy's mother or aunt?

6.5–2   What are some of Lucy's strengths?

6.5–3   What are some of Lucy's limitations?

6.5–4   What is your preliminary diagnosis for Lucy?
Axis I

Axis II

Axis III

Axis IV

Axis V

DIFFERENTIAL DIAGNOSIS

The most common challenge in making diagnoses among the mood disorders relates to the "rule-out" criteria included in nearly all of the disorders in this chapter. Specifically, clinicians are expected to ensure that the symptoms are *not* generated through the direct physiological effects of a substance (e.g., recreational drugs, prescription drugs, toxins, etc.) *or* by a general medical condition. There is, however, a strong tendency among clinicians to assume nonphysiological etiology as evidenced by the case examples in this chapter. Only in Case 6.1, Helen Stonewall, were physiological considerations made, and these efforts were clearly not generated by the mental health practitioner.

6.DD–1   Choose one case from among Cases 6.2, 6.3, and 6.4. List four questions you would ask to help rule out physiological causes.

Inherent in making mood disorder diagnoses is differentiating the intensity and length of symptoms. For example, the symptoms for Dysthymic Disorder are similar but not as intense or as debilitating as those for a Major Depressive Disorder. The distinction between Bipolar I and Cyclothymia is quite similar. Also, the distinction between hypomanic and manic episodes is simply that in Hypomania, the intensity of mood disturbance is not sufficient to cause serious psychosocial impairment and/or result in hospitalization. Similarly, a set of symptoms that has not lasted for the requisite time period to be a particular mood episode may well result in a NOS diagnosis (at least until the time frame is reached).

6.DD–2   What would be your diagnosis of Maggie Weinzapfel if she had come to you with the same symptoms 10 days after the breakup?

6.DD–3   Write a description of Connie Kellogg's "up" episodes that would be consistent with either a manic episode *or* a mixed episode.

Making a differential diagnosis when the client is exhibiting psychotic symptoms can be challenging as well. For example, the agitation that can accompany paranoid delusions in Schizophrenia may be easily confused with the expansive affect common in manic episodes, particularly when speech is pressured and the content is bizarre. Generally, a thorough history of the previous course of symptoms, knowledge of medication use (and the client's response to various medications), and/or family history can help in distinguishing these disorders. This approach may not be possible in the initial phases of psychiatric symptoms, and in those cases, it is not unusual for a number of different diagnoses to be made before a clear pattern emerges.

6.DD–4   What additional symptoms would you expect to see in Herschel Jarboe (Case 5.2) if he suffered from Schizoaffective Disorder?

A final consideration involves the presentation of symptoms typical in certain age groups. For example, depressive disorders among the elderly are often mistaken for Dementia. In this instance, a careful consideration of the onset of symptoms (particularly the temporal sequencing of depressive and cognitive issues) and a thorough medical history (and possible examination) can be particularly useful.

6.DD–5   What information would you need to rule out Schizophrenia in Della Corbin (Case 3.1)? List both questions for the client and sources of collateral information.

Similarly, among children, either general distractibility in depressive states or the agitation, impulsivity, and/or poor judgment associated with manic or hypomanic episodes can be mistaken for ADHD. Although considering the age of onset can be useful in making the distinction between ADHD and mania, the primary distinguishing feature will involve determining whether the course of symptoms is more chronic than episodic.

Furthermore, children are increasingly being diagnosed with Bipolar Disorder rather than ADHD or Conduct Disorder. In order to be diagnosed with a Bipolar Disorder, the child must display symptoms of Mania. However, the practitioner should be careful not to make this diagnosis without a full understanding of the family situation. Some children can display manic symptoms when they are under stress. These symptoms may disappear once the stressful situation is remedied.

6.DD–6   Choose one case from among Cases 2.1, 2.2, and 2.5, and write a scenario in which you would want to rule out Bipolar Disorder as a secondary diagnosis.

 InfoTrac keywords

Bipolar Disorder, Bipolar Mania, Depression, Depression in adolescence, Depression in children, Dysthymia

Anxiety Disorders | 7

DISORDERS

Anxiety is a normal human emotion that is often adaptive. For example, many of us may study for an examination because of anxiety about failing (rather than because of a real love of learning). The diagnoses in the Anxiety Disorders section of the DSM-IV-TR (APA, 2000) represent more extreme states of anxiety as well as behaviors developed to forestall anxiety. In any event, the specific diagnoses presented in this section relate to anxiety that is sufficiently severe to cause significant clinical distress and/or disruption in psychosocial functioning.

Similar to the section on Mood Disorders, this section of the DSM-IV-TR presents two noncodable "building blocks" that are relevant to several codable disorders. The first, agoraphobia, involves anxiety focused on situations or places from which the client may not be able to escape and/or receive help if the anxiety were to become too acute. In fact, with agoraphobia the client develops patterns of avoiding the situations or places *or* enduring exposure to them with significant distress *or* requiring support (e.g., a companion) in order to "handle" the anxiety. The second noncodable issue is that of a panic attack, an episode of anxiety usually lasting less than a half hour during which the client experiences a number of physical complaints and/or cognitive fears about the outcome of the "attack" (APA, 2000).

Three disorders relate directly to these noncodable building blocks. In Panic Disorder Without Agoraphobia, the client has experienced recurrent, *unexpected* panic attacks that have led to excessive worry and behavioral changes to avoid more attacks. For Panic Disorder with Agoraphobia, these concerns about additional panic attacks have developed into agoraphobia, thereby systematically limiting the client's interaction with the outside world. For Agoraphobia Without a History of Panic Disorder, the limitations of agoraphobia have developed even though there has not been a period of recurring, unexpected panic attacks. Of these three disorders, Agoraphobia Without a History of Panic Disorder is by far the least common (APA, 2000).

The next two anxiety disorders are related to better-specified, anticipated fears. Although some clients suffering from these disorders may experience actual panic attacks, others may simply feel a heightened level of anxiety. For example, in Specific Phobias, the client fears some specific object or situation. Consequently, he or she predictably experiences increased anxiety or a panic attack whenever exposed to the feared stimuli. Quite frequently, the phobia is directly related to a discernible event and is understood by the client to be an "overreaction." Similarly, in Social Phobia, the specific fear involves at least one type of social or performance situation that involves being "judged" by others (e.g., public speaking, parties) (APA, 2000).

At the other extreme, the anxiety and worry associated with Generalized Anxiety Disorder is *not* focused on the specific fears listed above. In this disorder, concern is usually focused on everyday events and tends to shift over a number of events or activities. Although the client may not view the worries as excessive, he or she does experience distress associated with an inability to control the concerns. For this disorder, the condition is more chronic; specifically, the excessive worry has persisted for at least 6 months (APA, 2000).

Obsessive-Compulsive Disorder is characterized by the presence of recurrent obsessions and/or compulsions. Obsessions are intrusive and persistent thoughts, ideas, impulses, or images that are associated with marked anxiety or distress. The specific content of obsessions does not usually involve any real-life problems. Compulsions are repetitive behaviors that are performed to prevent or reduce anxiety. However, these behaviors are clearly either excessive or not realistically associated with preventing or reducing the feared situation. Although by definition, clients suffering from this disorder have at one time realized that their symptoms are excessive or unreasonable, such insight may be tenuous (APA, 2000).

The next two diagnoses are associated with direct exposure to extreme traumatic events involving threats of serious injury or death to the client or another person. In Acute Stress Disorder (ASD), symptoms begin during or immediately after the trauma, last for at least 2 days, and resolve within 4 weeks. The symptoms in this disorder tend to be largely dissociative in nature, include some form of reexperiencing the trauma, and lead to patterns of avoiding reminders of the event. It should be noted that if the symptoms are not resolved in the time period, another diagnosis is in order (e.g., a depressive disorder, other anxiety disorders, substance-abuse problems) (APA, 2000).

In Posttraumatic Stress Disorder (PTSD), the symptoms have persisted for at least 1 month, although the exposure to trauma may have occurred at any time prior to symptom onset. Specifically, this disorder is characterized by persistent reexperiencing of the traumatic event and avoidance of stimuli associated with the trauma. Further, the client evidences both numbing of general responsiveness and persistent symptoms of arousal that were not present before the traumatic event (APA, 2000).

Two of the diagnoses in this section are determined by the etiological factors relevant to the anxiety disorder. Specifically, Anxiety Disorder due to a General Medical Condition is used when the anxiety is directly related to a diagnosable organic problem. Similarly, Substance-Induced Anxiety Disorder is used when the problematic anxiety is directly related to the use of recreational drugs, prescribed medications, or a toxin (e.g., lead, carbon monoxide). Finally, a diagnosis of Anxiety Disorder NOS is included for when an individual's symptoms fail to fit any of the more specific diagnoses but clearly are related to increased levels of anxiety (APA, 2000).

People suffering from Anxiety Disorder do not necessarily seek treatment even when symptoms become fairly disruptive. Several issues contribute to this lack of help-seeking behavior. The course of most anxiety disorders tends to be variable, and many clients attain some symptom relief through avoidance strategies. The natural waxing and waning of symptoms is frequently related to stress. Further, "self-medication" is not uncommon for clients experiencing Anxiety Disorder. Whether relieving symptoms with prescription or recreational drugs, transient symptom relief is quite possible.

Stigma may also play a significant role, with some clients being embarrassed by their anxieties and thereby being reluctant to acknowledge their symptoms. Similarly, some clients may view their symptoms as childish or something they "should be over by now." Particularly for clients who experience panic attacks, the message from medical practitioners that their symptoms are not indicative of a physical disorder may be interpreted by the client as a dismissal and/or judgment.

ASSESSMENT

When assessing someone who you suspect may have an anxiety disorder, particular attention will be focused on the person's fears and worries. Although a thorough history is required to make a diagnosis of a specific anxiety disorder, it may be difficult for clients to present detailed and accurate information. They may deliberately minimize symptoms because of internalized stigma. It may be difficult for them to discern their internal thought processes. They may be embarrassed by details that, in their minds, are clearly excessive (and perhaps "crazy").

Because fear and worry are primarily internal processes, consulting collateral sources may not be useful, particularly in cases when stigma is high. Clients may actively hide the details of their anxieties or may minimize the impact of their situation. Significant others may be "fooled" by such strategies or may actively collude in minimization.

It should be noted that, particularly when panic attacks are involved, collateral medical referrals are warranted. Even in situations where the client seems healthy, ruling out serious medical problems is an essential part of the assessment process.

Assessment Instruments

Adults The State-Trait Anxiety Inventory (STAI) (Speilberger, Gorsuch, Lushene, Vagg, & Jacobs, 1983) is the most common self-report general measure of anxiety for adults. It consists of two separate scales, the state anxiety scale and the trait anxiety scale. The state anxiety scale is intended to measure transitory feelings of nervousness, worry, tension, and/or apprehension. In contrast, the trait anxiety scale reflects individual differences in the characteristic response to stress. Generally, an individual with strong trait anxiety is more likely to experience strong state anxiety when exposed to stress. Both subscales have shown sound psychometric properties; however, the state subscale is used more commonly than the trait subscale in clinical settings. The internal consistency for the state subscale is very high, with median alpha coefficients of .90. It has shown good concurrent and discriminant validity.

A number of more focused scales are commonly used. The Mobility Inventory for Agoraphobia (MIA) (Chambless, Caputo, Jasin, Gracely, & Williams,

1985) is a 27-item instrument designed to measure agoraphobic avoidance and the frequency of panic attacks. Specifically, 26 items address avoidance (both when the client is alone and when accompanied), and the final item defines panic and asks the respondent to report the number of panic experiences during the previous week. Estimates of internal consistency have ranged above .90 for this scale, and test-retest reliability has been good over a 1-month period. Known-groups validity has also been demonstrated (Fischer & Corcoran, 1994).

For a more detailed examination of panic attacks, the Panic Attack Symptoms Questionnaire (PASQ) (Clum, Broyles, Borden, & Watkins, 1990) is a 33-item instrument that covers symptoms of panic attacks by having the respondent indicate the duration of symptoms. In addition, the scale allows clients to list additional symptoms and to estimate the frequency of attacks in the past week, month, 6 months, and year. The scale has shown good internal consistency, with a coefficient alpha of .88 and known-groups validity (Fischer & Corcoran, 1994).

The Obsessive-Compulsive Scale (OCS) (Gibb, Bailey, Best, & Lambirth, 1983) is a 20-item instrument designed to specifically address the presence of obsessive thoughts and/or compulsive behaviors. The scale has high internal consistency and good stability (.82 test-retest reliability over a 3-week period). The OSC has evidenced good concurrent validity with clinical ratings (Fischer & Corcoran, 1994).

The Social Phobia Scale (SPS) (Mattick & Clarke, 1998) and the Social Interaction Anxiety Scale (SIAS) (Mattick & Clarke) are two companion measures for assessing social phobia fears. Both scales were shown to possess high levels of internal consistency and test-retest reliability. They discriminated between social phobia, agoraphobia, and simple phobia samples, and between social phobia and normal samples. The scales correlated well with established measures of social anxiety but were found to have low or nonsignificant correlations with established measures of depression, state and trait anxiety, locus of control, and social desirability. The scales were found to change with treatment and to remain stable in the face of no treatment.

The Acute Stress Disorder Scale (ASDS) (Bryant, Moulds, & Guthrie, 2000) is a 19-item, self-report inventory that indexes Acute Stress Disorder (ASD) and predicts PTSD. The ASDS includes 5 dissociative, 4 reexperiencing, 4 avoidance, and 6 arousal symptoms items. Preliminary analysis has shown good internal consistency, with coefficient alphas ranging from .84 to .93 for total score, dissociation symptoms, reexperiencing symptoms, avoidance symptoms, and arousal symptoms.

Most of the measures addressing PTSD have been focused on a particular traumatic event. For example, the Trauma Symptom Checklist-33 (TSC-33) (Briere & Runtz, 1989) is designed to measure the impact of child abuse, particularly child sexual abuse. It has shown excellent internal consistency, with an overall coefficient alpha of .90. It also has successfully discriminated between abused and nonabused women. The most commonly used instrument for combat exposure is the Mississippi Scale for Combat-Related PTSD (Keane, Caddell, & Taylor, 1988). This 35-item scale has demonstrated both reliability and validity and has been recommended as the best self-report instrument for combat veterans in a review of the literature (Watson, 1990).

In contrast, the Impact of Event Scale (IES) (Horowitz, Wilner, & Alvarez, 1979) allows the client to focus on any particular event that has been traumatic. The 15-item scale then measures the emotional reaction in two categories: intrusiveness and avoidance. Internal consistency estimates of the two subscales average .86 for the avoidance component and .90 for the intrusiveness. The IES has also demonstrated known-groups validity (Fischer & Corcoran, 1994).

Children   The most widely used self-report anxiety scales for children have been derived from adult scales. For example, the State-Trait Anxiety Inventory for Children (STAIC) (Speilberger, 1983) was derived from the adult scale mentioned previously. Although this scale has been used in numerous research and clinical settings, it has not reliably distinguished anxious children from children with other disorders (Perrin & Last, 1992). In particular, these scales based on adult models tend not to distinguish between anxiety disorders and ADHD.

The Multidimensional Anxiety Scale for Children (MASC) (March, Parker, Sullivan, Stallings, & Conners, 1997) is a relatively new scale designed specifically for use with children and adolescents. The MASC consists of 39 items distributed across four major factors, three of which can be parsed into two subfactors each: (1) physical symptoms (tense/restless and somatic/autonomic); (2) social anxiety (humiliation/rejection and public performance fears); (3) harm avoidance (perfectionism and anxious coping); and (4) separation anxiety. Test-retest reliabilities have generally been greater than .85. Most important, the MASC has demonstrated discriminant validity among samples of anxious and ADHD children (March et al., 1999).

Interestingly, studies have consistently demonstrated low concordance between child self-reports and parent or teacher ratings in terms of anxiety (Greenhill, Pine, March, Birmaher, & Riddle, 1998). This suggests that the typical reliance on adult reports to diagnose children may be inappropriate with anxiety disorders.

CULTURAL CONSIDERATIONS

As anxiety is a normal part of the life experience, culture undoubtedly influences what is viewed as anxiety-provoking. For example, the interpretation of unfortunate occurrences may be conceived as witchcraft and, consequently, viewed with intense anxiety by those cultures that subscribe to beliefs in magic (e.g., Haitian and other Caribbean cultures). Similarly, in cultures that have traditionally shielded women from public contact (e.g., some Asian and Arabic cultures), women may exhibit marked fearfulness in certain social interaction, at least initially.

Also, culture can influence what level of anxiety is considered problematic. For example, worrying can be normative in Jewish cultures, and there may not be a level of worry that is viewed as pathological. Among certain Germanic cultures in which displays of emotions are discouraged, a relatively low level of anxiety might be judged pathological.

Typically, the standards for displays of emotion vary by gender. This, in turn, may influence the occurrence of certain conditions. Among anxiety disorders, there is little difference between the sexes in the occurrence of Social Phobia, Acute Distress Disorder, PTSD, Generalized Anxiety Disorder, or Obsessive-Compulsive Disorder. These all share either a link to an intense psychosocial stressor or a relatively private set of symptoms. Among the specific phobias or panic disorders, however, the female-to-male ratio is at least 2:1. These disorders are comparatively public in symptom display and, thus, less likely to be diagnosed among men. Some evidence indicates that males suffering from panic attacks are more likely to "self-medicate" and may eventually come into treatment because of substance-abuse disorders.

SOCIAL SUPPORT SYSTEMS

Anxiety disorders typically do not cause disruptions in psychosocial functioning as serious as those caused by mood or schizophrenic disorders. Many people suffering from anxiety disorders can manage their lives while still avoiding the "triggers" of their anxiety. In these instances, only close friends or family members may be aware of the person's fears.

However, there are individuals for whom an anxiety disorder results in profound occupational and social impairment. Some of the specific phobias may rule out a realm of occupational choices. Certainly, agoraphobia (with or without a history of panic disorder) puts tremendous strain on most social support systems. Even though in the computer age there may be more occupational choices for someone suffering from agoraphobia, at least some limitations in occupational functioning should be expected in most instances.

There is also wide variation in how the symptoms of anxiety disorders affect clients' social support systems. Although many clients may acknowledge that their fears are unreasonable, such insight does not usually change behavior. Some people in the social support system may become frustrated that the person can't just put his or her fears aside. In other instances, one or more members of the client's social support system might actually bring some symptom relief by their presence. In these instances, there is some danger that such dependency could disrupt the relationship.

The social isolation that usually accompanies agoraphobia or social phobia may affect partners and family members as well. It may limit their social interactions, or they may feel guilt if they continue more "normal" social activities. A number of symptoms (e.g., panic attacks, compulsions) may be viewed as embarrassing and lead to avoiding the symptomatic person.

Perhaps because the symptoms of anxiety disorders are usually less disruptive, fewer support groups and psychoeducational groups have developed around these disorders. Nonetheless, there are a number of Internet resources available.

www.anxietynetwork.com/gahome.html—Description of Generalized Anxiety Disorder

www.ocfoundation.org/ocf1050a.htm—Discussion of medication issues for Obsessive-Compulsive Disorder

www.trauma-pages.com/articles.htm—Research articles related to PTSD

www.athealth.com/Practitioner/newsletter/FPN_4_13.html—Assessment and treatment of anxiety disorders

www.athealth.com/—With subscription to this Web site, weekly e-mails received related to mental health topics in the DSM-IV-TR; two sites related to anxiety disorders and social phobias in the 2000 archives

Case 7.1

Identifying Information
Client Name: Gloria Kuhlenschmidt
Age: 33 years old
Ethnicity: Caucasian
Marital Status: Married
Occupation: Computer sales representative

First Contact

Gloria Kuhlenschmidt, a 33-year-old Caucasian female, is a sales representative for a large computer corporation and has made an appointment with you to talk about a new software package designed specifically for mental health counselors. While she is in the waiting room, she picks up several brochures related to anxiety and depression and places them in her notebook.

You meet Gloria in the waiting room. She is a very attractive, stylish-looking business-woman who is dressed in a dark gray suit, pumps, and a matching shoulder bag. She has long dark hair, a light complexion, and beautiful brown eyes. She would be considered thin for her height of approximately 5 feet 8 inches tall. She greets you enthusiastically and seems eager to tell you about her company's software.

In her discussion about the software product she is selling, Gloria appears to be a very engaging and self-confident woman. However, after conducting her sales pitch for about 15 minutes, she tells you that she really doesn't want to push you to buy the software and to take your time and think about it.

Gloria then slips the brochures out from her notebook and asks you if you could help someone who had some of the symptoms in the pamphlets. You ask her if she could give you a little more information. Gloria opens one of the brochures and says, "Well, if someone had feelings of shortness of breath, shakiness, numbing sensations, dizziness, heart pounding, and chest pain, do you think you could help the person?"

You state that you work with a lot of people with a variety of emotional issues and that you have successfully worked in the past with people with those symptoms. Gloria's eyes brighten and she says, "Then, can I make an appointment to see you?"

You ask rather tentatively, "So, you have had some of these symptoms?"

Gloria emphatically explains, "Oh, yes, I've been taking Xanax four times a day for the last 8 months ever since this incident when I wound up in the emergency room at the hospital thinking I was having a heart attack. The doctor said everything checked out normal, but gave me these pills to take. Now, I'm afraid to leave home without them, and I don't know if I want to be on them the rest of my life."

"Did the doctor recommend you see a therapist?" you query.

Gloria states that he just told her to go to her family doctor for a refill of the prescription, but somehow she feels medicated all the time and often feels very tired even at the beginning of the day.

You decide to set up an appointment for Gloria for the following week.

7.1–1   At this point, what kind(s) of disorder do you think Gloria might have?

First Session

The following week, Gloria arrives for her appointment 10 minutes early. She, once again, is dressed in a very businesslike manner and appears to be very organized.

You start the session by asking her how and when these symptoms first occurred.

Gloria tells you that she got married for the third time a year and a half ago to a man who is also in computer sales. He is a very gregarious man who loves his job. He also loves to race dogs, which he does on the weekends. She, on the other hand, is a musician. She loves to stay at home and play the piano and cook when she has the time. Gloria states that one night she and her husband, John, went to a concert and halfway through the show, she began to have this feeling that her heart was pounding too hard and she couldn't catch her breath. She said she had to leave the concert with John almost carrying her out, which she found very embarrassing. He took her to the emergency room, where the doctor ran some tests, said she was perfectly okay, and gave her Xanax to take four times a day. "He said to go to my family doctor when the prescription ran out. My family doctor ran all kinds of tests and kept asking me if I was using drugs or alcohol! I told him my husband and I don't even drink beer or wine, much less do drugs! Finally, he said I was perfectly healthy and just wrote another prescription, asking me if I felt like I had been under a lot of stress lately." Gloria states that this incident occurred about 8 months ago.

Gloria states that several of these incidents have occurred since the first one at the concert. She tells you that once her heart starts pounding and she feels like she can't breathe, then she gets shaky, and sometimes it takes a couple of hours to get over the feeling. She states that she worries about having more attacks and is most fearful of an incident happening when she is out. To try to make sure she'll be safe, she has been taking Xanax for the past 10 weeks before she leaves the house.

You ask her how these feelings have affected her job. She states that she really isn't cut out to be a sales representative. Her previous jobs have involved working with people, but she doesn't like making "cold calls" and feels a lot of pressure to sell since she works solely on commission. "My husband just doesn't understand why this job is so hard for me," she sighs. "I feel that he doesn't think I try hard enough. He gets up at the crack of dawn and can't wait to go out and sell all day long. Maybe I just don't have the right attitude. I don't really want to push people to buy a product they aren't interested in. I'm afraid my husband also thinks I'm just lazy. I have a very hard time getting up in the morning, and he doesn't like that trait of mine. He almost drags me out of bed. I guess I should get up and going, but it's just hard for me to do."

You ask Gloria how long she has known her husband. She states that they dated for 3 years before they got married. "He's 10 years older than I am, and sometimes he treats me like I'm a child. I feel like I have to do everything perfectly or I'll get in trouble. He is somewhat of a perfectionist and wants the house clean and everything put away before we go to work in the morning. If I were to do that, I'd have to get up at 3 A.M."

Gloria tells you that since these incidents have occurred, her husband doesn't push her so much to get everything done and get out of the house so early in the morning. She states that it seems to take her forever to get out of bed, showered, dressed, and the house cleaned up before she can leave for work. "I feel that everything has to be in perfect order or he'll be upset."

You decide to explore this issue concerning her husband and ask her to explain further what she means when she says, "He'll be upset." Gloria assures you that it's just a feeling and that he actually never has gotten upset with her. "He's never really said anything about it. He just is always trying to get me to be more motivated to schedule my day like he schedules his day."

Gloria states that both she and her husband have a college education and that both of their families are from the eastern part of the state. They don't plan on having children since her husband has a child by his first marriage that he sees every other weekend. John's son is 17 years old and gets along with Gloria quite well. John and his son go to the racetrack on weekends when they are together. John's participation in dog racing takes up a lot of his free time. Gloria states that she goes along with them oc-casionally, and that it's really an enjoyable way to spend the weekend.

You suggest that perhaps the pressure of her job might have something to do with these incidents she has been experiencing. Gloria says that she has never thought about that possibility, but "it's food for thought." You tell Gloria that you believe you can help her figure out what might be triggering these episodes and ways to help her be more relaxed. She states that she would like to continue to see you for at least 10 sessions.

7.1–2   What further information would you want to get from Gloria the next time you meet with her?

7.1–3   What are some of Gloria's strengths?

7.1–4   Would you want to see Gloria with her husband, John, for a session? Why or why not?

7.1–5   How would you diagnose Gloria?
Axis I

Axis II

Axis III

Axis IV

Axis V

Case 7.2

Identifying Information
Client Name: Maya Pena
Age: 23 years old
Ethnicity: Hispanic
Marital Status: Single

Intake Information
Maya Pena is a 23-year-old Hispanic female who currently resides in Houston, Texas. She was born and raised in "the Valley," the southernmost region of the state. Maya is the youngest of three children. Her parents have been married for 32 years and continue to live in the Valley. They recently moved from McAllen to Brownsville after living in their previous home for over 25 years. Her oldest sister is married and has a baby girl. Maya's middle sister is married and lives in Houston. Maya is 8 years younger than her middle sister.

Immediately following high school, Maya attended a community college in her hometown. After 2 years, she was admitted to a larger university in Houston where she received a degree in history and philosophy. After completing her college education, Maya returned to her hometown to work while living with her parents. She obtained a job at the McAllen Chamber of Commerce. Approximately 6 months ago, Maya returned to Houston, where she is currently working for a temporary agency while she looks for a permanent job. Maya enjoys reading, dancing, going to bookstores, and writing.

Information Received from a Former Therapist
Maya gave your agency permission to contact a former therapist she saw for a couple of years in junior high school. The therapist forwarded you her records.

The records indicated that Maya began having problems around the age of 10. When Maya was confronted with stressful situations, she would begin counting under her breath, washing her hands several times every hour, and checking behind her every time she stood up. Her need to wash her hands frequently created problems for her in the classroom, as she was constantly asking permission to leave the class and go to the bathroom. It would take her 5 to 10 minutes to wash her hands, and she began missing large segments of each class period. The teacher informed the school counselor of this problem, and Maya was referred to an outside therapist for counseling. Maya told the counselor that besides the hand washing, she had a feeling sometimes that she had to count. The counselor also noticed that Maya had to check behind herself every time she stood up. When pushed to explain these behaviors, Maya would vaguely respond that they kept "bad things" from happening. During the time that she was seeing the counselor, the symptoms seemed to recede somewhat, although under stress, the symptoms would intensify. The counselor's notes indicated that she had used some behavior modification techniques with Maya in order to reduce the symptoms she was displaying.

Interview with Maya
Maya arrives for her appointment with you a few minutes early and sits quietly in the waiting room reading a book. She is of average height, has long dark brown hair tied back in a ponytail, and is slightly below average weight. She is wearing a pair of brown trousers with matching shoes and socks and a tan blouse. She is carrying a small brown purse and is exceptionally neat in her appearance. She smiles when you greet her in the waiting room and readily walks with you to your office.

Maya states that she isn't sure why she made the appointment and feels a bit silly for being there. You ask her what made her think about making the appointment, and she states: "There have been some things bothering me lately, and I thought it would help to talk to someone."

You suggest that it can be helpful at times to talk to someone who can be objective. "Why don't we start by you telling me a little about yourself and what you're doing right now?"

"Well, right now, I'm working for a temporary agency as a secretary, but it's not what I want to do. I just took the job until I can find something else that I really want to do."

"What is it you're interested in doing?" you ask.

"Well, I'd really like to work for a museum, I think. I majored in history and philosophy and working at a museum, like a natural history museum, sounds like a very interesting job to me. There aren't too many jobs in that area, though. I've also thought about going back to school to get my master's degree in something a little more useful than history, but I've got to save up the money before I can go back to school."

"Have you thought about other jobs you'd like to have for a year or two until you can save the money to go back to school?" you inquire.

"I think I'd like a job in a bookstore or library. I read a lot, and I'd be good at helping people pick out books to read. I definitely don't want to work in a hospital. I did that for a while, and it really bothered me."

"What bothered you about it?" you ask.

"I just couldn't handle all the germs in that place. I guess it's one thing I wanted to talk to you about. I feel this urgent need to wash my hands all the time. See how red they are? That's because I'm constantly washing them. I feel like there are germs everywhere and I can't ever get clean enough. Some days I spend most of my time just washing my hands, and then the minute I touch something that I think has germs on it, I have to wash them again. It's hard to get anything done because of all these thoughts and feelings inside about needing to get rid of the germs. It's kind of driving me crazy these days."

"How long have you had these feelings like you need to wash your hands?"

"Really, for a long time, since I was a little girl. But sometimes it doesn't bother me so much. In fact, it seems to almost go away, and I'm not so worried about germs. Then, for no reason, those feelings come back, and no matter how hard I try, I still feel like I need to wash my hands."

"What do you do if you can't wash your hands?" you ask.

"Then, I count. I just begin counting, and I don't feel like I can stop until I reach a certain number. Other times, I just count up to 25 over and over again. I know it probably sounds crazy, but I just can't stop it."

"Are there any other things you have an urgent need to do?"

"Ever since I was a little girl, I've felt the need to check behind me every time I stand up. I really have no idea why I feel a need to do that, but I always do."

"Do you feel better after you've engaged in one of these activities like washing your hands or counting or checking behind you?"

"Oh, yes, absolutely. I have a big sense of relief for a little while, but then I feel the urge to do it again."

"Do all of these activities get in the way of other things you're doing?" you ask.

"Sometimes they do. When I was at the hospital, it was a real problem because I couldn't stop thinking about all the germs. Sometimes, I just allow time for needing to wash my hands, but I'm not always in a situation where I can make the time. Then, it becomes a big problem. Sometimes it doesn't seem to get in the way too much, but I'm embarrassed if someone notices me doing one of these things."

"It sounds like you're a very insightful and intelligent person who tends to be on the quiet side. How would you characterize your mood most of the time?"

"I've had times when I feel real depressed about my life. I've always felt this huge responsibility toward my family. Even when I was young, I thought it was my job to take care of all of them. Right now, I feel terrible because I'm not earning enough money to send some home to my parents. I feel like I should be able to take care of them, especially when they get old. It makes me tense just thinking about it. Sometimes, I feel like I should be working two jobs just so I could help them out some. They don't have much, and I always thought that when I grew up, I'd get them things they've always wanted."

"Have you felt depressed recently?" you ask.

"No, not really. More anxious than depressed. I'm always anxious, it seems. I worry about everything."

"Do you ever take anything to control the anxiety?" you ask.

"Like what?" she says.

"Some people have a drink or take some kind of drug, like marijuana or a prescription or even an herbal remedy."

"No, I've never done anything like that. My family is very strict about things like that."

"What about friends? Do you have friends you do things with?" you ask.

"I've gotten to know one person at work a little bit, but she's married so she doesn't have much time to do anything. It's been one of my problems. I think people think I'm weird or something because of all these urgent feelings I have. It's been hard to have friends because all my time is taken up with these activities," Maya says sadly.

Because the session is almost over, you ask Maya what her goals for therapy may be. She states that she would like to get more control over her urges so they don't run her life and that she would like to feel less tense all the time. You suggest to Maya that you would like to meet for eight sessions and then evaluate her progress during the eighth session. If she needs to continue in therapy at that time, then you will make those decisions with her after the eighth visit. You also explain to Maya that there may be more information you'd like to obtain at a later time, but you feel that counseling could be beneficial to helping her resolve some of the issues you've discussed. Maya ends the session by telling you that her aunt Juanita wants to give you more information about her. She signs a release of information so that you will be able to speak with the aunt when she calls.

Information Received from Maya's Aunt in Houston

Maya's aunt, Juanita Garza, calls you to express her concern about Maya's behavior. She begins by saying that she has spent a great deal of time with Maya since her first move to Houston. Juanita is an art therapist at a rehabilitation hospital and has some background in psychology.

She tells you that she has been very concerned about Maya over the years. Maya appears to go through periods of depression that aggravate her symptoms of washing, checking, and counting. She states that Maya has always been a good child, easy to get along with but somewhat shy, reserved, and easily prone to depressed moods. She states that Maya was always very responsible, even as a young child. She worked part-time through high school and financed her way through college with student loans and a job.

She states that the last 2 years of college were difficult because Maya was working full-time 3 P.M. to 11 P.M. at the hospital in Houston while attempting to go full-time to school. Juanita tells you that during Maya's senior year, she became very withdrawn and was washing her hands so much they were rough and red.

"When I asked her about her hands, she said that she felt a need to wash her hands frequently due to all the germs in the hospital." Juanita feels that the job in the hospital was not ideal for Maya but that she needed the money to cover her school expenses. She states that Maya often will go to the restroom when they are out at a restaurant, wash her hands, and then take the paper towel and open the door with the towel in order to avoid touching the door handle.

7.2–1   What are some questions you might like to pursue in the next session with Maya?

7.2–2   What are some of Maya's strengths?

7.2–3   What are some possible diagnoses you would like to rule out in Maya's case?

7.2–4   How might a physician be of assistance to you in this case?

7.2–5   What is your preliminary diagnosis for Maya?
Axis I

Axis II

Axis III

Axis IV

Axis V

Case 7.3

Identifying Information

Client Name: Caroline Collins
Age: 38 years old
Ethnicity: Caucasian
Marital Status: Married
Occupation: Nurse
Children: Josephine, age 14; Carter, age 12

Intake Information

Caroline Collins called the Family Counseling Center to make an appointment with a counselor. She asked the intake worker if there was anyone at the Center who specialized in "working with people with fears." She stated that she has been having trouble driving her car lately due to "some fears I have." She was scheduled for an appointment with you for the following day.

Initial Session with Caroline

Caroline comes to the initial session with you the following day after her shift at the hospital is over. She appears weary as you step into the waiting room to greet her. She is wearing blue hospital scrubs and is simply staring into space when you ask her to come to your office with you. She smiles and follows you down the hall.

Caroline tells you that she has been married for 15 years to her husband, Alex. She has two children, a girl named Josephine, age 14, and a boy, Carter, age 12. Caroline works a rotating shift at the hospital on the surgical floor. She switches between the 7 A.M.–3 P.M. shift and the 3–11 P.M. shift. She rarely has to work the 11 P.M.–7 A.M. shift unless they really need her to work. She has 15 years of experience as a registered nurse.

Caroline begins the session by explaining that she has trouble with certain fears, which have been gradually increasing. She feels that the fears are beginning to interfere with her work

and the rest of her life, and she doesn't know how to get control of them. She states that her husband recommended she go to counseling and that she just needs to learn how to relax.

She states that her initial fear concerned driving. "I just began to feel very nervous about driving the car by myself. I can drive the car to work, but it is difficult. I'm always so relieved when I get into the hospital. My house is only about 2 miles from the hospital, so it's not too bad, but I begin to get nervous about an hour before I have to go every day. Driving around town is a whole other story. I really don't do it unless I absolutely have to."

"How do you get errands done?" you inquire.

"Well, I just try to wait until the weekends when my husband is home. If he's driving, I'm okay. It still bothers me, but it's not as bad. During the week, I just pretty much stay at home except to go back and forth to work. I've noticed lately that it's much worse when I get off at 11 P.M. and have to drive home in the dark. I don't like to be out when it's dark."

"Okay, from what you're telling me, it sounds as if the difficulty at night is due to it being dark outside, not that it's harder to drive at night because of poor vision, for example. Is that correct?"

"Yes, exactly, I have a fear of being out at night . . . anywhere, anytime. I just don't like to be out in the dark. It makes me very anxious," Caroline tells you.

"So, driving the car and being out at night can make you fearful. Are there other times when you feel fearful?" you ask.

Caroline looks at you anxiously as if she's trying to decide what to tell you next. "Yes, there are other fears I have. I really hate to stand in line at the grocery store. It scares me for some unknown reason. I begin to feel really uncomfortable, like I have to get out of there. So, I just refuse to do it. I make my husband or one of my children go to the grocery store with me and stand in line. I know they think I'm crazy, but I can't help it. It just scares me to death." Caroline looks distraught and anxious just talking about these issues.

"Let me see if I am understanding you correctly," you say. "You have several different fears. You get fearful driving the car, especially when you're alone; you have a fear of being outside at night; and you have a fear of standing in line at the grocery store. Do you feel fearful when you're standing in line at other places where you go to do errands?" you ask.

"Anytime I have to stand in line, it unnerves me. Makes me feel boxed in and like I'm going to scream or something," Caroline states.

"How long have you been having these fears?" you ask Caroline.

"I guess it started about a year ago. I didn't used to have any of these fears. I could go anywhere, and it didn't bother me. It's been a gradual thing that I've noticed lately is getting worse, so I thought I better try to do something about it before it gets really bad. I think my husband may be right. I just need to learn how to relax."

"I'm really glad you came in, too, before it got really bad," you reply. "Caroline, I'm going to ask you some questions now that may or may not apply to you. And if they don't apply to you, just tell me."

"Yes, that's fine," Caroline replies.

"Have you ever felt that you've had an episode where you were so afraid that you felt like your heart was beating too fast or you couldn't catch your breath or you felt like you were choking or sick to your stomach?" you inquire.

"Well, yes, about a year and a half ago, I think it was. We were moving from California back to the East Coast, and I was traveling alone with my dogs and cats and a carload of stuff, and there were these long tunnels out West that I had to go through. I remember getting into this one tunnel and the traffic slowed down to a crawl because of an accident. All of a sudden,

I thought I wasn't going to get out of there alive. I remember feeling like I couldn't catch my breath and like I was having a heart attack or something. It was one of the scariest experiences of my life." Caroline shifts uneasily in her chair.

"Okay. And this was before you had all these fears you described earlier, is that correct?" you ask.

"Yes, before I got scared to drive. But for a long time after that incident I was really scared that would happen again. You know, that feeling like I'm having a heart attack. I was really afraid I was going to die in that tunnel."

"And did you have another episode like the one in the tunnel?" you ask.

"Not that bad, but I did have one like it one evening going to work. That time I had chest pain and was short of breath. I was shaking all over and sweating, too. Since I was on my way to the hospital, I decided to get a doctor to check me and make sure I wasn't having a problem with my heart. He did an EKG, and everything was normal," Caroline said. "Come to think of it, he told me I needed to relax, too," Caroline says with a little smile.

"So, it's only been those two occasions that you can remember having an episode of intense fear that affected you physically," you inquire.

"Yes, but ever since the first one, I've been scared of having more. They really are horrible! I feel like I'm going crazy," she says.

"Are there any other things going on in your life that seem very stressful to you?" you ask.

"No, not really. I love my job and my family. I think it's been stressful for my husband and children to have to cope with my problems, but we love each other very much and it's a good family. The situation with my parents has been a little stressful, though."

"Tell me a little bit about that situation," you suggest.

"Well, my parents live about 40 miles up the road in Millville," Caroline explains. "They have lived there all their lives. I go visit them every Sunday. They're getting older now, and they want things done in a certain way. For example, I have to go on Sundays, and I have to be there to have Sunday dinner with them. I can't change the day or the time, and they expect me to stay until 6 o'clock Sunday evening before I drive back home. It's just that sometimes I have other things I need to do on Sundays. Sometimes they ask me to work at the hospital on Sundays, and I always have to say I can't. My husband is very understanding about it, but sometimes I think he'd rather be doing other things with me and the kids than going to Millville every Sunday. Lately, he's had to work some on Sundays, too, so I've had to go by myself. You know, I'm a grown woman, and I think I should be able to decide sometimes what I do on my day off."

"How long have you been going up there on Sundays?" you ask.

"Oh, for 15 years, ever since I got married and moved out of the house, except while we lived in California. Then I called them every day since I couldn't see them," Caroline says.

"What do you think would happen if you called your parents one weekend and told them you had other plans and couldn't make it for Sunday dinner?" you ask.

"Oh, well, that would be totally unacceptable. They wouldn't understand that at all. They would be mad as all get out. I couldn't possibly do that; they'd never forgive me," Caroline says urgently.

"It sounds like it could be fairly stressful to always feel like you have to go visit your elderly parents every Sunday. And do you think that's the biggest stress in your life right now?" you inquire.

"Yes, I'm sure it is. It has caused a lot of problems for me and my family, and I don't know what to do about it," Caroline replies.

"Okay. Maybe that's something we can work on in conjunction with figuring out some of the fears you have. Would you be willing to come in again so we can work on these issues?" you ask.

"Yes, I really want to get control of my life. Everything lately has seemed out of control," Caroline tells you. "I just need to get my life back."

7.3–1 What impact(s) do you think Caroline's fears are having on her social support system? What other questions about the impact would you like to explore next session?

7.3–2 What strengths do you see in Caroline or her environment?

7.3–3 Would you recommend that Caroline see a doctor for medications? Why or why not?

7.3–4 What, if any, connection do you see between Caroline's relationship with her parents and her fears?

7.3–5 What is your preliminary diagnosis for Caroline?
Axis I

Axis II

Axis III

Axis IV

Axis V

Case 7.4

Identifying Information
Client Name: Celia Fernandez
Age: 30 years old
Ethnicity: Hispanic
Marital Status: Single
Occupation: Computer customer representative

Intake Information
Celia Fernandez, a 30-year-old Hispanic woman, contacted the Family Crisis Center on the referral of her physician and her employer, First Express Computers. She stated that she would like to see a counselor to discuss her job situation and something that happened while she was working. She didn't want to give any further details. An appointment was scheduled for her to see you the following week.

Initial Interview and Assessment
Celia appears to be a young, attractive woman with long brown hair and a slender build. She is dressed in a light blue suit and jumps up from her chair when you greet her in the waiting room. She appears to be somewhat anxious about the session, but also seems very willing and eager to talk with you. She tells you on the way to your office that she has been given time off from her job to come see you, but that she only has an hour before she has to be back at work.

You ask her if she'd like something to drink, and she accepts a glass of water. "What brings you to the Family Crisis Center?" you begin.

Celia hesitates for a moment and then says, "My boss thinks it might be helpful if I come talk to you about some things that happened while I was attending a training session in Careyville for my job at the computer center. It was about 3 weeks ago."

You are familiar with Careyville, a large city approximately an hour north of town. Celia sounds anxious about what she is about to disclose, and you decide to slow her down a little so she doesn't tell you too much, too fast.

"So, you work for the computer center. What is your position there?" you ask.

"Right now, I am a customer representative. I've been there for 2 years, since I finished my associate degree in business from the community college. I have been working on the help line, which is a pretty stressful job, but I went to the main office in Careyville to get trained so I could become a software specialist."

"So, the computer center sent you for the training? Is that correct?" you inquire.

"Yes, it was a 4-week training. I was staying in Careyville during the week and coming home on the weekends," Celia tells you. "I live with my parents in Oakdale just north of town."

"Okay, and you're single. Is that right?" you say to Celia.

"Yes, I was dating someone, but I broke up with him about 2 or 3 weeks ago," Celia says with a dismal look on her face.

"Did something happen while you were in Careyville for the training?" you surmise.

"Well, yes, that's what I thought I'd better talk to someone about. You see, the company put me at this motel that was close to downtown so I could walk to the training every day. It wasn't a very nice motel, and it wasn't in a good part of town. It's especially dangerous at night. Anyway, I had been there the week before and gone home for the weekend. Then I came back for the second week of training. On Tuesday, I had been in a training session from 8 A.M. until 6 P.M., and by the time I got back to the motel it was around 7 P.M. I was really tired and decided I'd just call out for pizza since I didn't feel like going out to eat. The motel didn't have a restaurant or anything—just a front desk. So I called the pizza delivery place, and they said it would be about half an hour. Well, I took a shower and put on comfortable clothes, and there was a knock on the door. Since I was expecting the pizza delivery person, I just opened the door, and this guy just pushed his way into my room and slammed the door shut. I was absolutely terrified. He grabbed me and forced me onto the bed and told me he had a gun. I've never felt so scared in my entire life."

Celia stares out the window. Her eyes are full of tears. She has been talking in a steady voice and doesn't appear to be in distress. In fact, she appears to be lacking the affect that you would normally expect to see in someone describing a terrifying event such as this one.

"Take your time, Celia," you say in a comforting voice. "If it gets too uncomfortable for you, you can stop anytime."

"I'm okay," Celia replies. "He told me to take off my clothes. When I hesitated, he grabbed my shirt and ripped it down the front. I didn't want to make him angry, so I took off my blouse and my skirt. He lay down on top of me and jerked my underwear down, and he raped me—first with his hand, and then he took off his pants and forced me to have intercourse with him. I was afraid he was going to kill me."

"That must have been a terrifying experience for you," you say gently.

"It was horrible, the worst day of my life," Celia says evenly. "I guess I've just been telling myself I'm lucky to be alive. The phone rang."

"The phone rang?" you say.

"Yes, the phone rang, and the guy asked me who was calling me," Celia said. "I told him it was my husband. He got the idea that I lived there and my husband must be in another room at the motel. I told him he would be coming to the room to get me for dinner if I didn't answer the phone. Then there was a knock on the door, and it must have been the pizza delivery person. He put his hand over my mouth so I wouldn't scream. For some reason, that scared him, and he grabbed me and threw me in the bathroom and closed the door. A minute or two later, I heard the outer door slam shut."

"So, he left you in the room alone?" you ask.

"Yes, I waited a few more minutes—it felt like an eternity—and then I opened the bathroom door and he was gone," Celia tells you.

"Then what did you do?" you ask.

"I had seen these two girls who looked like they were in town on business, and they had the two rooms next to mine. I didn't trust the guy at the front desk, so I called the girl in the room next to me and was screaming that I had just been raped and needed help. She came flying out of her room and got her friend who started running down the street looking for the guy. They called the police and an ambulance, and I was rushed to the hospital."

7.4–1   What diagnoses are you considering? How do you hope to direct the interview from this point?

Celia continues to remain very calm while she describes the events of that night. She blinks back her tears and says, "You know the thing that's bothering me the most right now is that I have these times throughout the day when I don't feel real. It's the worst feeling."

"What exactly do you mean when you say you 'don't feel real?'" you ask.

"Well, it's like I'm observing myself from a distance. I'm watching myself like a third, disinterested party. It's hard to describe, but it's a very unreal feeling. Sometimes, I feel like I'm real but nothing else is. Like everything in my surroundings is unreal, like in a dream or something."

"That sounds pretty disturbing. Does it happen when you're thinking about your experience in Careyville?" you ask.

"There doesn't seem to be any rhyme or reason as to when it happens," Celia says calmly. "It just happens periodically throughout the day. I can be talking to a customer on the phone and suddenly feel like this conversation isn't really happening. Like I'm watching myself and I look like a cartoon character rather than a real person. It's like I'm not really in the picture or I'm watching my body go through the motions, but my real self isn't there at all."

"Let me see if I understand. Sometimes you feel like you're watching yourself from a distance, and at other times, you feel like things outside yourself aren't real. Is that right, so far?" you ask.

"Yes, and I guess I just feel numb, almost like I'm made of rubber rather than flesh and blood a lot of the time these days," Celia states.

You notice that Celia doesn't look upset or anxious when telling you about these horrible events. In fact, she appears to be almost in a state of shock. "Can you tell me how you've been feeling since this terrifying incident took place?" you ask.

"Well, I've had to go back to Careyville on two occasions to talk to the investigators. The first time was before they had a suspect, and the second time I had to pick a man out of a lineup at the police station and give a positive identification," Celia tells you with little expression in her voice.

"How did that make you feel to have to do that?" you ask.

"A little nervous, I guess, but I knew he couldn't see me, so it wasn't too bad," Celia replies. "I just want to forget about all of this and get on with my life."

"How have you been feeling since you've been back to work?" you ask.

"I've been okay except for that feeling like nothing is real or I'm not real. That bothers me a lot. I feel like I'm going 'crazy' or something. Sometimes, I have to lock up the store at night, and that makes me nervous. I told my boss I don't want to be the only one left alone if I've got to lock up. It reminds me of being alone at the motel, and I start to 'relive' that night."

"How have you been sleeping since this incident occurred?" you ask.

"The first few nights after I came back from Careyville, I had a hard time getting to sleep, but after a week or so, it was better. But I'm still not able to sleep through the night without waking up with weird dreams that really scare me," Celia says. She slowly uncrosses her legs as though it requires a great deal of effort.

"Are there any other things that have become hard for you?" you ask.

"I did have some problems with my boyfriend touching me. I just didn't want anyone to touch me because it made me feel 'unreal,' and I don't think he could understand that at all. This whole thing just threw him for a loop, and I told him I didn't think we should see each other for a while. It was just too much for me to handle."

"Have you been feeling depressed or anxious about things?" you ask.

"I've been concerned about my job. My boss has been extremely nice to me since this incident happened, and I think it's because the company is worried that I'll sue them since it happened while I was working. It wasn't a good motel, and it was not in a good part of town, and they should have put me in a safer environment. I don't want to jeopardize my job, though, and the other women who work there are talking behind my back and making me real uncomfortable."

"What are they saying about you. Do you know?" you ask.

"Well, a friend of mine said she overheard a group of them talking about what happened to me and that I was getting special treatment now," Celia says glumly. "I'm hoping I'll get transferred to another department soon, though, and get away from them."

"What about your family?" you ask. "How have they reacted to you?"

"My parents have been very supportive, but they think I should just put it behind me. I think they've tried to make me feel safe at home. They won't leave me there alone at night. That's probably good right now. I'd probably get nervous at night if I were by myself."

"Do you think about it a lot?" you ask.

"I try not to think about it at all. I try to get my mind on other things. I haven't been out much with my friends since this happened, and I probably need to start doing things with them pretty soon. I've just felt so weird and unreal that I haven't wanted to do much of anything," Celia says.

"Okay, so let me see if I can summarize what you've been telling me today. A man who broke into your motel room raped you while you were working in Careyville a little less than a month ago. Since then, you've been having feelings of observing yourself from a distance or feeling like everything is kind of unreal. Sometimes, you feel somewhat nervous about being alone either at work or at home, and you're not real sure about going out yet because of some of these 'unreal' feelings you've been experiencing. Is that correct so far?"

"Yes, exactly," Celia says.

"You've also been feeling kind of numb, like rubber almost. Is that correct?" you ask.

"Yes, like I'm not quite real," Celia says.

"But you haven't had any nightmares about the incident or felt real anxious or depressed? Is that right?" you ask.

"Yes, just numb, I guess," Celia responds.

"And you've been concerned about your job," you say.

"Yes, not that I think I'll lose my job, just what other people are thinking about me, I guess," Celia haltingly explains.

"Okay, and are there any other feelings you've had since the incident?" you ask one more time.

"No, that's about it," Celia says.

"Okay Celia, I'm really glad you felt you were able to come in and talk to me today. You are a very courageous person. It takes a lot of strength to deal with a traumatic event like the one you've been through. From what you've told me today, I think I can help you with those 'unreal' feelings you've been having. Those feelings don't mean you're 'crazy.' It's not unusual for someone who has been through such a terrifying experience to have feelings like you're having."

Celia sits back in her chair and looks relieved for the first time during the session. "I'm so glad you don't think I'm crazy," she says. "And I feel better just having talked to you about the whole thing."

"I think it might be helpful if we set up an appointment for 1 day a week so we can work on those feelings of unreality. Would that be okay with you?" you ask.

"Yes, I'd like to come talk, and my boss said he'd give me the time off to come here," Celia states.

"Okay, we'll set up an appointment and see how things are going next week," you respond.

7.4–2   What impact has the sexual assault had on Celia's social support systems?

7.4–3   Are there aspects of her environment that you would like to explore more at the next session? Are you thinking of any particular areas that might require intervention?

7.4–4   What is your preliminary diagnosis for Celia?
Axis I

Axis II

Axis III

Axis IV

Axis V

7.4–5   Are there additional diagnoses that you would "watch out for" in working with Celia?

Case 7.5

Identifying Information
Client Name: Mark Abbott
Age: 29 years old
Ethnicity: Caucasian
Marital Status: Single

Intake Information
Mark Abbott, a new surgical resident at the hospital where you work, telephoned you and stated that he has been having some difficulties with his job and would like to talk with a therapist. An appointment was scheduled for the following day for Mark to meet with you.

Initial Intake Session
Upon meeting Mark in the waiting area, you observe that he is a tall, attractive young man who appears to be nervous. He paces back and forth in front of a large window overlooking the hospital grounds. He shakes your hand but has difficulty making eye contact with you. He follows you to your office without making any conversation.

Mark seems anxious and uncomfortable seated in a chair next to your desk. You ask him if he'd like some water, which he accepts gratefully. He glances at the pictures on the walls as he taps his foot on the floor. After explaining what you do as a counselor, you ask Mark what he wanted to discuss with you.

Mark states that he is a first-year surgical resident at the hospital. He did well in medical school and in his internship in another, smaller hospital, but he is having difficulties with his new job as a surgical resident. He is beginning to wonder if he's chosen the wrong field.

"Why do you think surgery might not be the right field for you?" you ask.

"Well, it's been a difficult adjustment for me coming to this large metropolitan hospital. Maybe I'm just a small-town type of guy. I'm not used to having to perform for so many people," Mark tells you. You notice that Mark's voice is a bit shaky.

"What do you mean exactly that you have to perform?" you inquire.

"Well, unlike the small hospital where I did my internship, this is a huge hospital. The operating rooms have observation booths, and there are senior physicians and medical students up there all the time watching everything I do when I'm operating," Mark says anxiously.

"And it bothers you that they are watching you?" you ask.

"Well, yes, it makes me extremely nervous. In fact, it's making me so nervous my hands begin to shake, and there have been times when I didn't think I could stand up. I've got a microphone attached to my scrubs, and I'm supposed to be explaining what I'm doing. I can hear my voice shaking when I talk. It is so embarrassing, and I'm sure everyone can tell I'm nervous as a cat."

"How long has this nervousness been going on?" you ask.

Mark thinks for a moment and then says, "Well, if you want to know the truth, I've always hated performing in front of other people. I'm just not good at it. I never played sports in high school or college because I didn't like the idea of people watching me perform. I learned to play the violin when I was very young, and I hated having to play in recitals. I can remember throwing up before big recitals where I was being graded. I guess some people might have considered me a nerdy kind of guy. But it never really bothered me because I always made good grades and did well in school, so I never really worried about it much before. I just didn't put myself in situations where I'd have to perform."

"Okay, so you can remember getting nervous when you had to play the violin in front of people when you were young, and you avoided other situations where you might have to perform in front of others. So, it's been okay until recently. Is that correct?" you inquire.

"Yes, I've been okay until I came to this hospital a couple of months ago. I do okay with one-on-one situations. For example, if I'm talking to one other person, I'm not too nervous about it. But if I've got to get up in front of an audience, I worry about it for hours before doing it, and then I'm a mess when I'm trying to do something in front of a crowd. I know it's really ridiculous how I react, but I just can't seem to control it," Mark responds.

7.5–1   What diagnoses are you considering at this point? What aspects of Mark's situation are of most interest to you to explore?

"It's not that uncommon for people to feel uncomfortable when they are presenting to an audience," you suggest. "Let me ask you some questions about your experiences when you're in front of an audience. You said that you feel very shaky and your voice trembles a little. Do you have a hard time breathing?" you ask.

"No, but I do break out in a sweat," Mark responds.

"Does your heart feel like it's beating too fast?" you ask.

"No, not really, but I'm aware of the fact that I'm nervous," Mark responds.

"What about nausea? Have you ever felt like you're going to throw up?" you inquire.

"No, just overly anxious, I guess," Mark states.

"Have you ever felt panicky or like you're going to faint?" you ask.

"No, I just feel like I can't control the shakiness in my voice or my hands," Mark states. "And when I'm in the operating room, that's a big problem."

"I'm sure it could be," you suggest. "What about in other situations? For example, if you go to a party, do you feel the same kind of nervousness or anxiety?" you inquire.

"Well, honestly, I don't go to many parties. I don't really like parties much. Probably because they do make me anxious and uncomfortable. I don't mind going out with a small group of people, like if I have a date and another couple comes along. That's okay with me."

"Okay. Are there any other situations that you can think of that make you feel anxious?" you ask.

"Well, the only other one is when I have to do a case presentation in front of a big group of doctors. Grand rounds, for example. That makes me very nervous, too," Mark tells you.

"So, it sounds as if whenever you have to get up in front of an audience and either perform or speak that it can make you feel very anxious. Is that right?" you ask.

"Yes, exactly. I'm okay as long as I don't have to get up in front of an audience, but I can't avoid it at this hospital, so I need some help getting this anxiety under control," Mark says.

"Mark, I think this anxiety you're experiencing is something that can be resolved. Would you be willing to come for several sessions so we can work on it?" you ask.

"Sure, I'll do anything to get rid of this problem," Mark says with relief.

You schedule another appointment, and Mark appears much more relaxed when he leaves your office.

7.5–2 Clearly, Mark's focus is on how his fears might influence his career. What impact do you think Mark's fears have had on his social functioning?

7.5–3 What do you see as Mark's primary strengths? Do you think he sees these as strengths?

7.5–4 Would you explore why Mark chose a big hospital for his residency even though he knew he had these performance fears?

7.5–5 What is your preliminary diagnosis for Mark?
Axis I

Axis II

Axis III

Axis IV

Axis V

Case 7.6

Identifying Information
Client Name: Nicole Gibson
Age: 25 years old
Ethnicity: African American
Marital Status: Single mother
Children: 2 children, ages 5 and 6

Background Information

Nicole Gibson is a 25-year-old single mother who has two children, a boy and a girl, ages 5 and 6, respectively. Nicole works for a non-profit organization supported by AmeriCorp that offers self-improvement programs for at-risk youth. Green House is an organization designed to teach young people home-building skills while they earn minimum-wage salary and an annual stipend of $4,000 to pay for college tuition and books. Additionally, the program provides paid time off to pursue a GED or high school diploma along with individual or group counseling opportunities several times a week. Nicole also participates in a program that allows her to live independently in a low-income housing unit while attending school and working.

Nicole is raising her two children on a salary of $800 per month and an infrequent child-support check of $200 per month. She has no telephone or car and must travel by public transportation to work and the day-care center. Traveling from her apartment to work, including dropping her children at the day-care center, requires her to take six buses each way every day. Nicole must get up at 4:30 A.M. in order to get her children to day care and herself to work by 8:30 A.M. She gets home at 7:30 at night, despite the fact that she finishes her work day at 4:30 in the afternoon.

As a case manager at the housing unit, you meet Nicole during a home visit. Nicole ex-presses a desire to obtain counseling to assist her with her life skills and family-of-origin issues that have made it difficult for her to function well at work. You agree to see her for counseling once a week for 2 hours. One hour will be used to assist Nicole with life skills such as parenting and home maintenance skills. The second hour will be utilized for counseling.

Progress Note from Your First Session with Nicole

As a child, Nicole lived in New Orleans with her parents and older sister, Marcia. Nicole's parents remained married until she was a teenager. Nicole's father sexually abused her from the time she was 8 years old through her mid-teens. He forced her to have sexual intercourse with him approximately three times a week. Several of her father's friends were allowed to sexually abuse her as well.

Nicole's mother was physically, verbally, and mentally abusive, often striking her, calling her names, reading her private journals out loud to other family members, and watching her in the bathroom. On one occasion, Nicole's mother struck her across the face with a belt buckle, leaving a permanent scar above her upper lip. On another occasion, Nicole's mother took a poem that Nicole had written and submitted it to a magazine under her own name. Her mother claimed a prize but never acknowledged the fact that it was Nicole's poem. Her older sister was also physically and verbally abusive to her.

Nicole left home when she was 18 years old and married the father of her two children. She referred to this as "getting married to escape hell," stressing the fact that although she couldn't stop the "torture" of her family situation, she could leave it behind by getting married. She stated that she left the marriage because her husband was a very "passive" person, and she didn't want to turn into someone like her mother.

Before her marriage, she fell in love with a man named Douglas with whom she now has an estranged relationship. Nicole and Douglas were never sexually involved even though they have been intimately involved on and off for about 8 years. Nicole stated that sex makes her feel "dirty, ashamed, and sick to her stomach." She hasn't spoken with or seen Douglas for about 6 months, as he will not return her calls.

Nicole has severed all ties with her family of origin since if she speaks with them she will only end up "feeling like dirt and getting real mad." Although Nicole is not involved at the present time in an intimate relationship, she does find support at her job with coworkers and has one close friend, Vickie, in whom she can confide.

Nicole has had difficulties at her job, however. She stated that she gets very upset when anyone gets "in her space." When the pressures at work become more than Nicole can handle,

she feels angry and panicky and "just wants to be left alone."

During the first session, Nicole stated that she didn't want to do anything but lie in bed. She stated that she often cries all weekend, becomes easily angered by her children, and often resorts to yelling and spanking them.

Nicole also stated that she was having difficulty doing chores (e.g., going to the Laundromat or grocery store, cooking, cleaning). There were piles of laundry in her bedroom and trash everywhere, including old food, which reeked. She stated she has had difficulty sleeping at night due to recurrent nightmares of "childhood stuff" and always feels "too tired." She avoids any situation that reminds her of "family stuff," but is afraid that she's turning out just like her mother.

Nicole possesses a great deal of intelligence and has the ability to seek out support and help when it is needed. She also has a very good sense of humor that she displayed throughout the interview.

7.6–1   What diagnoses are you considering at this time? What will be your primary area(s) of exploration at the next session?

Second Session with Nicole

Nicole begins the second session with you by describing a situation that occurred during the week at work. A male coworker asked her if she would like to go out for dinner after work one evening, and when Nicole declined the invitation, the coworker lightly touched her shoulder and said, "Oh, come on Nicole, you need a little fun in your life." Nicole states that she overreacted to this gesture by swinging at the man and striking him on his chest. She tells you she doesn't know what came over her, but she felt like she was warding off an attack of some

kind and couldn't tolerate having this man touch her.

When you ask her if this type of thing has happened on other occasions, she admits that she doesn't like to be touched by anyone. "It even bothers me sometimes if my own kids grab me when I'm not prepared for it."

Nicole states that she was so upset by this incident that she stayed home from work the next day because she was just "too tired" to get there on time. "My supervisor gets real mad when I'm late, even though I tell him I can't do anything about it if the bus isn't running on time. I just didn't want to deal with it the other day."

You ask her why she thinks she reacted so strongly to her coworker's touching her the other day. Nicole pauses for several moments and then sighs deeply. "I think it's related to all that 'childhood stuff' with my father. I just can't get it out of my head. I think it's going to haunt me for the rest of my life."

Nicole describes several depressive episodes to you in which she felt she just couldn't move because it took too much energy. During those times, she would forget to eat and would be unable to get to sleep until early in the morning. Her children would constantly ask her, "What's wrong, Mommy? Why can't you play with us?" Nicole states that her children's comments made her feel like a "terrible mother."

When you ask her about her goals for the future, Nicole states that she really doesn't have any goals, although she would like to go to college and become a teacher. She says she isn't sure she'll live long enough to complete an education.

7.6–2   What are some of Nicole's strengths?

7.6–3   Are you concerned about the potential for Nicole to commit suicide? If so, how would you assess the potential for danger in her situation?

7.6–4   What resources might be available to assist Nicole?

7.6–5   What would be your preliminary diagnosis for Nicole?
Axis I

Axis II

Axis III

Axis IV

Axis V

_____

DIFFERENTIAL DIAGNOSIS

Differential diagnosis can be challenging because there are a number of diagnoses that may have panic attacks as associated features. For example, panic attacks may occur among people diagnosed with various psychotic and mood disorders. In these instances, no anxiety disorder diagnosis will be made if there are not associated symptoms (e.g., worries, behavior changes, avoidance). If these symptoms are present, both disorders should be diagnosed, and the clinician must decide which is the principal one in that particular case.

Within anxiety disorders, it is critical to distinguish between unexpected, situationally bound, and situationally predisposed attacks. For example, although the diagnosis of Panic Disorder depends on a history of panic attacks, at least some of those prior attacks must be unexpected. It should be noted that some people with Panic Disorder have situationally bound or situationally predisposed panic attacks as well. In contrast, situationally bound panic attacks are common in both specific phobias and social phobias. In those instances, unexpected panic attacks would be extremely unusual. Similarly, situationally predisposed panic attacks would be most common in diagnoses like Generalized Anxiety Disorder or PTSD. Most important to differential diagnosis is a careful discussion of the focus and thought content associated with the panic attack.

7.DD–1   For Cases 7.5, Mark Abbott, and 7.6, Nicole Gibson, construct a brief narrative that you think would accurately reflect the circumstances under which each might experience a panic attack.

Self-medication triggered by panic attacks may lead to comorbid substance-related disorders. However, if anxiety symptoms occur only when a client is under the influence of a substance, the diagnosis would be Substance-Induced Anxiety Disorder. To make the differential diagnosis when substances are involved in anxiety disorders, the practitioner must take a careful history of both the anxiety symptoms and substance use.

7.DD–2   What are some questions you would ask Rachel Steffenbaum (Case 4.5) to determine whether she has or has had an anxiety disorder?

Finally, a common challenge in making diagnoses relates to the "rule-out" criteria included in nearly all of the disorders in this chapter. Specifically, clinicians are expected to ensure that the symptoms are *not* generated through the direct physiological effects of a substance (e.g., recreational drugs, prescription drugs, toxins, etc.) *or* through a general medical condition.

7.DD–3   In which of the cases in this chapter do you believe these "rule outs" have been adequately addressed?

7.DD–4   Pick one case in which the possibility of either a substance-induced or general medical condition cause has not been adequately addressed. List the questions, procedures, and/or referrals that would allow you to rule out these other possible diagnoses.

InfoTrac keywords

Anxiety, Obsessive-Compulsive Disorder, Panic Attack, Panic Disorder, PTSD

Somatoform and Factitious Disorders | 8

DISORDERS

Somatoform Disorders comprise disorders in which physical concerns are presented for which no medical basis can be found (e.g., a general medical condition, substance-induced, and/or another mental condition). These diagnoses infer that the physical symptoms are associated with psychological factors. As with all DSM-IV-TR (APA, 2000) diagnoses, the set of symptoms is associated with clinically significant distress and/or impairment in psychosocial functioning. In Somatoform Disorders, the production of symptoms is *not* under voluntary control (i.e., intentionally produced by the client).

The specific diagnoses within this section depend on the number and kinds of physical symptoms, as well on the cognitive process that may occur. Somatization Disorder is a chronic disorder that begins before the age of 30. The physical symptoms are varied over time and must include at least four pain symptoms, two stomach or intestinal symptoms, a sexual symptom, and a pseudoneurological symptom. Throughout this history, either no physical basis has been discovered or the complaints and/or resulting impairment exceed what would be expected based on the general medical condition or substance-related difficulty that is determined. In the first 6 months of this chronic disorder, the diagnosis of Undifferentiated Somatoform Disorder is appropriate (APA, 2000).

In Conversion Disorders, the symptoms or deficits are focused more narrowly on voluntary motor or sensory functions (e.g., impaired coordination, paralysis, blindness, deafness, seizures). Among people with this disorder, a preceding psychosocial conflict or stressor can be identified. Again, as with all Somatoform Disorders, the symptoms are *not* under voluntary control and do result in distress and/or impairment (APA, 2000).

Similarly, in Pain Disorder, the symptom presentation is narrowly focused on the occurrence of pain. A distinction is made between pain disorders in which general medical conditions are not present or play a minimal role in the onset and maintenance of pain and those in which both psychological factors and a general medical condition seem to be involved. In this second instance, the severity or continuation of pain is judged excessive for the specific situation (APA, 2000).

The diagnosis of Hypochondriasis is less focused on physical symptoms and more focused on fears regarding having a serious disease. Clients with this diagnosis are believed to misinterpret normal bodily signs and symptoms. This condition is chronic and leads to preoccupation with bodily functions and the associated worries. Somewhat similarly, in Body Dysmorphic Disorder, the preoccupation or fear is based on an imagined or slight physical anomaly (APA, 2000).

In contrast to the Somatoform Disorders, the Factitious Disorders are under voluntary control. In this group of disorders, differentiated by the type of symptoms produced, the client engages in conscious fabrication, falsification, exaggeration, and/or self-infliction of physical and/or psychological symptoms. The motivation for these behaviors is believed to be that the client wants to assume the sick role (i.e., to be cared for and/or to fool medical personnel). Any evidence that the symptoms are being produced for external gain (e.g., economic gain, avoiding legal problems) rules out these diagnoses (APA, 2000). Persons who do consciously produce symptoms for external gain are diagnosed with Malingering (a diagnosis in the DSM-IV-TR [APA, 2000] section on Other Conditions That May Be a Focus of Clinical Attention).

The diagnosis of Factitious Disorder by Proxy (or Munchausen by Proxy) has been popularized in the media in recent years. In this disorder, the deliberate production of medical or, much more rarely, psychological symptoms is targeted toward a third party who is under the client's care. In the DSM-IV-TR, this diagnosis is mentioned in Appendix B, which contains suggested diagnoses for which there was insufficient data to support their inclusion in the manual. For persons who seem to meet this profile, the appropriate diagnosis would be Factitious Disorder NOS (APA, 2000).

ASSESSMENT

In almost all of the diagnoses in the Somatoform and Factitious Disorders sections, in-depth medical screening is the primary form of assessment. The only consistent exception to this pattern would be in the instance of Factitious Disorder with Predominantly Psychological Signs and Symptoms. People with this diagnosis are feigning psychological disorders (rather than physical ones). Although the presentation of symptoms in these instances may be discernible because they do not correspond accurately with any known mental disorder, some clients are relatively sophisticated in their knowledge of the mental disorder they are producing.

For most Somatoform and Factitious Disorders, the MMPI-2, MMPI-A, and SCL-90-R (see details in chapter 1) are the most commonly utilized self-report instruments for both diagnosis and outcome studies with adults. For younger clients, the Children's Somatization Inventory (Walker, Garber, & Greene, 1991) is a 36-item inventory designed for children and adolescents. Coefficient alphas for the instrument have ranged between .88 and .92. The 35-item Parent Form of this instrument has shown reasonable concordance with the client self-report (Garber, van Slyke, & Walker, 1998).

Although not particularly useful in diagnosis, the West Haven–Yale Multidimensional Pain Inventory (Kerns, Turk, & Rudy, 1985), more recently referred to as simply the Multidimensional Pain Inventory (MPI), is used to measure chronic pain. More specifically, the MPI has subscales that address the impact of pain on the client's life, the responses of others to communication about the pain, and the extent to which the client participates in activities of daily living. The instrument has good psychometric properties and may be most useful in monitoring outcomes in Pain Disorder cases.

For Hypochondriasis, the most commonly utilized scale is the Illness Attitude Scale (IAS) (Kellner et al., 1985). This 28-item instrument has several subscales for measuring various aspects of attitudes, fears, and beliefs about illness. The IAS has demonstrated test-retest reliabilities of greater than .75 for periods as long as 4 weeks. It has also shown good known-groups validity and is sensitive to changes during treatment (Fischer & Corcoran, 1994).

CULTURAL CONSIDERATIONS

The type and frequency of specific physical symptoms are likely to be influenced by culture. Consequently, it should be remembered that the specific symptoms in the DSM-IV-TR (APA, 2000) were derived from studies conducted in the United States. Generally, the majority of persons diagnosed with these disorders are female, although there are instances of higher report rates for males of certain ethnic groups (e.g., Greek, Puerto Rican). The interesting exception to this pattern is with both Hypochondriasis and Body Dysmorphic Disorder, in which the prevalence data are inconsistent or suggest a fairly even distribution by gender. Also, persons diagnosed with Somatoform Disorders tend to be somewhat "unsophisticated" (e.g., rural, lower socioeconomic class, or relatively uneducated about medical and/or psychological problems).

Females are more commonly diagnosed with Factitious Disorders than are men. However, those men bearing this diagnosis tend to have a more severe symptom presentation and a more chronic course of the illness.

SOCIAL SUPPORT SYSTEMS

In both Somatoform and Factitious Disorders, initial presentation of symptoms is likely to generate concern and support from the client's social support system. Society generally makes allowances and renders support in the event of medical problems. Such positive responses may be somewhat less likely in the event of a Factitious Disorder with Predominantly Psychological Signs and Symptoms because of the stigma generally associated with mental illness.

Chronic presentations of either Somatoform or Factitious Disorders would likely result in severe impairment of psychosocial functioning. The unrelenting focus on illness without the relief of a diagnosis or some treatment success can simply exhaust friends, family, and caregivers. In chronic cases, occupational functioning will inevitably begin to suffer. In more extreme instances, the client may become an invalid who is socially isolated and emotionally and economically dependent.

Because of the deceptive nature of these disorders, there are no organized support or psychoeducational interventions known for these disorders. Consequently, the online resources that follow are primarily informational.

www.psyweb.com/Mdisord/somatd.html—Provides information on the diagnostic types and variety of treatments available for Somatoform Disorders

www.campus.houghton.edu/depts/psychology/abn7a/—An online lecture concerning Somatoform Disorders

www.athealth.com/Practitioner/newsletter/FPN_4_21.html—An online mental health newsletter devoted to mental health issues; this edition deals with Somatoform Disorders

www.gulflink.osd.mil/dsbrpt/ptsd.html—Looks at the comorbidity of PTSD and Somatoform Disorders

www.medscape.com—Contains the latest updates on a variety of psychiatric illnesses as well as free, downloadable publications in Medline; free registration

www.shpm.com/articles/chronic/factit.html—Overview of Factitious Disorder and Munchausen by Proxy Disorder, including case vignettes and treatment considerations

www.priory.com/psych/factitious.htm—Case reports and treatment considerations for Factitious Disorders

Case 8.1

Identifying Information
Client Name: Lisa Jennings
Age: 35 years old
Ethnicity: Caucasian
Occupation: Receptionist at husband's automobile dealership
Children: Husband has two children by a prior marriage; no children living at home

Intake Information
Lisa Jennings called to make an appointment with a therapist at the Family Counseling Center upon referral from her plastic surgeon. She stated that he wanted her to talk to a counselor before making any decisions about having plastic surgery performed on her breast. She agreed to make an appointment although she feels it is a waste of time. She is determined to have plastic surgery due to the discomfort she is experiencing in regard to one of her breasts.

Initial Interview with Lisa
Lisa is a tall, attractive, slender young woman with long blond hair and blue eyes. She is seated quietly in the waiting room reading a magazine when you meet her. She appears to be very poised with an air of confidence about her. She is dressed in a black jacket, short skirt, and black heels with white stockings. Her appearance is striking.

She begins the session by stating that her plastic surgeon, Dr. Faulkner, said that he would not consider doing plastic surgery on her breast until she had consulted with a counselor. Although this suggestion infuriated her at the time, later Lisa agreed to make an appointment only because she knows she is not "crazy." She crosses and uncrosses her legs continually as she explains her situation to you in a somewhat angry tone of voice.

Three months earlier, Lisa made an appointment with a well-known plastic surgeon in town. She told him that she had detected a deformity of her left breast and wanted plastic surgery to repair the deformity. She further explained that she had recently noticed that one of her breasts was smaller than the other breast, and it appeared to be shrinking. She also had detected a blemish on her left breast that was unattractive, and she wanted it removed. After extensive examination, the plastic surgeon indicated to her that her breasts were the same size, and if the left breast was smaller, the amount was so small as to be insignificant. As for the blemish, he told her that the surgery to remove it would possibly leave a bigger scar than the blemish itself and it would not make both breasts look identical. He thought that her concerns were extreme and that she didn't require any treatment.

Lisa was disappointed by this information but decided to wait to see if her breast would continue to shrink. She began checking her breast in the mirror several times a day for any signs of shrinkage. She also examines her breast constantly at home. She tells you that she can't go to bed at night until she's spent up to an hour in front of the mirror in the bathroom checking her breast for further shrinkage.

You ask her why she thinks the possibility that her breast has shrunk a little is so distressing to her.

"Well, isn't it obvious? I will look lopsided. People will begin to notice I'm deformed, and it's so unattractive," she states.

"You know, sitting here with you right now, it's not obvious to me with your clothes on that there is any difference at all between your two breasts. Have other people made comments about it?" you inquire.

"Oh no, people would be too embarrassed to actually say anything to me, but I can tell they're staring at my breasts," Lisa asserts. "It's horrible. I just want to go hide somewhere and never go out again."

"Has your husband said anything to you about how your breasts look to him?" you inquire.

"Well, he knows how upset I am about this situation. He knows I spend hours and hours in front of the mirror because it bothers me so much. He told me that if I wanted to have plastic surgery that he would support me," Lisa says beseechingly.

"But does he notice the difference?" you ask.

"Well, no, he said he couldn't tell any difference and even if there was a difference, he didn't care. He said he'd love me no matter what I look like, but you know, men don't really mean that. What they mean is as long as you stay attractive, they'll love you," Lisa clarifies.

"Okay. So your husband isn't telling you you're ugly and you need to get this physical problem fixed. Is that right?" you ask.

"Yes, but at the same time, he wants me to go to the beach with him and wear this teeny-weeny bikini that shows the whole world just how lopsided I really am. I dread going to the beach these days. We have a trip scheduled in a few weeks, and I just don't know how I'm going to handle it," Lisa groans.

It is apparent to you that Lisa is very unhappy and uncomfortable about her breasts and their appearance, whether the shrinkage is real or imagined. She seems very anxious discussing this problem with you and almost seems to be daring you to say she's "crazy," just like the plastic surgeon did. It is important not to alienate this client during the first session, so you decide to choose your words carefully when discussing this sensitive issue with her. You are also aware that you don't want to go too far or too fast with her because she could be considered an involuntary client. You feel that you might need some supervision before proceeding with this client.

"I can tell that this issue with your breasts causes you a lot of distress," you comment. "Has it interfered with your ability to work?"

"Yes, I think it does interfere with my job. You see, I'm at the front desk of the automobile dealership. It's my job to greet customers as well as do a lot of the paperwork when someone buys a car. It's not that it's such a problem that I can't perform my job. I'm actually a very efficient and organized person. It's just that I feel a need to constantly get up from my desk and go into the bathroom and check to see if my breast has shrunk. It takes time away from my desk, and I'm stressed out because I need to be at my desk most of the time, so I don't have a lot of time to check. I try to delay it and check only a few times a day, but by the end of the day, I'm totally exhausted."

"How often do you think you get up to go into the bathroom to check your breast?" you inquire.

"It depends on the day, but I'd say on average, about 10 or 15 times a day," Lisa says matter-of-factly. Lisa doesn't sound as if she thinks there's anything out of the ordinary about this behavior.

"Okay. And about how much time do you spend in the bathroom each time you check?" you ask.

"Probably about 10 minutes when I'm at work," Lisa responds.

"How about when you go home at night? How much time do you think you spend looking in the mirror at home?" you inquire.

"Probably about an hour and a half before dinner and a couple of hours before I go to bed," Lisa says as a matter of course. "Frankly, I don't know why it matters how much time I'm spending worrying about it. It's the most important thing in my life, and anyone in my shoes would spend a lot of time concerned about it."

You can tell Lisa is becoming more and more defensive about her situation. You decide not to go any further questioning her about this issue until you've talked to your supervisor and the plastic surgeon. You ask Lisa if she will give you permission to talk with her plastic surgeon about his recommendation not to perform surgery at the present time. Lisa agrees to let you call him and signs a permission form.

8.1–1   What are some of the possible diagnoses you are considering at this point?

8.1–2   Are there any psychosocial problems you suspect?

Case Conference with Supervisor

You decide to discuss this case with your clinical supervisor because you're not sure how to proceed. You explain the presenting problem to your supervisor and tell her that you decided not to try to force Lisa to divulge too much information all at once out of concern that she would refuse to return for another appointment. You have three major questions about this case for your supervisor: (1) How do you know whether Lisa's physical problems are real or imagined? (2) If the problem is real, is her anxiety over the problem extreme? (3) If the problem is imagined, how do you help Lisa understand that her problem isn't physical, given her adamant stance that it is a real physical problem?

Concerning your first question, your supervisor agrees with you that it would be appropriate to talk with the plastic surgeon about his findings. The results of his medical evaluation are likely to be accurate given his outstanding reputation in the community. This plastic surgeon is known for being careful not to do surgery for cosmetic purposes only.

Your supervisor tells you that whether or not Lisa's physical problem is real or imagined, it is real to her. Lisa is quite clear about her opinion. Your supervisor does agree that Lisa's anxiety about the problem seems out of proportion to what the problem might actually be. She asks you to think about why there might be so much anxiety surrounding this issue.

Finally, your supervisor suggests you obtain a more complete social history from Lisa. There may be underlying reasons for her anxiety that are not readily apparent to you from the presenting problem.

Discussion with Plastic Surgeon, Dr. Faulkner

The following day, you have a short conversation with Dr. Faulkner about Lisa. He tells you that she is a 35-year-old, very attractive female who came to him regarding plastic surgery on her left breast. He states that she told him her left breast was shrinking and no longer the same size as her right breast. He says that he carefully examined her breasts, measuring them carefully, and that he could find a difference of only a few micrometers between her two breasts. The difference was so small that it was absolutely insignificant.

She also complained of a blemish that she wanted removed that appeared to be the size of a pencil eraser on the underside of her left breast. He told her that the scar that would be left would be larger and more discernible than the small blemish visible at present. In his medical opinion, Lisa's problems are more psychological than physical. He realizes that she was angry when she left the office but says that no reputable plastic surgeon would do surgery for such a minute problem. In all likelihood, due to the psychological component, she would be unhappy with any surgery that was undertaken.

Second Interview with Lisa
With the information from your supervisor and the plastic surgeon in mind, you decide to attempt to get a more thorough social history from Lisa during her next visit. Although you weren't sure whether or not Lisa would come back for a second interview, she arrives early for her second interview with you.

Today Lisa is dressed in black form-fitting pants and a white cowboy jacket and boots, both with fringe on the sides. You notice what an attention-getting outfit it is.

"Wow, that's quite an outfit you have on," you begin.

Lisa smiles and says, "I've been making an advertisement this morning for my husband's business. This outfit should get their attention, don't you think?"

"Absolutely. You look outstanding," you reply. "How have things been going this week?"

"About the same," Lisa replies. "It hasn't changed much this week. I mean my breast, you know; it's shrunk a little but not too much."

"Okay. So you've noticed a slight difference but not a whole lot of change this week?" you inquire.

"Yes, that's right. Some weeks it changes a lot, and other weeks it doesn't," Lisa replies.

"Lisa, what I'd like to do today is to get some additional information from you about your family and the time in which you were growing up so that I can get to know you better and be able to help you in the best possible way. Is that all right with you?" you inquire.

Lisa sighs and looks doubtful but nods her head in agreement. "I'm not sure what this has to do with my current problem, but I'll tell you about my family if you need to know."

"Okay, good. Why don't you tell me a little bit about your family as you were growing up?" you suggest.

"Well, I was born in Middleville about 30 miles from here. I am the oldest daughter and then I have a brother who is 3 years younger than I am and a sister who is 5 years younger. My father has a hardware store in Middleville, and my mother was a counselor at the high school. I guess we were a pretty typical middle-class family. My mother died when I was 13 years old."

"Oh, that must have been very difficult for you," you comment.

"It was. Being the oldest, I felt very responsible for my father and taking care of him. I began taking care of the house and fixing meals and taking care of my little brother and sister. My father was extremely depressed for a long time after my mother died, so it wasn't a fun place to be—home, I mean."

"So, just as you're entering your teenage years, you lose your mother," you respond.

"Yes, and my teenage years weren't all that great. With all that responsibility, I also felt like I had to do well in school because my father wanted me to go to college and become a lawyer. He made it really clear that's what I needed to do. I did very well in school, but I tend to be very perfectionistic, and it would tear me up if I made a bad grade or didn't do well in a course. And I also felt like I'd be letting my father down. He isn't a very easy person to get close to. He never shows any emotion, and he can be pretty cold at times. He had very high expectations for all of us, and if we let him down, he would come down hard on us."

"In what way would he 'come down hard' on you?" you ask.

"He'd usually punish us by spanking us with his belt and grounding us to our rooms," Lisa continues. "I used to be so scared that he'd come home and I wouldn't have dinner made or the house would be a mess or something that would make him really angry. I tried as hard as I could, but sometimes, I just couldn't live up to his demands. I think he got angrier after my mother died, too. No matter what I did, it was never enough. So, I really don't have many fond memories of high school." Lisa looks despairingly out the window.

"Were there any other relatives living in Middleville that you could talk to?" you ask.

"I had an aunt and uncle and cousins that lived in town, but they were all a lot older than we were, and I didn't see much of them. And then there were these other people we called aunt and uncle, but they weren't really, and I hated them."

"You mean, they weren't really related to you?" you inquire.

"Right, they were my parents' friends, but they weren't related to us. They moved to California a few years ago, thank God, so I don't have to deal with them anymore," Lisa says angrily.

"Why did you dislike them so much?" you inquire.

"Well, my 'uncle,' who wasn't really my uncle, molested me one day when I was home alone after school," Lisa says coldly.

"Oh, that's horrible. What happened?" you inquire.

"Well, he came to the house one afternoon, and I was the only one home. I was sitting in the living room watching television, and he came in and sat down beside me. I didn't really think anything of it since he was always over at the house. After a while, he put his arm around me and told me how sorry he was that my mother had died, but that he'd take care of me and I had nothing to worry about. Then, he put his hand in my shirt and began rubbing my breast. I was only 13 years old, and I didn't know what to do. I think I was afraid to do anything. I just sat there, like an idiot, and let him do it to me. I was really afraid to move. Then he moved his hand under my skirt and began rubbing me there. I just remember feeling so angry and upset afterward. I didn't ever want to see him again. I've never been so glad that anyone moved far away, but I still hate him for what he did to me," Lisa says between clenched teeth. "I will always hate him."

"That must have been terrifying for you when you were only 13 years old," you suggest. "Was there anyone you could talk to about what happened?"

"Actually, the only person I've ever told is my husband. At the time, there was no one. I was afraid my father would find out and punish me for letting him in the house. I felt like it was my fault that it happened. And I was sure my father would think it was my fault. So, I never mentioned it to anyone. I just tried to push it out of my mind. I didn't know what else to do," Lisa says.

You are concerned that Lisa will feel that she's told you too much, too fast. So, rather than making the connection between her adolescent experience of being molested and her current issue with her breast, you decide to talk about her present feelings.

"How do you feel about telling me about what happened?" you inquire.

"Actually, it's kind of a relief," Lisa says. "I didn't think I wanted to tell anyone. It was a long time ago, and I didn't think there was any need to talk about it anymore. But, it just came bubbling out of me, didn't it? I'm still feeling very angry about it, and I'll always hate him for what he did to me."

"You know sometimes when people have been through traumatic experiences in their lives and never gotten a chance to resolve those issues, the experiences can interfere with their present lives even if it's not readily apparent. I was wondering if you might be interested in working on these issues so that you can really put them behind you?"

"You mean, come in here and talk to you?" Lisa asks. She doesn't seem completely committed to counseling yet.

"I mean, maybe you'd like to come in for six sessions. At the end of six sessions, we'll see where you are and evaluate whether or not it's been helpful to you. Does that make sense to you?" you inquire.

"Well, okay, six sessions would be all right. Do you really think you can help me?" Lisa wonders out loud.

"I think there is definitely a chance it could help. You have some very good coping skills, and you've clearly come a long way since you were a teenager. I think it could be very beneficial to you," you suggest.

"Okay. I'm willing to try it," Lisa tells you. "I guess it couldn't hurt."

8.1–3   What do you see as Lisa's strengths?

8.1–4   What would be your diagnosis for Lisa at this time?
Axis I

Axis II

Axis III

Axis IV

Axis V

8.1–5   Are there any other diagnoses that you would still want to rule out with Lisa? Explain your answer.

_____

Case 8.2

Identifying Information
Client Name: Sheila Hanson
Age: 32 years old
Ethnicity: Caucasian
Marital Status: Married
Children: Four children, ages 1, 3, 5, and 7

Intake Information
Sheila Hanson came to the Mindspring Center for Health and Mental Health upon a referral from her primary care physician. She asked to see a therapist, and the receptionist explained that she would need to talk to the intake worker, who would then schedule an appointment for her. She told the intake worker that she had been having severe headaches on a daily basis and other physical problems. Her doctor told her he wanted her to get an "evaluation." She said she thought her doctor believed her symptoms "are all in my head," but she knows she's in pain. In order to comply with his orders, she agreed to see a therapist. The intake worker scheduled an initial interview and assessment for her for the following week. Sheila Hanson signed a consent form allowing you to talk with her primary care physician.

Telephone Consultation with Physician
In order to obtain information about Sheila Hanson's medical problems, you obtain a release of information and call her physician, Dr. Randolph. He tells you that he has seen Sheila on numerous occasions over the past 12 months for complaints of severe headaches, gastrointestinal distress, and menstrual problems. Laboratory tests each time revealed no physical or medical reason for the pain she has been experiencing. He prescribed pain medication that appeared to alleviate the symptoms initially, but she came back a few weeks later complaining that the medicine was no longer effective. He is concerned about prescribing stronger medications without a psychological evaluation. He states that previous medical history revealed that Sheila had been treated by a gynecologist for endometriosis after her third child was born.

8.2–1   What diagnoses are you considering based on the background information on Sheila?

Initial Interview with Sheila
Sheila begins the session by stating that she doesn't know why her doctor feels this interview is necessary. "I've been having medical problems for the past year that have not been alleviated by medication. I have so much pain that, at times, I can't care for my four young children. My husband is so alarmed that he hired a full-time housekeeper so that the children would be supervised when I'm unable to get out of bed." Sheila appears distressed about her experience and says she just wants to feel better soon.

"I've always been a very active person. I was on the swim team in high school and the track team in college. When I got married, my husband and I got road bikes and joined a biking club. We would bike 40 or 50 miles on the weekends. I'm not used to being disabled like I am these days. These aren't just ordinary aches and pains like I had when I worked out. These problems have caused me to be unable to do anything. Sometimes I can't even go to the grocery store I feel so bad. And, you know, I've got four children that I have to take care of. I can't just stop."

"When did these physical problems begin?" you ask.

"It was about 12 months ago, right after the birth of my fourth child," Sheila says with a sigh. "A few weeks after Carrie was born, I began having severe headaches. The doctor said they were tension headaches, not migraines, but they're so painful I have to lie down somewhere quiet and wait for the pain to go away."

"And you've continued to have these headaches for a year?" you ask.

"Well, the headaches haven't been as bad with the medicine I've been taking, but I have had several other problems besides the headaches," Sheila states. "In the last year, I've had severe pain in my lower back that I thought might be a ruptured disk, but nothing showed up on the X rays. Then, I had some serious stomach problems, and the doctor said that even though it wasn't showing up on the X rays, it might be an ulcer, so I started taking ulcer medication. I've also had shooting pains down both my legs that come and go. I never know whether I'll be okay or not. It's just been miserable."

You wonder why the physician with whom you spoke didn't mention all these problems. "And have you been seeing the same doctor for all these problems?" you ask Sheila.

"Oh, no," Sheila says. "I've been to several different doctors. I went to a chiropractor for the pain in my back and legs, and I saw a gastroenterologist for the problems I've had with my stomach. The chiropractor has been doing adjustments and said I was out of alignment. And I was having so much trouble with my stomach that I thought I'd better see a specialist."

"What kind of trouble have you been having with your stomach?" you ask.

"Well, it started with just severe pain, but it got worse and I began to feel very nauseated and couldn't eat certain foods or I'd get very bloated." Sheila rubbed her forehead and looked very disconcerted. "I just don't know what's wrong. I feel like I've just been constantly sick for a year."

"It sounds as if you've been through a lot in the last year. Let me see if I understand everything you've told me so far. You've had severe headaches and back pain. Sometimes, you have shooting pain that goes down your legs. You've also had pain in your stomach that includes a bloated feeling and nausea. Is that correct, so far?" you ask.

"Yes, but the bloating and nausea sometimes happen without the severe pain in my abdominal area. It doesn't happen all at the same time, but it can. Do you see what I mean?" Sheila asks. "I've also been so sick to my stomach through all my pregnancies. For 6 of the 9 months, I couldn't even go into a room that smelled like certain foods or I'd throw up. I haven't had one easy pregnancy. I thought I'd die having this fourth baby. I told my husband this was the last baby I was going to have. He has always wanted a big family, and I told him four children are enough."

"Yes, I understand what you're saying. Have there been any other physical problems you've experienced in the past year?" you ask.

"Not in the past year," Sheila states, "but about 6 years ago, after Mikey, the oldest, was born, I was having problems getting my menstrual period regulated, and the doctor said I had endometriosis. I had a D & C, and it seemed to take care of the problem," Sheila states.

"Okay, have there been any other physical problems you've experienced?" you ask.

"Well, the only other problem I've had that I haven't even talked to my doctor about is this numbness in my hands. I get this tingling sensation in my hands like the feeling when you've been sitting on your leg and it goes to sleep. It seems to happen for no reason at all. My hands just go numb. It's very uncomfortable and makes it difficult to pick anything up or hold anything." Sheila looks very anxious and taps her foot constantly while describing these symptoms. She looks around your office and asks you how long it took you to get a counseling degree. You explain to her that you went to graduate school after obtaining an undergraduate degree and that it takes 2 or 3 years of additional education depending on the program.

Sheila leans back in her chair and looks wistfully out the window. "I always wanted to go to graduate school. I have a degree in biology and was premed in college. I thought I would become a doctor. Of course, those plans changed dramatically when I got married. My husband just wanted me to stay home and have children. He's old-fashioned and comes from a very traditional family. The woman stays home and cares for the children while the man goes to work. So, I spend all my time running after kids and changing diapers while my husband spends two or three nights a week out of town on business trips staying in nice, luxurious hotels and going out for expensive dinners. Not that I'm really complaining. He makes a very good living, and we have a nice lifestyle."

"But it sounds like taking care of four children can be pretty stressful and draining at times," you respond.

Sheila nods her head and sits up in her chair. "I just never get a minute for myself. My day starts at 5:30 A.M., and I don't stop until midnight. And that's a good day. Sometimes, I'm up in the middle of the night when one of the children wakes up. I'm constantly trying to catch up. I'm always behind schedule. My husband thinks I have nothing to do all day and can't understand why might not be able to get to the cleaners or why I didn't call the plumber. He has no idea what my day is like. He comes home and dinner is on the table, and he thinks I've just had all day to do whatever I like. He doesn't realize what it takes to manage four children. Even with a housekeeper to help me, I'm on the go every minute of the day. I've given up everything I used to do. Sometimes, I wonder if I haven't given up myself."

"So, it sounds very stressful at times. Are there things you do when you begin feeling really stressed out?" you ask Sheila.

Sheila cocks her head sideways and appears to be thinking. "Well, like I said earlier, I've had so many physical problems in the last 6 years that I haven't been able to do a lot of things I used to do."

"Are there other mothers you know with whom you can talk or go out to lunch occasionally?" you inquire.

"I know some mothers who have children Mikey's age, but, you know, I've really been so incapacitated lately, I haven't really been able to do anything," Sheila tells you with a worried look on her face.

"So, your physical problems have really prevented you from doing many things that you used to do. Is that correct?" you ask.

"Yes, it's been difficult. Howard, my husband, hasn't been able to take as many trips, and I've needed help with the children, and I just feel like my whole life is falling apart. The worst part about it is that the doctors can't seem to figure out what is wrong, and that scares me to death." She bursts into tears and throws her head in her hands. "Why can't anyone understand I'm too sick to take care of everything right now?"

You suggest that perhaps if Sheila is willing to come talk to you, maybe you can uncover the underlying reasons for her physical problems. You explain to Sheila that sometimes physical problems can be caused by psychological mechanisms. It doesn't negate the fact that she is having real symptoms. They just may be caused by psychological rather than physical factors. Sheila states she had never thought about it from a psychological perspective. Although she has some misgivings, she agrees to come back and talk with you for six more sessions. After six sessions, you'll reevaluate her situation.

8.2–2   What would you consider Sheila's strengths?

8.2–3   Would you refer Sheila for any further medical screening? Why or why not?

8.2–4   What would be your diagnosis for Sheila at this point?
Axis I

Axis II

Axis III

Axis IV

Axis V

8.2–5   Are there additional diagnoses you would want to rule out over time?

InfoTrac keywords

Body Dysmorphic Disorder, Factitious Disorder, Hypochondriasis, somatization

9 | **Disorders of Dissociation**

DISORDERS

As a psychiatric term, *dissociation* refers to instances in which the normally integrated aspects of cognitive functioning (e.g., consciousness, memory, identity, perception) are disrupted. More concretely, some aspects of an individual's thoughts, feelings, or behaviors are not under his or her conscious awareness and/or control. It should be noted that dissociative symptoms might be present in a number of other DSM-IV-TR (APA, 2000) diagnoses, particularly in Acute or Posttraumatic Stress Disorders.

In the first diagnosis in this section, Dissociative Amnesia, the client has one or more episodes in which he or she cannot remember important personal information. The material forgotten is too extensive to be attributed to normal forgetfulness. In most instances, the forgotten material is of a traumatic or stressful nature. For a diagnosis to be made, the symptoms must be associated with distress or psychosocial impairment. Further, any of the remaining dissociative disorders have precedence if those symptom profiles are met (APA, 2000).

In Dissociative Fugue, the client is also unable to recall some or all of his or her personal history. In this disorder, sudden and unexpected travel that removes the person from his or her home and/or usual place of daily activities occurs. The client has some degree of confusion about his or her identity and may actually assume a new identity. For the diagnosis, the episode may not be part of Dissociative Identity Disorder (see following discussion) or be a result of substance use or some general medical condition. As can be easily imagined, clinically significant distress and/or psychosocial impairment is experienced as well (APA, 2000).

In Dissociative Identity Disorder, two or more distinct identities or personalities are present and recurrently take control of the individual's behavior. Further, there is an inability to recall personal information while the client is in at least one of the distinct identities. The situation, similar to that in other diagnostic categories, is not due to substance use or a general medical condition and results in distress and/or psychosocial impairment. This diagnosis was formerly labeled Multiple Personality Disorder (APA, 2000).

Usually, clients with this disorder have a primary identity that carries the individual's legal name. Each alternative identity frequently has a different name and can vary from the primary identity in terms of age, gender, knowledge, affect, and so forth. Each identity has an enduring pattern of viewing and relating to the environment and the self. The primary and alternative identities may or may not be aware of the existence or experiences of one another. Rather obviously, persons with this disorder may have frequent gaps in memory for both recent and remote events (APA, 2000).

The fourth diagnosis in this section, Depersonalization Disorder, is somewhat different from the others. The key symptom is depersonalization rather than dissociation. Depersonalization is characterized by feeling detached or estranged from one's self. This may be described as feeling outside the self, as if viewing one's self as a character in a movie. For this diagnosis, reality testing must remain intact during the episodes. Brief instances of depersonalization are not unusual or may be associated with another mental disorder. For this diagnosis, depersonalization is the major symptom and causes distress and/or psychosocial dysfunction (APA, 2000).

A final diagnosis of Dissociative Disorder NOS covers other instances in which dissociation is a major symptom but the full criteria for a more specific disorder are not met (APA, 2000).

ASSESSMENT

Diagnosing dissociative disorders can be quite challenging, at least partially due to possible memory problems related to the incident(s). For many clients, the first clue that a dissociative disorder is occurring is simply "holes" or unaccounted-for time periods. Careful history focused around times of stress can be particularly informative.

The MMPI-2, MMPI-A, and SCL-90-R (see details in chapter 1) can be utilized as self-report instruments for both diagnosis and outcome studies. The oldest of the more specific instruments addressing dissociation is the Dissociative Experiences Scale (DES) (Bernstein & Putman, 1986). This 28-item instrument has shown reasonable reliability with a test-retest reliability coefficient of .84 and split-half reliabilities ranging from .71 to .96. The instrument has yielded a predicted continuum of scores with steady progression from "normal" subjects to those with Dissociative Identity Disorder (Fischer & Corcoran, 1994).

A newer instrument, the Dissociation Questionnaire (DIS-Q) (Vanderlinden, Van Dyck, Vertommen, Vandereycken, & Verkes, 1993) is a 63-item instrument divided into four subscales: Identity Confusion/Fragmentation, Loss of Control, Amnesia, and Absorption. Cronbach's alphas range between .67 and .94 for the subscales, and 4-week test-retest reliabilities range between .75 and .93. This instrument may be more useful across the range of dissociative disorders.

For children, the Child Dissociative Checklist (CDC) (Putnam, Helmers, & Trickett, 1993) is one of the few available measures. The CDC has a 1-year test-retest reliability of .69 in a sample of normal and sexually abused girls. The instrument has also shown good discriminant validity with both boys and girls.

CULTURAL CONSIDERATIONS

Dissociative experiences, particularly fugue-like states, may occur within a number of cultural groups as an accepted expression of cultural activities or religious practices. In those instances, no clinical distress or psychosocial dysfunction occurs. Nonetheless, if the individual is distressed or suffers psychosocial impairments, a diagnosis is warranted.

Dissociative Identity Disorder is diagnosed much more frequently in women than in men. Further, men with this disorder tend to have fewer distinct identities. Some data suggest that the occurrence in children is more evenly distributed between the two sexes. It remains unclear what factors may be associated with the significant difference in diagnosis among adults.

Although not recognized as a diagnosable condition according to the DSM-IV TR, in some cultures, persons are perceived to be in a "spell." A "spell" is a trance-like state in which the individual may communicate with deceased relatives. This condition has been seen in African American and Southern U.S. cultures. During the experience, a person may appear to be in a dissociative state (APA, 2000).

In addition, some societies such as in Ethiopia, Egypt, Sudan, and certain Middle Eastern countries recognize a condition known as "zar." During "zar" episodes, persons appear to be in a dissociative state in which they may shout, cry, laugh, sing, or hit their heads against a wall. The belief is that these people are possessed by a spirit, and the state is not considered pathological (APA, 2000).

Scott (1999) suggests that some form of the dissociated self exists in most cultures and is associated with past histories of childhood trauma and pain. She suggests that in England and North America, "mediumship, channeling, speaking in tongues, possession and multiple personality" are all socially acknowledged labels for dissociation (p. 455). Other cultures that engage in shamanism and possession associate these practices with traumatic experiences. She suggests that, rather than asking "what's wrong with the person" who is experiencing dissociation, we should be asking what underlying causes (i.e., childhood trauma, pain, ritualized physical and sexual abuse) have made it so difficult for the person to experience the self in an integrated manner.

SOCIAL SUPPORT SYSTEMS

Dissociative Disorders can obviously be quite disruptive to one's interpersonal and/or occupational functioning. Unexplained absences and/or personality fluctuation can certainly strain relationships and employers' patience. Depersonalization Disorder may be the least disruptive of these diagnoses but also carries the potential to impact one's functioning for at least short periods of time. In those instances, the potential impact is probably a function of when depersonalization occurs.

Because of the relative rarity of these disorders, fewer resources in terms of groups and/or self-help–oriented supports are available. There are some primarily informational Internet resources available.

www.nami.org/helpline/dissoc.htm—Fact sheet published by National Alliance for the Mentally Ill concerning dissociative disorders

www.voiceofwomen.com/VOW2_11950/centerarticle.html—Discussion of diagnosis and treatment of dissociative disorders

www.rossinst.com/dddquest.htm—A somewhat broadly focused discussion of assessing and diagnosing trauma-related disorders

Case 9.1

Identifying Information
Client Name: Lucy Johnson
Age: 19 years old
Ethnicity: Caucasian
Educational Level: College student

Intake Information
Lucy Johnson called the Family Counseling Center, which is located in a small Virginia town, from her college dorm in Washington, D.C., where she is attending college. She told the intake worker that she received counseling from you approximately 4 years ago when you were a counselor in the school system (see chapter 6). She stated that she was coming home for semester break and wanted to make an appointment with you. She told the intake worker, "She is the reason I'm in college now rather than married with two kids, and I really need to talk with her again." The intake worker made an appointment for her to see you on a Friday afternoon as soon as she gets home.

Initial Interview
You greet Lucy in the waiting room, and she appears to have grown into a very attractive adult since the last time you saw her, when she was 15 years old. On the other hand, she looks very tired, and there are tears in her eyes when she sees you. She quickly gets up to go with you to your office.

You ask Lucy how she's been doing and comment on the fact that she is attending a university that has a reputation for being very academically rigorous. She tells you that she received three different scholarships from the Junior League, the Civitan Club, and the university and that her board and tuition have been covered for all 4 years.

"I'm really impressed, Lucy. You have really come a long way since the last time we talked," you suggest.

With great sadness in her voice and tears in her eyes, Lucy says, "I suppose so. I've been doing okay until the last few weeks. That's why I needed to talk with you."

"Lucy, you look really sad. What's been happening recently?" you inquire searchingly.

"Well, I've just been having a very hard time concentrating lately in school. It's gotten so bad, I haven't been able to get any of my assignments turned in on time, and I'm afraid I'm going to get put on academic probation this semester," Lucy tells you.

"Has something been distracting you from school?" you ask.

"I don't know; I don't think so, but I feel like I'm trying to juggle a lot of things right now," Lucy responds.

"Tell me what you've been doing," you urge.

"Well, in addition to the five courses I'm taking, I'm also working part-time as a lifeguard on the weekends at the YWCA, and then at night I'm a waitress for this little restaurant in Georgetown," Lucy states.

"Wow, those are a lot of different jobs to juggle," you suggest.

"I know, but I have to work or I won't have any money for expenses," Lucy tells you. "Even though my room and tuition are covered by the scholarships, I don't have any money for other expenses. And I'm barely making enough to cover it all with the two jobs."

"Okay, so how have you been feeling?" you ask.

"Well, sometimes I feel like I'm going crazy," Lucy replies.

"Going crazy?" you respond. "What feelings are associated with those thoughts?"

"It's sort of hard to describe," Lucy begins. "I get this feeling like I'm not really in my body."

"Can you tell me a little more about that feeling?" you ask.

"Well, sometimes I feel like I'm watching myself from outside my body. I told you it would sound crazy, but that's the way it feels. I feel like I'm floating outside my body, and sometimes I feel like I'm moving around in a dream rather than real life," Lucy suggests.

"Okay. When you're feeling this way, Lucy, are you aware of the fact that you aren't really in a dream, or do you have a hard time telling whether or not you are in a dream?" you ask.

"Oh, no. It's just a feeling. I know I'm not really in a dream, but it still feels very weird. Like I'm detached from the real world and nothing seems real to me. Sometimes, I feel like everyone I'm around is a cartoon character," she explains.

"Okay. I think I understand what you're talking about. Do these feelings stay with you, or do they come and go?" you inquire.

"Oh, they come and go. Sometimes I'm fine, but even when I'm not having those 'unreal' feelings, I'm feeling very dulled, like a light bulb that's about to go out. I don't exactly feel happy or sad about anything. It's like all my feelings about anything are blocked off by something. It's hard to explain," Lucy tells you.

"Even when you're not having those feelings like you're observing yourself from outside your body, you feel that your feelings are blunted or dulled. Is that correct?" you inquire.

"Yes, exactly," Lucy says.

"Has there been anything that's happened recently that you think might be related to these feelings?" you ask.

Lucy ponders this question for a few moments and then replies, "You know, I think I've had feelings like this periodically for a long time. It seems to happen when I get stressed out about something. I can't really put my finger on any one thing, but I remember one time when I felt this way and I just went to bed for about a week and slept more hours than I was awake. I think it just felt so weird I wanted to get away from it, so I slept."

"How old were you when that happened, Lucy?" you ask.

"I was probably about 13 years old," Lucy states. "It was around the time that my father left, and my mother was upset all the time."

"Okay, and it's happened several times since that time?" you ask.

"Yes, maybe four or five times since then. It seems to go away after a while, but it always makes it hard for me to get anything accomplished. Now that I'm in college, I can't afford to lose a lot of time or I'll flunk out of school. It's felt so hard lately, I've thought about just dropping out of school for a while," Lucy says with her head lowered. She runs her hands through her hair and looks very unhappy.

"Lucy, would you say you've been feeling down or depressed lately?" you ask.

"No, not really, not like I was when I saw you before. Just overwhelmed with school and jobs. You know my family isn't very supportive of me going off to school. My mother asked me if I thought I was too good for them. That really hurt me." Lucy looks very dismayed.

"When did she say that to you, Lucy?" you ask.

"Last summer when I came home for a couple of weeks before school started. I took some classes last summer in school and stayed in Washington. I think my mother was hurt that I didn't come home for the whole summer."

"Okay, so you haven't gotten a whole lot of support from your family for your effort to finish college. Is that right?" you ask tentatively.

"I feel like I'm completely on my own," Lucy says. "Sometimes, it feels like too much to handle."

"Have you talked to anyone at school?" you inquire. "For example, have you gone to the student counseling center?"

"No, but maybe it would help, huh?" Lucy responds.

"It might be a good idea to have someone to talk to as you're trying to juggle all this work," you suggest.

"That might be a good idea," Lucy admits. "Can I come back and see you again before I go back to school?"

"Yes, I want to see you again in a few days and see how things are going," you suggest. "In the meantime, if it's okay with you, I will contact the student counseling center and tell them I'm referring you to them. I will need you to sign a consent form in order to talk to them. Would that be all right with you?"

"Yes, I am already beginning to feel more centered," Lucy says with a deep sigh. "I knew you would understand what I was talking about."

"Okay, let's go set up another appointment for you." You and Lucy walk out to the receptionist's desk and make an appointment for the following week.

9.1–1   What are some of Lucy's strengths?

9.1–2   Do you think Lucy's present difficulties are related to her prior history (see Case 6.5)? If so, describe how the earlier issues in Lucy's life may be affecting her now.

9.1–3   What are some diagnoses that you would want to rule out in Lucy's case?

9.1–4   What are some resources that would be helpful to Lucy?

9.1–5   Based on this interview, what would your current diagnosis be for Lucy?
Axis I

Axis II

Axis III

Axis IV

Axis V

Case 9.2

Identifying Information
Name: Larry Schenk
Age: 36 years old
Ethnicity: Caucasian
Marital Status: Divorced
Occupation: Retail store manager

Background Information
You have been seeing Larry Schenk for 6 weeks in individual psychotherapy sessions. He presented with a mildly depressed mood focused on his recent divorce. His wife of 10 years left him because she suspected him of infidelity. Specifically, she had become suspicious because of numerous, significant time periods when the client was "missing." Along with unaccounted-for time, she found unexplained mileage on his car. Although your client maintained his innocence, his wife eventually filed for divorce. Your initial sessions have been a bit unfocused, but you have helped him acknowledge and accept his feelings of loss. However, he continues to worry about his wife and to feel "misjudged" by her regarding the alleged infidelity.

You receive a call from the local hospital emergency room one evening. The nurse indicates that Mr. Schenk has been in an automobile accident, although he is not badly injured. "He's acting kinda crazy and says you're his therapist. We need somebody to clear releasing him in the state he's in. Can you come down?" she inquires.

Interview at Emergency Room
When you arrive at the emergency room, you ask the nurse for details of what has happened. She tells you that Mr. Schenk ran a red light and crashed into another vehicle. Although he received only cuts and bruises, a passenger in the other vehicle is in surgery, and it is uncertain whether she will live.

"He seemed okay until the police officer talked to him. Then he got really agitated and started talking out of his head," she relates.

"Can you describe what he was doing exactly?" you prompt.

"You'll see. He's in Exam Room 3." She points the way.

As you enter the room, your client jumps to his feet and runs to embrace you. "Thank God, you're here! This is a nightmare! You have to help me!"

This strikes you as very unusual behavior. Your impression of the client is that he is very reserved about his emotions. "Okay, Larry. Why don't you tell me what's going on?" you respond calmly.

"This is the worst! I haven't been entirely honest with you. I haven't been having any affair as far as I know, but I lose track of time. It's been going on since I was a kid. I don't know how I got here!" he rambles. Larry continues to pace and wring his hands.

"Why don't you get back on the gurney, Larry. I think maybe you're still in shock. Tell me what you do remember about this evening."

Larry reluctantly climbs back on the gurney, although he continues wringing his hands. "I remember being at work. I wanted to finish up some inventory that I've been putting off, so I let the clerks go home once they'd finished closing out. The next thing I know I'm sitting here and this cop is telling me to calm down. Do you know what's going on?" he asks.

"Larry, what I've been told is that you ran a red light and crashed into another vehicle."

"Oh my God!" he interrupts. "Was anyone hurt?"

"At least one person in the other vehicle is in surgery right now. I take it her injuries are serious," you answer.

Larry starts to get off the gurney again but relents when you ask him to "stay put." "Am I in serious legal trouble now? Do you have any idea what's going on with me?" he asks.

9.2–1   What diagnoses are you considering at this point?

9.2–2   Is there additional collateral information you wish you had?

"At this point I'm not sure, Larry. I need you to try to calm down so we can talk this through. Do you think you can do that?" you ask.

"Of course he can't! He's hysterical! What a pansy!" Larry says aggressively.

"I beg your pardon?" you respond, completely surprised by his change in demeanor.

"'I beg your pardon?'" Larry says sarcastically. "Like you've done a damned thing to help him out! You've been helping him feel sorry for himself. What good is that?"

"Larry? I know you're upset, but you don't have to get angry with me," you respond.

"Don't give me no bullshit! You need to get Larry an attorney. He doesn't know it, but he doesn't have a driver's license. If that lady croaks, he could be in big trouble!" Larry continues.

"Why are you talking about yourself in the third person, Larry?" you ask.

"I'm not Larry! I'm not anything like him!" he shouts.

"Well, then who are you?" you persist.

"I'm the one with some guts around here. I'm the one who knows how to have a good time. I'm the one who cares about something other than pleasing everyone all the time!" he responds.

9.2–3   What is your preliminary diagnosis for Larry at this time?
Axis I

Axis II

Axis III

Axis IV

Axis V

9.2–4   What other diagnoses do you want to rule out?

9.2–5   What strengths do you see in Larry? What resources or referrals do you want to alert him to immediately?

InfoTrac keywords

depersonalization, Dissociative Identity Disorder, Multiple Personality Disorder

Sexual and Gender Identity Disorders | 10

DISORDERS

This section in the DSM-IV-TR (APA, 2000) contains three distinct categories of disorders. The first subsection comprises a variety of problems related to sexual functioning. As in all psychiatric diagnoses, the symptoms for each disorder cause significant distress and/or interfere with the individual's psychosocial functioning. In the case of sexual dysfunctions, the focus of impairment is relational in that the symptoms tend to create barriers in establishing or maintaining intimate relationships.

Sexual Dysfunctions

The first set of diagnoses regarding sexual dysfunction is focused on sexual desire. In Sexual Aversion Disorder, the client expresses persistent or recurrent aversion and avoids sexual contact with a partner. The potential range of this response varies from moderate anxiety to extreme psychological distress. In Hypoactive Sexual Desire Disorder, there is an absence or deficiency in sexual interest that extends to both fantasies and actual sexual activity. This diagnosis obviously calls for a clinical judgment about what is normative although no normative data exist. Consequently, most clinicians tend to rely on the client's and/or his or her partner's expectations (APA, 2000).

The next grouping of diagnoses is focused on the physiological process of sexual arousal. For men, the diagnosis of Male Erectile Disorder is based on a persistent or recurring inability to attain or maintain an adequate erection during sexual activity. For women, the diagnosis of Female Sexual Arousal Disorder is based on a persistent or recurring inability to achieve or maintain an adequate genital lubrication–swelling response during sexual activity. In both instances, it is important to rule out general medical conditions and the use of substance(s) as causal factors (APA, 2000).

The next set of sexual dysfunction diagnoses focuses on orgasms. For both Male and Female Orgasmic Disorder, the key feature is a persistent or recurrent

237

delay in, or absence of, orgasm following normal sexual excitement and activity. Again, clinical judgment in the absence of any normative data is necessary, particularly if the complaint is about orgasmic delay. For men, an additional diagnosis of Premature Ejaculation is made for persistent or recurrent episodes of ejaculation and orgasm before the person wishes. Usually, there should be evidence of relatively limited genital contact prior to ejaculation to make the diagnosis (APA, 2000).

The next set of diagnoses involves pain associated with sexual activity. In Dyspareunia, men or women report recurrent or persistent genital pain associated with sexual intercourse. The diagnosis of Vaginismus is a more specific episode of pain characterized by involuntary vaginal muscle spasms associated with penetration (APA, 2000).

Finally, the sexual dysfunction diagnoses include Sexual Dysfunction due to a General Medical Condition, Substance-Induced Sexual Dysfunction, and Sexual Dysfunction NOS. To make a diagnosis of sexual dysfunction other than these, causality related to a medical condition or substance use must be ruled out (APA, 2000).

It should also be noted that there are important specifiers related to all the diagnoses in this category. The first specifier indicates whether the specific sexual dysfunction is lifelong or was acquired after a period of satisfactory sexual functioning. The next specifier distinguishes between dysfunctions that are pervasive or generalized and those that occur only in specific situations. Finally, there is a specifier describing causal factors. If general medical conditions and substance use play *no* role in a particular disorder, the specifier "due to Psychological Factors" is used. If the problem is accounted for by a general medical condition or substance use, those specific diagnoses are used. If there is a combination of factors, the specifier "due to Combined Factors" is included (APA, 2000).

Paraphilias

The next subsection of diagnoses involves variations in the object or conditions of sexual fantasies, urges, and/or behavior. For any of the Paraphilia diagnoses, the symptom presentation must have persisted for at least 6 months. For those Paraphilias that involve nonconsenting partners (and are consequently illegal), the diagnosis is made if the client has acted on the urges and/or if he or she experiences distress or interpersonal impairment in relation to the urges. For those Paraphilias that do not involve potentially illegal behavior, the diagnoses are usually made based on the presence of clinical distress or psychosocial problems (APA, 2000).

The specific Paraphilias listed in the DSM-IV-TR (APA, 2000) include Exhibitionism (exposure of genitals), Fetishism (use of nonliving objects), Frotteurism (touching and rubbing against a nonconsenting person), Pedophilia (focus on prepubescent children), Sexual Masochism (receiving humiliation or suffering), Sexual Sadism (inflicting humiliation or suffering), Transvestic Fetishism (crossdressing), and Voyeurism (observing sexual activity). A Paraphilia NOS category exists for diagnosing people with attachments to less frequently encountered situations or objects (APA, 2000).

It is essential to distinguish the nonpathological use of fantasy, behavior, or objects in consensual sexual relations from Paraphilias. In these disorders, there must be clinically significant distress or psychosocial impairment, such as being unable to perform sexually in the absence of the paraphilic material, legal complications, interference with intimate relations, and other dysfunctional behaviors (APA, 2000).

Gender Identity Disorders

In the last subsection of diagnoses in this section, the focus is on feeling intensely uncomfortable with one's own biological sex. These clients evidence strong and persistent identification with the opposite sex. In fact, many insist that they are actually members of the opposite sex. These clients also express significant discomfort with their actual sex and/or the gender role(s) of that sex. These diagnoses are not appropriate in instances when an individual has a physical intersex condition. As in all diagnostic categories, the client must also suffer clinically significant distress and/or have psychosocial impairments associated with his or her desire to be a member of the opposite sex (APA, 2000).

Separate diagnostic codes are used based on the age of the client with a Gender Identity Disorder. If the disorder occurs in childhood, the code 302.6 is used. Clinicians are cautioned against employing this diagnosis lightly with children. The vast majority of children who evidence these sorts of symptoms do not carry them into adulthood (APA, 2000).

The code 302.85 is used with adolescents and adults. It should be noted that among adolescents, the symptoms of Gender Identity Disorder are sometimes resolved by realizing a bisexual or homosexual sexual preference. If clients are sexually active, a specifier regarding sexual attraction (i.e., to males, to females, to both, or to neither) is included (APA, 2000).

A Gender Identity Disorder NOS diagnosis is included in this subsection to address situations in which a specific gender identity disorder diagnosis is inappropriate. Similarly, a Sexual Disorder NOS diagnosis is available for coding any sexual disturbance not covered in this section (APA, 2000).

ASSESSMENT

The essential focus of assessment with sexual dysfunctions is to rule out and/or identify and treat any aspect of the problem related to a general medical condition. For nonmedical personnel, the most common instrument used to determine the existence and severity of sexual problems is the Golombok-Rust Inventory of Sexual Satisfaction (GRISS) (Rust & Golombok, 1986). Both forms of this instrument (GRISS-F for women and GRISS-M for men) have 28 items answered with a 5-point Likert scale (i.e., "always" to "never applies"). The GRISS-F evidences slightly higher full-scale split-half reliability (.94) than the GRISS-M (.87) (Touliatos, Perlmutter, & Straus, 1990). In addition, both the MMPI-2 and MMPI-A are reputed to be useful in determining psychogenic sexual dysfunction and gender dysphoria (Butcher & Williams, 2000).

CULTURAL CONSIDERATIONS

The diagnoses in this chapter require that clinicians take into account the individual's ethnic, cultural, religious, and social background, as these aspects will dramatically influence expectations and attitudes about sexual and gender identity issues. The client's age and relational status also influence expectations regarding these matters.

Generally speaking, social mores about male sexual behavior are more stringently "enforced." For example, sexual functioning is a primary area of concern for many males, whereas society focuses more interest on fertility among women (rather than desire or performance). Cross-gender role interests are usually well tolerated for girls but engender excessive concern with boys. Consequently, the diagnostic criteria of clinical distress and psychosocial impairment may vary dramatically based on the sex of the individual.

Women are almost never diagnosed with Paraphilias, with the exception of Sexual Masochism. The reason or reasons for this variance are not known.

SOCIAL SUPPORT SYSTEMS

The primary psychosocial problems faced by persons with the various disorders in this chapter are usually in the area of relational functioning. People with these symptoms may face unusual challenges in forming and maintaining intimate relationships. For example, deciding when to disclose a sexual dysfunction when forming a new relationship can be problematic. If done before developing emotional intimacy, the client may well fear that the potential partner will be unwilling to invest in exploring the relationship. If the information is withheld until more intimacy is attained, the potential partner may feel that he or she has been lied to or manipulated.

In addition to facing relational challenges, many clients with Paraphilias may face serious legal problems if they act on their impulses. Those clients whose desired sexual circumstances are not illegal may face serious problems in forming intimate relationships.

The potential relational impact for persons with Gender Identity Disorders is even broader. Although gender identity and sexual orientation are not necessarily linked, these clients usually incur the stigma associated with homosexuality in our culture. Indeed, because of such stereotypical beliefs, these individuals may face extreme ambivalence and confusion about their sexual orientation. In any event, the potential for social isolation extends far beyond intimate relationships. Family members and friends may also reject an individual when his or her confusion is known, particularly if the person decides to seek sexual reassignment surgery.

Unfortunately, few self-help or group therapeutic approaches have been developed for persons with these diagnoses. Some primarily informational Internet resources are available.

www.mentalhelp.net/guide/sexual.htm—Diagnosing and treatment of sexual disorders

www.athealth.com/Consumer/rcenter/resource_ data.cfm?TopicCF=Paraphilias—Assessment and treatment of Paraphilias

www.biopsychiatry.com/paraphilias.htm—Discussion of pharmocotherapy for Paraphilias

www.narth.com/docs/childhood.html—Discussion of the controversy surrounding Gender Identity Disorder

www.transgender.org/tg/gic/what.html—Information and referral for transgendered individuals provided by the Gender Identity Center

www.leaderu.com/jhs/rekers.html— Online text chapter written by George Rekers, Ph.D., on Gender Identity Disorder of childhood and adulthood

Case 10.1

Identifying Information
Client Name: Chris Hawkins
Age: 32 years old
Ethnicity: Caucasian
Marital Status: Single

Background Information

Chris is a 32-year-old youth director at a large metropolitan church in a large southeastern city. He is highly regarded by everyone in the parish for his commitment of time and energy to the youth ministry at the church. As a single male, he has been a role model to many of the young boys who attend church school during the year and church camp during the summer. Chris has gone the extra mile in providing leadership and direction to the youth program. He has spent many long hours developing relationships with the young boys and their families.

Chris has been in charge of the youth Sunday school, sports activities, outings, and special events designed for the youth at the church. He has been singled out as an outstanding minister in the community by the local community of churches. He is always positive, enthusiastic, and hardworking. He never complains about working overtime to accomplish his goals. He has been able to establish the admiration, respect, and trust of both youth and parents alike.

Chris has spent a great deal of time working with boys from single-parent homes. He often takes on the "big brother" role to these children since the father is usually absent. He has taken them on day trips and overnight camping excursions. Because boys grow to trust him, they often go to him when they have trouble at home or school. He has spent many afternoons tutoring boys who were having trouble in school with a particular subject, such as math, and has been working on the implementation of an after-school program for boys ages 5–12 at the church.

On several occasions, Chris has had boys over for dinner and a slumber party. Chris explains to the parents that this gives them a night off to do as they please. On one occasion, an 11-year-old boy who had been in trouble at school spent the night with Chris, with his mother's permission, so that Chris could counsel him.

The following day, the young boy told his mother that Chris had sexually molested him. The mother immediately contacted the head minister of the church. The minister brought Chris in for questioning, and Chris denied the allegations. He alleged that the boy was a "mixed-up" kid who was angry at Chris for not letting him stay up past midnight to watch MTV.

Following these allegations, Chris has been suspended from all activities that involve contact with the youth and has been admonished to get a lawyer since the mother is reportedly filing charges against him. His lawyer has referred Chris to a sex-offender treatment facility for a series of tests.

Psychologist's Records

Chris is given the following tests: the Wechsler Adult Intelligence Scale, the Millon Clinical Multiaxial Inventory III, Substance Abuse Subtle Screening Inventory, Third Edition (SASSI-3), Jesness Inventory, Multiphasic Sex Inventory, and the Shipley Institute of Living Scale. The sex-offender treatment provider, a psychologist, provides the following report after scoring and analyzing the scales.

The results of the administered standardized instruments are based on Chris' responses. As such, the validity of the test results are limited to Chris' unique history and present circumstances.

Chris' level of intellectual functioning is in the average range (Full IQ 95–110). Abstract reasoning is also in the average range in relation to Chris' ability to think in terms of general principles, solve logical problems, and generalize between situations. Chris appears to have read the tests and did not respond randomly. The results indicate a moderate set of good fake responses. Chris answered some questions in a socially desirable manner in order to minimize pathology. This social desirability factor may limit the validity of the following results, as underlying pathology may be more extensive than indicated by the scales.

Anger responses are very low, indicating the possibility of repressed anger. Chris may have difficulty acknowledging and coping with angry feelings. Anger could build up, resulting in explosive behaviors.

Impulse control is poor. Chris acts impulsively without consideration of alternatives. He desires immediate gratification without considering the consequences. Chris exhibits chronic tendencies toward illogical, disjointed thought, which can lead to poor judgment and odd, eccentric behavior. Results also indicate moderate levels of interpersonal mistrust and suspiciousness that can lead to defensiveness and withdrawal. On the personality scale, Chris scored in the severe range of character pathology. His scores are consistent with schizoid, avoidant, and obsessive features that are likely to affect daily functioning. Scores are highest for the schizoid factors.

Results reveal Chris as a person who fears rejection, which culminates in a sense of humiliation, low self-esteem, and withdrawal. He denies having normal sexual drives, interests, and attraction to age-appropriate heterosexual relationships. Instead, he presents himself as asexual. These results may indicate that Chris is minimizing sexual pathology in testing or may indicate a low sex drive. He also exhibits mild to moderate cognitive distortions and immaturity typically found in sex offenders.

Results indicate that Chris engages in a moderate degree of rationalization justifying his sexual deviancy, blames others, and makes excuses for his acting-out behaviors. His profile indicates significant pathological behavior similar to that found in child molesters. Chris also admits to engaging in public masturbation and acknowledges actively looking for opportunities to carry out his sexual fantasies. Results also indicate mild impotence and significant feelings of sexual inadequacy. Chris appears mildly motivated to seek treatment for sexual problems, but this alone may be insufficient for successful treatment.

The psychologist concluded this report with a diagnosis.

10.1–1   What would your preliminary diagnosis be?

Axis I

Axis II

Axis III

Axis IV

Axis V

10.1–2   Do you think Chris has any strengths? If so, what are they?

Follow-Up Information

Several weeks later, Chris is charged with indecency with a minor and child molestation. His lawyer plea-bargains an agreement. Chris pleads guilty to a lesser charge and serves 6 months in jail followed by 4 years of probation, including weekly attendance in a court-mandated sex-offender program. After a year of treatment, Chris admits in therapy to having fondled at least one child under the age of 18 years old. He also admits to having ongoing fantasies about having sex with young boys. He has some insight into the fact that these behaviors emanated from having been shamed and physically abused by his father, who was an alcoholic, and having had an unsupportive mother. Chris currently is employed as a manager of a fast-food restaurant. He has complied with the terms of his probation and has regularly attended group and individual therapy sessions.

10.1–3   What prognosis would you give Chris? Why?

Case 10.2

Identifying Information
Client Name: Alexia Hazelhurst
Age: 35 years old
Ethnicity: Caucasian
Marital Status: Married with three children

Intake Information
Alexia Hazelhurst, age 35, was referred to the Marriage and Family Counseling Center by her OB/GYN physician, who recently saw her for a complete physical workup. Alexia stated that she had been experiencing a gradual lack of interest in "making love" with her husband, Jim. She told her doctor that Jim thought perhaps something was "wrong" with her and that she should get a physical exam. Alexia stated that she was not experiencing any pain or discomfort, but that she just wasn't as interested in sex as she had been in the past. Her physician found no physical or medical problems and referred her to a counselor for an assessment. The intake worker scheduled an appointment with you for the following week.

Initial Interview
You greet Alexia in the waiting room and walk with her back to your office. Alexia is dressed in a soft pink, sleeveless sundress and sandals, with pearl earrings and necklace. Her long blond hair is pulled back in a ponytail and tied with a pink ribbon, and she appears to have an appropriate amount of makeup on. Alexia tells you she's glad you're on time for the appointment since she has one child with a baby-sitter, another child at a swimming lesson, and a third child on a play date at the neighbor's house.

"How old are your children?" you inquire.

"Oh, well, Alex is 7 years old, Lottie is 4 years old, and Jimmie is 2½ years old. They are a handful right now," Alexia says, laughing nervously.

"So, I guess Alex is the only one in school so far," you suggest.

"Yes, Lottie still has a year before she'll be in school due to her birthday being in September," Alexia sighs deeply. "I'm running around all day long just trying to keep up with them."

"How long have you been married?" you ask.

"It's been 14 years," Alexia states. "We didn't have kids for a while after we got married because both Jim and I were in graduate school and working, so we decided to finish school before starting a family."

"I see. And what did you get your degrees in?" you inquire.

"Jim has a Ph.D. in chemical engineering and works for a big oil and gas company. My degree is in art history. I worked at the Museum of Fine Arts before Alex was born. I decided to stay home with him until he started school, and then I had two more children and I was definitely a housewife after they were born."

"Wow, that sounds very interesting. Do you miss your job?" you ask.

"Well, a little. I don't have any time though, and I couldn't possibly work with three children. Besides, I'd make just enough to pay for child care so it really wouldn't be worth it."

"It sounds as if you have a full-time job as a mother these days," you respond.

"You bet. I'm on call 24/7, and there's never any letup. Jim works 10 hours a day and often has to go away on business trips, so I'm left to handle everything," Alexia says with another sigh. She props her elbows on the arms of the chair and looks a little more relaxed.

"So, tell me why you decided to come here today," you suggest.

"Well, this is a little embarrassing to talk about, but as I told that other woman whom I talked to on the phone, my OB/GYN doctor told me to make an appointment here since she said there was nothing physically wrong with me." Alexia begins to appear anxious again.

"Okay, so she said there was nothing physically wrong with you, but she thought something else might be going on?" you inquire.

"Yes, you see, I'm just not very enthusiastic about making love to my husband these days, and it's been going on for about a year, and he says there must be something wrong with me, that I never used to be this way, but suddenly, I'm just too tired or, to be perfectly honest, it just doesn't appeal to me much anymore," Alexia says with an anguished tone of voice.

"Can you think of any reasons why you might not be as interested in making love as you were previously?" you tentatively ask.

"Well, of course, I've thought about it a lot. My husband won't let me forget about it, which is what I'd really like to do." Alexia laughs hesitantly. "For one thing, after running around with three kids all day, I don't feel too attractive. There are days when I don't even get to take a shower without one of the kids screaming for me, and I end up getting about 2 minutes to shower and get dressed. I pull my hair back with a rubber band, don't put on makeup, and dash off with the kids. Like this morning, I was trying to get everyone organized before coming here, and Lottie decided to make pancakes on the kitchen floor for her dolls. Pancake batter all over the kitchen. Here I am in a huge rush and I have to stop and wash the floor and Lottie before I can get out the door. And it sometimes goes like that until 9 o'clock at night when they go to bed. It's exhausting. I don't have much left over when Jim walks in the door at 8 P.M. I sometimes think he expects me to have a romantic dinner and evening waiting for him, and all I want to do is to sit down and watch television and relax after a full day of kids."

"So it sounds as if one very good reason may be that you're just too tired to be interested in making love after a long day with the children. Can you think of any other reasons?" you respond.

"Well, now that I stop and think about it, even though Jim acts very disappointed when I tell him I'm too tired or I need to get some sleep, he often seems to be having some problems himself. It's something we end up arguing about. Like whose fault is it, anyhow? Sometimes, I think Jim is having his own problems with making love, and it may be partly why I'm not so interested these days." Alexia slumps further down in her chair.

"Do you mean, you don't think he's as interested as he once was, or are you referring to other problems?" you carefully question Alexia.

"Actually, I think he may be experiencing some physical problems," Alexia states hesitantly. "You know, like he's having trouble getting excited. I think he thinks it's my fault, though."

"Alexia, I know how hard this kind of very personal issue is to talk about. If it's okay with you, I'm going to be very candid with you so that I can provide you with the most effective assistance I can. Is that all right with you?" you ask.

"Yes, please, I'm relieved to hear you say that. I'm willing to be very honest about this situation since I don't really feel I have done anything wrong and I want to preserve my marriage. Jim is a wonderful man. It's just been difficult lately with his long hours and the three young kids to take care of."

"Okay, so you think, perhaps, Jim is having some difficulties with impotence. Is that what you're thinking?" you ask straightforwardly.

"Yes, I'm not trying to point the finger at him, but I think the reason we're having problems is not just me and not just him but that both of us are experiencing some difficulties in the sexual realm of life."

"Actually, Alexia, that makes a lot of sense. When I work with couples, the issues with which they are trying to cope usually involve both persons in the relationship. So, let me see if I understand what you have told me so far. First, it sounds as if over the past year, you have had a declining interest in having sex with your husband. Is that correct?"

"Yes, exactly," Alexia comments.

"How often are the two of you having sex, let's say in the last 6 months?" you inquire openly.

"I'd say maybe once in the last 6 months, and it wasn't very satisfying for either one of us," Alexia stares out the window thoughtfully.

"You also told me that you think Jim may be having problems with impotence lately. Is that correct?"

"Yes, I just don't think he'll admit it," Alexia states emphatically.

"Do you think he would be willing to go to a doctor?" you inquire.

"Maybe, if I told him he would be helping me. I think this is a very hard thing for a man to admit," Alexia says. "Our family doctor is also a good friend of Jim's, and he might be willing to confide in him."

"Okay, good. It might be important to talk to both of you together once we determine what the concerns are. Would you be willing to consider coming in for couples' counseling?"

"Oh, yes. I think that would be a good idea," Alexia agrees readily.

"Okay, very good. Before we end this session today, I want to ask you if there are any other concerns or issues that you are worried about in terms of your relationship with Jim. In other words, do you feel that you get along with each other in other aspects of your relationship, or are there other problems that concern you?" you inquire.

"No, Jim and I really do love each other very much. We are very invested in this marriage, and we enjoy our family life together. It seems that we have just drifted away from each other in our intimate relationship. I don't think either one of us knows exactly why this has happened," Alexia ponders.

"Perhaps we can figure the answer out in therapy," you suggest. "Do you think Jim would be willing to come here and talk to me one time by himself?" you ask Alexia.

"Sure, I think he'd do anything if he thought it would improve the situation at home," Alexia suggests.

"Why don't you talk it over with him and have him call and make an appointment for next week. Then, all three of us will set up a session after I talk to Jim individually one time."

"Sounds fine with me. Thank you very much for your help. I feel better already."

10.2–1   What are some of Alexia's strengths?

10.2–2   Do you think Alexia should be seen in individual sessions or as a couple with her husband, Jim?

10.2 – 3   What do you think are the underlying problems in Alexia and Jim's relationship?

10.2 – 4   What is your preliminary diagnosis for Alexia?
Axis I

Axis II

Axis III

Axis IV

Axis V

Case 10.3

Identifying Information
Client Name: Jim Hazelhurst
Age: 49 years old
Ethnicity: Caucasian
Marital Status: Married

Intake Information
Jim Hazelhurst, age 49, calls the Marriage and Family Counseling Center following an initial interview with his wife, Alexia. He tells the intake worker that his wife told him that the counselor would like to talk with him one time concerning their initial discussion. Jim tells the intake worker that he could come during a lunch hour, but that he is very busy during the week and can't come any other time. The intake worker schedules an appointment for Jim to talk with you at noon the following day.

Initial Interview with Jim
Jim arrives on time for his appointment with you, and you find him outside in the parking lot on his cell phone. He is leaning against his car with his notebook spread out on the hood and appears to be engaged in a discussion concerning his business. He is dressed in a light gray summer suit with a yellow shirt and blue-and-gray tie. He motions to you that he will be with you in a moment, and you go back inside and wait for him in the lobby.

A few minutes later, Jim rushes into the waiting room, looking busy and distracted. Jim appears to be a very engaging individual. He greets you with a warm, friendly smile and vigorously shakes your hand. He apologizes for the phone call, stating with a smile that "there's no place to hide now that we have cell phones." He follows you back to your office, conversing about how much his wife enjoyed talking with you the other day.

Jim sits down in a chair next to your desk. You notice that he is approximately 6 feet 4 inches tall with dark brown hair and blue eyes. He comments on the painting on your wall and asks if it is a work of a local artist. You engage in light conversation about the painting for a moment or two, allowing Jim time to get comfortable in this novel situation. After these preliminaries, you ask Jim if he has ever seen a counselor in the past. He laughs nervously and states that he probably has needed to see one many times but never has talked to a therapist in a professional capacity. You decide to start the session by referring to his wife's visit.

"As you know, Jim, your wife came to see me the other day because of some intimacy problems you have been experiencing in your relationship. I really want to talk with you to get your perspective on the situation and hear how you've been feeling about it recently."

Jim shifts in his chair slightly and says, "Well, okay. This is kind of a difficult issue to discuss, but I'm sure you've heard it all in your job as a therapist."

"That's fairly accurate, Jim. I want you to know that everything we discuss will be kept confidential, with the exception of sharing information with Alexia. When I work with couples, it's important for both partners to understand that I won't keep secrets between them. Not that I will turn around and tell her everything you tell me, but that anything you tell me could potentially become an issue when I'm working with you and Alexia as a couple. Do you understand that?"

"Oh, yes, that makes perfect sense. You aren't here to get in the middle of our relationship," Jim states emphatically.

"Exactly," you respond. "So, can you tell me a little bit about how you have been experiencing your relationship with Alexia over the past year?"

"Well, to be honest with you, it hasn't been so great lately. Don't get me wrong. I love Alexia and our three children very much, but we've been having some pretty substantial problems with intimacy." Jim leans back in his chair and appears to be pondering the situation.

"What do you think the problems with intimacy have been recently?" you ask.

"Well, Alexia just doesn't seem interested anymore. It happened kind of gradually starting about 2 years ago, right after our third child was born. She just began to seem less romantic and enthusiastic about having sex with me, and then it gradually declined to the point that she was not interested at all. Well, at first I was really angry, and then I began to think she didn't care about me anymore, which hurt. It really hurt. And then we discussed the situation, and I realized it wasn't that she didn't care but that there was something else going on with her that was causing the lack of interest. So, I told her I thought she should go to the doctor and now we're here."

"Okay, so you have been feeling like the main problem is Alexia's lack of interest or desire for a sexual relationship right now," you state.

"Well, yes, I mean initially anyway." Jim begins tapping his foot on the floor. "I think, though, that it's affected me, too," Jim conjectures.

"How do you mean, it's affected you? In what way?" you ask.

"Well, this is really embarrassing for me to talk about, but I've had some problems, you know, with the physical aspect, if you know what I mean, but I think it's just because Alexia doesn't seem interested. If she were more interested, I don't think I'd be, you know, having trouble getting aroused."

Jim looks around the room searchingly and adds, "Whew, this is really hard to talk about."

"You're explaining yourself very well," you say encouragingly. "It is a difficult subject for most of us to discuss with anyone, but espe-

cially with a complete stranger. So, what you're telling me is that Alexia has been experiencing some difficulties with being interested in sex, but that you also have had some problems in the area of sexual arousal. Is that correct?"

"Well, I guess that's true, although I hadn't really thought about it that way," Jim says hesitantly. "I guess I always have attributed my problems to Alexia's problems, and what you're saying is that maybe we're both having some difficulties that are keeping us apart."

"Do you think that makes sense to you?" you inquire carefully.

"It could be," Jim states. "But what do I do about it? You know, I'm an engineer and I tend to want to fix things immediately. So, what do I do?"

"Jim, this may take some time, but there are some important things you and Alexia can do to improve the situation if you're willing to explore them," you suggest supportively.

"Okay," Jim says.

"First of all, just as Alexia has done, you really need to see a doctor and get a complete physical exam to make sure that the problem isn't a medical one. Second, I think it could be very beneficial for you and Alexia to come to counseling together as a couple for a few sessions," you state.

"Okay, well, I can make a doctor's appointment this week," Jim states.

"That would be an excellent start," you remark. "Would you be willing to set up another appointment for you and Alexia to come here and talk about these issues?" you ask.

"Yes, that would be fine. I'll find out what Alexia's schedule is and call you tomorrow."

"Very good. I think it will be very helpful for the two of you to have the opportunity to talk openly about this stress in your life. Thank you for coming in today."

"I appreciate you helping us in this way," Jim says. "I'm actually glad I came."

10.3–1   What are some of Jim's strengths?

10.3–2   What are some of the roadblocks you might encounter in working with Jim and Alexia?

10.3–3   What do you think are some of the factors contributing to Jim's problems?

10.3–4   What further information would you like to obtain from Jim?

10.3–5   What is your preliminary diagnosis for Jim?
Axis I

Axis II

Axis III

Axis IV

Axis V

Case 10.4

Identifying Information
Client Name: Terri Widenmeyer
Age: 29 years old
Ethnicity: Caucasian
Marital Status: Never married
Occupation: Assembly worker

Intake Information
The client scheduled an appointment with your agency and specifically requested to speak with a female counselor. She indicated that she had some "problems" but was otherwise not specific about her concerns. She requested a late-afternoon appointment time so she would not have to take time off work.

Initial Interview
Terri arrives precisely on time for her appointment. She is dressed casually in jeans and polo shirt. You know she works a day shift at the local automobile assembly plant, but she looks freshly showered and dressed.

After you lead her to your office, she inquires about your diplomas. "You've got a lot of degrees, huh?"

"I suppose so," you respond, smiling.

"I guess you've seen about everything, haven't you? I mean there's probably not anything somebody could say that would shock you, is there?" she asks.

"Well, never say 'never.' I have worked as a therapist for about 10 years and can assure you that I've heard all kinds of problems," you respond.

"Like what's the wildest thing you've ever heard?" she asks.

"Terri, I don't talk about my clients, not even in a general sense. What they or you say to me is confidential," you say.

"So you'd never tell anyone what I said?" she asks.

"I'm afraid that's a never say 'never' again. There are two circumstances that might lead me to talk about you with other people. The first is if I felt that I needed help in deciding how to work with your situation. I have a supervisor with whom I might discuss your case if I thought that would help. She would also be bound by confidentiality. The other situation would be if a court of law subpoenaed me. In that case, I would have to answer any questions that I was asked," you explain.

"How would that happen?" she says, seeming alarmed.

"Well, frankly, the only way I can imagine that happening at all is if you get involved in some legal proceeding. And then you would have to tell someone you had seen a therapist. Then, it might be possible that I could get subpoenaed," you respond.

"I guess that's pretty unlikely," she comments.

"Yes, I would say so, but I want to be honest with you. I get the feeling that you're a little hesitant to talk with me," you say.

"I don't know how to get started," she responds.

"Well, why don't you start with what made you decide to talk with a therapist?" you inquire.

"Even that's hard to explain. I'm just not happy with my life," she says.

"How long have you been unhappy with your life?"

"I guess always. It just seems like things aren't the way they should be," she says.

"This idea that things seem wrong somehow—how does it make you feel?" you ask.

"Just wrong. I don't know," she responds. She slumps into her chair and stares at the floor.

"Would you say you're feeling depressed?" you inquire.

"What do you mean? Like sad and I want to kill myself?" she asks, seeming a little offended.

"Well, I'd want to know if you were thinking of killing yourself. But I was thinking more of feeling sad, maybe feeling worthless, having trouble eating or sleeping?" you clarify.

"I do worry a lot. Sometimes that means I don't fall asleep as quick as I'd like when I go to bed. But I don't really think it's depression," she states.

"What do you think is wrong?" you ask.

"Like I said, things just aren't right," she repeats.

10.4–1   What diagnoses are you considering at this point?

10.4–2   What ideas do you have about how to engage Terri in talking about what's really bothering her?

"Okay, Terri. Let's try going at this from a different angle. If you went to bed tonight and a miracle happened that took care of all the things that aren't right, what would you be like tomorrow?" you pose.

"I'm afraid to tell you," she says.

"Terri, I can see that you're really worried about telling someone what's 'wrong.' I imagine since you said there's 'always' been something wrong that you've been keeping something secret for a long time. All I can tell you is that there's no way I can try to help if you don't tell me."

"I'd be a man," she blurts out and then blushes deeply.

"Okay, how would that make your life different from what it is today?" you ask.

"I'd be who I'm supposed to be. I wouldn't feel like a freak. I could date, maybe even marry," she says tearfully.

You hand her a tissue and continue. "Do you not feel that you can be intimate with anyone now?"

"What do you mean? Be a lesbian?" she gasps.

"Well, yes. I'm not trying to insult you or even suggest anything. I'm just trying to understand how you feel. I assumed because you said that if you were a man, you could date or get married that you're sexually attracted to women. Is that right?" you ask.

"Yes, but not that way. I'm not saying lesbians are evil or anything, but that's not how I feel. It wouldn't be right for me to be with a woman as a woman. That's as 'wrong' as being alone. I don't know why I'm telling you this stuff! What could you possibly do?"

"Well, that depends on what you want, Terri. I don't have a magic wand or anything, but I don't think you should have to feel 'wrong' and be alone your whole life. If you don't think it would do any good to try to work on changing those feelings, I can put you in contact with people who could change your sex. It's called sexual reassignment surgery and is certainly something you'd have to think about seriously. But I can help you think all this through. It can't be worse than holding it all inside, can it?" you ask.

Terri cries louder now. "It feels so weird that somebody knows. I've always felt 'wrong.' I kept saying I wanted to be a boy when I was little until my parents finally put their foot down. Then it was nothing but frilly dresses and ballet lessons! Can you imagine? I figured out I needed to keep this stuff to myself. After a while, it was okay again to be a 'tomboy.' I just had to balance it with acting like I liked girl things."

"What about friends, Terri?" you inquire.

"I've never had many. It was sorta okay with at least some guys to hang out with me when I was little. Then it got real weird when I was a teenager. Now, all my friends are guys. We like the same things—football, girls—I mean women."

"Have you had female friends at all?" you ask.

"Some when I was younger . . . other girls who were tomboys. But not since I was a teenager. How can I be someone's friend when that's not what I really want?" she asks.

"I can see you've been in a very difficult situation for quite a while. Have you looked into sexual reassignment surgery or anything like that?" you ask.

"No, I wasn't sure that could really happen for me. I read some book about them making a guy into a woman in Europe or something but, you know, not the other way."

"Okay, Terri. That's where I think we should start. Now I'm not saying that that's the only option here. I just think you need to understand *all* of your options before we try to decide how to proceed. What do you think?"

"That would be great! I can't believe I actually told you. Tell me the truth. Do you think I'm a freak?" she implores.

"Certainly not. I think you've been very lonely and scared for a very long time. We need to figure out how to fix that. It doesn't make you a freak," you reply.

"Thank you," she says.

10.4–3 What resources would you want to gather for Terri initially?

10.4–4 What is your preliminary diagnosis?
Axis I

Axis II

Axis III

Axis IV

Axis V

10.4–5   What other areas of Terri's life would you want to assess at the next appointment?

 InfoTrac keywords

Erectile Dysfunction, Gender Identity Disorder, Paraphilias, sexual aversion, sexual dysfunction, sex offender, Transsexualism

Eating Disorders

11

DISORDERS

Although the section on eating disorders in the DSM-IV-TR (APA, 2000) is subsumed under the broad category of Adult Disorders, eating disorders often originate in childhood or adolescence. Approximately 5 to 10 million Americans suffer from some form of eating disorder. Anorexia Nervosa is the third most common chronic illness in adolescent women, with a prevalence rate of .5 to 3% of all teenagers. Since 1960, the incidence of eating disorders has increased threefold in young adult women (Peckham, 1999).

Fifty percent of females between the ages of 11 and 13 see themselves as overweight; 80% have attempted to lose weight; and 10% report the use of self-induced vomiting (Costin, 1999). Additionally, the death rate for individuals with anorexia has been 5.6% per decade (Herzog, 1997).

Anorexia Nervosa is characterized by significant weight loss resulting from excessive dieting. Specifically, the body weight of anorexic individuals is less than 85% of the ideal weight for their height and age. They also have an unreasonable fear of becoming fat regardless of their low body weight. This intense focus on being thin is often accompanied by a distorted body image; that is, the individuals experience their weight or shape as greater than what it actually is. For females who have begun menstruating, there has been a cessation of menstrual periods for at least three consecutive cycles (APA, 2000).

There are two subtypes of Anorexia Nervosa: Restricting Type and Binge/Purging Type. Individuals with the Restricting Type severely restrict their food intake without engaging in bingeing or purging behaviors. Individuals with the Binge/Purging Type of Anorexia maintain their weight at an abnormally low level through food restriction but also engage in binge eating and purging behaviors, such as self-induced vomiting or laxative or diuretic abuse (APA, 2000).

Individuals suffering from Bulimia Nervosa generally maintain a normal weight for their age and height. The primary issue for the individual diagnosed with Bulimia is a pattern of binge eating that occurs at least two times a week over a 3-month period. A binge consists of a large amount of food consumed in a relatively short period of time. During the actual binge episode, the individual feels a lack of control over the eating. In addition, the person with bulimia engages in inappropriate activities to prevent weight gain, such as vomiting; laxative, diuretic, or enema abuse; fasting; or excessive exercise. Two subtypes of Bulimia Nervosa include Purging Type (a pattern of self-induced vomiting or laxative, diuretic, or enema abuse) and Nonpurging Type (a pattern of fasting and/or excessive exercise to prevent weight gain)(APA, 2000).

The DSM-IV-TR (APA, 2000) lists a third category, Eating Disorder NOS. Individuals are given this diagnosis when the pattern of disordered eating does not quite meet all the criteria for Anorexia or Bulimia. However, these individuals definitely have an eating disorder because they take extreme measures to control weight and have some distortion in how they view their own bodies and/or in the importance they put on weight.

ASSESSMENT

In assessing a client with a potential eating disorder, it is important to conduct a thorough psychosocial evaluation, including demographic information, reason for visit (which may be different from the principal diagnosis), support systems, family information, medical history, and any other history of mental health intervention (see chapter 1). The practitioner should note the client's presentation, specifically noting the following: baggy clothing; sallow complexion; dark circles under the eyes; bite marks on the hands, fingers, or nails; excessive fine body-hair growth (lanugo); deteriorated teeth and gums; unhealthy head of hair; and unusually thin limbs or bony facial appearance (APA, 2000).

Clients who present with eating-disordered symptomatology may not initially feel comfortable discussing behaviors associated with the disorder due to the stigma, shame, and fear of being discovered. Often, the behaviors have been held secret for a significant period of time. The clients may be afraid of family and friends pressuring them to change the behavior before they are ready to make any changes.

Even when the eating-disordered person appears confident, accomplished, fearless, and intelligent, the internal experience is painful (e.g., terror of "getting caught," pervasive feelings of confusion or turmoil, concern about "going crazy"). Although it may be obvious that the client has an eating disorder, several sessions may be required before the client is willing to acknowledge the problem. Family members may even maintain or support such denial because eating-disordered behaviors (e.g., dieting, overeating, abstaining from eating, overexercising) are learned from the previous generation.

Even at the point a client is able to talk about the eating disorder, the client or his or her family may question the validity of such a diagnosis. For example, the parents of an anorectic girl might suggest that their daughter just wants to look like all the models in the magazines. In order for the practitioner to address this defensive stance, it is crucial to join with the family and establish good rapport and communication; a nonjudgmental and empathic attitude; and a calm, neutral, matter-of-fact tone concerning the eating-disordered symptoms. If the clinician infuses the assessment interview with too much emotion, the client and family may intensify their guardedness and withdraw from treatment.

Adolescents with eating disorders are often pressured into therapy by their parents, school counselors, friends, or relatives. Their resistance to therapy may force the practitioner to focus on other non-food- or weight-related issues for a considerable length of time before the adolescents develop enough trust to confide in the therapist. Adults with eating disorders may be motivated to come into therapy for a variety of reasons other than wanting to recover from the eating disorder. Such reasons may include wanting to assuage the family's or friends' worries; fear of a particular medical manifestation, such as bleeding, tachycardia, or incontinence; or problems with interpersonal relationships.

Assessment of an individual who the practitioner suspects might have an eating disorder involves exploring several specific areas that pertain to eating behaviors and attitudes. First, the practitioner should obtain a history of dieting or compulsive eating habits. Second, the client should be assessed for present symptoms of specific eating-disordered patterns (e.g., restricting food intake, vomiting, abusing laxatives, hiding food, hoarding food, having strict lists of "safe" foods, being obsessed with recipes and cooking, and engaging in excessive exercise routines).

Often these behaviors are accompanied by symptoms of depression, low self-esteem, distorted body image, hopelessness, anxiety, and, in more severe cases, suicidal tendencies. Due to the possibility of comorbidity, specific assessments can be conducted to rule out concurrent mental disorders such as substance abuse, major depression, Body Dysmorphic Disorder, and Obsessive-Compulsive Disorder. In addition, personality disorders such as Borderline Personality Disorder, Dependent Personality Disorder, Histrionic Personality Disorder, and Avoidant Personality Disorder should be considered.

People with eating disorders tend to have very rigid, fixed thought patterns. This may affect their social relationships, interpersonal skills, and ability to maintain intimate connections with other people (e.g., close friends, partners, close work relationships, family ties). If the client is under 18 years old, the family situation should be thoroughly assessed.

Family factors that have been found to contribute to anorectic behavior in adolescence include enmeshed family systems, blurred boundaries between parents and children, and lack of separation and individuation. Family factors that may influence bulimic and compulsive overeating behaviors include chaotic family dynamics, power imbalances, lack of flexibility, and a lack of clear family structure. In all types of eating disorders, factors that characterize families could potentially include a history of sexual abuse or traumatic events, squelching of emotional expression, and power and control issues.

Finally, it is essential that the eating-disordered client's case be followed by a medical doctor while the client is in therapy for the eating disorder. Clients with anorexia who fall below a minimum weight are often hospitalized because of the life-threatening risks that emaciation poses. Bulimic clients can develop electrolyte imbalances and other physical problems that can lead to medical complications. It is often necessary to have a written contract with eating-disordered clients stating that if they fall below a certain minimum weight, they understand that they will be hospitalized. In addition, the practitioner must obtain written consent from clients to exchange information with the physician.

Assessment Instruments

One body image assessment scale is the Perceived Body Image Scale (PBIS) (Costin, 1999), developed at British Columbia's Children's Hospital. The PBIS provides evaluation of body image dissatisfaction and distortion in eating-disordered patients. It is a visual rating scale consisting of 11 cards containing figure drawings of bodies ranging from emaciated to obese. Subjects are asked to pick which of the figure cards best represent their answers to the following four questions:

1. Which body best represents the way you *think you look?*
2. Which body best represents the way you *feel you are?*
3. Which body best represents the way you *see yourself in the mirror?*
4. Which body best represents the way you *would like to look?*

The PBIS is useful not only as an assessment tool but also as an interactive experience facilitating the therapy (Costin, 1999).

The next two standardized tests are well-known instruments that have undergone close scrutiny in the scientific research on eating disorders. They are widely utilized for diagnosing anorexia and bulimia.

The Eating Disorders Inventory-2 (EDI-2) (Garner, 1991) is one of the most popular and influential of the available assessment tools. The EDI-2 is a self-report measure that assesses the thinking patterns and behavioral characteristics of clients with Anorexia Nervosa and Bulimia Nervosa.

The EDI-2 provides standardized subscale scores on several dimensions. Three of the subscales assess attitudes and behaviors concerning eating, weight, and shape. These are the Drive for Thinness, Bulimia, and Body Dissatisfaction subscales. Five of the scales measure more general psychological traits relevant to eating disorders: ineffectiveness, perfectionism, interpersonal distrust, awareness of internal stimuli, and maturity fears. The EDI-2 is a follow-up to the original EDI and includes three new subscales: Asceticism, Impulse Control, and Social Insecurity (Costin, 1999). Respondents must rate whether each item applies "always," "usually," "often," "sometimes," "rarely," or "never."

The test-retest reliability has ranged from .79 to .95. The validity of the instrument is supported by a significant body of literature indicating that the EDI-2 subscales measure the experiences of eating-disordered patients in clinically relevant dimensions (Garner, 1991).

The Eating Attitudes Test (EAT-26) (Garner, Olmsted, Bohr, & Garfinkel, 1982) is a rating scale designed to distinguish patients with anorexia from weight-preoccupied, but otherwise healthy, females. This test is a 26-item questionnaire and is broken down into three subscales: dieting, bulimia and food preoccupations, and oral control. Respondents must rate whether each item applies "always," "usually," "sometimes," "rarely," or "never." Clients who score above 20 are referred for a diagnostic interview.

The EAT-26 does not yield a specific diagnosis of an eating disorder. A disorder must have a prevalence approaching 20% in order for the test to be efficient in detection. Thus, it is very difficult to achieve high efficiency in detecting eating disorders that have prevalence between 2 and 4% in populations of adolescents or young women (Garner et al., 1982). This test is used primarily with female college students. The EAT-26 can be useful in measuring pathology in underweight girls but also shows a high false-positive rate in distinguishing eating disorders from disturbed eating behaviors in college women.

The EAT-26 has a children's version, which researchers have already used to gather data. It has shown that almost 7% of 8- to 13-year-old children score in the anorexic category, a percentage that closely matches that found among adolescents and young adults (Maloney, McGuire, & Daniels, 1988). Lack of honesty or accuracy in self-reporting can limit the usefulness of the EAT, particularly with anorexia. However, the EAT-26 has been shown to be useful in detecting cases of Anorexia Nervosa, and the assessor can then combine information gained from this assessment and other assessment procedures to make a diagnosis (Maloney et al.).

Emergency Considerations

Anorexia Nervosa and Bulimia Nervosa are two of the most lethal psychiatric illnesses in the DSM-IV-TR (APA, 2000). Due to the physical complications that can develop from starvation, laxative abuse, diuretic abuse, and vomiting behaviors, clients with eating disorders can develop life-threatening medical conditions that require emergency medical procedures. Therefore, the practitioner who is working with eating-disordered clients must develop a "team" approach to treatment and include a physician or nurse practitioner, a dentist, a nutritionist, and other medical professionals on the treatment team to effectively treat the client.

Clients with eating disorders also often suffer from severe depressive episodes that may lead to feelings of hopelessness and, ultimately, suicidal behaviors. If the practitioner assesses the client to have depressive symptoms, the severity of the depression along with suicidal ideation should be considered. Crisis intervention strategies should be utilized and a psychiatric evaluation conducted if necessary to stabilize the client and keep him or her safe.

CULTURAL CONSIDERATIONS

It is important to recognize that in the developed Western European and North American countries, food is taken for granted, and only in countries in which there is an abundance of food do eating disorders flourish. Poor and underdeveloped countries in which food is scarce have virtually no eating-disordered individuals among their populations. Cultural values, therefore, are an important aspect of this illness.

There is a growing controversy over why the number of minorities with eating disorders is relatively low. Some studies show that the experiences of African American and Caucasian female adolescents are extremely different, with African American girls being proud of their bodies regardless of the cultural pressure to be thin (Woodrow Wilson International Center for Scholars, 2000). Due to these cultural differences, African American females may be at a lower risk than Caucasian females for developing eating disorders that focus on thinness. On the other hand, in the last 5 years, eating disorders have become prevalent in almost all socioeconomic and ethnic groups.

Young minority women are entering male-dominated fields and experience the same kinds of pressures to be thin as their Caucasian counterparts. However, the prevalence rates of eating disorders among African American women remain relatively low. African American culture does not tend to embody the same emphasis on thinness as the dominant culture.

In terms of gender differences, although males are in the minority, statistics on males with Anorexia Nervosa have been steadily increasing from a 1:10 ratio to a 1:8 ratio to a 1:6 ratio. A recent study showed that 36% of third-grade boys had tried to lose weight, and in the past 10 years, more than a million males have been found to have eating disorders (Dickinson, 2000). Therefore, even though males may be less likely than females to develop eating disorders, they are not immune to the same cultural pressures to be attractive and thin with which women must contend.

SOCIAL SUPPORT SYSTEMS

Individuals with eating disorders often report an unusual amount of disruption in their social and intimate relationships due to their symptoms. Anorectic clients frequently report avoiding social interactions with others where food is the focus of attention, fearing that their abstention from food will be noticed. Also, anorectic clients may spend a great amount of time thinking about food, cooking for others, exercising, and avoiding people who might sabotage their efforts to restrict their food intake.

Bulimic individuals often hoard food, eat secretly, and purge in private, and therefore, frequently search for times to be alone. Bulimic clients also describe spending large amounts of time buying food, hiding food, eating and purging, and exercising.

Persons with compulsive eating problems also avoid social activities and instead, purchase and consume large amounts of food. In sum, persons with eating disorders are often left with few friends. If the individual is involved in an intimate relationship, the person can experience difficulty maintaining the relationship while engaging in eating-disordered behavior.

On the other hand, eating-disordered individuals often struggle to maintain social relationships in an effort to disguise the fact that they have a problem. Anorectic individuals may feel that friends are necessary ingredients to being "perfect." However, as the eating disorder becomes more noticeable and severe, the person generally becomes more and more reclusive in the pursuit of thinness.

Due to these pervasive feelings of isolation in individuals with eating disorders, group therapy has become a common treatment modality for such clients. Eating-disorder groups facilitated by a therapist with expertise in this illness can provide social support as well as other therapeutic benefits.

For adolescents with eating disorders, it is highly recommended that families become involved in family therapy. Families are often resistant to treatment and must be educated about the nature of the illness and ways to cope with the teenagers' symptoms.

For college-age students and adults, group therapy that focuses on the underlying reasons for the eating problems rather than issues about food can be very beneficial to clients. Group therapy can be both supportive and confrontive, thereby preventing the individuals from denying their symptoms.

At nearly every large university health services center, there are resources available to men and women with eating disorders. There are also a number of Internet resources that provide information and referral sources for eating-disordered clients, such as the following sites.

www.eating-disorders.com/—Information and referral sources on eating disorders from St. Joseph's Hospital, Townson, Massachusetts www.edap.org/—Eating Disorder Awareness and Prevention, a nonprofit organization

www.acadeatdis.org/—A multidisciplinary eating-disorder association focused on treatment of and research on eating disorders

www.eatingdisorders.about.com/health/eatingdisorders/—Guide to over 700 eating disorder–related Web sites

www.gurze.com/—Books and publications on eating disorders

Case 11.1

Identifying Information
Name: Bonnie Deal
Age: 24 years old
Ethnicity: Caucasian
Educational Level: Graduate student in law school
Marital Status: Single

Background Information
As a counselor at the student health center at a large university, you see many young women who have concerns about their self-image, confidence, and weight-related problems. You work primarily with women who have come voluntarily to the mental health center of student health services. The center serves all students at the university, providing individual counseling, group therapy, crisis intervention services, psychoeducational seminars, and resources and referral information. Students can access services free of charge. The center has an intake worker who gathers basic information about the student and sets up appointments with the therapists.

Intake Information
Bonnie Deal called the student mental health clinic and requested an appointment with a therapist due to feelings of depression, difficulty completing her schoolwork, and ongoing eating problems. She told the intake worker that she has been experiencing the current problems for approximately 1 month. She stated that she has been having difficulty getting herself to classes, can't concentrate on her homework, feels drained of energy, and wants to do nothing but sleep all day.

Initial Interview
During the first appointment with Bonnie, you gather information about the history of the presenting problem, a social history, and a family history. The first session is 90 minutes in duration in order to obtain enough information to make an initial assessment.

Bonnie is a noticeably thin, tired-looking young woman who is curled up in a chair in the waiting room when you meet her. She is wearing a pair of baggy blue jeans, a long-sleeved shirt covered by a heavy sweatshirt, and heavy socks and sneakers, despite the fact that it is July. Her hair is tousled as though she forgot to brush it after getting up in the morning. You notice that she has very dark circles under her eyes, and her face, including her forehead, appears bony.

Bonnie states that she developed an eating problem 7 years ago at age 17 after graduating from high school as class valedictorian and gaining admittance into a prestigious university in Boston. Prior to the eating problem, she weighed approximately 130 pounds (an ideal weight for her height and age). Bonnie moved away from home into the dorms at school and began limiting her food intake and exercising, sometimes 4 hours a day.

Initially, Bonnie lost about 20 pounds and found she couldn't lose any more weight without further restricting her diet. She started eating very small quantities of food, counting the number of bites she could have each day. At one point, she allowed herself only 4 bites of food per day. If she ate more than that, she would make herself exercise an extra hour.

Bonnie reports that by spring break of her first year, she weighed only 82 pounds and hadn't had a menstrual period for 4 months. When she went home to visit, her parents were shocked at her appearance and took her to her old pediatrician. She managed to convince the doctor that she did not have anorexia and that she had simply lost her appetite because of the pressures at school. The pediatrician recommended that she drink three cans of Ensure each day in order to bolster her weight. Bonnie was unwilling to do this because of the high calorie content of the drink. Assuring her parents that she would eat, she returned to school. She refused to think she had a problem; rather, she just wanted to lose weight and be popular. She felt that she had always been characterized by her peers as a bookworm, and she desperately wanted to "fit in" at college.

She states that on one occasion she was rushed to the hospital by ambulance after fainting in class. She stayed at the hospital for a week due to dehydration and electrolyte imbalance. She begged her parents to allow her to finish the semester since it would "ruin my grade-point average" not to complete the classes. At that time, she got her weight up to 98 pounds to "prove" she didn't have an eating disorder.

Later, she lost weight again, and her weight has hovered around 85 pounds since that incident. Bonnie states that she has been hospitalized on five different occasions over the past 7 years for dehydration, exhaustion, electrolyte imbalance, and starvation/emaciation. She has rarely seen a counselor for more than a few sessions, stating, "They just thought I should start eating and that would resolve the problem."

Due to her eating problems, her heavy school schedule, and her exercise regime, Bonnie reports that she has had little time for "having fun." She states that she had a boyfriend for about a year, but he couldn't handle her problems with food.

Currently, Bonnie weighs 90 pounds and feels "heavy." She considers her ideal weight to be 85 pounds. She suggests that she can "see fat" on her thighs and stomach when she weighs more than 85 pounds. Due to the 5-pound increase in her weight, Bonnie has recently begun to use laxatives and occasionally induces vomiting, although she states that it hasn't helped her lose weight. She feels very anxious because she thinks she has lost control of her eating, at times bingeing on ice cream and chocolate bars

when she gets extremely hungry. Bonnie does admit that she thinks she may have an eating problem. She also states that she has been amenorrheic for 5 years.

Family Session

After you have met with Bonnie on three occasions, she tells you that her parents are coming for a visit. You ask Bonnie if they would be willing to come to a session with her, and she agrees to ask them. Bonnie appears to have developed a working relationship with you. She has kept her scheduled appointments and has been on time for them.

The session with Bonnie and her parents lasts approximately 1 hour. It is apparent from the beginning of the session that certain dynamics prevail in this family. Bonnie, who has previously been very articulate and insightful in individual sessions with you, becomes quiet, unassertive, and passive during the family interview.

Her mother makes numerous attempts to speak for Bonnie and appears aggressive and overbearing. She admits that she, herself, has dieted most of her adult life in order to "stay fit," but that she thinks Bonnie is overdoing it a bit. Her father, on the other hand, appears passive and emotionally distant. He does not speak unless he is asked a question or spoken to directly. He often glances at his wife while offering his opinion about the family situation. He does suggest he is very concerned about Bonnie's problems.

Bonnie's mother states that Bonnie has always been the "perfect" child—an overachiever, a straight-A student, president of the student council, and an exceptionally well-behaved adolescent. "We never had any problems like other parents have with their teenage children," she states proudly.

As her mother speaks, Bonnie becomes increasingly uncomfortable, despondent, and withdrawn. She curls up in her chair as a small child might. It is apparent that Bonnie disagrees with her mother's description of her life at home. When you ask her how she is feeling at the moment, Bonnie replies, "Oh, yeah, everything was just great as long as we all agreed with Mother and her opinions, never letting anyone else have a say-so in anything. Then, Dad would get real quiet for a while until everything just blew up and all hell would break loose. Yeah, it was perfect all right."

At this statement by Bonnie, her mother becomes extremely angry, saying that she cannot continue the session. You calm the situation by discussing the importance of not talking for other family members and of using "I statements" when speaking about feelings. Although you are able to establish some order, it is obvious that the family will need additional counseling related to communication and family functioning. The family is clearly enmeshed and needs to see the value of Bonnie becoming an independent adult in her own right.

11.1-1   What are some of Bonnie's strengths?

11.1-2   With whom would you want to consult in order to ensure that Bonnie receives the best possible treatment?

11.1-3   What resources might be beneficial to Bonnie?

11.1-4   What issues would you want to include in a contract with Bonnie?

11.1-5   What is your diagnosis for this case?
Axis I

Axis II

Axis III

Axis IV

Axis V

_____

Case 11.2

Identifying Information
Client Name: Jill Warren
Age: 16 years old
Ethnicity: Caucasian
Educational Level: 11th grade

Intake Information
The intake worker received a phone call from the mother of Jill Warren, who had been referred by her physician, Dr. Amanda Welby, for mental health therapy. Jill's mother stated that Jill has been having problems with eating for the past 9 months and seems depressed and withdrawn much of the time. She has been seeing her physician every 3 months for physicals and weight checks. She is 5 feet 7 inches tall, and her current weight is 102 pounds. The problem has persisted despite Jill's mother's efforts to ameliorate the situation. Jill was discharged 1 week ago from the hospital after being admitted after a fainting spell. She was treated for dehydration.

Initial Interview
Your initial interview with Jill Warren lasts 90 minutes. During that time you obtain information concerning the presenting problem, a social history, and a family history. You establish rapport with the client, discuss issues of confidentiality, and schedule another appointment with her. In your files you have made the following reports.

Presenting Problem
Jill Warren is a 16-year-old Caucasian female who came to the Eating Disorders Clinic at her family's request after being hospitalized for a fainting and dehydration episode. Dr. Amanda Welby referred her to the clinic over concerns about the client's weight loss over the past 9 months.

Jill stated that she doesn't think she has an eating problem, although she admitted to wanting to lose weight to look more like the other girls at school. She stated that she used to be overweight at 130 pounds (although 130 pounds would be an ideal weight for someone 5 feet 7 inches tall). She stated that being overweight gave her low self-esteem and that she didn't feel that she "fit in" with the other girls.

She reported that she has been trying to lose weight since she was 13 years old and had tried several diets but never seemed to lose much weight until recently. During the past school year, Jill began skipping breakfast and lunch. For dinner, she primarily ate broiled chicken and salad. She stated that eventually she was able to eliminate the salad and eat only a piece of boneless, broiled chicken each day. She has found that she can lose weight rapidly on this sparse diet.

In response to a question about her exercise regime, Jill stated that she started walking 30 minutes a day about a year ago. After a month, she began running about 3 miles a day, which quickly escalated to running approximately 10 miles a day. She also begged her parents for a stationary bike that she exercises on approximately 2 hours a day. "Sometimes, if I can't fit all the exercise in during the day, I wait until my parents go to sleep at night and get up and work out on the stationary bike until 1 A.M."

Jill admits to being very tired and having no energy. She states that sometimes it is exhausting to exercise, but she feels that she has to in order to lose more weight.

When asked what she thinks of her weight now, she replied that she would like to lose a few more pounds because weighing less than 100 pounds is her goal.

Jill stated that she is not having problems in school and that she is a straight-A student. She hopes to get into Princeton, Yale, or Harvard

University, and she has been studying hard for the SAT exams.

Social History

Jill stated that she has always liked school and has done well throughout her school experience. She also plays the violin in the school orchestra, is in the choir at her church, belongs to a chess club, takes art lessons, and rides horses. She stated that her parents never let her sit around and watch TV; she is always busy doing something.

She has a few good friends but not a lot of friends. "I guess I'm kind of shy, and people sometimes mistake that for being snooty," she told you.

Jill appeared embarrassed when you asked her if she's had any boyfriends. She stated that because she was overweight, none of the boys in her class really liked her. About a year ago, she overheard a boy talking to her best friend in the cafeteria at school say that if she just lost a little weight in her thighs, she'd be quite pretty. Jill stated that she's always felt left out of a really popular group of girls at school because she doesn't have a boyfriend. "They get together and go out to a movie or for a pizza and never invite me because I don't have a boyfriend to go with."

Although she is not in the most popular group, Jill stated that she was always so busy with other activities that it didn't really bother her until this past year. She said she has always had one or two good friends with whom she engaged in activities and who also rode horses or played the violin. During the past year, however, her good friends have become involved with boys, thus leaving Jill out of their group.

Family History

Jill stated that her family is very close. Jill has a younger brother, Bobby, age 14, and an older sister, Clancy, who is 20 and away at college most of the time. Her father is an executive at a major electronics corporation and is often out of town on business. Her mother is a homemaker and does volunteer work for numerous nonprofit organizations.

She said that her mother is always bugging her about her eating. Jill felt that her mother has an eating problem also, but would never admit it. "My mother is a very controlling person and has always watched over me like a hawk whenever I put a bite of food in my mouth," said Jill. "I'm either eating too much or too little. I can never seem to please her."

Jill said that her mother is a chronic dieter and has always been on a diet as long as Jill can remember. Jill described her mother as being of average weight but a little on the heavy side.

Jill described her sister, Clancy, as "nothing like me. She's real social and has lots of friends and doesn't care what anyone thinks about her." She stated that her sister is also slightly overweight but not obese. Jill described her brother as just a normal boy. He plays soccer and tennis and doesn't really care much about school but does okay, with about a B average.

Jill said that she doesn't feel very close to her father since he is gone on business so much. Without prompting, she related an incident in which her father stated that Jill is "his little princess" and he wishes she would never grow up. It was apparent that Jill was upset by that remark. When asked if the remark bothered her, Jill replied that she doesn't know how she can stay little all her life when she is growing up and it is out of her control.

During the past year, Jill's relationship with her parents has grown tense due to her losing so much weight. "They are constantly telling me how, when, and where to eat, and if I don't, they get upset." She also stated that "being the middle child and always having to live up to their expectations is not easy all the time."

When asked about arguments at home, Jill said that no one ever argues at home. She stated that it isn't polite to argue or get mad about anything at home. When asked if she thought she was angry about anything, Jill replied that she never really gets angry and that she doesn't like conflicts with anyone.

11.2-1 Briefly describe what you think are Jill's strengths.

11.2-2 What are some of the contributing factors that seem to be involved in Jill's problems with food?

11.2-3 Are there diagnoses that you would want to rule out? If so, what are they?

11.2-4 What is your diagnosis for this case?
Axis I

Axis II

Axis III

Axis IV

Axis V

11.2–5 What would be some resources that you could suggest to Jill and her family that would assist them in Jill's recovery?

_____

Case 11.3

Identifying Information
Name: Karen Black
Age: 17 years old
Ethnicity: Caucasian
Educational Level: 12th grade

Background Information

Karen Black decided to enter counseling after an initial intake session where you assessed her as having low self-esteem and a possible Major Depressive Disorder. During the initial intake, she told you that she is going off to college in the fall and that she just doesn't feel good about herself anymore. She stated that she has never felt she is very pretty; however, it didn't really bother her that much until this year, her senior year at Golden High School.

Karen appears to be an attractive girl of average weight and height. She stated that her parents are divorced. She lives with her mother and two younger brothers, Mike, age 15, and Scott, age 13. Her parents divorced about 2 years ago, and her father lives in an apartment on the opposite side of town. Karen gets along well with both parents although she confessed that the year her parents separated was chaotic. Her mother accused her father of seeing another woman. Karen doesn't feel that allegation was true although she thinks her father may be dating someone else now.

First Session

After you discuss issues of confidentiality, Karen tells you that her biggest problem is being worried about going to college and nobody liking her there. She feels like the "ugly duckling" at school and doesn't have a boyfriend. She has had boyfriends in the past and just recently broke up with someone she says was more of a "friend" than a "boyfriend."

Nevertheless, it bothers her to have no one to call on the phone or go out with, and the loss of the relationship with her boyfriend makes her feel even worse about her already poor self-image. With some pride, she tells you that she is a straight-A student and has received a scholarship to Golden State University for the first year of college. She indicates that she doesn't like sports and isn't athletic, but she does ride bikes with her brothers occasionally and enjoys walking her golden retriever, Nugget.

Karen thinks that she and her mother have a good relationship. However, Karen states that her mother is always nagging her about what she wears, how she fixes her hair and makeup, and what she eats. She likes to go shopping with her mother, and sometimes they go to lunch and a movie when her mother isn't working. Her mother is a buyer at a large department store, Canary's, at one of the malls and often has to work on the weekends or go on buying trips for 3 or 4 days during the week. Karen is expected to stay home and take care of her brothers when her mother is gone.

11.3–1 At this point, what are the issues that you consider important in assessing Karen?

Second Session

Karen arrives on time for her second session with you after school on Wednesday at 4 P.M. She appears happy to see you when you go to the waiting room. She is wearing blue jeans and a pink top. You notice she has dark circles under her eyes and looks very tired. You mention that she looks fairly tired today, and she shrugs her shoulders and says that she had a term paper due that she worked on late the previous night.

She sighs and says, "Everyone has been telling me that I look tired, and I don't really know why they keep saying that. It makes me feel really self-conscious." When you tell her that she has dark circles under her eyes, she says, "Oh, that's nothing to be worried about."

You decide to summarize the first session with Karen and continue your assessment of her situation. You discuss her parents' divorce, her scholarship to college, her fears about attending the university in the coming school year, and her concerns about her self-image.

"Is there anything I left out from our discussion last week?" you ask.

"That's probably all we talked about, since I'm scared to tell you the rest of it," Karen replies.

"What do you think is making you scared to tell me something?" you respond.

Karen looks despondently out the window. "I'm just afraid you'll think I'm dumb or weird or crazy or something if I tell you. It's something that's really been bothering me lately, and I just don't feel like I can talk to anyone about it."

You remind Karen that anything she tells you will be kept confidential, unless it's about harming herself or someone else, and that you are there to help her work on issues that are bothering her. She sits quietly for a few moments staring out the window and then begins talking in a quiet, measured voice.

"Well, I told you I feel really bad about myself and how I look, and I feel like everyone thinks I'm just an ugly, overweight, boring person to be around. So, for about a year, I've been trying to lose weight. At first, I went on all these crash diets, and I'd lose a few pounds, but then I'd gain it right back because I'd get so hungry I'd eat everything in sight. It was really frustrating to me because I had this friend who lost about 20 pounds and everyone was saying how good she looked, and she kept saying all I had to do was exercise more and I'd lose weight, too. Well, I tried that for a little while, but I hate running and quit after about a month. While I was in one of my starvation phases, my former boyfriend asked me out for pizza one night. I went and sat there with a glass of tea. He asked me why I wasn't eating, and I lied and said I wasn't hungry. He told me I'd look good the way I was if I'd just lose a little weight in my thighs. That comment was mortifying to me. I don't know what happened, but I sat there and ate almost a whole pizza and when I got home, I just stuck my finger down my throat and threw it all up. I was so angry with him for saying that to me. The next day I got on the scale, and I had lost 2 pounds. I felt so good about having lost 2 pounds that I decided maybe I could eat and lose weight at the same time by, you know, throwing up. It sort of got me on a cycle. For a while, I tried to eat one meal a day like I'd been doing, but it got harder and harder not to binge. So, I would binge in the afternoon when my mother was at work, and then I'd vomit it all up. It's just gotten to be a vicious cycle."

"Karen, I don't think you're weird or crazy. A lot of girls your age have problems feeling good about themselves and their bodies. From what you're describing, it sounds as if you're struggling with food and body image. I'd like to ask you some specific questions about these issues if it's okay with you."

Karen shrugs her shoulders and says, "Okay, I'm sort of glad I've finally told someone."

"What do you mean by binge? Tell me a little bit about what you ate when you 'binged,'" you ask.

"Huge amounts of food," Karen responds. "I mean everything I could get my hands on. It was like this uncontrollable urge that I just couldn't stop. For example, a few weeks ago when I broke up with my boyfriend, I went home after school and ate a whole box of chocolate cookies, a carton of ice cream, three Hostess Twinkies, two candy bars, and a peanut butter and jelly sandwich. Then, I was thirsty so I made about a quart-sized glass of frappuccino. After that, I felt so bad about myself, I just went into the bathroom and threw it up. It sounds terrible, I know, but I felt better afterward."

"It doesn't sound terrible, but it does sound like a problem for you. How often does this happen, Karen?" you ask.

"It started out just like once a week," Karen replies. "But now, I do it every day, sometimes two or three times a day. Sometimes, I feel like I've vomited so much, I can't vomit anymore. So then I take laxatives."

At this point, you decide to ask about Karen's feelings before, during, and after a bingeing and purging cycle. Karen tells you that she usually gets an uncontrollable urge to eat a lot of food and tries to distract herself with other things to do until it becomes unavoidable. She then begins looking for ways to obtain the food without her mother noticing. She sometimes goes out to fast-food restaurants and buys food so her mother won't wonder where all the food went. She then finds a secluded place to eat it—either in her car or her bedroom—and then finds a place to throw up.

"I'm so nervous someone's going to walk in on me when I'm vomiting. It almost happened a couple of times when I got sick at school. I went into a bathroom that no one ever uses, and a teacher walked in right after I had thrown up. I told her I wasn't feeling well and needed to go home. She sent me to the main office to get a permission slip to leave. I was so embarrassed."

"How long ago did this problem start?" you inquire.

"About 6 months ago, I guess," Karen sighs. "It's been a roller coaster ever since. The worst part about it is that I feel better after I get rid of the food, so I can't seem to make myself stop."

You ask Karen if she thinks her mother is aware of the problem with food that she has been having. Karen thinks her mother has some idea but hasn't said anything to her. She has asked Karen about missing food at times and wonders out loud what happened to it. Karen feels extremely guilty when her mother questions her but avoids telling her the truth about the food.

"I just don't know what I'm going to do. I don't want to go to college with this problem. Everyone will know something's wrong with me. I just don't know what to do about it."

11.3–2   How concerned are you about Karen's medical status? Explain why you would or would not involve a physician.

11.3–3 What are some of Karen's strengths?

11.3–4 From this assessment, what would be your diagnosis for Karen?

Axis I

Axis II

Axis III

Axis IV

Axis V

11.3–5 What are some resources that might help Karen cope with these issues?

Case 11.4

Identifying Information
Client Name: Laurel Jackson
Age: 48 years old
Ethnicity: Caucasian
Marital Status: Married, no children
Occupation: Middle school math teacher

Intake Information
Laurel Jackson, a 48-year-old schoolteacher at a large metropolitan public school, makes an appointment to see you for counseling at Community Mental Health Center. The intake form states that she has a college education, is married, and has no children. Under the heading "Presenting Problem," the intake worker has written, "The client stated on the phone that she is concerned about problems she has had with her recent eating habits."

Initial Interview
Upon meeting Laurel for the initial interview, you notice that she appears to be older than her stated age of 48. She is a petite woman, approximately 5 feet 3 inches tall. She has gray hair that is pulled back in a bun, and she is dressed rather conservatively in a black skirt, a pink blouse with lace around the collar, and a black cardigan sweater. She appears to be of average to slightly above average weight. She smiles cordially and carries on small talk about the traffic getting to the agency while she gets settled in your office.

You explain your position as a counselor at the agency and issues of confidentiality. Then, you ask her what brought her to the agency. She states that she was referred to you by a physician, Dr. Miller, at the hospital across the street from the agency. She explains that she had been in a program called "Mediquik" at the hospital for the past 3 months. The program is designed for persons who are more than 30 pounds overweight. It involves a liquid diet for optimal weight loss. Participants are medically supervised during weekly group sessions at the hospital.

She explains that over the past 3 months she has lost 85 pounds. "I weighed over 200 pounds when I started the program, and you can imagine how awful I must have looked since I'm such a short person. I felt really good about losing all that weight."

You ask her if she was allowed to eat any solid food on the diet, and she states that it is a completely liquid diet that involves three liquid supplements per day, water, and nothing else.

You comment that a strict diet like that must have required a great deal of willpower, and Laurel states that initially it was very hard, but that after a couple of weeks, she got used to not eating and it got easier. Laurel stuck to the diet religiously for the 12-week period of time. After 12 weeks the hospital gave her an eating plan that consisted of solid food for a week, and then the program was over.

Laurel states that recently she finds herself getting up in the middle of the night and eating huge quantities of food, especially carbohydrates, and then feeling so sick the next morning she has a hard time getting to school on time. She says that no matter what she does, she can't seem to stop this midnight bingeing, and she is beginning to panic because she has begun gaining weight.

"I'm so scared I'll gain all the weight back that I lost that the other night, after I went on a major binge and ate everything in the house, I forced myself to throw up. It actually made me feel better, so the next night, I binged and then vomited again." Laurel states that she knows this behavior isn't healthy and that's why she decided she needs some help.

11.4–1   What other information would you want to obtain from Laurel before you could make a comprehensive assessment and diagnosis?

You decide that you need more information about Laurel's personal and professional relationships. You ask her about her family.

Laurel states that she has been married for the past 8 years. "I've known Darin since high school. He went into the Navy after school and got married. He came back home after a divorce about 12 years ago. I didn't think I'd ever get married, but Darin and I just hit it off. He has two daughters who are grown and on their own now. So it's just the two of us at home."

Laurel states that her relationship with Darin is very good. Darin works at a local grocery store chain as a manager and sometimes works long hours, but they usually have time together during evenings and weekends. She states that Darin is very proud of her for losing so much weight but never pressured her about being overweight.

Laurel states that her 80-year-old mother lives in the same neighborhood as she does. She talks to her mother every day on the phone and visits her after school three or four times a week. She says her mother has lived in the same house for the last 50 years. Laurel states that her younger sister is married, has three children, and lives in another state. Laurel's father died 10 years ago, so she feels a need to take care of her mother now.

When you ask Laurel about the quality of her relationship with her mother, she states, "Mom and I are a lot alike. She has always had

a weight problem, too, although since she's gotten older she's slimmed down. To my mother, food was love. She always cooked big meals for our family. We always had big breakfasts and lots of desserts. I was overweight when I was 5 years old! My whole family was obsessed with food, and I'd get stuck on one certain kind of food and eat it every day."

Laurel's last statement strikes you as unique, and you decide you want more information about her desire to eat the same food every day. You say, "So, you wanted to eat the same thing every day?"

"Oh, yes," Laurel sighs. "Once I ate nothing but potatoes for an entire year. Then, I switched and I ate nothing but spaghetti for another year."

"So, you got stuck on one kind of food and ate nothing but that specific food every day?" you query.

"For lunch and dinner, every day, for an entire year, like I was obsessed with it," Laurel states while rubbing her forehead. "I haven't gotten stuck like that on one kind of food since I got married because Darin likes regular meals and can eat anything without gaining weight," Laurel states with a deep sigh.

You suggest to Laurel that food has been problematic for her for a long time. She explains that she feels food has been "the enemy" ever since she can remember.

11.4–2   What are some possible emotional problems you would want to rule out in assessing Laurel's situation?

You ask Laurel if she has noticed any changes in her mood recently. She tells you that she has been upset about gaining back some of the weight she lost but that she is normally a fairly happy person.

You ask her if there is anything going on in her life that has been making her feel anxious lately. Laurel states that at the end of the school year, she always has a lot of work to do at school. You decide to get more information about Laurel's job.

"Do you teach specific classes or grades at school?" you inquire.

Laurel replies that she teaches sixth-, seventh- and eighth-grade math, including general math and Algebra I. "I have been teaching math for 27 years now," Laurel states proudly. "I really love math, but at the end of the year, I am in charge of a County Math Fair that I developed about 5 years ago. It involves middle schools from all over the county. There are over 1,500 students and parents involved in this week-long event. I'm in charge of the whole thing, and it just stresses me out. I tend to be a perfectionist about my work, and I worry all the time about being prepared for classes and getting all the homework assignments graded. I want my students to see how fun math can be, so I work very hard at making my classes interesting."

Laurel states that she tends to work nights and weekends on her classes. "I have a hard time relaxing. Darin and I play bridge on Saturday nights with some friends, but we don't do much else. Darin and his brother go fishing on the weekends, and I usually stay home and work. Sometimes we go out to eat."

11.4–3   What are some of the strengths that Laurel has mentioned in the session?

11.4–4   What are some resources in your town that might be beneficial to Laurel?

11.4–5   Laurel's husband, Darin, comes to a session with Laurel. What are some questions you could ask Darin that might benefit Laurel in therapy?

11.4–6   What is your preliminary diagnosis for Laurel?

Axis I

Axis II

Axis III

Axis IV

Axis V

 InfoTrac keywords

anorexia, binge eating, bulimia, compulsive eating, obesity

Sleep-Related Disorders | 12

DISORDERS

This section in the DSM-IV-TR (APA, 2000) contains diagnoses related to disturbances in the sleep process that cause clinically significant distress and/or psychosocial impairment. There are two major categories of sleep problems: Dyssomnias (in which a person sleeps too little, too much, or at the wrong time) and Parasomnias (in which abnormal things occur during sleep or immediately before or after sleep). Further distinctions are made related to the causal agents of the problems. In diagnosing sleep problems, one must determine whether they are related to another mental condition, a general medical condition, use of a substance, or none of the above (in which case, they would be labeled primary sleep disturbances)(APA, 2000).

It must be emphasized that sleep disturbances are expected in a number of instances. For example, sleep disturbances are part of the diagnostic criteria for several mood and anxiety disorders. Similarly, sleep disturbances are not unusual in clients suffering from cognitive, schizophrenic, or somatization disorders. When the sleep disorder is related to another mental condition, a separate diagnosis of the sleep disorder is made only when that symptom is excessive or has become the primary focus of intervention. Similar logic is applied in determining whether to make an additional diagnosis if sleep disturbance is expected as part of a general medical condition or with the use of particular substances.

The first of the Dyssomnias is Insomnia, or sleeping too little. Insomnia may take the form of problems in falling or staying asleep or it may be characterized by nonrestorative sleep (i.e., the time asleep seems adequate but the individual does not feel rested). For diagnosis, insomnia must last at least 1 month and be causing distress or psychosocial impairment. Depending on the presumed etiology of insomnia, the possible diagnoses include Primary Insomnia; Insomnia Related to Another Mental Disorder; Sleep Disorder due to a General Medical Condition, Insomnia Type; or Substance-Induced Sleep Disorder, Insomnia Type (APA, 2000).

The next Dyssomnia is Hypersomnia, or sleeping too much. This disorder is characterized either by prolonged sleep episodes or by daytime sleep episodes that occur daily or almost daily. Again, the problem must have lasted at least 1 month or be recurrent (i.e., lasting at least 3 days several times a year for at least 2 years) and be related to distress and/or psychosocial impairment. Possible diagnoses include Primary Hypersomnia; Hypersomnia Related to Another Mental Disorder; Sleep Disorder due to a General Medical Condition, Hypersomnia Type; or Substance-Induced Sleep Disorder, Hypersomnia Type (APA, 2000).

The remaining three specific Dyssomnias include Narcolepsy, Breathing-Related Sleep Disorder, and Circadian Rhythm Sleep Disorder. Narcolepsy is characterized by irresistible episodes of refreshing sleep that occur daily over at least a 3-month period. In addition, the client experiences episodes of cataplexy (brief episode of loss of muscle power) or recurrent intrusions of REM sleep in the transitions between being awake and sleeping (experienced as hallucinations or sleep paralysis) (APA, 2000).

Breathing-Related Sleep Disorder involves sleep disruption that leads to excessive sleepiness or insomnia. This disruption is caused by a sleep-related breathing condition, but not by some other general medical condition, mental disorder, or substance use. When diagnosing this condition, the practitioner should list the underlying breathing-related medical condition on Axis III (APA, 2000).

Circadian Rhythm Sleep Disorder is diagnosed when there is a persistent or recurrent pattern of sleep disruption due to disruptions in the normal sleep-wake schedule. The origin(s) of this problem is made clearer by the specifiers used. For example, Shift Work Type describes disruptions that occur because one works the night shift (and is consequently trying to sleep during the day) or changes shift assignments often. Jet Lag Type occurs when sleeping patterns are disrupted by travel across time zones. In the Delayed Sleep Phase Type, the individual is unsuccessfully trying to move his or her sleep to an earlier cycle (APA, 2000).

Finally, Dyssomnia NOS includes any other disruptions in sleeping patterns not described previously. As in all Dyssomnias, this diagnosis includes intrapersonal or psychosocial problems and excludes conditions related to general medical conditions, substance use, or another mental disorder (APA, 2000).

The other grouping of disorders covered in this section is Parasomnia, in which some disruptive event occurs during specific sleep periods and/or transitions. More specifically, these conditions refer to instances in which behaviors or physiological processes are activated inappropriately while the individual is asleep (APA, 2000).

Nightmare Disorder usually begins in children between the ages of 3 and 6 and causes significant disruptions for both the children and their parents. Although most children simply outgrow this disorder, it can persist into adulthood. Specifically, the individual experiences repeated awakenings with detailed recall of frightening dreams. Upon awakening, he or she rapidly becomes oriented. These episodes generally occur during the second half of the sleep period (APA, 2000).

In contrast, Sleep Terror Disorder occurs both among children and adults. In this condition, the individual experiences repeated episodes of abrupt awakening during the first third of a sleep cycle. Typically, the individual awakes with a scream and physiological symptoms similar to those of a panic attack. Further, the individual is generally unresponsive to attempts to be comforted and when finally fully awake, has no memory of any dream activity or of the episode. Fortunately, this is the least common of the Parasomnias (APA, 2000).

Sleepwalking Disorder usually begins in childhood and ends in adolescence. Initial onset of sleepwalking in adulthood is unusual. Specifically, sleepwalking involves the client getting up and walking around, usually during the first third of the sleep cycle. The individual is very difficult to awaken and has no memory of the incident. Finally, Parasomnia NOS describes any other unusual sleep behavior not already covered in the more specific disorders (APA, 2000).

ASSESSMENT

Assessment of sleep disorders has become a technologically advanced medical procedure in recent years. Clinics designed to diagnose the various sleep disorders are usually found as part of general hospitals, although some freestanding clinics also exist.

The procedures performed at these facilities are called polysomnography, or more simply, sleep studies. In the most common procedure, the client usually checks into the facility around 7:30 or 8:00 P.M. and leaves whenever he or she awakes in the morning. Typically, before going to bed, the client fills out instruments developed by the clinic to cover history about his or her concerns. Then, the client is taken to a "bedroom" equipped with observational devices and is fitted for several electrodes. The client is then monitored throughout the night, resulting in a complete set of information about breathing patterns and efforts, heart rate, oxygen saturation, brain activity, and muscle activity. From these data, a physician can diagnose sleep disorders and suggest appropriate treatments.

Less common sleep studies usually involve spending a day at a sleep clinic, where the frequency and length of daytime sleepiness is measured. There has been a proliferation of sleep centers, and each seems to have developed questionnaires for history and symptom description. Typically, nonmedical clinicians do not administer self-report sleep instruments because the data generated by sleep studies are much more helpful in diagnosing and formulating treatment.

SOCIAL SUPPORT SYSTEMS

Most people have had the experience of temporarily disrupted sleep at one time and consequently can well imagine the potential impact of long-standing Sleep Disorders on the individual. Excessive sleepiness resulting from either having a Dyssomnia or caring for someone with a Parasomnia can result in impaired functioning in school or at work. Although suffering from some of the Dyssomnias might have little potential for disrupting relationships, others can prompt separation in sleeping arrangements between intimate partners. Particularly if other strains are present in the relationship, this separation can have serious consequences. Caring for someone with a Parasomnia can be frightening and, over time, burdensome.

With the recent increase in medical interest in this area, there has been a corresponding increase in support services and information. The following list indicates some resources available on the Internet.

www.mentalhelp.net/guide/sleep.htm—Contains links to a host of sleep disorder links on the Web

www.websciences.org/nsf/disorder.html—Information about the variety of sleep disorders

www.srssleep.org/—Sleep research society providing information, research, and training concerning sleep and sleep disorders

www.bisleep.medsch.ucla.edu/—Sleep home pages provide research and information resources concerning sleep disorders

www.medlineplus.adam.com/ency/article/000809.htm—Information and resources concerning Night Terror Disorders

Case 12.1

Identifying Information
Client Names: John and Samantha Wildeman
Ages: Samantha, 35 years old; John, 40 years old
Ethnicity: Caucasian
Marital Status: Married
Children: One child from John's first marriage

Presenting Problem
John and Samantha Wildeman contacted the Family Counseling Agency for marital counseling. John is a 40-year-old, well-muscled individual who works as a sales distributor for a well-known frozen-pizza company. His job involves calling on grocery and convenience stores throughout the region and convincing them to buy his line of frozen pizzas. He is the sole distributor in a five-county area. Samantha is a slender, 35-year-old woman who teaches math and science at the local high school. John has one son, Robert, from his first marriage. Robert is 20 years old and away at college. He comes home periodically but has an apartment of his own.

John and Samantha have been married for 15 years and are seeking help due to increasing stress in their marriage. They both feel that they are having difficulty communicating effectively with each other, and Samantha feels that John's behavior and personality have changed dramatically over the past year. She states that she feels John is depressed, although he denies feeling down. Samantha explains that John works on his own schedule, and there have been many days over the past several months when he just hasn't bothered to work. She says that John is usually a highly motivated self-starter, and this behavior is very unusual for him.

John states that he has been feeling unusually tired and may be getting bored with his job. Several times, he has been on the verge of falling asleep in the middle of an important monthly business meeting with his regional director. His regular physical exam indicated no physical problems, with the exception of John's recent weight gain of 25 pounds. It appears that the couple's marital problems are focused on changes in John's behavior and personality. John finds no fault with Samantha except that she doesn't seem to understand that he has been under a lot of pressure with his job and that he may just need some time away from work.

You have seen John and Samantha on four occasions for couples' counseling. After the fourth session, John calls and asks to see you for an individual session. You explain to him that you can see him if he wants to come and talk about his personal issues, but he should know beforehand that he shouldn't disclose anything he doesn't want you to share with Samantha since you are seeing them as a couple. John says, "Oh, it's nothing secret. I just wanted to talk to you about some individual problems I've been experiencing lately."

12.1–1 What underlying issues do you suspect are affecting John and Samantha? What do you expect John to disclose?

Individual Session with John

John begins the session by stating that he feels he could use some individual help with his feelings of exhaustion and malaise. He states that he has always been "a very active" sleeper, but that lately, he has been waking up several times a night with a tight feeling in his chest. He says that his mouth is so dry that he drinks several glasses of water during the night. Upon awakening in the morning, he often feels more tired than when he went to bed. This problem has gotten worse over the past year, and he feels it's affecting his marriage and his job. He goes to work tired and has difficulty staying awake driving from one location to another. His job involves a great deal of driving, so this problem has been of major concern to him because he's afraid of falling asleep at the wheel.

You ask John whether this problem has developed suddenly or gradually. He tells you that Samantha used to get irritated because he was so active at night that he'd wake her up. Lately, however, she has complained of his snoring so loudly that it prevents her from being able to get to sleep. There have been many nights in the past several months when Samantha has taken a pillow and blanket and slept on the living room couch due to his snoring and restlessness at night. John feels that this has definitely created more friction and distance between them.

Due to his problems sleeping, John often has difficulty concentrating on his job during the day and feels tired and distracted. "I'm so tired by the time I get home at night, I'm just ready for an argument. I really don't think that Samantha is to blame for the problems we've been having in our marriage. I just can't cope with the pressures during the day, and I take it out on her when I get home at night. I think she's right when she says I'm not the same happy-go-lucky guy I used to be. I'm actually pretty miserable to be around right now. I am much more pessimistic and depressed than I've ever felt in my life. I can't really pinpoint what the problem is, but I think it has something to do with how poorly I've been sleeping at night."

"Did you mention any of these symptoms to your doctor when you went to see him for a physical?" you inquire of John.

"I did mention that I was feeling tired, but I also said I had been working long hours, and I think the doctor just dismissed it as a case of work overload," John tells you.

"And he gave you a clean bill of health?" you ask.

"Well, almost," John replies. "He said that my blood pressure was high, but he thought if I'd just lose some of this weight I've put on, it would improve my blood pressure. I guess that's what happens when you turn 40 and sell pizza for a living," John responds with a hearty laugh.

"It sounds as if you might have a specific kind of sleeping problem," you suggest. "Would you be willing to go to the hospital's Sleep Disorders Clinic and have them evaluate the problem you've described? I can call them and make a referral."

"I'd do just about anything if I could get a good night's sleep," says John. "It's been a long time since I've felt like I was alive and awake when I got up in the morning."

"Good, I'll develop a preliminary report and send it over to the doctors at the Sleep Clinic. I will need you to sign a consent form allowing me to release information to them. After you've been for an assessment, we'll get together and see where we go from there."

"Sounds like progress to me," says John. "I certainly appreciate you taking me seriously today."

12.1–2   What would be your preliminary diagnosis for John?
Axis I

Axis II

Axis III

Axis IV

Axis V

12.1–3   What would you recommend be communicated to Samantha at this point? How should this information be communicated to her?

Case 12.2

Identifying Information
Client Name: Katherine Carmichael
Age: 42 years old
Ethnicity: Caucasian
Marital Status: Divorced
Children: Two adolescent children

Intake Information

The intake worker reports that Katherine Carmichael called the Family Support Agency to make an appointment with a counselor. She said she hadn't been sleeping well for several months and thought it might help to talk to a counselor. She gave no further information about the cause of her sleep problems. Ms. Carmichael's schedule was full for the next 3 weeks, so an appointment was made a month in advance. The intake worker will call and remind her of the appointment 1 week prior to the time.

Initial Interview with Katherine

Katherine is an attractive, well-dressed woman who is seated in the waiting room reviewing her schedule book when you meet her. She immediately gets up, shakes your hand, and walks with you to your office. She is dressed in a light gray business suit with matching shoes and handbag. She appears to have come directly from work for this appointment.

After explaining your role as a counselor and the issues of confidentiality and informed consent, you begin by asking Katherine why she decided to make an appointment. Katherine brushes her hair back from her face and tells you she hasn't been sleeping well for about the past 4 months, and nothing she tries to resolve the problem seems to work.

"I own a real estate company here in town and have 45 agents working for me. I also sell houses myself. Recently, I've started a corporate real estate division, and we've been extremely busy getting that started as well. As you probably know, people in real estate work all hours of the day and night and weekends, and, well, business is just always on my mind. There are so many little pieces of a transaction that have to be taken care of when you sell a house, and I'm always thinking about my 'to do' list, which never seems to get any shorter."

"It sounds like you work a lot of hours," you suggest.

"I probably average 70 hours a week, especially in the past year or two. People have been buying houses like crazy," Katherine states. "I rarely get through a dinner without the phone ringing. Not that I don't enjoy it. I love my work and have been very successful at it, but there's very little leisure time available when you own your own business. And then I have my children to think about, too."

"And how old are your children?" you ask.

"Tony is 15 and plays soccer after school, and Theresa is 13 and she's got ballet and art classes every day after school. I try to work it out so I can attend some of Tony's games and take Theresa to her ballet classes, but it's hectic at times," Katherine explains.

"Sounds like you're very busy," you suggest.

"Extremely busy. I don't have time to breathe most of the time. You would think I'd sleep like a log, but I just haven't been able to," Katherine replies. "It should be better next year when Tony can drive. That will be a big help to me."

"I'm sure that will be," you reply. "How are you juggling all of this work and children as a single mother?"

"Well, my ex-husband helps some with getting the kids to their activities when he's in town. But he's gone a lot on business, so he's not always around. We still have a friendly relationship, but we communicate mostly through answering machines," Katherine states.

"Besides being extremely busy with your job and the children, are there other things that have been bothering you lately?" you ask.

"No, not really. I just can't seem to turn my mind off until late at night. When I finally get to sleep, I sleep for a few hours and then I'm wide awake again at 3:30 or 4 A.M. And I'm afraid if I go back to sleep, I won't hear the alarm and will be late getting the kids to school."

"So you're having a difficult time getting to sleep," you note. "About what time do you get to sleep?"

"Oh, it's about 11:30 or midnight before I get to sleep, so I'm existing on 3 or 4 hours of sleep every night, and I'm just exhausted if you want to know the truth," Katherine responds.

"Are you taking any medications?" you ask.

"Well, I tried an over-the-counter drug to help me get to sleep, but it didn't really help, so I quit taking it," Katherine replies.

"Anything else, even if it's not for sleep?" you ask.

"No, I don't take anything prescribed," Katherine responds.

"What about alcoholic beverages?" you ask. "How often do you consume alcohol?"

"Only occasionally, when I go out for dinner or on special occasions," Katherine states.

"Nothing on a routine basis. For my children's sake, I don't keep alcohol in the house."

"How has your mood been lately?" you inquire. "Have you noticed any changes in your mood?"

"I'm probably a bit more grouchy because of lack of sleep and, in general, just tired all the time," Katherine explains.

"Have you felt anxious or depressed lately?" you ask. You wonder if there have been any changes in Katherine's emotional state recently.

"No, I wouldn't say I'm anxious or depressed, but I do worry a lot about the business. I'm just responsible for so much that it's overwhelming at times."

"Okay, so you really feel that the primary difficulty you've been experiencing lately has been related to sleep?" you inquire.

"Yes, that's the only thing that's really bothering me right now. I think if I could sleep better, I'd feel more energized and able to handle all the demands of work and home," Katherine tells you.

"That sounds like something we can work on together. Would you be willing to make time to come in and see me once a week for the next few weeks?" you ask.

"Yes, I'll make a point to clear out a time to come in. I really want to get back to sleeping better," Katherine explains.

12.2–1   What strengths did you notice in Katherine and/or her situation?

12.2–2   List the stressors she is currently experiencing.

12.2–3   What would be your preliminary diagnosis?

Axis I

Axis II

Axis III

Axis IV

Axis V

12.2–4   Are there additional diagnoses you would like to rule out?

InfoTrac keywords

hypersomnia, insomnia, narcolepsy, sleep disorder, sleep disturbance

Impulse-Control Disorders Not Elsewhere Classified

13

DISORDERS

Numerous diagnoses in the DSM-IV-TR (APA, 2000) include a component focused on problems with impulse control. For example, the Substance-Related Disorders all include an element of continuing substance use despite negative consequences. The Antisocial Personality Disorder, the Paraphilia, and Conduct Disorder diagnoses all include engaging in activities for which there may be substantial negative consequences. Even persons with a Schizophrenic or Mood Disorder diagnosis may act on ideas (or impulses) without regard to consequences.

In this section, the diagnoses include a variety of situations in which the client fails to resist an impulse, drive, and/or temptation to engage in behavior with a clear potential for negative effects. In most of the disorders, the client's actions are believed to be an attempt to relieve some growing sense of tension or arousal. After performing the behavior, the client experiences a sense of relief or gratification that may be followed by feelings of regret or guilt (APA, 2000).

The first of these disorders is Intermittent Explosive Disorder. The key criterion consists of discrete episodes of failing to resist aggressive impulses that result in actual assault and/or property destruction. Although frequently the client may isolate a "cause" or "trigger" for these destructive outbursts, the degree of aggressiveness involved is judged to exceed a reasonable response to the specific provocation. The final criterion is ruling out a wide range of other mental disorders that could include such outbursts. Although some clients with this diagnosis describe these outbursts as relieving some inner tension, the diagnostic criteria do not reference such an underlying cycle (APA, 2000).

In Kleptomania, the cycles of growing internal discomfort and a sense of relief when performing the theft are part of the diagnostic criteria. Further, the objects stolen are not needed for personal or monetary use or to express anger or revenge toward their owner. Again, several other mental disorders should be ruled out before making this diagnosis (APA, 2000).

Quite similarly, the diagnosis of Pyromania includes criteria related to building and relieving tensions. Clients with this disorder evidence a general fascination with fire. Again, the fire setting is not motivated by receiving material gain, expressing some ideological viewpoint, or concealing other criminal activity. Also, various other mental disorders should be ruled out (APA, 2000).

The last diagnosis that follows this clear pattern is Trichotillomania. In this disorder, the individual pulls out his or her own hair (in sufficient quantities to be noticeable) to relieve the building sense of tension and to achieve some sense of relief or gratification. In this instance, there is no question of some alternative gain related to the behavior, but other mental or physical disorders should be ruled out (APA, 2000).

Pathological Gambling is the final specific disorder in this section. This diagnosis is based on a persistent and recurrent pattern of behavior in which gambling is continued despite negative consequences. Generally, individuals with this disorder exhibit addictive-like behaviors with preoccupation, an apparent need to escalate the amount of money involved, and/or an inability to control the behavior. Somewhat similar to clients with other diagnoses in this section, the client with Pathological Gambling Disorder reports gambling as a means to "feel better" and/or "solve problems." As in other addictive disorders, the client often engages in lying to conceal the amount of gambling, engages in illegal activities to fund the gambling, becomes reliant on others for financial support, and/or jeopardizes a variety of important relationships or occupational opportunities because of his or her gambling A diagnosis of Impulse-Control Disorder NOS exists to cover any other impulse-related problems not constituting a more specific diagnosis (APA, 2000).

ASSESSMENT

Few specifically focused assessment instruments have been developed for the diagnoses in this section. To some extent, general personality profiles like the MMPI-2 or the MMPI-A may be useful if the content scales that address broader issues like anger or obsessiveness are included in the administration and analysis. More commonly, in-depth interviewing regarding the problematic actions is used. Such interviews should focus particularly on the internal experience of the client in the times prior to, during, and after action.

The exception to this pattern is in the area of Pathological Gambling, where there has been more instrument development. The South Oaks Gambling Screen (SOGS) is a 20-item questionnaire that has demonstrated reasonable reliability and known-groups validity in a variety of settings and several different languages (Lesieur & Blume, 1987, 1993). These authors have also developed a companion screening tool, South Oaks Leisure Activities Screen (SOLAS) (Lesieur & Blume, 1993), for use with significant others, but its psychometric properties remain unknown.

It should also be noted that the Addiction Severity Index (ASI) (see chapter 4 for detail) has been expanded and modified for use with clients with gambling problems (Lesieur & Blume, 1992). Because of the rate of comorbidity between Pathological Gambling and substance-abuse problems, this instrument is particularly useful in substance-abuse treatment facilities.

Finally, an assessment instrument designed to screen for the potential of Pathological Gambling in adolescents and young adults has been developed.

The 19-item Problem Gambling Scale (Moore & Ohtsuka, 1999) focuses primarily on cognitive factors related to control over gambling. While beginning work evidences reasonable psychometric properties (i.e., coefficient alphas above .80 for most subscales), no work has demonstrated its predictive validity.

CULTURAL CONSIDERATIONS

With the exception of Pathological Gambling, the disorders in this section of the DSM-IV-TR are relatively rare (i.e., probably affecting less than 1% of the population) (APA, 2000). Consequently, few data are available for estimating distinctive prevalence rates. With that caution, it appears that Intermittent Explosive Disorder and Pyromania occur more frequently in males. Similarly, Kleptomania seems to occur more frequently in females, whereas the incidence of Trichotillomania is similar for both males and females.

Although Pathological Gambling apparently occurs at a more substantial rate (i.e., roughly 3.5% of adult populations and as high as 8% among adolescents and young adults), there is not a clear picture regarding differential occurrence (APA, 2000). As the availability of legal gambling has increased, the overrepresentation of males has steadily decreased. Indeed, female gamblers are often faced with more social stigma, which in turn may further obscure the prevalence of Pathological Gambling Disorder in women.

SOCIAL SUPPORT SYSTEMS

The potential for disruption to both social and occupational functioning for people diagnosed with these disorders should be evident. The self-help systems for clients with Pathological Gambling Disorder are the best developed. The following Internet resources may be useful to both clients and their significant others.

> www.mhsource.com/expert/exp1120197d.html—Information on the causes and cures of Kleptomania

> www.personalmd.com/news/a1999022214.shtml—Information about the use of Prozac for the treatment of Kleptomania

> www.psyweb.com/Mdisord/impud.html—Discusses the definition and treatment alternatives for Impulse-Control Disorders

> www.psychnet-uk.com/clinical_psychology/clinical_psychology_impulse_control_disorders.htm—Provides links to information about specific Impulse-Control Disorders

> www.cnn.com/HEALTH/9609/05/born.gamblers—Articles examining the possibility that compulsive gambling could be linked to one's genes

> www.healthanswers.com/library/MedEnc/enc/2832.asp—Information regarding the signs and symptoms of compulsive gambling

Case 13.1

Identifying Information
Client Name: Jerry Parker
Age: 21 years old
Educational Level: Graduate student
Marital Status: Single

Background Information

You are a counselor at the University Counseling Service. Your caseload consists primarily of undergraduate and graduate students who attend the university. The counseling center is paid for with university fees, so students do not pay for services on a session-by-session basis. Students are seen on average for 10–20 sessions, but there is no limit to the number of sessions they can have.

Intake Information

Jerry walked into the University Counseling Service and requested to see a counselor due to problems with a relationship in which he had been involved over the past 6 months. He stated he would prefer to see a female counselor since he wanted a woman's perspective regarding his relationship with his girlfriend. He appeared to be an attractive young man who seemed somewhat nervous about requesting services. The intake worker attempted to put him at ease and stated that he could see a counselor later in the afternoon.

Initial Interview

You meet Jerry in the waiting room and ask him to join you in your office. Jerry smiles and seems eager to talk with you. You note that Jerry is slightly balding in an unusual spot on the top of his head, but appears to be a very nice-looking, well-groomed college student.

To begin the session, you ask Jerry where he is from and what courses he is taking at the university. He tells you he came from a small town about 3 hours from the university and is majoring in business and accounting in the School of Business. He has a 4.0 average so far and will be a senior next year. He also states that he is the oldest in the family and will be the first person in his family to graduate from college. His father has a degree from a technical school in computers and has a good job with a computer corporation; his mother works at the phone company. They are both very happy that Jerry is going to be a college graduate. Jerry also tells you that he has two younger sisters, one of whom will be attending the university next year.

"What made you decide to seek counseling right now?" you ask.

"Well, I've been having some problems in my relationship with my girlfriend, Marsha," Jerry explains. "We've been seeing each other for about 6 months and I really like her a lot, but lately she seems to be getting more and more irritated with me for some reason."

"What's she been getting irritated about?" you ask.

"Oh, I don't know. She says I have these quirky little habits that she doesn't like," Jerry offers.

"Quirky habits?" you wonder out loud.

"Yeah, I think I'm sort of like my dad in some ways," Jerry states.

"Okay. How are you like your dad?" you ask.

"Well, you know, he's kind of particular about certain things—like he keeps everything in perfect order all the time. You know, like he has all this paper, I mean tons of it, and he has to know where every piece of paper is at all times. He's like perfectly organized. I mean perfect," Jerry says.

"So, he's a very organized person. Anything else?" you inquire.

"Well, he's a collector," Jerry tells you. "He collects old books and rare coins and stuff like that. He has bookshelves up to the ceiling in the den at home, and he has a system for keeping his books in order. And his coins are all neatly put in these boxes, and he knows where every coin is. He's got about a hundred boxes of coins."

"And do you collect things, too, like your dad does?" you ask.

"Well, not exactly, but I have a lot of stuff—it's not like collector's items or anything like that. But I do like to organize it," Jerry states.

"What kind of stuff do you have?" you ask.

"Well, I have a lot of tapes and CDs, and my girlfriend says I spend too much time messing with them," Jerry says.

"So that's one of the quirky habits she doesn't like," you wonder.

"Well, sort of, it's not that big a deal, but I think it does irritate her a little," Jerry says.

"So, there are other things that bother her?" you ask.

Jerry squirms in his chair a bit and looks around the room uncomfortably. It seems that he's having a hard time talking about the more important issues that brought him in for counseling.

"Well, yeah, there are," Jerry says. "You know, this is really a lot harder than I thought

it would be. Maybe I should think about this whole thing a little more and come back some other time."

"Talking about these habits makes you feel pretty uncomfortable," you say in an attempt to let Jerry know you understand how he's feeling.

"Yeah, I've never really talked about these things before," Jerry says. "It's sort of been—well, actually, it's been a big secret up until recently."

"So, it sounds as if maybe your girlfriend has figured out your secret or something like that and doesn't like it?" you ask tentatively.

"Yeah, exactly," Jerry says. "She's figured out exactly about the habit, and she thinks I should just be able to stop."

"And it's really hard for you to just stop?" you ask.

"Exactly. In fact, I don't think I can and that's why I'm here," Jerry says.

"You know, Jerry, I see people with all kinds of things that are bothering them. Sometimes, when they begin talking about those things, the problems don't seem so hard to cope with as when the people are just keeping those things to themselves," you suggest.

13.1–1   What diagnoses are you considering at this point?

Jerry sits quietly for a few minutes, apparently mulling over what you've just told him. You allow the silence to give him a chance to think.

"Well, okay. I hope you don't think I'm totally crazy, but I have this terrible habit of pulling out my hair," Jerry says.

"Okay, I understand," you say.

"You do? Whew, that wasn't so bad—telling you I mean. You can tell a little bit on my head,"

Jerry points to the top of his head, "but let me show you the real problem." Jerry begins rolling up the sleeve of his shirt, and you notice that he has no hair on his right arm. Jerry rolls up the other sleeve, and his left arm is also completely devoid of hair. "See what I mean?" Jerry asks beseechingly. He looks very tense and worried about your response to his divulgence.

"Yes, Jerry, I see exactly what you mean. And I know how hard it was for you to tell me about it. Do you mind if I ask you a few questions about it?" you ask carefully.

"No, it's okay," Jerry says. "Actually, it's a relief to have told someone."

"Jerry, can you describe how you feel before you begin pulling at your hair?" you query.

"Geez, it's like there's this big buildup. Believe it or not, I try really hard not to pull out my hair, but the harder I try not to, the more uptight I get until I just can't stop myself and I feel like I have to do it," Jerry explains.

"Okay, and how do you feel after you've pulled out some of your hair?" you ask.

"You know, this is going to sound crazy, but I actually feel better," Jerry comments. "It's almost like it's a huge relief."

"So, it's as if there's this tense feeling that builds up inside you, and then when you give into the feeling that you need to pull out some hair, it feels better," you suggest tentatively.

"Yeah, in fact, you might even say it feels enjoyable in an odd kind of way," Jerry says.

"Okay, I think I understand what you're describing," you say. "You've shown me your arms and the top of your head. Are there other places where you pull your hair?" you ask.

"Sometimes on my legs," Jerry motions to both of his calves. "But it's not nearly as bad as on my arms and my head. Sometimes, I don't even realize I'm doing it, it's become such a habit," Jerry says.

"I understand what you're saying. How long do you think you've been doing this, Jerry?" you query.

"Well, I probably started pulling at my hair when I was just a kid. I remember sitting in school pulling at my eyebrows and eyelashes. The teacher used to tell me to stop. For some reason, I don't do that anymore. Maybe I figured out it was too obvious, or maybe it just embarrassed me when the teacher would say something about it, so I switched to my arms," Jerry suggests pensively. "For a long time, it was just my arms and sometimes my legs, but probably in the last couple of years, I've started pulling at the hair on my head."

"Okay, do you think you do this when you get anxious about something, or do you connect it with any particular way you are feeling?" you ask.

"No, it seems more of a mindless thing to me. Except that I do feel this tension building up inside me if I try not to do it, and then there's relief afterward."

"I think I understand, Jerry," you say calmly. "I know how difficult this has been to talk about, and I really appreciate the fact that you told me about this habit. And I think there are some things we can work on to help you get over this habit. Would you be interested in working with me for a while to see if it would help resolve this problem?" you ask.

"Yeah," Jerry responds, "I think I'm finally ready to do something about it. It's begun getting in the way of my life, and I really want to get rid of this habit."

13.1–2   What strengths have you noticed in Jerry?

13.1–3   What monitoring assignment(s) would you give Jerry until the next session?

13.1–4   What diagnosis would you give Jerry?
Axis I

Axis II

Axis III

Axis IV

Axis V

Case 13.2

Identifying Information
Client Name: Sandra Jenkins
Age: 38 years old
Ethnicity: Caucasian
Marital Status: Married
Occupation: "Retired" attorney
Children: Jessica, age 6

Referral Information

Sandra has been mandated to get counseling as one of the terms of her probation for a conviction of shoplifting from a local department store at the mall. She stated that she meant to pay for the diamond earrings that were found in her coat pocket, but she got distracted and forgot. From her probation records, you discover that she has had two prior convictions of shoplifting, but because she retained a well-known lawyer, she was given community service without probation. This time, however, the judge placed her on probation and mandated her to counseling for the duration of the probationary period.

Initial Interview

Sandra Jenkins, a 38-year-old Caucasian female, is a very poised, attractive woman who attended a prestigious college and graduate school. She received a law degree when she was 26 years old and worked as a corporate tax lawyer making over $100,000 per year. Sandra reports that she has excellent analytical skills and a very high IQ. She met her husband, Jim, during her first year of practice. Jim is also a corporate lawyer.

Sandra and Jim married a year after their first date. They live in a wealthy suburban neighborhood with their only child, Jessica, age 6. Sandra states that she had two miscarriages before having Jessica and doesn't plan on having other children. Sandra quit her job after Jessica

was born and has engaged in volunteer work at the hospital for the past 4 years.

Sandra's grandparents were from Italy, and they passed away by the time Sandra was 5 years old. Her paternal grandfather had a history of alcoholism. Sandra's parents moved to the United States when she was only 2 years old. She had two older brothers and a younger sister. Sandra came from a low-income family and worked her way through college and law school. Her mother suffered from depression and stayed at home. Her father worked in the garment industry in New York.

In giving this information, Sandra appears to be nonchalant and unconcerned about the shoplifting incident, but also a bit defensive in her responses to your questions. After talking for some time, however, she begins to seem more willing to engage in a relationship with you as the counselor.

Beginning where the client is, you ask Sandra what she would like to work on during these sessions. She states that she is concerned about her marriage and isn't sure if she wants to stay married to Jim.

"Life has seemed so unfulfilling lately. Jessica is in school all day, and I just don't know what to do anymore to fill the hours I have to myself. I feel bored and lonely a lot of the time. I admit I need a lot of stimulation in my life. I've always gotten bored easily. Jim says I should be happy not having to work and that I can do anything I want to do. Besides, I'm bored in our relationship, too. We used to go on trips and have a very exciting sex life, but now, it's just dull. Jim doesn't want to go to interesting places. He likes to go to the beach and fish. And we don't even have sex that often anymore. Partly because it's boring to me, but Jim doesn't seem that interested either. I don't know; maybe I just need a change."

"Do you think these feelings are related to the shoplifting incident?" you ask.

Sandra looks flushed and guiltily turns her head away. "I just don't know what comes over me. I go into a store thinking I'm just going to do some window-shopping. I don't really intend to buy anything, and then this intense urge to take something just overwhelms me. It's not like I couldn't just buy it. We have plenty of money. I don't know what happens, but I just feel like I've got to have something and I take it."

"How does it feel once you've taken the item?" you query.

"Actually, I feel better—unless I get caught, and then I feel terrible about myself," Sandra relates.

"Can you tell me how many times this has happened when you haven't gotten caught?" you ask.

Sandra eyes you warily. "Who says I've ever done it when I wasn't caught?"

"You did just a few minutes ago when you were telling me how it made you feel," you suggest.

"Well, I guess there have been a few times when I didn't get caught. It wasn't anything expensive though. Just some fake jewelry and stuff like that. I didn't even really like the things I took," Sandra responds.

"What do you usually do with the items you take from the store when you get home?" you ask.

"I just throw them in a drawer in my dresser or put them away in the closet. The urge goes away for a while and then it comes back again."

"How often do you have this urge? Is it once a week or once a month or just every once in a while?" you ask her.

"It's really odd. Sometimes, I feel the urge every time I go shopping, about twice a week. Then, it disappears for months at a time before it comes back. If you want to know the truth, it's been happening to me for years. Even back in college, I was taking stuff from stores. Sometimes I'd take stuff I didn't even need and give it to other girls in the dorm. In fact, most of the time, I stick it in a drawer and end up throwing it away without ever having used it," Sandra states.

"Do you have any idea what causes this urge to come over you?" you ask.

"No idea whatsoever," Sandra states. "I just see it, I begin to feel this intense urge to take it, and then after I have it, the urge goes away and I feel better. I know it's against the law. After all, I'm a lawyer, for goodness sake. What do you think is wrong with me?" Sandra wonders.

"I think that's what we're going to work on when you come in to see me for these sessions. You're required to come to counseling on a weekly basis for a year. Hopefully, by our working together, you'll be able to change some of these behaviors you've been engaging in. Are you willing to work on making some changes?" you ask.

Sandra agrees to come for weekly counseling sessions. You feel that you've established some initial rapport with her since she was willing to admit some of her past behaviors.

13.2–1   Sandra has several strengths. List three of them.

13.2–2   Are there other questions you would like to ask Sandra? If so, what are they?

13.2–3 What are some resources that might be helpful to Sandra?

13.2–4 What diagnosis would you give Sandra?
Axis I

Axis II

Axis III

Axis IV

Axis V

InfoTrac keywords

compulsive gambling, Kleptomania

Personality Disorders

| 14

DISORDERS

The diagnoses in this section of the DSM-IV-TR (APA, 2000) are listed on Axis II. The Personality Disorders refer to pervasive, persistent, relatively inflexible personality traits that lead to functional impairment or subjective distress. In this sense, departures from expectations of the individual's culture may include the cognitive approaches to viewing the self or others, emotional range, intensity, stability and/or appropriateness, interpersonal functioning, and/or impulse control. The pattern in question should be stable across a broad range of situations, be established by early adulthood, and not be due to another Axis I disorder, a general medical condition, or substance usage (APA, 2000).

Although the criteria for the specific personality disorders do *not* preclude their use with children or adolescents (with the exception of Antisocial Personality Disorder), clinicians are encouraged to be extremely circumspect in applying these labels with young people. Usually, problematic personality traits exhibited in early years will often not persist into adulthood. In any event, for these diagnoses to be applied to persons under the age of 18, the specified behavior needs to have been present for at least 1 year (APA, 2000).

The specific diagnoses in this section are divided into three "clusters" or subgroupings based on similarities in symptom presentation. Often, an individual warranting a diagnosis of a particular personality disorder will exhibit traits related to other diagnoses within the same cluster. Less frequently, an individual may exhibit a grouping of traits related to a particular cluster of personality disorders without fully meeting any specific diagnosis; this may also be diagnosed as a Personality Disorder NOS. Clinicians may simply list such personality traits on Axis II, particularly if their presence is deemed to have relevance to treating a coexisting Axis I disorder (APA, 2000).

The first cluster, Cluster A Personality Disorders, refers to a pattern of behavior that is generally viewed as odd or eccentric. Commonly, clients with one of these disorders tend to isolate themselves and/or be suspicious. Frequently, a pattern of social isolation can be traced into childhood. People with Cluster A Personality Disorders seldom seek treatment (APA, 2000).

The first Cluster A diagnosis is Paranoid Personality Disorder. A pervasive distrust and/or suspiciousness of others characterize clients with this diagnosis. More specifically, they may suspect others of having malevolent motives, be pre-occupied with concerns about others, be reluctant to confide in others, be extremely sensitive to perceived criticisms, and/or bear grudges against others (APA, 2000).

The next Cluster A diagnosis is Schizoid Personality Disorder. Clients with this diagnosis are characterized by a general detachment from social relationships and a restricted range of emotional expression. More particularly, they consistently prefer isolation to social relations, generally have few interests or hobbies, seldom engage in intimate relationships, seem indifferent to others' opinions of them, and/or are described as cold or emotionless (APA, 2000).

The diagnosis of Schizotypal Personality Disorder completes Cluster A. Clients with this diagnosis typically have restricted interpersonal relationships and evidence marked peculiarities in thinking and perception. More specifically, they show thinking and perceptual processes similar to, but not as severe as, those in persons diagnosed with Schizophrenia or other Psychotic Disorders. For example, someone with this personality disorder may have ideas of reference but not so pervasively as to be considered delusions of reference (APA, 2000).

The Cluster B Personality Disorders refer to a pattern of behavior that is generally viewed as dramatic or emotional. In particular, clients with one of these disorders often display erratic or impulsive behaviors. Further, there is generally a marked self-absorption that results in a diminished capacity for empathy (APA, 2000).

The first Cluster B Personality diagnosis is Antisocial Personality Disorder. It should be noted that this diagnosis is not given to clients under the age of 18 (a diagnosis of Conduct Disorder would generally capture the same types of behavior among these younger people). Clients with this diagnosis usually engage in illegal activities, routinely practice deceit, are often aggressive or violent, are typically irresponsible, and generally ignore the rights and feelings of others. Further, these clients rarely show remorse for their behavior. Typically, they do not seek treatment but may be referred because of interactions with the legal system or in conjunction with substance-abuse treatment (APA, 2000).

The next Cluster B diagnosis is Borderline Personality Disorder. Clients with this diagnosis typically evidence erratic interpersonal relationships, fluctuating self-image and/or affect, and marked impulsivity. They frequently engage in suicidal or self-mutilating behaviors. They are noted for extremes in affect and in judgment; people diagnosed with this disorder rarely see themselves or others in a balanced way. These clients are the most likely of people with Personality Disorders to seek treatment (APA, 2000).

The next Cluster B diagnosis is Histrionic Personality Disorder. Clients with this diagnosis evidence emotionality and attention seeking. They generally are only comfortable when they are the "center of attention" and will use physical appearance, speech, and emotions to command others' attention (APA, 2000).

The final Cluster B diagnosis is Narcissistic Personality Disorder. A grandiose sense of self-importance, a need for attention, and a reduced capacity for empathy characterize clients with this diagnosis. They often seem to have an exaggerated sense of entitlement and expect to be admired and obeyed by others.

With these last two Personality Disorders, clients usually seek treatment to address their frustration with other people (APA, 2000).

The Cluster C Personality Disorders include patterns of behavior that are essentially fearful and/or anxious. Clients with these disorders tend toward being perfectionistic or rigid in standards or expectations for themselves or others. Like people with Cluster A diagnoses, clients with Cluster C disorders are relatively unlikely to seek treatment (APA, 2000).

The first of the Cluster C diagnoses is Avoidant Personality Disorder. Clients with this diagnosis show marked feelings of inadequacy that are associated with hypersensitivity to negative feedback and/or social inhibition. More specifically, these clients seldom put themselves in "risky" or even new situations in which they may perform poorly. They seldom develop intimate interpersonal relationships and may even constrain occupational choices based on fear of negative judgments and/or a demand for high levels of social interaction (APA, 2000).

The next specific diagnosis in Cluster C is Dependent Personality Disorder. Clients with this disorder seek someone to take care of them, even to the extent of being submissive, clinging, and fearful of separation. These clients avoid decisive action and encourage others to make decisions for them. The characteristic subservence makes it quite difficult to express disagreement, even when asked to undertake unpleasant activities. These clients fear being alone and quickly substitute a new relationship if an old one is lost. They systematically underestimate themselves and their ability to function independently (APA, 2000).

The final Cluster C diagnosis is Obsessive-Compulsive Personality Disorder. Clients with this diagnosis have well-controlled, perfectionistic patterns of behavior at the expense of spontaneity, flexibility, and even efficiency. More particularly, there is often such preoccupation with planning and details that tasks are not completed. These clients have difficulty delegating responsibilities and, in fact, tend to work long hours in order to meet their own standards regarding productivity. Also, they tend to collect and hoard things even when those things have little value. Unlike persons with Obsessive-Compulsive Disorder, individuals with Obsessive-Compulsive Personality Disorder do not necessarily have obsessions or compulsions. Rather than have full-fledged obsessions and compulsions, they tend to be rigid in their actions and thinking, adhering to strict and controlled patterns of thought and behaviors (APA, 2000).

ASSESSMENT

Detailed and thorough histories are necessary for the diagnosis of a Personality Disorder. Often the level of detail needed to substantiate a pattern of persistent and pervasive personality traits is not obtained when the clinical focus is on an Axis I mental disorder. Consequently, it is not unusual to defer diagnosis on Axis II when evaluating adults who have more prominent or pressing issues.

The MMPI-2 (see chapter 1 for detail) can be useful in assessing the presence of the various Personality Disorders, particularly as the Content Scales are included in its administration. Due to the target age range of the MMPI-A, there is much less emphasis on the possibility of Personality Disorders in its interpretation.

Two other broad-based assessment instruments have been designed to address the presence of a Personality Disorder more directly. The Millon Clinical

Multiaxial Inventory (MCMI-III) (Millon & Davis, 1997) consists of 175 true-false items designed primarily to detect a variety of Personality Disorders, including some that are listed only in the DSM-IV-TR Appendix (APA, 2000) for diagnoses under consideration. The MCMI-III has additional subscales for detecting some of the more common Axis I mental disorders as well. Similar to other NCS Pearson products, the MCMI has been well researched and validated in its various versions.

Another set of instruments designed to detect Personality Disorders has been developed by Coolidge and associates. The Coolidge Axis II Inventory (CATI) (Coolidge & Merwin, 1992) consists of 200 questions self-rated on a 4-point scale, ranging from "strongly false" to "strongly true." Two other companion instruments are available. The CATI—Significant Other Form (Coolidge, Burns, & Mooney, 1995) is designed for completion by a person familiar with the client, and the Kids' Coolidge Axis II Inventory (KCATI) (Coolidge et al., 1990) is designed to assess Personality Disorders or their precursors in children and adolescents (ages 5–17). All of these instruments have demonstrated reasonable psychometric properties.

CULTURAL CONSIDERATIONS

Judgments about persistent and pervasive personality traits cannot be made without consideration of a person's cultural background. Caution should be exercised when evaluating clients whose culture of origin is unfamiliar to the assessor. Particular care should be exercised in diagnosing members of minority groups with Paranoid Personality Disorder. There is a tendency to underestimate the existence of prejudice and discrimination by people who are not members of the group in question.

The incidence of certain Personality Disorders seems sharply divided along gender lines. For example, men are much more likely to be diagnosed with Antisocial Personality Disorder, whereas women predominate in diagnoses of Borderline, Histrionic, and Dependent Personality Disorders. Even though this may, in fact, reflect an actual difference in prevalence, clinicians should be cautious about over- or underdiagnosing these disorders based on gender role stereotypes.

SOCIAL SUPPORT SYSTEMS

In contrast to the impact of other mental disorders, the impact of Personality Disorders on both social relationships and occupational functioning is more accurately described as "constraining" than "disrupting." Because these are persistent patterns of behavior established by early adulthood, the characteristics directly influence both social and vocational choices. For example, individuals with a diagnosis of Dependent Personality Disorder would not likely seek or be comfortable with an egalitarian relationship. Similarly, people with a Cluster A Personality Disorder are not likely to become salespeople.

These constraints are also evidenced in patterns of seeking treatment. As has been indicated, few people with Personality Disorders actively seek treatment. Those who do are frequently "motivated" by circumstances that prevent them from comfortably continuing their pattern of behavior. For example, someone with Antisocial Personality Disorder may seek intervention only to minimize the intrusion of the legal system into his or her life. People with a Cluster A Personality Disorder may be "forced" into treatment when changing circumstances force them to interact more broadly with the world (e.g., when their parents die).

With these characteristics in mind, it is not surprising that most community resources and Internet sites are devoted to "explaining" Personality Disorders to those who may be associated with the client.

www.medscape.com/NATCO/PiT/2000/v10.n04/pit1004.04.dobb/pit1004.04.dobb-01.html—Article presented in Medscape concerning Personality Disorders and the prognosis for transplant patients with Personality Disorders; includes a good discussion of two ways of defining and classifying Personality Disorders

www.medscape.com/medscape/psychiatry/journal/1997/v02.n09/mh3253.carver/mh3253.carver.html—Medscape article that describes the clinical aspects of Borderline Personality Disorder

www.medscape.com/medscape/psychiatry/journal/1998/v03.n03/mh3155.dono/mh3155.dono.html—Discussion of disruptive behavior disorders and the antisocial spectrum

www.medscape.com/medscape/cno/2000/APA/Story.cfm?story_id=1170—Lecture on "Personality Disorders and Other Issues in Adolescent Psychiatry" by Elizabeth Weller

www.mentalhelp.net/disorders/sx36.htm—Discussion of Narcissistic Personality Disorder, including symptoms and treatment issues

www.psychcentral.com/resources/Personality/—A listing of Web resources regarding Personality Disorders with abstracts on the topics in the links

Case 14.1

Identifying Information
Client Name: Natalie Loftin
Age: 29 years old
Ethnicity: Caucasian
Educational Level: College graduate
Occupation: Administrative assistant

Intake Information

Natalie Loftin contacted the Marriage and Family Counseling Center due to concerns about her relationship with her boyfriend, Larry Watkins, over the past 6 months. She reported that she has been so upset that she hasn't been able to function at work and her coworkers told her she needs to get some help.

When the intake worker asked her what she meant by "upset," Natalie stated that she felt so depressed and empty that she didn't think she could stand it. A friend of hers gave her the name of this agency since it has a sliding-scale fee structure. Natalie said she also was having financial difficulties and hoped her insurance would cover the cost of counseling. The intake worker assured her that the cost of sessions was based on the client's ability to pay and that if Natalie had insurance coverage, the cost would be minimal. Natalie agreed to come in for an initial interview the following week. Her case was assigned to you.

Initial Interview

You find Natalie restlessly moving around in the waiting area chewing on her fingernail and flipping through a magazine while she walks. She is a petite, well-groomed woman wearing a dark blue suit, a yellow blouse, and small heels. Her long, brown, curly hair is pulled back in a large clip, and she has applied a considerable amount of makeup.

You introduce yourself as the counselor and ask her to come with you to your office. Natalie readily agrees and begins talking as you walk down the hall.

"My friend, Denise, told me that this was a good place to come to talk to someone. Do you know Denise?" she asks.

"No, I'm afraid I don't, but even if I did, I couldn't tell you because everything we discuss here is confidential. We don't even tell anyone that someone is being seen by a counselor at this agency," you reply. "Won't you come in and have a seat?"

"Oh, I see. Well, I guess that's a good thing," Natalie responds. "What is your degree? I have a bachelor's degree in math and computer science."

"That's impressive," you respond. "My degree is in mental health counseling. All the counselors at this agency are master's level counselors, and we work with people who are attempting to cope with a variety of emotional issues. Everything we talk about is confidential, but I must tell you that if you tell me that you may harm yourself or someone else, I cannot keep that confidential and I must report that information to either the police or my supervisor. Do you understand that?" you ask.

Natalie thinks for a minute and then replies, "Yes, that makes sense. I haven't really thought about suicide this week. That's what you're talking about, isn't it?"

You decide to note that Natalie inferred that she has thought about suicide in the past but to wait before delving into that issue since it might be too much divulgence too fast for Natalie to handle. "Yes, maybe we could begin by you telling me why you decided to make an appointment."

"Okay. Well, I've been dating this guy, Larry—Larry Watkins—for about the last 6 months. He and I just seemed to have a whole lot in common, and I really thought this was going to turn into a permanent relationship. We just seemed to get along so well and, you know, after seeing each other for about a month, he moved in with me and it just seemed to be great. I just don't know what happened." Tears well up in Natalie's eyes, and she looks as if she's about to burst into tears.

"I see. You were living together for the past 5 months and everything seemed to be going well. Then what happened?" you inquire.

"Well, we got into this big argument about my parents. I mean it was a huge argument one night. We stayed up all night arguing, and in the morning, he just said he couldn't take it anymore and packed a bag and left."

"Okay. Did you ever argue before this?" you ask.

"Well, sometimes, usually over little things. One time I remember thinking I had some kind of love-hate relationship with Larry, but then things got better, and I just felt like this guy could really take care of me. But since the other night, I'm wondering what's wrong with me. This has been the sixth time I've been involved with someone and had the relationship just blow up in my face. I hate it and I hate myself when this happens." Natalie slumps down in her chair, and tears well up in her eyes again, but she doesn't actually cry.

"Okay, so you've had other relationships that have ended abruptly," you suggest.

"Yes, five other relationships that were serious. I guess I dated other boys in high school, but those don't really count. I just don't understand it."

"Can you tell me what you and Larry were arguing about the other night? You said it was about your parents," you acknowledge.

"Yes, you see, Larry doesn't like my parents or, at least, he thinks I'm too involved with my family. He got mad because I talked to my mother on the phone about the car accident I had a few weeks ago, and she just infuriated me because she refused to help me out. My car was totaled, and I really need to get another car, but I don't have enough money to get the one I want. My parents have plenty of money and could

help me if they wanted, but my mother can be a real 'witch' sometimes. She said that they had already bought me two other cars and they weren't going to buy me another one. I couldn't believe what a witch she was being. She can be crazy, I'm telling you. She had the nerve to suggest I need to get a better job where I could use my college education, but she doesn't realize how hard it is to get a job in the computer industry, and besides, I think she just hates me. Sometimes I think I hate her, too."

She continues, "So, I'm just telling Larry about this conversation, and he gets really angry and says I'm too dependent on my parents and that I still act like I'm a teenager and should let go of them since they always make me furious. He knows that the whole subject of my parents is a 'hot button' for me. I think he said that just to make me mad and he did. He knows what a temper I have! He made me so angry I thought I was going to explode. Actually, I did explode. I told him what an idiot I thought he was. Just because he doesn't have a relationship with his parents doesn't mean I shouldn't have one with my parents. It's weird—sometimes I am so in love with Larry and other times I hate his guts. Is that the way it is for most people?" Natalie curiously inquires.

"I don't think it's unusual to have disagreements with people you love," you suggest. "How did the argument end?"

Natalie stares out the window for a moment and then says matter-of-factly, "He just said he couldn't take it anymore and went to the bedroom and packed a suitcase and left. I actually thought he was joking. I told him if he walked out the door, he'd be a stupid fool. And then when I realized he was serious, I begged him not to leave me, and he just shrugged his shoulders and said, 'Life is too short, Natalie; you are always running hot and cold. I just can't take it anymore.'"

"What do you think he meant by that statement?" you ask.

"Well, I think he's referring to the fact that I sometimes hate him and then, other times, I love him. It just seems too empty inside when he's not around. I wonder if it's all really worth it," Natalie responds.

"So, sometimes you feel really empty when you're not involved in a relationship. Is that right?" you ask.

"Maybe that's why I've had so many," Natalie ponders. "It seems like the times in between relationships are awful, like sitting in the bottom of a black hole. Nothing, there's just nothing worth living for. And I hate everyone and everything. But sometimes, I feel that way when I'm in a relationship, too. I don't know. It's very confusing to me." Natalie rubs her forehead and pulls her legs underneath her.

"How do you feel about yourself when you're in or out of a relationship?" you ask.

"That's simple. I usually hate myself when I'm not in a relationship. I think I'm stupid and ugly and can't do anything right. I feel that way when I'm in a relationship sometimes, too, but it comes and goes. Initially, when I first meet someone, I feel really good about myself, but then it gradually disappears."

"And when you're thinking you hate yourself, how does that make you feel?" you ask Natalie.

"Very down in the dumps and worthless and hopeless," Natalie replies. "Like I said before, sometimes I've been so depressed I've felt suicidal. Like I just want to end it all."

"Have you ever actually tried to hurt yourself?" you ask.

"A couple of times when I was a teenager, I scratched my wrists and a couple of times after I broke up with a boyfriend, but I haven't done anything serious lately," Natalie replies.

"Okay, can you make a contract with me that if you start feeling suicidal, you will not do anything before talking to me?" you inquire seriously.

"I think so," Natalie states. "I'm sort of feeling more hopeful about things now that I've talked to you. Do you think you can help me figure all this stuff out?" Natalie asks pleadingly. "I'm just scared to death I'm going to be left alone for the rest of my life."

"Natalie, I think I may be able to help you, but you have to make a commitment to counseling, and sometimes it may feel uncomfortable for you. I'd like you to think about whether or not you really want to get involved in counseling, and if you decide this is a good idea, call and make another appointment. Okay?"

"I'm pretty sure I need to get some help," Natalie considers.

"Okay, but why don't you think about it overnight, and if you are still sure tomorrow, you can call and make an appointment."

"Okay, that will be all right," Natalie sighs. "I guess this isn't going to be easy."

14.1–1 Describe Natalie's presenting problem. Do you think this is her primary problem? Why or why not?

14.1–2 What are some of Natalie's strengths?

14.1–3 What potential diagnoses would you want to rule out in this case?

14.1–4 What resources might be helpful for Natalie to access?

14.1–5 What is your preliminary diagnosis for Natalie?
Axis I

Axis II

Axis III

Axis IV

Axis V

Case 14.2

Identifying Information
Client Name: Jack Keller
Age: 40 years old
Ethnicity: Caucasian
Marital Status: Married
Occupation: Corporate accountant

Intake Information

Jack Keller has been referred to you, a counselor at a large corporation's employee assistance program (EAP), due to recent problems he has had with coworkers. His boss, Chris, strongly recommended that Jack contact the EAP because of several complaints he had received concerning Jack's interactions with other employees.

Jack is a hardworking employee whom Chris values. He is a competent accountant who always completes his work on time and often works overtime in order to make deadlines. His work is always accurate and detailed.

Chris suggested Jack talk to a counselor since Chris has received several complaints from assistants and coworkers over the past 2 months. Although Jack stated that he "had things under control," Chris insisted that Jack make an appointment with a counselor. Chris suggested that perhaps Jack was under a lot of stress, but Jack maintained that there was nothing wrong with him other than working long hours on several big projects recently.

He told Chris, "I don't know why you want me to see a counselor. My work is flawless; I get things in on time; and I work harder than anyone else in this department. Just because I expect others to do their jobs doesn't make me crazy."

Chris told Jack that he (Jack) expected perfection and was being overly critical of others when they did not measure up to his expectations. "You've got to stop berating others when they aren't as perfect as you, Jack," Chris told him in exasperation. This comment made Jack wonder what he was doing that bothered people so much, and he decided to make the appointment with a counselor to get a better handle on the situation.

Initial Interview

You meet Jack in the waiting room and observe that he is an immaculately dressed man about 6 feet tall and of average weight. He is wearing a white shirt, a blue-and-white tie, and black pants. His black shoes are polished so they shine, and his wire-rimmed glasses give him a studious appearance. Jack glances at his watch as you walk into the waiting room.

You introduce yourself as a counselor at the EAP and escort him to your office. Jack questions the time of the appointment, suggesting you are late (it's 3 minutes past the hour). You explain that sometimes you are running a minute or two behind in order to get messages or make a phone call between clients.

Jack responds matter-of-factly, "Well, it did seem like you must be running behind today." You note the fastidiousness of this comment.

"Well, first, I want to tell you that everything we talk about in these sessions is confidential. It is important for you to know that, especially since we are a counseling center within this larger corporation. Unless you tell me you are going to hurt yourself or someone else, the information we share in this room will not be discussed with anyone other than my direct supervisor. Do you have any questions concerning confidentiality?"

"No, that's pretty clear. I've never actually seen a counselor before," Jack says hesitantly. "I'm only here because my boss thought I should come for a session."

"I see. So, you aren't sure you really need counseling," you reply.

"Well, it might be a good idea to talk to an expert about some things that have been going on in my department as long as it's confidential," Jack states.

"Okay, tell me what's been going on," you say.

"Well, you see I'm the senior CPA in my division, and I report to the head of the finance department. I have 10 people working under me and am responsible for all their work. Sometimes it seems like I'm the only one in my division that takes work seriously. I work very hard to see that everything is running smoothly and that all the figures are accurate. Sometimes that means I work late at night and on weekends, double-checking everyone else's work to make sure it's correct. I shouldn't have to do that, but I've found that if I don't, mistakes are made and I get called on the carpet because other people aren't doing their jobs. So, I tell people that they must be precise and accurate when it comes to these figures and they can't be lazy about doing it right. If they'd do it right the first time, then I wouldn't have to be on their backs all the time to get the numbers correct."

"And how do they respond to what you tell them?" you inquire.

"Well," Jack throws his hands in the air, "they just get irritated and angry with me. Apparently, they are running to my boss and telling him that I'm hard to get along with or something like that. I can't understand it. No one works as hard as I do in that department, and if they'd take a little more pride in being accurate, then I wouldn't have to be on their cases all the time. I don't really see it as my problem." Jack leans back in his chair and shrugs his shoulders. "So, that's why I'm here, I guess."

"Let me see if I understand what you're saying. You are telling me that people who work for you are getting upset because you are correcting their mistakes and telling them they should be more careful about their work. Does that more or less sum it up?" you ask Jack.

"More or less," Jack replies. "From what my boss tells me, they think I'm being overly critical of their work. He told me that I needed to learn how to control my anger."

"Do you get angry when your employees don't do the work the way you want them to?" you ask.

"Well, it's very frustrating to me. I go over and over pages of figures to make sure they are accurate, and no one else seems to care. It just infuriates me that they don't take their jobs seriously. These numbers are either right or wrong. It's all very black and white. When I tell them that they need to check their work again, they get angry and say that if they spent all their time rechecking every number the way I did, they'd never accomplish anything. Sometimes, they even leave work early and say they've finished for the day. I don't understand how they can do that when they've rushed through their work and done a sloppy job. I've told them that according to their job descriptions they are supposed to be at their desk from 8 A.M. until 5 P.M., Monday through Friday. Recently, I had to tell them that they had to stick by the rules and only take 1 hour for lunch since they were coming back 15, or sometimes 20, minutes late. No wonder they don't get their work done right the first time! They just don't care. I've told my boss that I can't get the spreadsheets to him on time since I've got to check everything that other people are doing three or four times."

"Okay, I can see that this issue is a very upsetting one for you," you respond. "Do you have similar experiences with people outside work?"

"Well, it's not the same thing, but if you mean do people get under my skin because of their slovenly behavior, you bet!" Jack replies. "I have a 12-year-old son who just refuses to follow the rules in my house."

"What exactly do you mean?" you ask.

"Well, he plays sports at school, and when he gets home from soccer practice, he just drops his muddy soccer shoes at the foot of the stairs even though I've told him a hundred times that his dirty shoes belong on the back porch. He just doesn't listen to me. And that's just one example. There are numerous times when he disobeys my orders. He'll walk out of the house without making his bed, or he'll leave the toothpaste tube open on the sink. He knows that he's breaking the rules, but he does it anyway. My wife will take his side sometimes, which makes me even more angry."

"What happens when your son breaks the rules?" you ask seriously.

"Well, I tell him he's grounded, or he can't do something he wanted to do until he straightens up his act. I slave away at this job all week long in order to buy him $80 soccer shoes, and then he drags those muddy things into the house and I have to clean up after him. The last time I bought myself a new pair of shoes was 10 years ago. Look at the soles of these shoes I have on." Jack throws his foot up in the air so that you can see the bottom of his shoe.

"Wow, it looks like you've really worn a hole in that shoe," you comment. "Have you thought about buying another pair?"

"I can't afford to buy another pair when I have an irresponsible son who needs expensive shoes and apparel all the time," Jack says mournfully.

"Okay, what I hear you telling me is that your 12-year-old son can get on your nerves at times. I guess most 12-year-olds are not always neat. Are there other people that you run into problems with in a similar way?" you ask.

"No, not really," Jack says. He looks tired and discouraged. "I just can't understand why people don't have the same values as I do. My wife and I argue about these issues all the time, but she knows who pays the bills and is head of our household," Jack states unequivocally. "I've told her when she starts making more money than I do, then she can make the rules in my house."

"Wow, how does she respond to that?" you ask.

"She usually just gets quiet and walks away," Jack states. "She knows I'm right."

"Okay, I think I've got a fairly good picture of what you're talking about," you respond. "I'm just wondering if you think that counseling could be beneficial to you in working on some of these issues."

"You mean so that people will listen to me and do what they're supposed to do?" Jack inquires.

"No, actually, I meant to help you be more effective in dealing with other people," you reply as convincingly as you can. "You see, Jack, people come to counseling to obtain help with something they want to change about themselves. As I'm sure you know, we really can't make other people change. We can only work to change things about ourselves. And what I do is assist people in making those changes about themselves that they would like to work on. Does that make sense to you?"

"Well, I guess I see what you're saying. I'm going to have to think it over. I'm not really sure how you could help me since I think it's other people who have the problem, but I'll think it over and talk to my wife."

"Good idea. Give it some thought, and if you would like to come back for another session, call the office and schedule an appointment. So, that will be our plan?" you ask.

"Sounds fine with me," Jack says. "Thank you for your time."

14.2–1   As the counselor interviewing Jack, how did you feel?

14.–2   Do you think Jack will agree to counseling? Why or why not?

14.2–3   What other resources might be useful to Jack?

14.2–4   What diagnosis would you give Jack?

Axis I

Axis II

Axis III

Axis IV

Axis V

Case 14.3

Identifying Information

Client Names: Sherry Black and Kyle Monroe
Ages: Sherry, 25 years old; Kyle, 28 years old
Ethnicity: Caucasian
Marital Status: Cohabiting couple
Occupations: Sherry, airline flight attendant; Kyle, operating room technician

Intake Information

Sherry Black contacted the Marriage and Family Counseling Center for assistance with a relationship that she is having with Kyle Monroe, her live-in boyfriend. Sherry is a flight attendant, and Kyle is an operating room (OR) technician at the local hospital.

Sherry told the intake worker that she and Kyle have been having increasing difficulty with their relationship due to Kyle's suspicious nature and constant questions about Sherry's loyalty to him. Sherry feels that Kyle has become overly possessive, and when she tries to talk to him about this issue, he states that her desire to be more independent is evidence that she can't be trusted and that she must be seeing someone else.

Sherry states that Kyle has become more and more suspicious of her whereabouts while she is flying and every phone call that she receives. Even though she has told Kyle he can listen in on the phone conversations, Kyle resents her accepting phone calls from anyone he doesn't personally know. In addition, he has told Sherry that her desire to get some help is just a way for her to get support when she leaves him.

Sherry states that his suspiciousness has "spilled over" to his job and is causing Kyle problems at work. For example, he feels that the OR nurses can't be trusted and that they may be trying to get him fired. He told Sherry that his friend Arnold at the hospital told him that the head OR nurse thought he was an excellent OR technician. Kyle felt that the comment meant that he wasn't as good as the nurses and he had to be careful about what he told the head nurse. The intake worker scheduled an appointment for the couple to come to the first interview together.

Initial Interview

Sherry and Kyle sit together on the couch in your office. You introduce yourself and explain to them that you provide counseling to couples who may be experiencing difficulties in their relationship. Kyle is very concerned about how this appointment will be reported on insurance forms and about issues of confidentiality. You explain that the appointment is confidential and that the agency operates on a sliding-scale fee. Kyle appears to be assessing you.

"What made you both decide to make an appointment for counseling?" you ask.

Sherry looks at Kyle and begins. "Kyle and I have been having some problems in our relationship," Sherry comments. "I think we care a lot about each other, but we've been getting into some big arguments lately." Kyle appears to be inspecting the office and your desk. You realize he's staring at the file with Sherry's name on it.

"Can you tell me what the arguments are about?" you ask. Kyle remains fixated on the file folder on your desk.

"Kyle seems to be having a hard time trusting me while I'm away at work," Sherry states. "You see, I am a flight attendant for Southern Light Airlines, but I fly locally and I'm always back in town each evening. So, I'm a little confused about why he thinks I'm playing around on him when I'm home every night."

Kyle grunts and continues to stare at the folder. Pointing to the folder on your desk, he asks, "What's that folder got in it?"

"Just the information that the intake worker got when Sherry called to make the appointment," you say.

"Wait a minute. Before we can go any further, you need to show me that folder."

"I'll be happy to show it to you at the end of the session," you remark. "Right now, I'd like to find out what you have been arguing about."

"Oh, no. I'm not giving you anything until I see what's in that folder," he insists.

Sherry blushes and says, "Kyle, I'm sure it's just basic information. Don't worry about it. It's nothing."

"Nothing? My personal life may be nothing to you, but it's my life, okay? It's bad enough that you tell everyone our business. Now it's in print!"

"Is this how the arguments go at home?" you comment. Sherry and Kyle both look at you and appear taken aback by your comment. You decide to gently reframe by stating, "Privacy seems to be a tense issue for you, Kyle, and Sherry doesn't seem to be so concerned."

Sherry quickly responds despite Kyle's glaring, "This is exactly the problem at home, only at home he's suspicious about my whereabouts and what I say to anyone."

Kyle leans back in the chair, nods, and says, "You've both already talked about this, haven't you? You don't even need me here, do you?"

Sherry sighs in resignation. "Do you see what I mean? Kyle doesn't trust anyone about anything!"

You realize that you have to establish some rapport or Kyle will leave. You say, "Kyle, this is the first time I've had the opportunity to talk with either of you, and I'd really like to get your perspective on how things are at home."

Kyle eyes you and then Sherry.

Sherry says, "Come on, Kyle. She's a counselor and wants to help."

Kyle looks pensive and begins hesitantly to discuss the relationship. "Well, as anybody can see, Sherry is a very attractive woman and flirty by nature. She's on that plane every day with all those businessmen and you can't tell me that they don't make moves on her. It all started when I picked her up after her Houston trip . . ."

"Oh, God. Here we go again!" Sherry says with disdain.

"Will this help me understand the situation?" you comment.

"It sure will. It explains everything. Let me finish. I go to pick her up, and there she is bending over her purse at the baggage claim and this idiot guy is standing there with her bags in his hands. It's quite obvious what's going on. Makes me sick to think about it."

Sherry says, "It was just a nice man trying to help me with my bags while I took out my claim stubs. I didn't even know his name. It was a 30-second interaction."

Kyle exclaims, "Bull! I saw how you looked at each other, and you were giggling away. It sure didn't look like 'nothing' to me."

Sherry sighs and throws her hands in the air in utter frustration. "This was one of our worst arguments, and he brings it up every time we try to deal with things. He's so jealous of everything I do. He can't let it go!"

"Have your arguments ever become physical?" you question.

"No, except he once threw my carry-on bag out the door of the house, telling me never to come back."

You respond, "Okay, so the arguments focus on Kyle's worries about your commitment to the relationship, and you feel these worries are unfounded. Is that correct?"

They both nod. Sherry urges Kyle to tell you about the work situation. Kyle glares at you again and says, "That's not what we're here for. We're here to figure out what's wrong with our relationship. If you weren't messing around on me, we wouldn't have any problems. Then I wouldn't have to be so concerned about my job."

Sherry in utter exasperation stands up and says she's going out for some water. "Maybe this is enough for today." She leaves the room, with Kyle glaring after her.

In one last attempt to establish some rapport with Kyle, you say, "How is all of this making you feel, Kyle? It's pretty hard to talk about personal stuff with a stranger."

He says, "Sherry just needs to get her ducks in a row, and everything will be fine. How about giving me a look at that chart?"

You hand him the chart and say, "Really, Kyle, this just contains your names and address."

Sherry returns with a cup of water. "Where do we go from here?" she asks you.

"I'd like you to consider becoming involved with some counseling. I think it could be bene-ficial to you at this time. I'd like to start with six sessions and see if you feel your relationship is improving. How do you feel about coming in for six sessions?" you inquire of both of them.

Kyle shrugs his shoulders and says, "If you think it will help, I'm willing to do it."

Sherry nods her head enthusiastically and agrees.

"Okay, so we'll schedule an appointment for next week," you reply. "If you need to talk before the next appointment, here is my card. Call me and if I'm not available, I'll call you back as soon as possible."

14.3–1   Describe your perceptions of the presenting problem.

14.3–2   Do you think Kyle and Sherry will be able to maintain this relationship? Why or why not?

14.3–3   What other information would you like to gather about Kyle? Include additional questions you might like to pose to him as well as collateral information.

14.3–4   What is your preliminary diagnosis for Kyle?
Axis I

Axis II

Axis III

Axis IV

Axis V

14.3–5 What, if any, diagnoses are you considering for Sherry?

Case 14.4

Identifying Information

Client Names: Phillip and Kim Garrett
Ages: Phillip, 40 years old; Kim, 36 years old
Ethnicity: Caucasian
Marital Status: Married
Occupations: Phillip, high school principal; Kim, middle school teacher
Children: Gary, age 5

Intake Information

Kim Garrett contacted the Family Counseling Center for assistance with her 5-year-old child, Gary, who has been having some conduct problems in his first year of kindergarten. She stated that the school counselor suggested that they contact the Family Counseling Center for help since there have been multiple incidents at school with Gary hitting and fighting with other children.

Kim stated that she and her husband, Phillip, have tried everything to get Gary's behavior under control and have not been successful. The intake worker suggested that both Kim and Phillip come to the agency for the initial interview with the counselor without their son. Another interview will be scheduled for Gary. Kim stated that it would have to be after 5 P.M. because her husband is a school principal and wouldn't be able to come earlier in the day.

Initial Interview with Kim and Phillip Garrett

You meet the Garretts in the waiting room and notice that both parents are dressed in professional-looking clothes. They are seated beside each other and are both looking at separate magazines when you enter. You introduce yourself, shake their hands, and escort them back to your office. They sit beside each other in chairs next to your desk.

You begin by explaining the purpose of the agency and the issue of confidentiality. You explain that your agency works with families and that when children are experiencing difficulties, it is very important for the parents to be involved in the child's counseling.

Phillip begins the discussion by stating that he is the principal at the largest high school in the city and that he has a very important position that requires a tremendous amount of time and effort. "Despite the fact that I hold a very important job, I always make time for my wife and son."

"Okay, good, can you tell me what's been going on with Gary recently?" you inquire.

"Well, to be perfectly honest, I'm not sure anything is wrong with Gary," Phillip replies. "Kim and I don't experience any of the problems they are talking about at school when Gary is at home with us. I think we're just trying to get an assessment done so that we can have some evidence that perhaps it's the teacher, not Gary, who has the problem. Of course, we'll leave the evaluation to you, but I have many years of experience working with children, and I just don't see Gary as having a problem. What kinds of problems would a 5-year-old have anyway? In my position, I work with teens with lots of problems. But, we're talking about a little boy who has good parents who care about him," Phillip states.

"Okay, so you don't really see this as Gary's problem. You think that it may be the teacher who is not able to cope with Gary. Is that correct?" you ask Phillip.

"Exactly. Kim and I are very educated and intelligent professionals, and we have excellent parenting skills. Kim leads a parenting workshop every year at her middle school, and I'd say parenting is a real strength of mine. Gary always behaves when he's around me. I make myself clear, so of course he obeys." Phillip straightens the lapels of his jacket.

"I see," you reply. "Have you been feeling that the school is blaming you for Gary's behavior?"

"Well, not exactly," Phillip replies. "However, they are saying that Gary's behavior is the problem, and we just don't believe that is the case. There may be some jealousy involved. After all, this is the same school district, and I'm a 'star.' It's possible that this teacher wants to try to embarrass me."

"Okay, I understand," you respond. "So, as you said, my job is to do an assessment of Gary. In order to do that, I'm going to need to ask you some questions that you may find unimportant, but I need to ask them anyway. Is that okay with you?"

"That's fine with us," Phillip states.

"Is Gary your only child?" you ask.

"Yes," Phillip states. "We don't plan on having more than one child because of our professions."

"How long have you been the principal at Southside High?" you ask.

"It will be 3 years in September," Phillip states. "I am in charge of 200 teachers and 2,000 students. It's quite a large responsibility. Not to mention all the other duties I have with the school district. It's a great school, though. I've really turned it around, and the administration has suggested there may be other positions in the district open for me to move into as time goes on. I've really been quite successful in my career, so far."

"Yes, he has," Kim states. "Everyone thinks Phillip is the greatest principal Southside has ever had. He has quite a loyal following of teachers that really appreciate his management style."

You note that Kim's comment about her husband was the first time she has spoken since the session started. "Wow, that's impressive," you

state. "What about you, Kim? How do you see Gary's behavior?"

"Kim feels the same way I do," Phillip answers. "We both feel that this kindergarten teacher is just not very competent. We've talked to her about Gary's behavior, and I just think she's really clueless about children. We may just need to move Gary to a different class."

"Okay, and how do you experience Gary's behavior, Kim?" you say directly to Kim.

"Well, Phillip really knows a lot about children. He took courses in child psychology in his doctoral program," Kim states. "Gary really isn't a behavior problem at home."

"Just to summarize, both of you feel that Gary's behavior may be a result of the teacher's interaction with him and that you see no problems with Gary's behavior at home. Is that correct?"

Phillip nods his head and adds, "Just make a note that Gary's parents are experts in working with children."

"All right," you acknowledge Phillip's remarks. You decide to get some information about Phillip and Kim's relationship. It is clear to you that Phillip does not believe Gary has a behavioral problem.

"Let me ask you about your relationship with each other. How long have you been married, and how would you characterize your relationship with each other?" you ask.

Kim begins to answer but is interrupted by Phillip. "Go ahead," Kim tells her husband.

"Well, Kim and I met in college when I was a senior and she was a freshman. We dated for 3 years before we got married. Kim began teaching and I was in graduate school. Then I taught and enrolled in a part-time doctoral program in order to get my Ph.D. Even though I had a full scholarship to complete the Ph.D. program, we both worked very hard for a number of years before we decided to have a child."

"Kim, how would you describe your relationship with Phillip?" you inquire.

Kim looks at Phillip and smiles, "Well, Phillip was everything I was looking for in a life partner. He is so bright and ambitious. I was so impressed by his intellect and his being 4 years older than I was. I thought he 'walked on water.' He was president of the student teachers' association and had a whole following of female undergraduate students who thought he was fantastic. I didn't think I stood a chance of dating him. Phillip asked me to go out for dinner one night after we finished working on a project for the student teachers' organization, and I couldn't believe he was interested in me. He could have had any girl he wanted."

Phillip looks very pleased with Kim's response. He laughs and adds, "Well, Kim was fairly outgoing herself. Even though she didn't excel in school the way I did, she was a good team player. I think we complemented each other."

You glance at Kim to see her reaction to Phillip's comment. She smiles and says, "Phillip has never had a problem with his ego."

You're surprised that Kim would so clearly state the obvious, but Phillip appears unconcerned about the comment.

Phillip responds with a smile on his face, "I just know my strengths and weaknesses."

"Okay, so you met in college and married after Kim finished her degree, when Phillip was still in graduate school. How was that time for you in your relationship?"

"It was great. Kim was teaching and I was going to school and teaching, and we both enjoyed what we were doing. Probably the most difficult time was when I was trying to finish my dissertation and I ran into some trouble with the chair of my dissertation," Phillip stated.

"What kind of trouble?" you query.

"Well, I just think he was an incompetent fool, if you want to know the truth. We had a disagreement about my research design, and he just decided he didn't like me or something. It was a real nightmare. Eventually, I had to fire him and get another chair for my dissertation committee, but it was not an easy time. He could have prevented me from completing my doctorate that I had aspired all my life to have." Phillip leaned back in his chair and sighed.

Kim added, "Yes, that probably was the most difficult time in our marriage, thus far. Phillip was really questioning himself and his career and felt like he wasn't being treated fairly. It was a difficult time for both of us."

"But you eventually got it worked out and then decided to have a baby?" you ask.

"Yes, after I finished my degree, we decided we wanted a baby," Phillip stated.

"And how was it for you, having been working professionals for a long period of time, to have an infant at home?" you ask.

"Well, Kim took a leave of absence from her job for a year and stayed home with Gary, and then we found a good day care so that Kim could go back to work," Phillip states.

"And how was that time for you, Kim?" you ask.

"Oh, it was great. Gary was a dream come true. I thought he was the cutest baby on earth. I guess all mothers think that about their babies, but Gary was a good infant who never really caused us much trouble. He seemed to be happy at the day-care center and always was happy to see me when I went to pick him up in the afternoons. Honestly, other than the normal stuff that infants go through, Gary was a fairly content little baby."

"How old was he when he began walking and talking?" you ask.

Phillip chimes, "Oh, he was really talking early, around 9 months. I think it's because Kim and I exposed him to books at a very young age, as well as classical music. He began walking early, too, as I recall. He was about 13 months when he started to walk. You know, now that we're talking about all of this, maybe the problem Gary is having in kindergarten is that he's just too advanced for the class and he's bored stiff!"

"What do you think, Kim?" you inquire.

"Well, I never thought of Gary as being advanced. He seemed to go through the normal developmental milestones about on time and always seems to blend in with the crowd until recently." Kim sighs, "I'm just not sure what the problem is right now."

"Has anything changed in your family's life this year?" you ask.

Phillip looks puzzled for a moment and then quite suddenly blurts out, "Well, I've had a lot of speaking engagements to attend now that I'm in such a prominent position in the community,

and maybe Gary is angry that I'm not at home as much as I used to be."

Kim looks at Phillip and says, "Phillip, you are so brilliant. You may have just discovered the problem. You've been gone two or three nights a week for the past year, and Gary asks me all the time, 'When is Dad coming home?'"

"Okay, well I'm glad we at least uncovered one possible reason why Gary may be having some difficulties in school. Can you think of anything else?" you inquire.

Both parents look at each other and shake their heads. You decide to schedule an appointment to meet Gary, but you feel your assessment of the parents has yielded some valuable information. You will meet with them again following your interview with Gary.

14.4–1   What are some of the strengths of these parents?

14.4–2   How would you characterize Phillip?

14.4–3   What would be your preliminary diagnosis for Phillip?
Axis I

Axis II

Axis III

Axis IV

Axis V

_____

InfoTrac keywords

avoidant personality, borderline personality, dependent personality, narcissistic personality, obsessive-compulsive personality, paranoid personality, schizotypal personality

Adjustment Disorders and V-Codes | 15

ADJUSTMENT DISORDERS

Adjustment Disorders are considered among the mildest forms of mental disorders described in the DSM-IV-TR (APA, 2000). Characteristically transient and of short duration, these disorders develop in response to an identifiable stressor with which the person has been attempting to cope. When normal coping mechanisms prove to be ineffective in response to the stress, the person may experience one of several different types of Adjustment Disorders. Both children and adults can be diagnosed with an Adjustment Disorder.

The stressor must have occurred within 3 months of the onset of the disorder. The symptoms of the Adjustment Disorder must be resolved within 6 months of the onset of the stressor unless the stressor is chronic in nature (e.g., prolonged illness, ongoing financial strains, serious relationship problems) (APA, 2000; Baum & Andersen, 2001). Stressors may include a single event (e.g., birth of a child), an ongoing strain (e.g., financial problems), a recurrent event (e.g., harassing phone calls from a former spouse), or several stressors at once (e.g., loss of job, failed marriage, and death of a parent). In addition, stressors can be related to the individual's or family's developmental transitions (e.g., entry into adolescence, in the case of an individual; or when all the children leave home, in the case of the family).

In the case of a prolonged stressor, the symptoms of the Adjustment Disorder may continue beyond 6 months, and the specifier "chronic" is used to indicate the ongoing nature of the problems. If the symptoms persist for less than 6 months, the specifier "acute" is used to designate the duration of the Adjustment Disorder (APA, 2000).

There are six major subtypes of Adjustment Disorders: (1) with depressed mood, (2) with anxiety, (3) with mixed anxiety and depressed mood, (4) with disturbance of conduct, (5) with mixed disturbance of emotions and conduct, and (6) unspecified. Each of the subtypes delineates the predominant symptoms and/or behaviors that the individual is experiencing due to the stressor in his or her life (APA, 2000).

The first three subtypes that relate to emotional states are often diagnosed in adults, whereas Adjustment Disorder with Disturbance of Conduct and Adjustment Disorder with Mixed Disturbance of Emotions and Conduct are often diagnosed in children. Children with these disorders may have behavioral problems at school or home, as well as feelings of worry, nervousness, or depression. Adults with these two subtypes may experience problems with the law or their occupations in the case of Adjustment Disorder with Disturbance of Conduct and Emotions, as well as problems with daily functioning in the case of Adjustment Disorder with Mixed Disturbance of Emotions and Conduct (APA, 2000).

Adults and children who are diagnosed with an Adjustment Disorder may also complain of physical ailments such as headaches, stomach upset, or other pain-related symptoms. In addition, although the individual with an Adjustment Disorder may experience intense feelings of anxiety or depression, the emotional disturbance can be directly tied to the particular stressor or multiple stressors in the person's life (APA, 2000).

V-CODES

V-codes are conditions that may be the focus of clinical attention but are not considered mental disorders. In most instances, third-party payers do not cover charges for delivering services to an individual who has been diagnosed with one of the V-code conditions. V-codes are grouped into three categories: (1) relational problems, (2) problems related to abuse and neglect, and (3) additional conditions that may be a focus of clinical attention (APA, 2000).

Broadly speaking, the category "Relational Problems" describes interactional problems between family members or partners that result in significant impairment of family functioning or development of symptoms in spouses, siblings, or other family members. For example, a Parent-Child Relational Problem involves interactional problems between one or both parents and a child that lead to dysfunction in the family system or other symptoms in a family member (APA, 2000).

Similar interactional patterns leading to problems in family relationships may include Partner Relational Problem or Sibling Relational Problem. Relational Problem Related to a Mental Disorder or General Medical Condition is described in the DSM-IV-TR (APA, 2000) as an interactional problem that is caused by an illness of one of the family members. Finally, any other significant relational dysfunction for which someone may seek treatment can be covered by Relational Problem NOS (APA, 2000).

The V-codes subsumed under the broad category of "Problems Related to Abuse or Neglect" include the following: Physical Abuse of Child; Sexual Abuse of Child; Neglect of Child; Physical Abuse of Adult; and Sexual Abuse of Adult. These V-codes are used when the focus of attention is on the perpetrator of the abuse. If the focus of the attention is on the victim/survivor of the abuse, the codes 999.5 for children and 995.81 for adults are used (APA, 2000).

The V-codes under the broad category of "Additional Conditions That May Be a Focus of Clinical Attention" include the following: Noncompliance with Treatment; Malingering; Adult Antisocial Behavior; Child or Adolescent Antisocial Behavior; Borderline Intellectual Functioning (listed on Axis II); Age-Related Cognitive Decline; Bereavement; Academic Problem; Occupational Problem; Identity Problem; Religious or Spiritual Problem; Acculturation Problem; and Phase of Life Problem. As can be seen, many of the V-codes are related to behaviors or situations that, if they are causing a sufficient level of distress or impairing psychosocial functioning, may be diagnosed as a particular mental disorder (APA, 2000).

ASSESSMENT

In assessing an individual with an Adjustment Disorder, it is important to obtain information about the person's emotional and behavioral state before the stressor or multiple stressors occurred. An individual with an Adjustment Disorder may present with emotional responses to the stress ranging from very distressed to only mildly distressed about the problem. Clients may tell the practitioner during the initial assessment that they have always been able to cope with problems in their lives until confronted with the present difficulty. While some clients can readily identify the particular stressor with which they are having difficulty coping, other clients focus on the symptoms and are unaware of their relationship to the stressful situation that caused the symptoms initially.

It is also important to find out how the client has attempted to cope with the problem before seeking professional assistance. Does the client use problem-solving strategies? Has the client been seeking other assistance from friends or family members? Or does the client simply avoid the problem until it seriously impairs functioning in important areas of the client's life?

Finally, it is important to allow clients to define what constitutes a stressful situation for themselves. Some individuals may feel very distressed about relatively minor life events, while other persons may define only major life changes as problematic. In addition, some individuals may have a history of overcoming some major obstacles in life prior to the present stressor. In terms of prognosis, this information indicates that the persons will be able to cope with the present stress.

On the other hand, other persons may indicate that they have been unable to deal with life problems over a long period of time. In this situation, the individuals may have other emotional or personality problems that should be explored in more detail. Therefore, a complete psychosocial assessment (see chapter 1) should be conducted by the practitioner, even when the identifiable stressor is quite apparent.

Assessment Instruments

Although the diagnosis of Adjustment Disorder is generally made from a clinical, psychosocial assessment, the severity of the emotional response can be measured with standardized assessment instruments that have been discussed in earlier chapters of this workbook. This would, of course, be most appropriate when the practitioner is uncertain whether the level of symptoms constitutes a more serious diagnosis. Generally speaking, the most appropriate instrument choices in these instances would be screening (rather than clinical) instruments.

Depressed moods and anxiety are the two negative emotional reactions specified in conjunction with Adjustment Disorders. For adults who seem to have more depressive symptoms, the Center for Epidemiologic Studies-Depression Scale or the Hamilton Rating Scale for Depression would be recommended choices; for children, the Hopelessness Scale for Children is recommended (see chapter 6 for detail regarding these instruments). For anxiety symptoms, the state subscales from the State-Trait Anxiety Inventory (for adults) or the State-Trait Anxiety Inventory for Children would be excellent choices (see chapter 7 for more detail).

Disturbances of Conduct—that is, behavioral symptoms—may also be specified in conjunction with Adjustment Disorders. There is no comprehensive survey of adult behaviors to use in this regard. However, for children the Child Behavior Checklist would be appropriate (see chapter 2 for more detail).

Because some clients may be focused on a single psychosocial stressor when, in fact, multiple stressors are occurring simultaneously, it can be useful to use a standardized approach to assessing the amount and type of stress in a person's life. The Social Readjustment Rating Scale (SRRS) (Holmes & Rahe, 1967) examines 43 different increasingly stressful life events and assigns a value to each item. Scores above a cutoff point can help to assess the probability of a problem in adjustment or a related health problem in the near future. It is important to recognize that the scale contains several "positive" items (e.g., marriage, vacation, holidays) that can also be experienced as stressful life events.

Emergency Considerations

Because clients with Adjustment Disorders may experience moderate to severe symptoms of anxiety and depression, it is important to probe regarding suicidal feelings in the initial interview. Even though Adjustment Disorders are considered mild mental disorders, there may be times when the person with an Adjustment Disorder feels very hopeless or depressed, and these symptoms should be taken seriously by the practitioner. Of course, a more comprehensive assessment of risk for suicide should be pursued if the client reports having these thoughts or feelings.

In addition, the stressful events that individuals with an Adjustment Disorder have experienced may be quite serious and may require clients to take emergency measures to ensure their well-being. For example, a client may have lost his or her home due to a fire. In this case, in addition to being anxious, the client may need to find emergency housing for a period of time until another residence can be obtained. Therefore, both emotional issues and environmental situations may constitute emergencies for the client.

CULTURAL CONSIDERATIONS

Stressors that may affect people adversely differ among ethnic groups and cultures. For example, an event that might be perceived and labeled as stressful to an Anglo American individual may not be considered stressful to an individual living in South America, Japan, China, or the Congo. In addition, how individuals cope with stress is largely defined by the culture and society in which they live. For example, in the United States, families and individuals consider divorce to be a stressful life transition that may require assistance from professionals. In other cultures, leaving a partner may involve only a verbal dissolution of the relationship and change of residence.

The symptoms that constitute an Adjustment Disorder in the United States and Western European countries may not be considered pathological in other cultures. It is important to be sensitive to cultural differences in this regard and not label symptoms as pathological when they may not be considered so in other cultures. By the same token, practitioners need to be cognizant of their own cultural biases and stereotypical ideas. Either minimizing or maximizing symptoms because of a person's cultural background alone could result in an inappropriate psychosocial assessment.

A large body of literature exists that examines the causes of stress, its impact on individuals' lives, coping strategies, and interventions designed to reduce the negative effects of stress on individuals' mental health. In recent years, researchers have turned their attention to the relationship between sociocultural factors and identifiable stressors experienced by people of different ethnic and social backgrounds in the United States and other countries worldwide. The relationship between stress and socioeconomic status has been examined in relation to behavior disorders in children (Andra & Thomas, 1998). A comparison of stressors between lesbian and heterosexual women has been studied (Bernhard & Applegate, 1999). The stressors related to being a gay adolescent and the incidence of suicidal behavior are the focus of attention in a study conducted by Rotheram-Borus and Hunter (1994) of 138 self-reported gay teens living in New York City. The stress and strain related to being a minority group member in a country (termed "acculturative stress") are delineated in studies of Hispanic college students (Saldana, 1994) and Puerto Rican women and children (Landale & Oropesa, 1999).

A widely researched model of stress and coping developed by Lazarus and Folkman (1984) suggests that stressors may impact individuals in a variety of ways depending on how they cognitively process the stressful event. First, the individual makes a "primary appraisal" of the stressful event (What has just happened? Am I in danger? How has this stressor affected me?). Second, the individual makes a "secondary appraisal" of the event (What can I do about this stressor? How will I cope with this event?). Third, the individual uses available coping skills (e.g., avoidance, problem-solving, and emotion-focused skills) to attempt to ameliorate the effects of the stressor. Finally, the individual adapts to the stressor, which results in positive, negative, or neutral consequences.

Slavin, Ranier, McCreary, and Gowda (1991) proposed the addition of a multicultural component to Lazarus and Folkman's model. Since the perception of stress is a culturally bound issue, it is important to take into account the cultural experiences of the individual in assessing the impact of stress on the individual. The authors suggest that, in addition to assessing the seriousness of the stressor, the practitioner should be aware of the stressor as related to minority status, potential discrimination, disadvantaged socioeconomic status, and specific cultural customs of the individual experiencing the stress-related event. Second, in regard to the primary appraisal of the event, the counselor should take into consideration the person's or family's cultural definition of the event and the person's or family's cultural frame of reference for understanding the event. Third, from a multicultural viewpoint, assessment of secondary appraisal options (coping mechanisms) should include the individual's culturally bound behavioral options, role definitions, ethnic identity, and definition of family, group, and social network. Attempts to cope with the stressful event should include consideration of the individual's cultural rituals, cultural and mainstream sanctions against certain coping strategies, and biculturation (the incorporation of both minority and mainstream coping skills). Finally, the outcomes of coping strategies should be assessed according to the person's cultural framework and norms for the cultural group. Each of these steps in the process can be added to the basic model proposed by Lazarus and Folkman (1984) when considering the multicultural factors related to stressful events and situations.

SOCIAL SUPPORT SYSTEMS

The impact of Adjustment Disorders and/or V-codes on an individual's social support system can vary dramatically. A primary consideration in assessing the impact is the degree to which one or more members are also being affected by the situation. A person who is not directly affected may be more willing to extend support. At the same time, this less involved individual may find it harder to really empathize with the client's situation. Clearly, when the issues are relational, the possibility of continued (and even escalating) conflict can result in other members of the social support systems withdrawing or aligning themselves with one of the parties.

Although it was common in the 1980s for insurance companies to reimburse practitioners for treatment of Adjustment Disorders, the managed-care shift in the new millennium marks the need for creative interventions and solutions for Adjustment Disorders. Support groups can provide critical resources in situations where more formal treatment is not available (or desired). Whether sponsored independently or as part of church-related or nonprofit organizations, most of the resources are organized around a particular concern. For example, support groups dealing with individuals with such difficulties as divorce recovery, relocation, empty-nest syndrome, school-based social networks, chronic illness recovery/caregiving groups, employee assistance programs, relationship/sexual support groups, single persons' support networks, parent education programs, and anger-management group interventions are widely available. There is a unique value in sharing experiences related to stressful situations with mutual-aid support groups. Such safe and confidential environments reduce shame, stigma, guilt, burden, and fear among members. Often, a combination of a few individual therapy sessions along with ongoing support groups can lead to satisfactory outcomes for the individual with an Adjustment Disorder.

Other community resources that might prove useful in certain situations may include recreation or after-school programs for youth, psychoeducational programs or workshops provided by nonprofit agencies, holistic approaches to health (e.g., yoga, meditation groups, or exercise programs), advocacy and service opportunities, meals-on-wheels, mentoring programs, and senior centers. The following list suggests other resources that can be found on the Internet.

www.athealth.com/Consumer/Disorders/Adjustment.html—Describes the symptoms and accompanying treatment issues associated with this disorder

www.psychcentral.com/disorders/sx6t.htm—Discusses the symptoms of Adjustment Disorder and the psychotherapeutic treatment available to help individuals experiencing this disorder

www.mentalhealth.com/rx/p23-aj01.html—Provides suggestions for treatment of Adjustment Disorders

www.umm.drkoop.com/conditions/ency/article/000932.htm—University of Maryland Medicine Web site that describes Adjustment Disorders and provides treatment considerations for this problem

Case 15.1

Identifying Information
Client Name: Nancy Kauffman
Age: 49 years old
Ethnicity: Caucasian
Marital Status: Separated
Occupation: High school teacher
Children: Two children, ages 23 and 25

Intake Information
Nancy Kauffman called the Family Support Center and requested an appointment with you after getting your name from a friend and co-worker at the local high school. Nancy's friend was a former client who had come to the Family Support Center for counseling regarding her daughter when she was an adolescent. Nancy stated that she needed to talk to someone about her recent problems with her marriage. She specifically requested an appointment with you.

Initial Interview
Nancy is a petite, attractive woman who arrives for her appointment wearing a white tennis skirt and top. Her hair is pulled back with a light blue headband that matches her blue-and-white tennis shoes. She appears to be an active and energetic woman. She is standing in the waiting room reading a brochure when you meet her. Nancy smiles and firmly shakes your hand as she makes your acquaintance. She immediately explains her appearance by telling you that she has a tennis match scheduled following your appointment and wouldn't have time to go home and change clothes.

You converse with Nancy for a few moments about the game of tennis. You discover that Nancy has been playing tennis since she was a teenager and she coaches the girls' tennis team at the high school where she teaches. Nancy plays tennis several times a week at a racquet club in town. She has won several women's tournaments over the past 10 years. Nancy is obviously very enthusiastic about the sport and engages easily with you in conversation.

After she is comfortably seated in your office, you begin the session by asking her if she's ever been in counseling in the past. Nancy tells you that she went to see a therapist several times about 10 years ago when her daughter was having some difficulties in school. It seemed to benefit her daughter, and she felt she communicated better with her daughter following therapy.

You ask her about her teaching position at the high school. "You teach French and history—is that correct?" you ask.

"Yes, I've been teaching juniors and seniors for the past 25 years. I teach advanced French as well as ancient history," Nancy tells you.

"Wow, those are difficult subjects," you remark.

Nancy nods her head in agreement and tells you that in most cases, she likes the teenagers she teaches and enjoys her job very much. She especially likes coaching the girls' tennis team.

"So, what's been going on that made you decide to make an appointment?" you ask.

"Well, I just felt like I could use some help right now," Nancy states. "You see, I've just recently separated from my husband. We have been married for 25 years, and I've been feeling very alone with no one to talk to lately."

"When did you separate from your husband?" you ask.

"About 2 months ago," Nancy says sadly. "He just came home one night from school and said he didn't want to be married anymore. I couldn't believe it. I was completely caught off guard. Right up until that moment, I thought we had a good marriage. In fact, I said to him, 'If this is your idea of a joke, it's a very bad one.'

He wasn't joking at all. Jay is 52 years old. He's the soccer coach at the high school. He seemed to be going through something, you know, like a midlife crisis or something. He wanted to buy a Mustang convertible. I didn't object. I thought it was a phase and it would pass. If he could be happy with a new car, it was okay with me. But I guess it wasn't that simple." Nancy looks down at her hands and looks very discouraged.

"That must have been a real shock for you. Did he give you any further explanation for why he didn't want to be married?" you inquire.

"No, he just said he wanted to live alone and that he had put down a deposit on an apartment that afternoon. He said he'd pack his bags and leave the next day. I pleaded with him to go to counseling with me and work it out, but he wasn't interested. He's not the type who would ever go to counseling, but I didn't know what to do. He was determined to leave, so there was nothing I could do about it," Nancy replies.

"It sounds like a very difficult situation for you. How have you been coping with the situation since he left?" you inquire.

"Well, I've been working a lot. But it's been difficult since we both work at the same school. I end up seeing him several times a week. Lately, I've just been feeling very depressed about the whole thing. I'm fine when I'm at school, but I go home to a fairly large house, and I just feel so alone walking around those empty rooms. I haven't ever lived alone my entire life. I got married right after graduate school, and I lived with my family or a roommate before I got married. The last couple of months have been very difficult for me." Nancy begins crying softly. "Oh, I just don't know what's wrong with me," she says.

"So, before Jay left, you weren't feeling down and depressed?" you ask as you hand her a box of tissues.

"Right, I'm usually a bubbly, outgoing person. It's just been since he left that I've felt so low. I'm having difficulty concentrating on my work and teaching. Some days I walk into class and have no idea what I'm going to teach that day. I've never been like that before. I'm always prepared for class."

"Are you and Jay communicating at all?" you ask.

"We've talked some, but he's not interested at all in coming home or working on our relationship. I feel pretty pessimistic about getting back together with him. I think he'll ask me for a divorce soon," Nancy says glumly. "I'm beginning to feel angry now, too. How could he do this to me after so many years?"

"How are you sleeping?" you ask.

"When I get to bed, I'm sleeping fine. I've never really had difficulty sleeping. My problem is that I just don't go to bed until late and I have to be up early. I'm usually at school by 7 A.M. So I'm not getting much sleep, but I guess if I'd just get to bed at a decent hour, it wouldn't be a problem. I just hate going to bed alone," Nancy replies.

"Okay. And how has your appetite been lately? Have you gained or lost weight since Jay decided to move out?" you ask.

"If anything, I might have lost a few pounds. That might be the only benefit to this situation," Nancy says with a smile. "I've been playing so much tennis lately that I don't really have to worry about what I eat. I just haven't been fixing meals lately. I'll stop on my way home and get a couple of things at the store, but I rarely fix a whole meal."

"It sounds as if it might help to have someone to talk to as you're coping with this situation," you suggest.

"I think it would help a lot if you want to know the truth. I don't know why it took me so long to make that phone call to your office. All my friends are Jay's friends since we work at the same place. It makes me feel like I can't talk to anyone since I don't want to put them in the middle of this mess."

You schedule another appointment with Nancy for the following week.

Letter from Nancy, Received between First and Second Sessions with Her

It's after midnight and I'm still rumbling around this house thinking about what we talked about the other day when I came to see you. I thought it might be helpful if I gave you a little history of my relationship with Jay.

Jay and I met 29 years ago when we were both aspiring teachers in graduate school at Yale University. It was the 1970s. Jay had long hair and wore bell-bottoms, and I had long hair and wore miniskirts. We were both on a mission to save the world through education. We believed in peace and love, and we joined in several marches and sit-ins against the fighting in Vietnam. We were the flower children of that generation. It's amazing any of us actually graduated with a degree. College campuses were fraught with tension, students were at war with the establishment, and we were all involved in politics.

Jay and I were no exception. We attended antiwar demonstrations and marched through the campus mall on a weekly basis. We moved in with each other about 6 months after we first met. We lived in a run-down apartment in an old house where five other couples lived. We believed we were going to make a difference in the world and shared the same personal and political values. We spent hours and hours sitting in our makeshift living room having serious discussions about society and how we were going to change it. I think we were happier during those days than we have ever been since.

We graduated from college and easily got jobs teaching and decided to get married in 1975 after I got pregnant. Lucy and Leo were born two years apart, and it definitely changed our lives. Now we were working to put food on the table rather than to further our lofty values about society. We also began focusing on the children rather than on ourselves.

During that time, Jay had an affair with another teacher at school. It was a devastating experience for me, but I wanted to hold our marriage together. My parents divorced when I was only 10 years old, and I didn't want that for my children. We muddled our way through it, and Jay finally gave up the affair and promised to be faithful forever. We managed to move on, but I think Jay resented being married and could never fully commit himself to it. He enjoyed being the superstar soccer coach and getting a lot of attention. He couldn't understand why I had to spend so much time with the children when they were little. You would think a teacher would know what children require, but he didn't seem to want to share my attention with anyone, including the children.

His way of coping was to just leave the house when I couldn't give him my undivided attention. He would become despondent when I couldn't attend to his every need. My way of coping was to become even more involved with the children and their activities. I was the primary caregiver, and Jay was the soccer star. I see this retrospectively because I think we both denied there was a problem at the time. He was highly involved with teaching and soccer, and I was equally involved with teaching, tennis, and the children.

When the kids were 15 and 17 years old, it happened again. He had another affair that I found out about through a lifelong friend of mine. She told me that while she was at a teaching conference in another city, she had seen Jay at a restaurant with his arms wrapped around another woman. I confronted him about it, and he said it was nothing—just a fling. He wasn't interested in her, and it just happened out of the blue at the conference. I told him if he didn't stop it right away, I was leaving him. Surprisingly, the thought of me leaving him scared him. And I honestly don't think he's had another affair since that time at the conference.

Now I think he's confronted with the fact that he's getting older and is not as attractive as he once was. He can't stand the idea that he might not be able to get all the attention. He's down on his job because he's no longer the young, attractive soccer coach that everyone adored. There are a couple of assistant coaches now that have moved in on his territory.

In essence, I think he's depressed. It worries me that he's moving into an apartment by him-self. I'm not sure it's so good for him to be alone right now. If this is a midlife crisis, I hope he comes to his senses quickly.

So, I'm coping as well as possible with the current situation. I just thought this information might help you better understand what's happened prior to our separation.

15.1–1   What would you consider the identifiable stressors in Nancy's current situation?

15.1–2   What support mechanisms are in place that Nancy can utilize? What additional support might be beneficial to Nancy?

15.1–3   What are some of Nancy's strengths? Would you refer Nancy to any other health professionals? Why or why not?

15.1–4   What is your diagnosis for Nancy?
Axis I

Axis II

Axis III

Axis IV

Axis V

15.1–5   What other Axis I disorders would you want to watch for and/or rule out?

_____

Case 15.2

Identifying Information
Client Name: Lynn Phillips
Age: 36 years old
Ethnicity: Caucasian
Marital Status: Married
Children: Dorie, age 8 (stepdaughter); Tommy, age 4

Referral Information
Lynn Phillips, a 36-year-old mother, contacts you at the request of the school guidance counselor over concerns about changes in her 8-year-old stepdaughter's behavior at school. Dorie is a third-grader at Clayton Elementary School.

Lynn tells you that her husband, Scott, age 38, gained custody of Dorie when he divorced his alcoholic and drug-abusing wife 7 years ago. Scott and Lynn got married when Dorie was 3 years old, so Lynn feels that she is the only mother Dorie has really known. She states that Dorie has always been a bright and bubbly child who is normally full of energy.

Recently, Dorie's teacher has seen a noticeable drop in Dorie's energy level as well as school performance. Lynn wants to make an appointment for you to see Dorie and evaluate her. You suggest that, before you see Dorie, you would like to talk with Lynn and Scott about what they have observed at home in terms of Dorie's behavior and mood. You schedule an appointment for Lynn and Scott Phillips.

Initial Interview
The following week you meet with Lynn and Scott Phillips. From outward appearances, they seem to be a wholesome, hardworking couple. Scott works for an auto parts supplier in the southeast region, and Lynn works as a secretary for a local bank. Lynn and Scott both shake hands with you and seem eager to talk.

Scott tells you that he and Dorie have a special bond between them due to the divorce and

inability of Dorie's mother to care for her. He states that for 2 years, he took care of Dorie by himself (although his mother baby-sat for him while he was at work). He took Dorie everywhere with him even after he met Lynn. He states that Dorie has always liked to fish and hike with him, ride on the back of his motorcycle, go bowling, or just play ball in the yard. Dorie is on the girls' softball team at school, and Scott coaches the team along with several other fathers. Scott is a husky, blond-haired, blue-eyed man who towers over Lynn.

Lynn, on the other hand, is petite, approximately 5 feet 2 inches tall, and has dark brown hair and brown eyes. Lynn states that she began noticing a difference in Dorie's behavior about a month and a half ago. "She usually loves to talk about school and everything that happened during the day, and lately, she comes home and doesn't say a word about school or what she did there. Her appetite also seems to be off. You know, she's picking at food she usually likes a lot. She seems bored with schoolwork that she has always been excited about in the past. Dorie is really smart like her dad. She likes to read and do math and always gets very involved in projects. Like one time she built a relief model of Antarctica out of plaster of paris; we had to go to the hardware store and get all the supplies, and she spent hours working on it. Now, it doesn't seem she cares much about anything like that. I've asked her several times if there's anything that's bothering her, and she just shrugs her shoulders and says, 'Not really.' She also seems to get real whiny, almost like a baby, when she gets frustrated by something. She did that when she was little but hasn't been like that for a long time. I just don't know what's going on anymore."

Scott agrees with his wife's observations and adds that Dorie has just withdrawn into "her own little shell." Scott feels like Dorie is going backward instead of forward. When you ask him exactly what he means, he states that Dorie is acting a lot younger than she used to rather than more grown-up. "Like she cries over silly little things that you would expect a much younger child to get upset about."

"Are there any other feelings or behaviors that you've noticed are different lately?" you ask the couple.

Scott and Lynn look at each other, and Scott says that the only other thing is that she seems to be having more nightmares and wants to come sleep with them several nights a week. "It just breaks my heart to see her standing at our door scared to death. She doesn't want to go back to her bed, and we don't make her. Of course, then we don't get much sleep with the three of us packed into a double bed like sardines," Scott chuckles. "Lynn and I have talked about it, and it seems like the best thing to do because Dorie instantly looks relieved and curls up and goes to sleep. And she is usually fine by the next morning."

You suggest you'd like to get some information about Dorie when she was a baby and was growing up. Lynn says, "Well, Scott would know more about that since I didn't know Dorie until she was 3 years old."

"Did you adopt Dorie when you married Scott?" you ask.

Lynn states that they'd thought about it but hadn't done anything about it. All custody rights were given to Scott when he divorced Susan, so they didn't feel it was necessary to go through the adoption process.

"What was Dorie like as a baby, Scott?" you ask.

"She was a very happy, normal baby who never was much of a problem. Her mother got into drinking and drugs about a year after Dorie was born. I don't think she was cut out to be a mother and never was much of one when Dorie was little. I was both mother and father to Dorie from the very beginning. I'd come home from work, and Susan wouldn't have done anything all day except sit and watch soap operas and read magazines. She didn't like to play with

Dorie much, and I think she thought it was just a hassle. She took care of her okay, I guess, but she didn't like doing it. She would complain all the time about being bored and having nothing to do. If I suggested she get together with other mothers, she said she wasn't interested in 'baby talk.' Then she started drinking and wouldn't stop. I told her she could get a job if she didn't want to sit home all day, but nothing seemed to satisfy her. After a while she just got so she wouldn't do anything. I did all the cooking and cleaning and taking care of Dorie. I'd take Dorie with me wherever I went on the weekends, trying to give Susan a break, but it was never enough. Finally, she got hooked up with some guy who was doing a lot of drugs, and that's when I told her I was taking Dorie and leaving her. She really didn't seem to mind too much."

"So, you and Susan got a divorce when Dorie was just a year old?" you query.

Scott leans back in his chair and sighs. "That's right. Dorie and I went to live in an apartment on the other side of town, and my mother helped me out with baby-sitting while I worked. It went on that way for about 2 years until I met Lynn."

"And how was Dorie during that time when it was just you and her together?" you ask.

"Oh, it was probably harder on me than it was for Dorie since my mom helped out," Scott replied with a smile. "She seemed like a happy child who loved her daddy. Of course, she had all the trying times any child has, but all in all, it seemed better for both of us. And she's real smart, so she figured things out pretty quickly. Like she was talking and walking before she was 2 years old."

"So then you and Lynn met?" you inquire.

"Yes, we met at a mixed bowling league we both had joined. So, we knew each other for about 6 months before we decided to get married," Scott reflected. "Lynn stepped right in and began caring for Dorie soon after we started dating each other. She knew we came as a package deal," he laughed.

"So you became a wife and mother on the same day," you comment to Lynn. "How did things go between you and Dorie when you first married Scott?"

Lynn states that it seemed to her that Dorie was just dying for a mother. Although initially she was a little timid around Lynn, Dorie quickly warmed up and became attached to her and began going to her instead of Scott when she needed help with something. By the time she and Scott got married, Dorie had gotten used to having Lynn around and would sometimes ask Scott why Lynn wasn't coming over every night. Lynn explained that she came from a big family with six children and she always liked kids and took care of her younger siblings growing up. "I never looked at it as a chore. It was just natural to have kids around," Lynn states.

After Lynn and Scott got married and were both working full-time, Dorie went to day care for 2 years before starting school. The couple described Dorie as a well-adjusted child who had no difficulties in the day-care program at the church they attended on a regular basis. Lynn became pregnant with their son, Tommy, a year after they were married. Tommy is currently 4 years old and will be going to kindergarten next year. Dorie and Tommy seem to have a normal sister-brother relationship. Dorie was excited about having a baby brother when Tommy was born.

"So, you have really had no major problems with Dorie until just recently. Is that correct?" you ask.

Both Lynn and Scott agree that nothing out of the ordinary had occurred until Dorie began having problems at school.

You ask them if they have had any concerns about Dorie being abused, either at home or at school. They quickly say that there has been nothing to indicate something like that had happened. They feel that Dorie has been supervised closely at school and in the after-school program she attends until they pick her up after work.

"One more thought," you suggest. "Does Dorie know that you, Lynn, are not Dorie's real mother?"

Scott and Lynn stare at each other for several seconds. Scott hesitantly states, "Well, no, she doesn't know. Lynn and I have talked about when the best time would be to tell her, but we haven't told her yet. Just never could find the right time. Since she can't remember anyone else in her life, we just decided to let it be for a while until she was old enough to understand."

"Is there anyone you know who might've told her, like friends or other family members?" you ask.

"Not that we know of," says Scott, looking perplexed. "The whole family knows that we haven't told her anything about Susan, so I don't think they would've said anything to her. And I don't think any of our other friends would have either."

"Okay, well, it's just something to consider. Children sometimes pick up on what adults are talking about, and it's possible that Dorie may have heard someone at school talking about it," you state. "Before you make any decisions concerning that subject, though, I'd like to see Dorie for a session. Would that be all right with both of you?" you ask.

They both readily agree to having Dorie come in the following day for an appointment with you.

15.2–1 What are some of this family's strengths?

Interview with Dorie

Dorie is a very cute, blond-haired, blue-eyed girl who is slumped in a chair in the waiting room next to Lynn when you meet her. She shyly tells you her name. You sit down in a chair beside her and talk to her for a few minutes about the book she has in her hands and then ask her if she'd like to come with you and play with some of the toys you have in your office. Dorie looks at Lynn. Lynn tells her that she'll be waiting right here in the waiting room and that it's okay to go with you to your office.

Dorie quietly gets up and walks with you to your office. You tell her about the toys you have in your office, and Dorie goes over to the doll house you have in the corner and begins picking up the dolls and placing them in a line in front of the doll house. You explain to her that there is a whole family of dolls for the doll house and ask her about her family.

She picks up the father and mother and little boy and little girl and says that these are the people in her family. She begins looking at the furniture in the house and talks out loud about each room in the house. "This is the kitchen. There's a stove and a refrigerator and a sink. This is the living room with a TV and a couch and a chair," Dorie remarks. "And this is the little girl's bedroom and this is the little boy's bedroom and this is the mommy and daddy's bedroom."

Dorie places each of the dolls in its respective bedroom and says that they are going to sleep. Then, she says that it's morning and takes the little boy and the mother and father dolls down to the kitchen.

"Why is the little girl staying in bed?" you ask.

"She doesn't want to go to school today," Dorie remarks.

"Why not?" you inquire.

"Because there are mean kids at school," she replies. Dorie pushes the little girl doll down on the bed and says, "You don't have to go to school today."

"What do the kids at school do that's mean?" you ask.

Dorie scowls and with a serious expression on her face, she takes the little boy and places him out of the house and says he's at school now.

"They say mean things to the little girl," Dorie states.

"What kind of things do they say?" you inquire.

Dorie picks up the mother and the little girl and places them face-to-face in the living room of the house. Then she gets two other dolls and holding them as though they are talking to each other says, "Your mom isn't your real mom. Your real mom was crazy and she ran away," Dorie says with an angry expression on her face.

"And what does the little girl say?" you ask Dorie.

"She says that they are wrong. They are stupid dummies," Dorie replies. She picks up the little girl and places her back in the bedroom with the mother.

"How does that make the little girl feel?" you wonder.

"It makes her mad and sad," Dorie says. "I don't think I want to play this game anymore."

Dorie goes over to your desk and sits down in the chair. You follow her and sit down in another chair.

"I like this chair that turns around," Dorie states. You let her play in the chair for a few moments.

You ask Dorie if she'd like to draw a picture with the big box of crayons you have at the desk. Dorie agrees, and you suggest that she draw a picture of herself in her family.

Dorie draws a picture of the mother, father, and little boy standing together and a little girl off to the side with a big question mark on her shirt. You ask Dorie about the question mark, and she tells you that the little girl doesn't know if she belongs in this family.

"Why wouldn't she belong in the family?" you inquire.

"I don't know," says Dorie, "maybe she belongs to someone else."

You ask Dorie if there's anything else that makes the little girl sad, and she goes over and picks up the girl doll in the doll house and says, "No, now the little girl is happy because she's home with her real mother."

You suggest to Dorie that the mother she lives with is the mother she loves, and Dorie agrees. "Yeah, the real mother is the one you love. Right?" Dorie asks.

"That's right. Mothers are the ones that love their little girls like your mother loves you," you suggest.

Dorie tells you she's ready to leave, and you walk with her out to the waiting room.

15.2–2   What would your preliminary diagnosis be for Dorie?
Axis I

Axis II

Axis III

Axis IV

Axis V

15.2–3   What resources would be valuable to Dorie and her parents?

15.2–4   With the parents' permission, what information would you want to impart to the school counselor?

Case 15.3

Identifying Information
Client Name: Tamara Johnson
Age: 42 years old
Ethnicity: African American
Marital Status: Divorced
Children: One daughter, Cindy, age 19

Intake Information

Tamara Johnson called the Family Support Agency and talked with an intake worker approximately 1 week ago. The intake worker reported that Ms. Johnson requested an appointment with a counselor due to problems she has been experiencing following the death of her mother approximately 2 months ago. Ms. Johnson stated that she thought it would be helpful to have someone with whom she can talk since she feels very isolated at this time.

Initial Interview

Tamara arrives for the first appointment at the scheduled time. She is wearing a dark blue suit and paisley blouse. She appears to have come from her job. She is an attractive, petite woman of average height. She is reading a book when you arrive in the waiting room.

Tamara smiles, shakes your hand, and follows you back to your office and sits quietly waiting for you to begin the session. After some conversation about the traffic at rush hour, you ask Tamara how you might be of assistance to her.

Tamara begins by saying that her mother died about 2 months ago. She has a painful look on her face as her eyes fill up with tears. She takes some tissues and explains that her mother and she were best friends ever since she divorced her husband 18 years ago.

"We did everything together. We talked on the phone several times a day and had lunch to-gether three or four times a week. I just miss her so much."

"How old was your mother when she died?" you ask Tamara.

"She was 75 years old, and she'd been dealing with some medical problems for a few years," Tamara states as she blots the tears from her eyes. "I could tell for the past few months that she wasn't doing too well. She talked a lot more about pain she was having in her chest, and it was getting hard for her to go anywhere. I had started going to the grocery store for her since that seemed to require too much effort for her to do."

"So, she lived close by?" you query.

"Yes, she lived less than a mile from my house. I told her last year that she could move in with me since my daughter went off to college, but she wanted to stay in her own home, which I could understand at her age. She didn't want anything to change. We still had lunch together, and I would go over there every night after work to check on her, you know. So we spent a lot of time together, especially after Cindy, my daughter, went off to school. I just feel at loose ends now. I feel like everyone thinks I should just 'get over it,' but it's not that easy, if you know what I mean."

"It takes time to get over a major loss in your life, and it sounds as if you were very close to your mother," you reply.

"I really was close to her. I don't think I even realized it until she was gone. We were like best friends. I could talk to her about anything. I find myself driving the car and thinking I've heard her voice. Sometimes, in the middle of the night, I wake up and think I've seen her, but then I think I must have been dreaming about her. I don't feel like anyone can understand what I'm going through right now, and I wonder if I'm going crazy since I don't seem to be much better. Someone told me the other day that I just need to get busy doing other things. I just don't feel like doing anything. I go home and mope around and go to bed. I work extra so I don't have to face going home and feeling so alone, but I don't feel like doing anything else. I'm just so sad about losing her I can't stand it."

"Are the sad feelings there all the time, or do they come and go?" you ask.

"I feel sad a lot of the time, but not all the time. When I'm working and around other people, I feel better, happier I guess. But then I'm driving down the street, and I just burst into tears thinking about her," Tamara says with a big sigh.

"So you're feeling sad a great deal of the time, but not necessarily every minute of the day. Is that correct?" you ask.

"Yes, exactly. It's not simply being down in the dumps. It's that feeling that you've lost something very precious to you," Tamara states.

"Do you ever think about hurting yourself?" you ask.

"You mean, like suicide or something? No, I mean, I've wished at times I could've just died along with her, but I'm not going to kill myself or anything like that. I've got my daughter to think about. Besides, I would never do anything to hurt myself. That would really make my mom mad. I don't think she'd appreciate that one little bit," Tamara halfheartedly smiles.

"So, even though you don't feel like killing yourself, you still feel very sad much of the time. Are there other things that have bothered you recently?" you wonder.

"Well, I've lost some weight because I'm just not hungry; I used to go over and fix my mother's dinner at night after work, and now I just eat a pack of crackers and go to bed. It just doesn't seem worth the effort," Tamara states. "I suppose that's a good thing, though."

"Where do you work, Tamara?" you ask.

"I'm a paralegal at the district attorney's office downtown," Tamara replies. " I have a very time-consuming job working for three prosecuting attorneys. They could use four paralegals, and they only have two of us in the office. Sometimes, I end up working 60 hours a week. I like my job, but it's not always an easy one to have."

"That does sound like a very hectic schedule. Do you feel that the loss of your mother has affected your work?" you ask.

Tamara fiddles with the straps of her purse and stares at the picture on your wall. "Well, I'm sure it has, but I'm able to keep my mind off of it when I'm really busy. It's when I'm home alone at night or early in the morning. Weekends are terrible. I feel like I've relived those last few days of her life a thousand times in the last 2 months. I keep thinking about every little detail, wondering if I could have made it easier for her."

"Do you feel like telling me about what happened?" you inquire.

"Actually, she was okay until she came down with pneumonia. She called me one night, and I could tell she was struggling to breathe. I rushed over there and called 911, and they took her to the hospital. It was very scary. They worked on her for several hours before they took her up to intensive care on a respirator. I didn't think she was going to make it through the night. I called my daughter who was in the middle of final exams and told her to come home immediately. She arrived the next day, and my mother was still in critical condition."

Tamara pauses for a minute to collect her thoughts. "So, Cindy and I waited together. The doctors weren't sure why she wasn't getting better. They treated the pneumonia, but she still couldn't breathe on her own. They kept running tests, and it took them a week to discover she had a large, fast-growing tumor in her lymph node. It was heartbreaking. The doctors said it wasn't possible to operate since my mother couldn't breathe on her own. They said the operation would kill her in her very weak state. There wasn't anything anyone could do. So, I had to make the decision to take her off the respirator. She died the next afternoon."

Tamara bows her head and sobs quietly. "That must have been extremely difficult for you," you say. "Are you an only child?"

"There were no other siblings. My mother was a single parent like me. It must be genetic. It was just her and me," Tamara says with a smile. "She worked her whole life as a house-keeper and saved enough money bit by bit so I could go to college. She was happier than I was the day I graduated."

"It's good you haven't lost your sense of humor," you observe.

"I've always been able to see the positive side of things, at least until recently," Tamara says in an exhausted tone of voice. "I am just so tired of crying. I didn't know there were so many tears in me."

"Do you think it might help to come in and talk about all you're feeling right now?" you ask. "It sounds as if you've had a lot bottled up inside for a while."

"Whew, I think it could help tremendously. Like I said, I can't talk to anyone about this whole thing since I'm supposed to be 'over it,' if you know what I mean," Tamara says calmly. "I feel like a big load has been lifted off my shoulders already."

"Good, then let's make another appointment for next week," you suggest.

15.3–1   What are some of Tamara's strengths?

15.3–2   What are some resources that would be helpful to Tamara?

15.3–3   What issues would you want to take into consideration in deciding between a V-code and an Adjustment Disorder?

15.3–4   What is your diagnosis for Tamara?
Axis I

Axis II

Axis III

Axis IV

Axis V

Case 15.4

Identifying Information
Client Name: Dagmar Elkin
Age: 28 years old
Ethnicity: Caucasian
Educational Level: High school graduate

Intake Information
Dagmar Elkin is an inmate at Central Prison, serving a 15-year sentence for burglary and assault with a deadly weapon. He has been to the infirmary 10 times in the past year for various ailments ranging from severe stomach pain to heart problems. The physician has referred Dagmar to you, the mental health counselor at the prison, for a mental health evaluation. He has been in the infirmary for the past 2 days complaining of heart palpitations and stomach pain. The doctor cannot find any reason for Dagmar's symptoms.

Initial Interview
You enter the infirmary and tell the nurse that you are there to see Dagmar Elkin. He escorts you to the cubicle where Dagmar and another inmate are lying in bed. Dagmar's chart states that he is 5 feet 7 inches tall and weighs 140 pounds. Although small for a male, Dagmar appears to have a muscular build and ruddy complexion. You approach Dagmar's bed and tell him that you are a mental health counselor and that you need to talk with him.

Dagmar looks over at you and says, "What do you want? Do you think I'm crazy or something?" The inmate in the bed next to him chuckles.

"That all depends, Dagmar. Are you crazy?" you ask.

"Nah, I ain't crazy. I'm sick. Can't you see I don't feel good?" Dagmar says with an anguished look on his face.

"Well, the doctor wants us to talk, and I'm going to ask the officer to let you go into that room over there so we can talk privately. Would that be okay with you?" you inquire.

"Yeah, I guess," Dagmar moans.

You ask the corrections officer to allow you to go into a small consulting room so that you can talk with Dagmar without others listening to your conversation. The officer opens the door and allows Dagmar to get out of bed and enter the room. He asks you if you want the inmate handcuffed, and you decline the offer.

"So, Dagmar, why are you in the infirmary again?" you question straightforwardly.

"Well, you see, I'm not feeling too good. Something's wrong with my heart, and it's affecting my stomach, too. I've had these bad pains in my chest, and it feels like I'm having a heart attack," Dagmar tells you.

"Okay, any other symptoms?" you ask.

"Like I said, I've had these bad pains in my stomach, and I've thrown up blood," Dagmar responds.

"Okay. Anything else?" you ask.

"Should there be something else?" Dagmar asks.

"Dagmar, you've been in the infirmary 10 times in the past year for various aches and pains, and it seems that these symptoms come and go in a very convenient way. The doctor can't find anything physically wrong with you, and he's wondering why you keep coming to the infirmary. Is there something else going on that you want to talk about?" you ask.

"Are you saying I'm lying about all this pain I'm in?" Dagmar asks incredulously.

"I'm just saying your symptoms are convenient," you respond. "I just want to help you out here. Why don't you tell me what's going on, and maybe I can help you find another way of coping with things."

"Are you going to run and tell the doctor everything I say?" Dagmar questions.

"Only if you keep lying about being sick when you aren't," you respond.

"I don't know what you're talking about. I am sick!" Dagmar says emphatically.

"Okay, so what's making you sick?" you ask.

"Well, I think I need to be moved to a different cell," Dagmar states.

"Why do you say that?" you ask.

"Because this guy in my cell, he's driving me nuts. I think I wouldn't be so sick if I had a different cell," Dagmar implores.

"What's the guy doing that's driving you nuts?" you ask.

"He's always talking to himself and pacing back and forth and keeps saying I'm the 'devil' and 'get away from me' and crap like that. Where am I supposed to go? I can't get away from him no matter how much I'd like to."

"Do they give him meds?" you ask.

"Nah, he just rants and raves all day and all night. Nothing seems to quiet him down unless he gets a fist in his face. Sometimes, I just can't take it no more," Dagmar tells you. "I feel like if I don't get out of there and get some relief, I'm going to kill the guy."

"Have you told anyone about this situation?" you ask.

"Nah, I'm afraid that'll just make things worse. You know how it is over on the unit. I'm not looking for no trouble. I just want to get some rest. Rollo, he's a mess. I'm afraid he is going to kill me one night thinking I'm the devil or who knows what." Dagmar taps his foot on the floor and looks nervous. "You can't tell nobody I said anything or you know how it is. They'll make me pay for opening my mouth."

"So, you've been getting sick in order to get away from Rollo?" you look Dagmar directly in the eye and ask.

"Let's just put it this way. If Rollo weren't in that cell, I might feel just fine," Dagmar points out.

"Now, let me tell you something," you say. "I may not be able to get Rollo moved, but I might be able to get him some medicine to calm him down. Do you think that might help with your trips to the infirmary?"

"Anything to get him quiet is just fine with me," Dagmar tells you. "I just need some peace and quiet for a change. That is one scary dude in there with me."

"Okay. I'll see what I can do," you say to Dagmar, "but I don't want to see you in the infirmary unless you're seriously sick again. Do we understand each other?"

"Gotcha," Dagmar nods once and walks out the door.

15.4–1   What diagnoses would you want to rule out in Dagmar's case?

15.4–2   What are some possible problems you must overcome in your interview with Dagmar?

15.4 – 3   What strengths do you see in Dagmar?

15.4 – 4   What diagnosis would you give Dagmar?
Axis I

Axis II

Axis III

Axis IV

Axis V

Case 15.5

Identifying Information
Client Name: Henju Lee
Age: 27 years old
Ethnicity: Asian (born in Korea)
Marital Status: Married
Educational Level: Graduate student
Occupation: Research assistant
Children: One daughter, Eunju, age 2

Intake Information
Henju Lee, a female graduate student at a U.S. university, contacted the student counseling service stating that she needed to talk with someone about her "confusion over living in America." She stated that her husband doesn't want her to be "too independent," and she feels that her other American friends are allowed to do more activities than she is. She said that her husband has become very angry about her behavior. "He is very strict with me and my daughter and won't tolerate when I misbehave." The intake worker referred her to you since you have knowledge about marital relationships. Henju agreed to come to the center for an appointment with you between her classes the following day.

Initial Interview
Henju is sitting quietly in the waiting room reading a book when you meet her. She smiles, stands, and tells you her name. She is a petite woman, approximately 5 feet 3 inches tall, and has long, dark hair. She follows you back to your office and asks permission to sit in the chair next to your desk. "Yes, absolutely," you tell her. "Would you like a cup of coffee?"

"Oh, no thank you," Henju replies.

"Okay, what made you decide to come talk to someone today?" you ask.

"Well, I think I have confusion about being in America," Henju replies.

"Confusion? Can you explain what you mean a little more?" you ask.

"Yes, you see, I am from Korea, and in Korea, women are, what is the word, less than their husband," Henju tells you.

"You mean subservient? They do what the husband tells them to do without questioning it?" you query.

"Yes, the husband rules the household. The wife does not ask questions," Henju responds. She begins looking around the room anxiously.

"Is this kind of hard for you to talk about?" you ask.

Henju's shoulders sag, and she says, "Yes, it is very hard to tell you since in Korea we keep the personal problems private. I do not tell anyone about, you know, my personal things."

"It sounds as if you have some things, though, that you really would like to talk about," you surmise.

"Yes, I am worried about how I misbehave and don't listen to my husband since I am in America."

"Okay, before you tell me about that, why don't you tell me how long you've been in America and what you're working on in school." You feel like you should take a step back and give Henju time to feel comfortable about the counseling situation.

"Yes, I live in Korea until I am 25 years old. I married my husband, Soekoo, ah, 2 years before I came to America. He is in engineering, a graduate student. When we come here, I am pregnant. I did not start school until my baby was born. Then I start school. We have been in America for 2 years now."

"Okay, and where do you live?" you ask.

"In international student housing," Henju tells you. She begins looking more relaxed talking about these areas of her life.

"And what are you studying in school?" you ask.

"I take physics and computer sciences," Henju tells you. "I do well in these areas of study."

"That's very impressive. Are you studying for a master's degree or a doctorate?" you question.

"First, a master's and then the Ph.D. degree," Henju smiles. "I get both degrees and then I teach and do research."

"Wow, that's a lot of school. Do you plan on going back to Korea after you and your husband have finished school?" you ask.

"Ah, we do not know. Perhaps, get a job in the U.S. but we must wait and see."

"Yes, of course. And how have you been managing with a small child with both you and your husband going to school full-time?"

"My little girl, she is in the child care from 7 A.M. until 5 P.M.," Henju replies.

"The child care here at the University?" you query.

"Yes, she likes it very much," Henju tells you.

"Good, that makes it easier for you to have her right here, I'm sure. So, let's talk a little about what you've been feeling confused about lately. Can you tell me a little more about that?"

"Well," Henju sighs, "I think I like better the way American women are free to do as they like, so I tell my husband I want to do things on my own."

"And how did he respond?" you ask.

"He does not like that at all. He wants me to go to school and to come home. That's all. Everything else, he wants to do it with me."

"Can you give me an example?" you ask.

"Well, like I say to him that I will go to the grocery store and get baby food or something. He says no; he says he must come with me to the grocery store. Or, well, I want to study with my girlfriends, and he says I have to study only at home. I don't like this at all. He goes out with his friends to study, but it is not okay for me to do the same. Do you see what I mean? I am confused. He says I misbehave. And I don't

see that at all. I think I am now in America, and I want to do what my American girlfriends do in this country. Oh, he gets very angry with me."

"Okay, and what happens when he gets angry with you?" you ask.

"He sometimes says I am not a good wife and that he is in charge of the household and I will do what he says. I feel very bad when he says that." Henju sighs and sits back in her chair. She twists her hair and looks uncomfortable again.

"So, when he gets angry at you for wanting to go out alone or with your girlfriends, he makes you feel bad. What do you do when he says those things?" you query.

"Sometimes, I think I get mad at him. But, I should not get mad. In Korea, the wife obeys her husband."

"Do you ever decide to go out with your friends even if your husband doesn't want you to take part in those activities?" you wonder.

"One time, I did that. You see, my friends decide to have a meeting because we have a big exam in the physics class. I tell my husband I need to go to the meeting so I can do well on the exam. He says, 'No, you cannot go.' I tell him I think this is very important and he can stay with our daughter one evening. So, I did not go home that night, and I went over to my friend's house to study. When I got home, he was so angry. He had been drinking the wine and was, how do you say, too much to drink? And he screams at me and says I am a bad wife and all, and he hits me with his belt. I was very, very upset after that for a long time."

"When did this happen, Henju?" you carefully ask.

"About 1 or 2 months ago," Henju replies.

"Did you tell anyone about this incident?" you ask.

"No, I felt very ashamed and did not want anyone to know," Henju says quietly.

"Okay, has your husband gotten angry and hit you other times?" you ask.

"No, just the one time, but I have not felt like I could go out on my own since that time. I feel I must be at home and please my husband or he will be very angry again."

"Are you fearful that he might become angry and hit you again?" you ask.

"I am always fearful of my husband when he drinks the wine," Henju replies. "I would like to not be so afraid all the time. And I would like to enjoy the freedom like American women do. I think maybe I should not want this, but I have tried and I cannot stop thinking I want some of this freedom like my friends."

"When you say 'fearful,' Henju, do you mean you are scared that your husband will hit you again?" you ask.

"Only if I do something to make him very angry and drunk. If I behave the way I should as a Korean wife, then I am not afraid. I love my husband very much. He is a good person. He just does not understand American way of life for women. I feel I must learn how to obey him better and get these thoughts out of my mind."

"How often does your husband drink too much wine?"

"Only on holidays and when he goes out with his Korean friends."

"Not every day or week?"

"No. Not that much."

"So you have been living in America for 2 years now. How many times have you gone out by yourself?" you query.

"Three times I go out. Once with my friends that I told you about; once to the pharmacy as my baby was sick and I needed the medicine; and once to buy food. My husband was not happy about these times at all. But he only hit me the one time when he had too much to drink and he became very angry that I was not home when he wanted me to be."

"The times that he gets angry with you but hasn't hit you, what does he do?"

Henju thinks for a minute. "He tells me I am a bad wife and I misbehave. He yells and in Korean says bad names. Sometimes he says I am not a good mother. One time, he made me sit and meditate about my bad ways until morning."

"When he tells you you're a bad wife, how does that make you feel?"

"I am very sad and ashamed of my ways. I think I should be good Korean wife. I think I should act that way for my daughter, too. But lately, I have been talking to my girlfriends, and they say I don't have to listen to my husband and that I am not a bad wife. So I have confusion."

"I see. This is a big dilemma for you. Have you been having trouble sleeping or eating?"

"Sometimes I am so tense that I lie in bed without sleeping. But I eat very well," she says with a big smile on her face, patting her belly. "I like American hamburgers and ice cream the best."

You smile and say, "I'm glad you like American food. But it must be hard not to be sleeping very well. How long have you had trouble sleeping?"

"Only since my husband got so mad at me when I went to the study group. I did not think I had a problem until that time."

You decide that you do not want to press Henju further during the first session and that you have enough information to make an assessment of her issues. Therefore, you end the session by thanking her for coming and being honest and open with you. You schedule a follow-up session in the next few days.

15.5–1　What are some of Henju's strengths?

15.5–2　What acculturation issues do you think are involved with this case?

15.5–3　About which aspects of Korean culture do you need to get information in order to diagnose Henju appropriately?

15.5–4　What resources might be beneficial to Henju?

15.5–5　If you were to form hypotheses of Soekoo's issues, what would they be?

15.5–6　What is your initial diagnosis for Henju?
Axis I

Axis II

Axis III

Axis IV

Axis V

15.5–7   What would be your next steps with this client and family system?

_____

DIFFERENTIAL DIAGNOSIS

With both Adjustment Disorders and V-codes, unsuccessful coping can indeed lead to more serious diagnoses. For example, in the case of Bereavement, grief following the loss of a loved one is a normal emotional process that may involve some depression or insomnia. The length of the bereavement period differs among individuals and cultures. However, if the person experiences symptoms of a major depressive episode after several months of grief, a diagnosis of Major Depressive Disorder would be used for that individual. Similarly, if an Adjustment Disorder with Depressed Mood continues and symptoms escalate, the Major Depressive Disorder diagnosis will become more appropriate.

15.DD–1   What additional symptoms would Tamara Johnson (Case 15.3) need to be diagnosed with a Major Depressive Disorder?

15.DD–2   Write a paragraph describing your rationale for your diagnosis of Dagmar Elkin (Case 15.4). Include your decision to rule out a Somatoform or a Factitious Disorder.

15.DD–3   What would be different about Maggie Weinzapfel's symptoms (Case 6.4) if she were diagnosed with an Adjustment Disorder?

15.DD–4   Why did Michael Barron (Case 2.6) receive a more serious diagnosis than an Adjustment Disorder? Which Adjustment Disorder would you consider in this case?

15.DD–5   Why did you rule out an Adjustment Disorder diagnosis for Natalie Loftin (Case 14.1)?

InfoTrac keywords

Adjustment Disorder, anxious mood, Bereavement, child abuse, depressed mood, marital problem, parent-child problem

16 | Additional Cases for Assessment

Case 16.1

Identifying Information
Client Name: Clarence Jones
Age: 51 years old
Ethnicity: African American
Marital Status: Married
Occupation: Part-time job at auto repair shop
Children: Three adult children

Intake Information
Clarence Jones has been referred by his physician to the Veterans Administration (VA) Counseling Center. He recently made an appointment with his doctor for a medical checkup because his wife was increasingly concerned about his irritability, his inability to sleep, his moodiness, and some bizarre behavior she had observed. Upon examination, Clarence appeared to be in good physical condition. The physician, however, felt that Clarence could benefit from counseling.

VA records show that Clarence Jones, a 51-year-old auto repair worker, served 4 years in Vietnam from 1967 to 1971. During that time, he spent a great deal of time on the front lines and witnessed many women, children, and fellow comrades die in battle. While in Vietnam, he received word from his family that his younger sister had been murdered in a park where she had taken her daughter to play. Clarence was unable to return to the United States for her funeral.

Clarence is currently in his second marriage. He married for the first time shortly after returning from Vietnam. After 5 years, his first wife took the two children and left him. She told Clarence that she couldn't handle his drinking, his moodiness, and his explosive anger. She told him that he was a recluse and they should never have gotten married. She feared for her children's safety because Clarence would often get "out of his head" and become destructive.

Clarence remained single for several years following the end of his first marriage. He worked only sporadically and had difficulty maintaining a job and a residence. He moved in and out of the homes of his "army buddies" but rarely stayed in one place for more than a few months. During that time, he was dependent on alcohol and abused marijuana. He spent some time in jail and then later, a rehabilitation center.

In 1980, Clarence was abstaining from drugs and alcohol and holding down a job repairing cars at an automobile dealership. Although still having difficulty with intermittent outbursts of anger and insomnia, he felt that he was coping well. During this time, he met another woman, Alice, with whom he lived for 6 years. They had a child together, but the relationship didn't last. Clarence states that he and Alice broke up due to his volatile moods and difficulty getting along with others at his place of employment.

In 1987, he married his present wife, Charlene. Charlene has told Clarence that if he doesn't get help for his problems, she will leave him. This demand appears to be the motivating force behind Clarence's desire for counseling.

Initial Interview
Clarence is slumped in a chair in the waiting room, staring out the window, with his hands in his pockets. He stands and shakes hands with you and goes to your office. He is quiet and seems somewhat withdrawn.

Clarence begins by telling you that his wife said she was going to leave him if he didn't get some help for his problems. He tells you that she has threatened him with leaving before, but this time, he thinks she really means it.

"So, you've been having some trouble in your marriage. What kinds of problems is she talking about, Clarence?" you ask.

"It's not drinking again or anything like that. I went to rehab and got away from all that stuff a long time ago. No marijuana either. I've been clean and sober since 1980. No, I think she's talking about my moods," Clarence suggests.

"What about your moods?" you inquire.

"See, I was in Vietnam from '67 to '71. I seen a lot of things I wished I never seen when I was over there. It kind of comes back on me from time to time and puts me in a mood," Clarence tells you.

"What happens when you're in one of those moods?" you ask.

"See, I get 'crazy' sometimes. It's like I'm right back there in the jungle, same feelings, everything, just like Nam. I get to thinking I'm going to be ambushed even though I'm in my own living room. See, it even feels like I'm in the jungle. Sometimes, I think I see Viet Cong coming out of the bushes. It scares me, I'm telling you. My wife says I'm not in my right mind when that happens."

"Okay, sometimes you feel that you're reliving what happened in Vietnam. Has this been going on just recently or for a long time?" you ask.

"Oh, off and on, ever since I came back to the States," Clarence responds.

"What kind of mood does this put you in?" you ask.

"Tears me to pieces, I'm telling you," Clarence says. "I'm all messed up after one of those times."

"Do you feel anxious or scared or angry, or how does it make you feel?" you ask.

"Real tense, like any little thing will set me off. Like when I hear a loud noise on TV or if the phone rings and I'm not expecting it. I get real tense," Clarence tells you. "Sometimes I just feel angry about it for no reason at all. And I yell at my wife, and then she gets upset. And then I get upset because she's upset, and it ends up in a big mess," Clarence says.

"Okay. Is there something that happens that causes this feeling like you're back in Vietnam to happen?" you inquire.

"Sometimes, I think I just see something on TV, or I hear something outside that sets it off," Clarence says.

"I see. So you sometimes feel like you're reliving experiences you had in Vietnam, sometimes you get very angry for no reason, and sometimes you get real tense," you summarize what Clarence has told you so far. "Do you ever have trouble sleeping?"

"You know, when I was in Nam, I could sleep through anything. Explosion goes off right beside me, and I'd sleep right through it. But now, I'm up half the night. I try to go to sleep, but I'm wide awake. I just stare into space for hours. Yeah, I have a lot of trouble sleeping these days," Clarence tells you.

"Okay. Is there anything else you can think of that's troubled you lately?" you inquire.

"Only other thing is sometimes I feel like I just want to be left alone. I don't want anyone bugging me. I just want to be by myself," Clarence says.

"So, sometimes being around other people bothers you?" you ask.

"Yeah, and I just don't feel like I belong anywhere. Like I'm an outsider everywhere I go," Clarence states.

"Okay. I understand what you're telling me, Clarence. You know, a lot of guys who served in Vietnam come in here for help with some of the same types of issues you've mentioned today. It's not uncommon after surviving something as terrible as a war to have some of the symptoms you're experiencing. But, it doesn't mean you're crazy and that you're just out of your head. It's something we can work on so some of the issues you carry around with you can be resolved. It means you would have to come in to this office about once a week and work with me. Would you be willing to do that?"

"Yeah, I don't want this marriage to break up like the others did. And I'm glad someone understands what I'm talking about. All these

years and it still bugs me to death sometimes—
you know what I mean?" Clarence asks you.

"Yes, I know what you mean. Let's make an
appointment for next week, and we can talk
more about your experiences," you respond.

16.1–1   Clarence has several problems. Make a list of the problems that Clarence presents for assessment.

16.1–2   Clarence also has some important strengths. Make a list of Clarence's strengths.

16.1–3   From the problems you have listed, which three would you assess are most important in terms of helping Clarence?

16.1–4   What resources in the community might be beneficial to Clarence?

16.1–5   What is your preliminary diagnosis for Clarence?
Axis I

Axis II

Axis III

Axis IV

Axis V

_____

Case 16.2

Identifying Information

Client Name: Harriet Fisher
Age: 11 years old
Ethnicity: African American
Educational Level: Sixth grade
Parents: Mary and Frank Fisher

Intake Information

Mary and Frank Fisher, a middle-class African American couple in their mid-30s, called to make an appointment at the Family Counseling Center concerning their 11-year-old daughter, Harriet. They were referred for counseling by their pediatrician, who had seen Harriet several times over the past 2 months for complaints of gastrointestinal problems. The intake worker suggested that Mary and Frank come to the first appointment without Harriet so that you could gather information about the family's history and current concerns.

Initial Interview

Mary and Frank come together to the first interview and appear to be very concerned about their daughter. Frank is an insurance salesman for a major health insurance company, and Mary works part-time in the mornings as a church secretary. They state that Harriet's problems began after Christmas vacation from school.

Harriet entered sixth grade at Simmons Middle School the previous fall. The couple states that Harriet is an excellent student who has always done very well in school. They describe her as "a little on the shy side" and "a sensitive child." She gets along well with other children, but she usually has one or two "best" friends.

Harriet plays soccer after school in the city recreation league and goes to Girl Scouts one evening a week. She also sings in the children's choir at church and attends choir practice on a weekly basis. Mary describes Harriet as a mother's "dream come true." Harriet is eager to please and helps her mother around the house without being asked.

Mary and Frank tell you that they started noticing a difference in Harriet's mood shortly after she entered middle school in the fall. Harriet seemed less happy than usual, and she often seemed to brood in her room for several hours at a time. When Mary asked Harriet if there was something bothering her, Harriet told her mother that she wasn't sure she was going to like middle school. Mary felt that Harriet was just making the adjustment to a different school and encouraged Harriet to invite friends over to play on the weekends.

Although Harriet had her best friends over to the house a few times during the fall, she seemed withdrawn and became quiet with a sad appearance about her. She told her mother on several occasions that she didn't like some of the boys in her class at school.

She also expressed some irritation that her friends were just "boy crazy" and didn't care about anything else. Mary states that she thinks Harriet is very smart but is less mature socially than some girls her age.

When you ask Frank if he has noticed anything different about his daughter, Frank states that he also senses that Harriet has been less talkative and seems "down" more than usual. He notes that he just started a new job and has to travel around the state, sometimes leaving on Monday and getting home on Friday.

He states that everything seemed fine until school started again after the Christmas break. Harriet seemed very unhappy about starting school again, and after the first week, she began having stomachaches every morning. She began crying every day, saying she couldn't get out of bed because her stomach hurt. Frank and Mary took Harriet to their pediatrician, who thoroughly examined Harriet and couldn't find anything physically wrong with her.

The stomachaches continued, and Harriet missed school almost every day during January. The couple became concerned about the number of days Harriet was out of school, as well as the fact that Mary had to miss work or have her sister come over and take care of Harriet while Mary was at work in the mornings. When the couple called the pediatrician again about Harriet's stomachaches, he suggested they take her to the Family Counseling Center.

You ask the couple about the family composition and how other members of the family get along. Frank and Mary tell you that Harriet is the second oldest child in the family. They have an older daughter who is 14 and a younger son who is 9. The couple describes their family as "close-knit"; they enjoy doing things together.

Frank and Mary state that they have other family members living in the same town. Mary's three sisters live nearby, and Frank's sister and two brothers live within 10 miles of the Fishers.

Mary's mother, who was a widow, remarried last summer and moved from the East Coast to California with her new husband. Mary says that she misses her mother, who she used to come over to the house frequently and often took care of the children when Mary needed to work. Frank's parents live on the other side of the state, and Frank and Mary visit them three or four times a year.

Mary describes her oldest daughter, Tenisha, as very outgoing. She is a cheerleader this year in high school and has a group of friends she enjoys. She recently started going out with a boy in the neighborhood to movies and the mall. Tenisha doesn't excel in school like Harriet does, but she loves art and music. She plays the flute and the piano and takes art lessons after school.

Frank describes their son as "all boy." He plays Little League, football, and basketball and belongs to the Cub Scouts. Frank states, "He is exactly like I was at his age."

You have obtained some important information about Harriet and her family thus far in the interview. You schedule an appointment to meet with Harriet separately in a few days.

16.2–1   List the strengths you have observed in this family.

16.2–2   What issues might you want to explore further with this couple?

Interview with Harriet

Three days after meeting with Frank and Mary Fisher, you schedule an assessment interview with Harriet. You meet Harriet in the waiting room where she is sitting quietly with her mother. Harriet is neatly dressed in blue jeans, a pink shirt, and white sneakers with pink socks. Her hair is tied back in a ponytail with a pink ribbon.

She willingly follows you to your office. You suggest she might like to draw a picture of her family while the two of you talk. She says she's not real good at art like her sister, but she'd like to draw a picture with colored marking pens.

You ask Harriet if she knows why her mother brought her to see you today. Harriet says that her mother told her you could help her with her stomach problems. You tell Harriet that you hope to be able to help her and that you would like to get to know her better so you can help. Harriet nods in agreement while continuing to draw her picture.

You ask Harriet how she likes sixth grade this year. Harriet replies, "It's okay. It's middle school, you know, and we move to a different classroom for each subject."

You ask her how she likes doing that, and Harriet responds quietly, "It's okay. I just don't like the boys in my class. They're always saying things about me and laughing at me because I wear glasses. Sometimes, I just feel like screaming at them."

You ask her if anyone else in the class wears glasses, and Harriet states that one other boy wears glasses, but they don't laugh at him. "He's just a computer nerd, anyway, and nobody bothers him like they bother me," Harriet mumbles.

You ask Harriet if there is anything she likes about her new school. Harriet says, "Well, I like reading and spelling and geography. And, I like to play soccer after school, and I like library time."

"So, it's the boys in your class that bother you the most?" you ask in a questioning tone of voice.

Harriet tells you that the boys are really mean and they don't seem to bother other girls. It makes her mad that just because she wears glasses, they pick on her.

You decide that although Harriet is having some problems at school, there may be other things that are bothering her beyond school. You ask Harriet about how things are at home. Harriet says she thinks everything is fine at home. She says she likes being at home, espe-

cially when her mother is there. Harriet tells you her mother works at the church in the mornings. She wishes her mother would be at home all the time.

You ask Harriet why she would like her mother to be home, and she says, "I don't know; it would just make me feel better."

When you ask Harriet how she gets along with her brother and sister, Harriet indicates that she gets along just fine with her siblings and doesn't have any problems with them. "My little brother gets on my nerves sometimes, but he can be pretty nice sometimes, too."

Harriet hands you her picture of her family. You immediately notice that there are five people, two adults and three children standing very close together in a circle and then there is one very small person in the corner of the page standing in what looks like waves of the ocean.

You ask Harriet to tell you about the picture, and she points to her family and says, "This is my family. This is my brother; this big girl is my sister and me in the middle and my father and mother."

"Who is this person over here in the corner?" you query.

Harriet tilts her head and squints her eyes and says, "Oh, that's my grandma. She's gone way far away to California because she had to get married. She's probably never coming back here. She's got a new husband, and she's just gone forever."

"How does it make you feel that your grandmother got married and left?" you ask.

Harriet opens her eyes very wide and then covers her face with her hands and responds in a muffled voice, "It makes me so mad that she just left all of us. She just doesn't care about anybody except that guy she married. She didn't even say good-bye to me."

Harriet drops her hands in her lap and puts her head down on the table. Her eyes are wet, and she obviously has some very strong feelings about her grandmother's recent marriage.

"She didn't say good-bye to you?" you query.

"No, after the wedding there was a party at the church, and there were lots of people there. I went to the store with my aunt to get more ice, and when I got back, my grandma was gone. I looked everywhere for her, and then my mother told me she left with her new husband on a plane. I don't think she'll ever come back," Harriet says tearfully. "I wish they had told me she was going to leave. All of a sudden she was gone," Harriet moans.

You ask Harriet if she is worried that other family members might suddenly leave her. Harriet tells you she's very worried about her parents disappearing while she's at school. "When I'm at school, I keep thinking I'll get off the bus and walk in the door and everyone will be gone," Harriet says anxiously. "I can't get it out of my head. It just scares me to death."

"Have you told your parents that you're worried about them leaving?" you ask Harriet.

Harriet tells you her parents have reassured her they would never leave her alone. Nevertheless, Harriet worries constantly that they might leave her.

"I just hate school," Harriet tells you. "I wish I never had to go back there."

While letting Harriet know you understand how she feels, you also explain to her that she has to go to school and you want to help her feel better about going to school. Harriet tells you she knows she has to go to school but she doesn't like it anymore.

You ask her if there's anything else that's happened at school that makes her dislike it so much. Harriet shakes her head and says, "No, I just don't want to go."

"Okay. I understand how you're feeling, Harriet, and we're going to try to make it easier for you to go to school every day," you conclude.

16.2–3   What are some of Harriet's strengths?

16.2–4   What are some resources that would be useful for this family?

16.2–5   What diagnosis would you give Harriet?
Axis I

Axis II

Axis III

Axis IV

Axis V

Case 16.3

Identifying Information
Client Name: Kim Garrett
Age: 36 years old
Ethnicity: Caucasian
Marital Status: Married
Occupation: Middle school teacher

Intake Information
Kim Garrett calls you 2 days after your initial appointment with Kim and her husband, Phillip (see Case 14.4), concerning their son, Gary. She states that she really would like to talk with you alone about some personal concerns she has.

Since you are working with her and Phillip as a couple, you tell her that you don't "keep secrets" between marriage partners and that you can't guarantee confidentiality if it relates to the relationship. Kim states that she understands and that she is really interested in working on her own growth and development and doesn't have any secrets from Phillip. You set up an appointment for Kim to come in for an individual session without her husband.

Interview with Kim
You greet Kim in the waiting room and notice she is grading student papers. "It looks like you have a lot of papers to grade," you comment as you escort Kim to your office.

"Yes, I have four language arts classes and two history classes that I teach every day, so it keeps me pretty busy," Kim replies.

"Maybe you can start by telling me what made you decide to make an individual appointment today," you suggest.

"Yes, well, when we met with you last week, Phil and I, well, it just made me realize, perhaps for the first time, some things about our relationship that I hadn't really thought about be-

fore that meeting," Kim states hesitantly. She seems to be searching for the right words to explain what she is thinking.

"What kinds of things were you thinking about?" you ask.

"Well, you know, I'm not really sure how to explain it. It was so embarrassing to me when Phil was telling you how dumb I am. I just wanted to disappear. And he does that a lot to me. I'm afraid to say anything because he can be so critical. Everyone sees Phil as so accomplished and bright, and they see me as just the stupid wallflower or something like that. I don't think I'm being very clear; do you know what I mean?" Kim looks at you with a perplexed expression on her face.

"So you think that Phillip overshadows you in social situations?" you inquire.

"Well, it's more than that. I feel like I'm incapable of handling situations that come up, whether they are social situations or other things like this situation with Gary. I feel like I've got to get a lot of support before I can make a decision about anything. Most of the time, Phil just takes over and makes the decisions for me, and I'm afraid to tell him how I feel because I'm afraid he'll just say I'm being stupid," Kim states.

"Okay, so it's more than just when you're in social situations. It occurs in everyday life as well," you suggest.

"Yes, I feel like I have no self-confidence in my own ideas," Kim states. "This problem with Gary has made me realize that I don't agree with Phillip about Gary's problem, but I'm afraid he'll just leave me if I tell him what I think."

"Really?" you say. "You really think Phillip would leave you because you disagreed with him about an issue?"

"I just can't stand the thought of being alone," Kim replies. "Before I met Phillip, I dated someone for a couple of years, and when

374 Chapter 16 Additional Cases for Assessment

we broke up, it was horrible. I didn't know how I was going to make it. And then Phillip came along and saved me."

"Saved you from what?" you ask.

"I was just falling apart and could hardly get to my classes. My grades were dropping, and I just felt like I was a worthless human being. Phillip came along just at the time I needed him the most."

"Okay, so you were having difficulty coping with the breakup of your former relationship, and Phillip came along and kind of 'rescued' you? Is that what you're telling me?" you ask.

Kim pauses for a moment and then nods her head. "Yes, at the time, I think I even said he was my savior. I just don't think I could've made it on my own."

"And do you still feel that way?" you question.

Kim nods her head and says, "Yes, in fact, more so than ever. Phillip makes all the decisions at home. He is in charge of our bank account and even goes to the grocery store every week and helps me buy food. I try very hard to please him because he's so important in my life."

"How about in your job? You obviously have a very responsible job and make decisions about your work on your own," you surmise.

"I suppose so," Kim says. "But when big issues come up at work, I go to Phil and get his opinion before I do anything. He's told me that he probably knows more than I do about how to handle student issues, so I just do whatever he suggests."

"How does that make you feel?" you ask.

"Well, I think I've begun to resent the fact that Phil is always right and I'm always wrong. I have some ideas about Gary's problem, but Phil thinks I'm making a big deal about nothing. I'm not sure he's right this time, but I'm afraid I'll make him angry if I say anything."

"And if he gets angry, then what happens?" you ask.

"I guess I'm afraid he'll leave me," Kim says despairingly. "I just don't know what to do."

"Do you think that's a fear or a reality?" you ask.

"I'm really not sure. What do you think?" Kim asks you.

"What I think may not be as important as your feeling comfortable with your own ideas. And I think that's something we could work on together."

"That would be okay with me. Maybe I should ask Phil if it's okay with him," Kim wonders out loud.

"Perhaps this is a decision you need to make on your own," you suggest. "I'd like to know what you decide. Call me if you want to make another appointment."

"Okay," Kim says with a smile. "I'll do that."

16.3–1 What are some of Kim's strengths?

16.3–2 What is your preliminary diagnosis for Kim?
Axis I

Axis II

Axis III

Axis IV

Axis V

16.3–3   Are there additional Axis I diagnoses that you want to rule out in this case? If so, what are they?

16.3–4   Are there other questions you would like to ask Kim? If so, what are they?

Case 16.4

Identifying Information
Client Name: Jamie Mason
Age: 10 years old
Ethnicity: Caucasian
Educational Level: Fifth grade
Parents: Joan and Sonny Mason

Background Information
Jamie Mason is a 10-year-old Caucasian fifth-grader. This interview with Jamie follows an initial interview with his parents (see Case 2.4).

Interview with Jamie
Jamie is waiting quietly in the waiting room when you and Joan enter. Jamie is a cute little boy who looks angelic when he smiles. He easily agrees to talk with you in your office. You notice on the way down the hall that Jamie touches the doorknobs of each office door twice on your way to your office. You start the conversation by asking Jamie about the doorknobs.

"I noticed on the way down the hall that you touched all the doorknobs twice. Can you tell me about that?" you query.

"I have to touch them twice to get rid of all these thoughts I have about doorknobs," Jamie says.

"Can you tell me about the thoughts?" you ask.

Jamie makes several odd gestures with his head and guttural sounds in his throat. "It's kind of like when I see a doorknob, I can't think about anything else until I touch it two times. Something really bad will happen if I don't, you know," Jamie says.

"What does that feel like?" you ask.

Jamie jerks his head back and forth. "It sort of bothers me," Jamie says. "I don't like it much."

"You don't like having to think about doorknobs, or you don't like touching them?" you ask.

"Thinking about them," Jamie responds. "It feels better when I touch the doorknob and walk through the door."

"Are you thinking about anything else when you feel the need to touch the doorknobs?" you ask.

"Uh, no, I don't think so, just the doorknobs. It's hard to explain. I guess it's silly, but I just *know* something bad will happen if I don't touch them."

"Okay, I think I understand," you comment.

You decide to change the subject so that Jamie can begin to feel more comfortable with you. "Tell me a little about yourself, Jamie. What kinds of things do you like to do?" you ask.

"Well, I like to play soccer, and I like to play the violin," Jamie tells you.

"Wow, you play soccer and the violin?" you respond.

"Uh-huh, I am the goalie for our team in soccer," Jamie states. Jamie suddenly gets up out of his chair, jerks his head back, touches the floor, and makes crying sounds in his throat. He sits back down in his chair.

"Does that happen often?" you ask.

"Sometimes," Jamie says, "well, mostly all the time."

"Do you know when it's about to happen?" you ask.

"Nope, it just happens and I can't help it," Jamie says. "I've told my mom and dad I try not to do it, but it happens anyway."

"What about the doorknobs? Do you know when you're going to touch the doorknobs?" you query.

"Sort of," Jamie says. "I think about it for a long time before I have to touch them. And it makes me real mad if someone tries to stop me."

"But the noises and the movements—you don't know when those are going to happen. Is that right?" you ask.

"Yeah, and the other kids at school, they think it's funny or weird or something. I wish I could make it stop," Jamie pleads.

"Do they tease you about it, Jamie?" you wonder.

"Sometimes. They think I'm doing it on purpose," Jamie says. "Mom and Dad did, too, but now, they think it just happens."

"Okay, and I believe you, too, Jamie, when you tell me you don't do it on purpose. I'd like to be able to help you with all the noises and movements you experience," you suggest.

"I'd be happy about that," Jamie tells you. "I feel like I'm the loneliest boy in my class."

"So, it's hard to have friends when you have all of these things going on inside you," you suggest.

Jamie rolls his eyes upward and tells you that it's very hard to have even one friend. Suddenly, he jerks his head from side to side and makes several barking noises and guttural sounds.

"Does this make it hard to think when you're at school?" you ask.

Jamie nods his head and tells you he used to make good grades when he was little, but now he makes all C's.

You tell Jamie that you're going to talk with his mom and dad again and that you will be assisting him in getting the help he needs for these problems. Jamie leaves your office and runs down to the waiting room.

16.4–1 What are some of Jamie's strengths?

16.4–2 What is your diagnosis for Jamie after meeting with him?
Axis I

Axis II

Axis III

Axis IV

Axis V

16.4–3   If you gave Jamie more than one Axis I diagnosis, how did you decide which was the principal diagnosis?

16.4–4   If you did not give Jamie more than one Axis I diagnosis, are there additional diagnoses you would like to rule out?

Case 16.5

Identifying Information

Client Name: Mary Searcy
Age: 34 years old
Ethnicity: Caucasian
Educational Level: High school graduate
Occupation: Waitress

Intake Information

Mary Searcy called the Truluck Mental Health Center, a public, governmentally funded agency, and requested an appointment with a counselor. She stated that she's about to lose her third job in 6 months due to an anger problem. When the intake worker asked her if she could expand on what she meant by anger problem, Mary stated, "It's just out of my control."

She further stated that her manager told her if she didn't get some help, he'd have to let her go. An appointment with you was scheduled for the following day.

Initial Interview

Mary arrives at the mental health center wearing her waitress uniform and her hair pulled back in a ponytail. She is sitting calmly in the waiting room reading a magazine when you arrive to greet her. She smiles and tells you she came a few minutes early because she's going to have to leave in an hour in order to get to work. She tells you as you're walking to your office that she can't afford to be late or she'll lose her job.

"So, you've been worried about your job lately?" you inquire.

"Yes, I just can't lose this job because I might never get another one," Mary says.

"What's been happening that makes you think that?" you ask. You wonder if Mary is being realistic or if she is exaggerating the problem.

"Well, it's my anger, I think," Mary tells you. "Although I'm not really sure my anger is the problem. But it must be."

"You think you may have a problem with your anger, but you're not sure," you suggest.

"Yes, you see it doesn't happen often, but when it does happen, it's really out of control," Mary says. She looks nervously around the room as though she's searching for the right words to express her thoughts.

"You mean your anger?" you ask.

"Well, I don't really know what else to call it, but it feels like anger. You see, it started about 2 years ago. I had a job out in California making good money waiting tables at a really upscale restaurant. I was doing a good job, and my boss wanted to make me head waitress. He gave me all the big parties, and I was finally getting some bills paid and keeping up with my rent and car payments. Then one night, this other waitress said something to me like, 'Could you hand me that pitcher of water?' She had a huge platter of food, you know, lobster and steak dinners, and I don't know what came over me, but I just hauled off and knocked the tray up against her and hit her upside the head. She landed on the floor, and the tray landed on top of her. Or at least that's what she said happened. I don't clearly remember, you see. It's all kind of a blur. I don't really remember being angry, but I guess I was. Anyway, $185 worth of food hit the floor, and my boss was so angry with me I knew I was going to lose my job. So, I just walked out of the restaurant and never went back."

"Did you have problems with this other waitress before the incident occurred?" you ask.

Mary scowls and rubs her forehead. "I think we got along okay as I remember," she says. "I remember I'd had trouble earlier in the day with my landlord claiming I owed him money for getting the carpet cleaned. I hadn't asked anyone to clean the carpet and didn't think I should have to pay for it. I also remember having an argument with my boyfriend because I had to work that night and he thought I was off and wanted to go out. So, I guess it had been a hard day before I ever got to work," Mary ponders.

"Do you remember how you were feeling at work that night?" you ask.

"I just remember being irritable, like in a bad mood," Mary suggests. "But I don't think I was really angry at Sue, the waitress I knocked down, just tense. Then when she asked me for the water pitcher, I just exploded."

"How often would you say this type of situation has occurred over the past 2 years?" you ask.

"Well, I'd say it's been happening once a month or so but not always at work. It's happened at home several times, and I've had two relationships that broke up because I just lost control of myself. One guy told me that I needed to get help after I'd thrown the frying pan through a window at the house, and he just left and never came back. That happened about a year ago. At the time, I didn't think he knew what he was talking about, but now, I think maybe he was right. I've had three jobs in the last 6 months, and I just can't afford to lose this one."

"So, you lost two jobs in the last 6 months because of your anger?" you inquire.

"Yes, well, it was the same type of thing that happened in California. I had this one job that I liked and I thought was going pretty well, and one day I came to work and had a big party of eight people I was waiting on by myself. Then the hostess gave me another party of six. Normally, I could handle it. But, I remember getting real tense because I didn't have any help, and I was rushing around trying to get all the orders. One obnoxious guy at the table of eight kept asking me for more coffee. I was doing my best, but I couldn't get to him right away. Finally, he puts his arm out and grabs me around

my waist and says, 'Why are you ignoring me?' I just lost it. I took the whole pitcher of water and dumped it on his head and was yelling, 'Can't you see I'm a little busy here? I'll get your damned coffee when I get a chance.' The guy tipped back in his chair so far that he fell over onto the floor and threatened to sue the restaurant. Needless to say, I lost that job."

Mary sinks into the chair and looks very unhappy. It sounds as if this is the first time she's admitted to having a problem or identifying her behavior as a problem for her.

"Looking back on it now, I'm not sure why I dumped the water on his head. He was obnoxious, but I've dealt with a lot of obnoxious people in my job, and I never went to that extreme or got that upset," Mary remarks. "The most recent thing that happened wasn't that bad. I just knocked a hole in the wall in the kitchen at work. It surprised me that I had that much strength, if you want to know the truth. Anyway, my boss said I better get control of my anger or he'd send me packing. I really don't want to lose this job. I've got bills to pay, and I'm tired of moving from one job to the next. You've got to understand. I'm really not a violent person. Something just comes over me and I blow," Mary tells you.

"Okay, so it sounds as if you've been having a lot of trouble controlling these sudden outbursts that seem out of proportion to the problem you're trying to handle. Is that correct?" you ask.

"Yes, I think that's pretty accurate," Mary says.

"What about other aspects of your life?" you inquire. "Do you live by yourself? Do you have a boyfriend now? Are there other things bothering you right now?"

"I'm living by myself right now, although I do have a boyfriend. We haven't been dating that long though, maybe 6 weeks. He's a nice guy and we get along. I don't want to ruin that relationship either. I've been having a little trouble paying all my bills but nothing out of the ordinary. Other than that, everything has been okay, I guess."

"Have you been sick at all recently?" you inquire. "Have you been taking any medications for any medical problems?"

"No, I'm a fairly healthy person. Don't get sick much. Maybe a cold in the winter, but that's about it," Mary replies.

"So, you're not taking any medicine right now?" you ask again.

"Only birth control, but nothing else," Mary responds.

"What about your family?" you inquire. "Has anyone in your family ever had similar problems to the one you've been experiencing?"

"I don't think so," Mary states. "My mom died when I was 12 years old, and my dad remarried about a year later. I never remember my mother getting upset about anything. She was a fun person who loved to take us out shopping and to the movies. My dad is kind of the quiet type, if you know what I mean. He sort of blends in with the walls. He's a carpenter and likes to build stuff. He was always out in the garage making something—a pretty easygoing fellow."

"What about your sister?" you ask. "Is she your younger sister?"

"Yes," Mary replies, "she's 4 years younger than I am. She still lives out in California, and I don't see her very often. She was the smart one in the family. She teaches preschool at a nursery out there and has two kids of her own. I guess she's like my mom. Loves children."

"And how would you describe yourself?" you ask.

"Well, I think of myself as a pretty outgoing person. I like talking to people and being outdoors. I run and ride bikes and like to go sailing when I have the chance. Most people tell me I have a good sense of humor, too," Mary responds.

"So these outbursts seem to come out of nowhere and don't necessarily fit with your personality," you suggest.

"Right, I mean I do begin to feel this tension building up inside me, but I don't know what it's about. It seems out of sync with what's actually going on at the time. And then I just have to get rid of it somehow—I just explode over some small thing," Mary says.

"Okay, I think I have the picture," you respond. "I think I can help you figure out what's going on and how to get your feelings under control. Would you like to make another appointment so we can talk again?" you ask.

"Yes, I think I really could use some help with this problem," Mary states.

16.5–1   What are some of Mary's strengths?

16.5–3   What has Mary already done that you would consider resourceful?

16.5–3   What is your initial diagnosis for Mary?

Axis I

Axis II

Axis III

Axis IV

Axis V

16.5–4   Are there other diagnoses that you would want to rule out in this case?

Case 16.6

Identifying Information
Client Name: Eric Connors
Name: 21 years old
Ethnicity: Caucasian
Marital Status: Single
Children: One child (no contact)

Intake Information
The client is a 21-year-old referred for evaluation by his attorney. The client is facing felony charges of theft and could be sentenced as a "career criminal." The attorney is interested in an evaluation and diagnosis since she feels Eric is in need of long-term treatment.

Prior History Provided in Written Form by the Attorney
The client presents with a long history of problem behaviors. He was frequently truant from school throughout childhood. His parents believe that he stole household items (for selling at a pawn shop) through much of his childhood. His first brush with legal authorities was for auto theft at age 15.

At that time, his parents began arranging treatment for him. Although he saw a substantial number of physicians, counselors, social workers, and psychologists and each reported that he was polite and apparently "working hard" in therapy, the offenses continued. At age 16, he was arrested for driving a stolen car across state lines. He was placed in a rehabilitation program at the state facility for juvenile delinquents. Although he reports he was released early because of his "exceptional response to treatment," records indicate that he was released the week of his 18th birthday (the "normal" release time for an adjudicated youth).

Upon return, he found employment and was viewed as energetic, bright, and enthusiastic by his employers. After several months, he began missing work and was again arrested for auto theft. At present, the client has been arrested as an adult a total of six times. Because these offenses have been in the adult system and in different jurisdictions, he has been able to avoid incarceration and is currently on probation in three separate jurisdictions.

The client has apparently never formed any substantial attachment for another person. Although he states he is "extremely close" with his parents, they indicated that they cannot trust him to be truthful in any circumstance.

He describes a history of sexual promiscuity. He was married at age 19 to a woman who had achieved considerable recognition as a prostitute. After 9 weeks, he left her and has not shown any regret about this ill-fated marriage. He states that she had a child by another man, but she named the child Erica and claimed the child was Eric's daughter in order to get child support. Eric denies this claim and has never accepted any emotional or financial responsibility for this child.

Following this short-lived marriage, Eric had a string of unsuccessful relationships with women. In each case, the woman left Eric due to his excessive drinking and drug use, which led to abusive behaviors. Eric has been arrested on multiple occasions on "assault with injury" charges. These cases were later dismissed due to inadequate evidence or the woman not appearing for the court date.

Initial Interview with Eric
When Eric enters your office, you note that he is a very attractive young man with thick, wavy brown hair and blue eyes. He appears to be very relaxed and comfortably sits back on your couch and attempts to engage you by commenting on your nice office. He seems unaffected by the gravity of the situation he is currently facing.

You ask him if he understands the purpose of the session with you. Eric smiles in a charming way and states that he seems to have gotten "into a little bind" with the law and his attorney wants to know if he's "crazy."

You ask him if he thinks he has a problem, and he replies that the only problem he has is that he's being "picked on" by the cops and he doesn't feel that he's done anything to warrant such a strong response by the law. "I'm only 21. It seems premature to say I'm a career anything," he quips.

"When you say you've gotten 'into a little bind' with the law, what do you mean, Eric?" you question him.

"You mean the latest thing?" Eric asks.

"Yes, your attorney has told me you've been arrested several times, but why were you arrested this time?" you inquire.

Eric leans back on the couch and stretches his arm across the back of it. He squelches a yawn and says, "Well, they say I stole a car, but they've got it all wrong. I was leasing it from a buddy of mine for a day or two so I could look for a job," Eric tells you.

"You were leasing it?" you ask doubtfully.

"Yeah, I paid him 10 bucks to use the car. How was I supposed to know it was stolen?" Eric asks innocently.

"Okay, so you were using the car to find a job, and you are currently unemployed. What was the last job you held?" you ask.

"Well, I was working for a carpet-cleaning service, but the boss and I didn't see eye to eye, so to speak," Eric tells you. He smiles and shakes his head.

"What do you mean? Did you get in an argument with your boss?" you ask.

"Yeah, he accused me of stealing some jewelry from some little old lady's house when I went to clean her carpets, but I didn't steal anything. Maybe my partner took something but not me. He wouldn't believe me, so I just quit," Eric states.

"How long did you work there?" you inquire.

"About 3 weeks, I guess," Eric says. "But it wasn't my fault that it didn't work out."

"Okay. And your attorney has told me that you've been in treatment for alcohol and drug abuse. Are you currently drinking or smoking pot?" you ask.

Eric smiles and says, "I'd say that I'm a 'recreational user.' These days, I only get alcohol or marijuana when someone gives it to me. It's the downside of unemployment, you know."

"That you can't afford drugs and alcohol?" you ask.

"Yup!" he smiles.

"Okay. Has using substances ever caused any problems in your life?" you ask.

"It's never caused me problems, but it sure seems to tick off other people. Like my parents—they're always asking me. Like probation officers—they always want to test me. So, I guess substances have given me headaches from other folks!" he moans.

"Well, I think I have a fairly clear understanding of your situation. Is there anything else you think I need to know?" you ask.

"Don't you want to know how my parents treated me as a child or anything? I thought shrinks always asked about that," he inquires.

"Not necessarily. Did anything unusual happen during your childhood that you think is important that I know?" you clarify.

"Just that they didn't really help me when the law was after me," he notes.

"I believe I was told they tried to get you into various treatment programs. Is that not the case?"

"Well, yeah. But they should have spent their money getting a good attorney. Even this lady I have now isn't top-notch! I'm sure they could afford better," he complains.

"Thank you, Eric. I'll make a note of that. I'll be sending a report to your attorney in a few days," you conclude.

16.6-1   Do you see any strengths in Eric's situation?

16.6-2   Do you think Eric would be a good candidate for treatment? Why or why not?

16.6-3   What is your preliminary diagnosis for Eric?
Axis I

Axis II

Axis III

Axis IV

Axis V

16.6 – 4   Is there any collateral information you would like to obtain before writing your report? Include both records requests and possible interviews.

Case 16.7

Identifying Information
Client Name: Maya Pena
Age: 25 years old
Ethnicity: Hispanic
Educational Level: Graduate student
Occupation: Part-time librarian

Background Information
Maya Pena calls you after having terminated therapy approximately a year ago (Case 7.2). The last time you saw her she was functioning much better. Many of her habits were under control, and she was taking medication prescribed to her by a psychiatrist.

When she telephones, you ask her how she's been in the last year. She tells you she's been doing all right, but that she has some other issues she would like to talk to you about. You make an appointment for her to come see you the following day.

Interview with Maya
Maya appears very happy to see you when you meet her in the waiting room. She is smiling and appears to have matured since you last saw her. She tells you that she's finally going to graduate school and working part-time at the library.

When she enters your office, she sighs with relief and says, "This is the problem-solving room. I don't know what you have in that chair, but it seems to make the problems go away." She laughs and takes a seat.

"Well, how have things been going this year?" you ask.

Maya sits back in her chair and says, "Fairly well, actually. I finally decided to go to graduate school in art history because I still would like to work at a museum and I think the graduate degree will help. I'm working part-time at the library where I was working full-time, and

they're being flexible with my hours so I can work around classes. It's been a little stressful with so much work to do, but I like my classes and job and everything."

"Okay, and how have things been going with those habits we were working on?" you ask.

"Well, just recently, I've had a little flare-up of some of the feelings, like I need to check everything. I'm not sure why, but it's bothering me a little," Maya says with a look of concern on her face.

"Is that why you wanted to talk today?" you ask.

"Well, not exactly," Maya says. "I think the stuff with the checking is just because I've been under a lot of stress lately, trying to get through this first year of graduate school and everything."

"Is there something else going on?" you query.

"Yes, actually there is," Maya says. "This is going to sound very weird, but I'm going to tell you anyway because it's bothering me a lot."

"Okay, good. What is it?" you wonder.

"Well, I've been having these terrible dreams lately, and I can't seem to shake them," Maya tells you.

"Bad dreams?" you question.

"Yes, really bad dreams of the nightmare variety," Maya says. "I mean they are so bad I wake up screaming in the middle of the night. I'm so shaken by the dreams that I have a really hard time getting back to sleep."

"I see. How often has this happened, Maya?" you ask.

"It's been happening for about the last 4 months; only they've gotten worse lately. At first, it was just every once in a while, and I figured everyone has bad dreams every now and then. But lately, I've been having these ferocious nightmares about three times a week, and it's really upsetting me."

"What are the dreams about?" you ask.

"Well, it's not like I'm dreaming the same thing over and over again, but one thing that seems to be the same in every dream is that someone is chasing me who I know is going to hurt me if the person catches me. So, I'm running and the person is right behind me and I'm very, very frightened. Sometimes, it almost seems like it's some kind of monster trying to catch me, and other times it seems like a person." Maya sighs and leans back in the chair.

"Can you remember what was going on when the nightmares first started?" you ask.

"Well, it doesn't seem like anything special really," Maya says thoughtfully. "I was trying to finish some papers for my classes before Christmas break, and I was staying up late at night. As you can imagine, I was really concerned about all this work since it was my first semester in graduate school and I was so afraid I might not make it. These papers were really important because they were the only grade I'd get for the class, so everything hinged on them. I was going over and over and over what I wrote, trying to make it as good as I could. Besides, I was working a lot of hours at the library, and I was just not getting much sleep. So, I thought at first it was because I was just so tired when I finally did get to bed that I was having these

bad dreams. But actually, they got worse over the break when I was getting more sleep, but still just happening every once in a while."

"Okay, so you remember the dreams when you wake up. Is that correct?" you ask Maya.

"Absolutely, and it frightens me even after I realize it was just a dream," Maya states.

"What about any other problems you may have been experiencing? Have you been having any medical problems recently?" you ask.

Maya thinks for a few moments. "No, nothing other than being tired," she states.

"When was the last time you went to your family doctor for a checkup?" you ask.

"Oh, probably about a year ago. I haven't really had any medical problems."

"Okay, Maya, I'd like you to make an appointment to see your doctor and just make sure there's nothing going on medically, and then we'll get together and talk again. Does that sound okay to you?" you ask.

"Yes. Do you think you can help me with all these bad dreams?" Maya asks.

"If everything checks out medically, I think we can work together to overcome them," you say convincingly.

"Okay, great. I'll make an appointment tomorrow."

16.7–1   What are some of Maya's strengths at this point in her life?

16.7–2   What are some possible reasons for the problems Maya is currently experiencing?

16.7–3 What diagnoses would you want to rule out in this case?

16.7–4 What is your preliminary diagnosis at this time?

Axis I

Axis II

Axis III

Axis IV

Axis V

Case 16.8

Identifying Information
Client Name: Delores Hoffman
Age: 27 years old
Ethnicity: Caucasian
Marital Status: Never married
Occupation: Office manager

Intake Information

Delores Hoffman called to make an appointment to see a counselor due to her "growing preoccupation with suicide." The intake worker screened her for suicide risk and discerned she had no history of past attempts or a present plan. Nonetheless, an initial appointment was arranged for later that day.

Initial Interview

As you meet Delores Hoffman in the waiting room, you notice that she is well dressed and attractive. Before you approached her, she had been staring out the window, virtually motionless.

As you enter your office, she says, "I guess I scared everyone talking about suicide. That is why I got an appointment so fast, isn't it?"

"Quite probably. Was that your intent?" you ask.

"Not really. I forget that not everyone feels like I do. It just doesn't seem like such a big deal to me," she explains.

"Well, based on what you said to the intake worker, it must concern you some. Isn't that why you wanted to see someone?" you clarify.

"Well, yes, it is. But not in the sense that I'm going to run out and do something. I think I've been depressed my whole life. Certainly as long as I can remember. So somehow, this seems logical—just more of the same."

"Can you tell me exactly what feelings you've had for so long?" you ask.

"Sure. I've just never been happy. I've never really liked myself. I'm just a big nothing. Always have been. No energy, no plans, no future, nothing to look forward to. I thought I was used to it and I had accepted it. Some people have lives worth living; the rest of us take up space," she observes.

"And you say you've always felt this way?" you prompt.

"Well, that's probably an exaggeration. Certainly I've felt this way since I was 10, maybe 12. Younger than that, I don't remember very well. I don't think I thought about much of anything. But around that age, I realized I didn't really have anything going for me. Do you know what I mean?" she asks.

"I hope to understand, but I need you to tell me more. How did you decide you didn't have 'anything going for you'?"

"Pretty simple. Some people are really smart; I'm not. I'm not retarded or anything but just not brainy. Some people are beautiful; I'm not. I'm not ugly or anything but just not remarkable. I'm not ambitious. I'm not clever. I'm destined to just go along, probably get married, get left by my husband after the kids are grown, and end up lonely," she explains.

"That sounds pretty hopeless," you observe.

"That's right. I don't mind too much, you know. It's just the way it is," she reports.

"Okay, I'm starting to get a picture, but I'd like to ask you some things about your childhood. Can you tell me what your family was like?" you ask.

"They're okay, I guess. Just dull people like me. I have two sisters, one older and one younger. We lived in a nice suburban neighborhood. If my parents had any problems, we kids didn't know about them. Everything was ordinary and orderly."

"Did you ever tell anyone about how you felt about yourself?" you ask.

"Not really. We didn't talk about much in my family. We just did the things we were supposed to do," she explains. "I can't tell you anything else about them really. I haven't really seen them since I left home."

"Okay. So if I understand you correctly, you've felt somewhat depressed or at least unhappy with yourself for most of your life. Has something changed, though, to make you concerned enough to want to see someone?" you ask.

"Well, yes. For the past 6 or 7 months, I've been feeling much worse. I think it's about my boyfriend. He moved in with me around the time things got worse. I know that sounds weird. I'm *supposed* to be happy to find someone who seems to love me. We're planning on getting married in the summer. But really, my life has sorta fallen apart since he moved in," she says.

"Can you tell me specifically what changes have occurred?" you ask.

"Well, it's almost everything! As soon as he moved in, I pretty much lost interest in him sexually. Of course, he hasn't lost interest, but it's just going through the motions for me. I can't sleep right either. At first, I thought it was just sharing a bed, but I don't know. When I try to go to sleep, it takes forever. Then, I wake up before my alarm goes off! I've never had a great deal of energy, but I'm really dragging now," she says.

"Okay, have you lost interest in any other things in the same time frame?" you ask.

"Well, I used to really enjoy cooking. Now it just seems like a chore. I've probably lost 15 pounds since he moved in just because I don't want to cook! He'll go ahead and get some fast food or something, but I just don't eat," she explains.

"Any other things you've lost interest in?" you persist.

"I guess. I mean I don't really enjoy anything anymore. I know how strange that sounds. I really feel bad about it! He's a nice guy, and I don't want to hurt him but . . . I don't know, I just feel like I'm ruining his life."

"Anything else?" you ask.

"Well, I've sorta lost interest in my job. I've worked for the same company for a long time. I've been the office manager for the past 4 years. It's been a good place to work, but it just seems like a drain now. People at work keep asking me what's wrong, and I really don't have anything I want to tell them. Does this make *any* sense?" she asks.

"I think so. I need to take us back to your initial concern. Tell me about wanting to kill yourself."

"Oh, that's a little strange. I daydream about it all the time. Instead of focusing on what I need to do or something, I dream up ways to end it all. Isn't that stupid?" she asks.

"No, I certainly wouldn't call it stupid. What you've described to me makes it clear that you are very unhappy with your life. Do you think you'll act on any of these plans you 'dream up'?"

"No, not really. I know that seems strange since I'm so preoccupied with it, but I'm afraid to die! I don't know why all these thoughts are in my head, really. Do you think I might be going crazy?" she inquires.

"No, I don't think you're crazy! I do think you need to take some hard looks at yourself and your life. No one can just go along being as unhappy as you are. Does that sound like something you're willing to do?"

"I think it is. Really, I know it is. I've thought about seeing a therapist for a long time. I wouldn't have made this appointment if I weren't ready to try something," she says.

16.8–1 How would you assess the threat of suicide with Delores at this point? Are there any changes you would watch for in working with her?

16.8–2 What strengths do you see in Delores?

16.8–3 What thoughts and/or behaviors would you like Delores to self-monitor?

16.8–4 What is your preliminary diagnosis for Delores?
Axis I

Axis II

Axis III

Axis IV

Axis V

Case 16.9

Identifying Information
Client Name: Victor Reynolds
Age: 36 years old
Ethnicity: Caucasian
Marital Status: Married
Occupation: Assistant manager at a grocery store
Children: Two children

Referral Information
Victor has been referred to you by the consumer credit counselor at the Family Counseling Center where you are employed as a counselor. Victor has been engaging in excessive spending and has amassed credit card debts in excess of $80,000.

He is employed by Bernie's, a grocery store chain, where he is an assistant manager. His salary is $40,000 per year. Ann, his wife, also is employed as a cosmetologist, earning approximately $30,000 per year. Although the couple enjoys a good income, Victor's excessive spending habits have created problems at his job and in his relationship with his wife.

The consumer credit counselor feels that Victor needs help beyond what he can provide. He states that he has set up Victor on the consumer credit program, in which Victor can gradually pay off his credit card debt by writing a check to consumer credit, who, in turn, disburses the money to his creditors. So far, Victor has been unable to comply with the program.

When asked why he misses payments and doesn't follow the rules of the program, Victor states that he never seems to have the money when he needs it. The counselor believes Victor is not being totally honest with him concerning his spending habits.

Initial Interview
During the initial intake session, after explaining the issues of confidentiality, you summarize the information provided to you by the consumer credit counselor and ask Victor if the information is accurate. He nods his head and admits that he hasn't been following the rules of the program.

He states that he feels he is under tremendous stress at work, and when he goes home, his wife is always nagging him about the bills. "I just have to get away from it sometimes. It drives me up the wall after a long day at work," Victor laments.

"Are the debts the main problem you've been having, or are there other issues that you are concerned about?" you ask.

Victor states that the credit card debt is a major problem but suggests that there may be other reasons why he has accumulated so much debt.

"Perhaps, it might be a good idea to start at the beginning and tell me when this problem first began and what other things were going on in your life when you began to get into debt," you suggest.

Victor sits back in his chair and appears to be thinking about what he is going to tell you. He looks as if he is having difficulty deciding what to say. You wait a few moments, and then he says, "Well, as long as this is all confidential, I might as well 'come clean' with you."

Victor explains that the problem with spending really began before he got into trouble with credit cards. "I've been married for 6 years, and I was having trouble even before I got married. It started out with the lottery, I guess. I used to go every Saturday afternoon and buy a couple of lottery tickets, just like a lot of people do. One time, I won $100 by getting four numbers right. The next week I bought 10 lottery tickets, and the week after that I bought 30 lottery tickets. When I didn't win anything with all those tickets, I thought I'd go try my luck at the dog races on Saturday night. I began betting on the dogs and won some money, and then I began betting on football games, too. At first, it was just small amounts of money, but later, I began betting most of my paycheck. I began borrowing money in order to place bets. It was unreal. It just got out of control, and I felt this urge to keep on playing because I just knew I'd win a big pile of money eventually."

Victor continued gambling for about 2 years, and then he met Ann. "After I met Ann and we were dating, I quit going to the races and placing bets on football games. I got rid of a lot of the debt I was in, and that constant urge just disappeared for a while. We got married about a year later, and everything was great for about a year. Ann and I were both working and earning good salaries, and we were saving money to have a baby. It seems like the year after our first child, Michele, was born, I started playing the lottery and everything just went from bad to worse. I started borrowing money on my credit card, and when I reached the limit on that credit card, I just went and got another one. Before I came to consumer counseling, I had 25 credit cards all maxed to the limit. What I haven't told the consumer credit counselor is that I also have debts from gambling. I have to try to pay on them before I can pay off the credit cards."

"How much do your gambling debts come to?" you ask.

"Well, I've paid a lot of them off, but I still owe about $10,000. Ann doesn't know about the gambling debts," Victor explains. "I'm scared that she'll find out and throw me out of the house. I've felt so desperate, at times I feel like she'd be better off if I were dead."

"Have you thought seriously about killing yourself?" you query.

"Nah, not really. I just sometimes get so down on myself for getting into this fix that I get to feeling real hopeless. Like I'm never going to get out of this mess. My relationship with Ann has been on the brink of disaster over all this debt. We'd never make it if she found out about the gambling. She and I have really been tense with each other lately, if you know what I mean."

"You mean in terms of intimacy?" you ask.

"Yeah, you got it. It's been almost nonexistent lately because she's so upset about all this debt. It's ruining our relationship. I've just got to figure out something, or I'm going to lose her." Victor seems visibly upset about the possibility of his marriage falling apart.

"It seems that you've made a first step to resolving these difficulties by coming here and seeking help. It sounds as if you've been feeling very overwhelmed by these problems," you suggest.

"Yeah, I sure hope you can help me out of this mess I'm in," Victor implores.

You decide to summarize what Victor has told you in this first intake session. "Let me see if I understand what you've told me so far. Although you came in to the agency for help with credit card debt, that's only part of the problem. The other part is that you've been gambling on a regular basis and have gone into a lot of debt as a result. You feel that the problem started about 9 years ago, before you were married. It went away for a while when you met Ann, but it's been a problem again since Michele was born. And you feel an uncontrollable urge to gamble, even when you know in your head you don't have the money to do it. In addition, you sometimes begin to feel really down because you don't know what to do about this difficulty, and you've also been having some problems with your relationship with Ann. Have I left anything out?"

"Nah, I think that about covers it."

You decide to gather some additional information about Victor's social history. You ask Victor to tell you about his life before he had this problem. Victor states that he grew up in a family with three sisters and a younger brother.

"Both my parents worked in a sock factory; my dad was on second shift, so we never saw much of him. When he was home at night, he usually wanted to sit in front of the TV and drink beer. He didn't want us kids to bother him. Mom worked first shift, 6:30 A.M. to 2:30 P.M., and was home when we got out of school. I was the oldest son, but two of my sisters are older than I am. We didn't have much money, and I remember always thinking that when I grew up I was going to make enough money to be rich. I didn't want to live my life always worried about money the way my parents did. We never had anything. I never got to do anything with other kids at school because it cost too much. I always felt like I never got to have any fun. I started working a newspaper route when I was 13 just to have spending money. I've been working ever since."

"Has the gambling caused problems for you at work?" you ask.

Victor implies that he's been able to function at work adequately although he finds himself making excuses for taking Saturdays off so he can go to the races. He indicates that he hasn't had as much energy for work as he had before he got into so much debt. He states that he is worried all the time, day and night, about how he is going to pay off his debts.

You question him about what he thinks he does well. Victor suggests that he used to do some carpentry work as a hobby and he built a deck on the back of his house. He also used to spend more time with his children before he got so caught up in the gambling.

"It's taken me a long time to admit it, but I think I finally realize I've got a problem. I just don't know what to do about it. Do you think you can help me with it?"

16.9–1   What additional information would you want to gather from Victor in future sessions?

16.9–2   What are some of Victor's strengths?

16.9–3   Give three examples of how this problem is affecting Victor's functioning.

16.9–4 From this initial assessment, what would your diagnosis be?

Axis 1

Axis II

Axis III

Axis IV

Axis V

Case 16.10

Identifying Information
Client Name: Shaun Gillespie
Age: 16 years old
Ethnicity: Caucasian
Parents: Glenda and Ralph Gillespie

Referral Information
The client is a 16-year-old, single Caucasian male who was brought to the emergency room by police after he was found wandering in traffic on a local bridge. Police report that he was somewhat resistant to being taken into custody but calmed slightly during transport to the emergency room. Emergency room personnel report that his medical condition is stable and that his drug screen showed the presence of amphetamines.

Initial Interview
When you enter the examination room at the hospital emergency room, Shaun is pacing and wringing his hands.

"Shaun, I'm here to assess your situation. I'm a counselor, and I work here at the hospital. The nurse has reached your parents, and they're on their way here. Would you be willing to talk with me now?" you ask.

Shaun initially stopped pacing but began again before you were finished speaking. "What about my parents?" he asks.

"They are on their way here. Do you know where you are?" you ask.

"I guess in jail," he says and stops.

"No, Shaun. You are at the hospital. The police did bring you here, though. They picked you up on the 318 bridge. Do you remember that?" you ask.

"What do you mean? Are you a cop? Are you trying to trick me? Where are my parents?" he yells, becoming more agitated.

"Shaun, I don't work for the police. I work for the hospital. Your parents should be here soon. Would you rather wait until they get here to talk with me?" you ask.

"Do I have to see them?" he asks, resuming pacing. "How did I get here?"

"The police brought you here, Shaun. Do you remember being on the 318 bridge?" you persist.

"This isn't good," he replies. "It might be a setup! I was at Jeff's house, I think. Did you have anything to do with this?"

"Shaun, I work for the hospital and am just trying to figure out what's going on with you. Do you remember what you were doing at Jeff's house?" you ask.

"No way!!!" he shouts. "Now I know you're with them. Just get out of here, okay?"

"Okay, Shaun, but I have to ask you just a few more questions. Do you know what day it is?"

"Who cares? Monday? Saturday? I don't know. Just leave me alone!"

"One more question, Shaun. Have you been thinking of hurting yourself?"

"What do you mean, 'hurting myself'? They're trying to hurt *me!*" he shouts.

Shaun moves toward you in a somewhat threatening fashion. You decide to leave the examination room and await his parents' arrival. You let the emergency room personnel know that you think Shaun should have someone with him until the situation can be better understood.

16.10–1   What diagnoses are you considering at this point?

16.10–2 What collateral information (either interviews or records) would you like to have?

Interview with Shaun's Parents

Shortly thereafter, Glenda and Ralph, Shaun's parents, arrive at the emergency room and are directed to you. You reassure them that Shaun is unhurt and medically stable.

"Is he on drugs? Did he hurt anyone?" Ralph inquires.

"The ER drug screen shows amphetamines, Mr. Gillespie. No one was hurt tonight. In fact, Shaun seems to be the only one who was in danger. He was on the 318 bridge darting in and out of traffic and leaning over the rail. A motorist called police, and they brought him in here," you explain.

"So he's not under arrest?" Glenda asks.

"Not to my knowledge," you reply. "I believe the officer who brought him in is still here, so you should ask him to be sure."

After conferring, Ralph leaves to find the police officer. Glenda remains to answer your questions.

"So I take it this isn't Shaun's first brush with the law?" encouraging her to tell you more.

"I'm afraid not. Shaun has been picked up for shoplifting and breaking into someone's car. The shoplifting was about a year ago. He served 6 months of probation with juvenile court and had to pay restitution. The car business just happened a couple of months ago. The people at juvenile court are still trying to decide what to do with him about that. I just assumed he was in more trouble," she says, beginning to cry.

You offer Glenda a tissue and continue when she quiets. "Has he been in other trouble?" you ask.

"Not with the police; that's relatively new. We've been worried about him for a couple of years now. He wasn't a bad kid before he started junior high school. He was a bit of a bully when he was younger. I never really understood that, but it stopped when the other kids caught up with him. He was quite large for his age until he was about 12," she offers.

"What happened when he started junior high school?" you ask.

"I think he fell in with the wrong crowd. His grades went down from mostly A's to mostly C's. Ralph thinks he takes 'pep pills' too. He certainly does act strange sometimes, but he always denies taking pep pills. Frankly, we don't know what to do anymore," she says despondently.

"What have you tried?" you ask.

"Well, all the regular things. We've laid down the law and set up 'consequences' when he breaks the rules, but then he just ignores them. He'd been skipping school, so we said he couldn't go to extracurricular activities unless he attended. So he just sneaks out of the house and goes anyway! He's even spent the whole night out several times. We call the police, but they can't do anything unless he's missing for a couple of days. Can you believe it? He's just *defied* us! And this started when he wasn't even a teenager yet! I've just never known problems like this!" she laments.

Ralph returns at this point and explains, "Well, there aren't any charges against Shaun tonight. I don't know if that's good or bad. The nurse says they are still concerned about his safety. I can see why. I spent a couple of minutes with Shaun, and he's just talking weird and crazy. I told her that we can't guarantee he won't leave the house again if we take him home. I'm not sure what will happen now!" Ralph slumps over and holds his head.

"Mr. Gillespie, your wife has been telling me that she feels that you've lost control of Shaun. I take it you feel the same way," you prod.

"It's embarrassing but you're right! I don't know what will happen next."

16.10-3   What do you see as the strengths in the Gillespie family?

16.10-4   Do you agree that if Shaun is released at this point, he might pose a danger?

16.10-5   What is your initial diagnosis for Shaun?
Axis I

Axis II

Axis III

Axis IV

Axis V

16.10 – 6   Are there additional diagnoses you would want to rule out?

_____

Case 16.11

Identifying Information
Client Name: Christopher T. Hager
Age: 62 years old
Ethnicity: Caucasian
Marital Status: Divorced
Children: One daughter, Catherine

Intake Information
Christopher T. Hager, a 62-year-old Caucasian male, contacted the Behavioral Health Center and said that he felt that his life was "out of control." When asked how he had heard of the Center, the client said that his family physician had sent him. He also noted that his daughter wanted him to "get some help."

Initial Interview
Chris appears for the first interview wearing a wrinkled cardigan, blue jeans, and a plaid shirt. He is unshaven and appears to have just gotten out of bed. His hair is uncombed, and he has dark circles under his eyes. Chris is slightly underweight and has a subtle tremor in his hands.

You administer the Mini-Mental Status Exam to Chris prior to beginning the interview. He scores within the normal range on this scale. He shows no signs of cognitive impairment, loss of memory, or thought disorder. He reports no history of cognitive problems. His thinking appears to be clear, focused, and well organized.

When you ask about his medical history, he reports that he recently has gone to the doctor for headaches. In addition, Chris reports that the doctor found no physiological reason for the pain he is experiencing. He also remarks, "My headaches really make it hard to eat, so I've lost some more weight. I think I really need to gain a few pounds."

When you ask about family history, Chris states that there has been no prominent family history of illness, though he notes having an uncle who committed suicide. When pressed, he says he didn't know this uncle well and doesn't know what, if anything, led up to his death.

When you ask him about substance use, he reports having tried Advil, Tylenol, and aspirin for the headaches but is taking no prescribed medication on a regular basis to alleviate the chronic pain. He also states that he sometimes has a "nightcap" to help him fall asleep, which has become more difficult lately.

Chris says he was employed as an electronics engineer for 30 years at a well-known high-tech computer corporation. He recently took early retirement because of the company's cutbacks in employees and their offer to provide a compelling severance package. Chris states, "I really miss the routine of getting up and going to work every morning, although I don't miss the pressure of trying to keep up with young, new college grads."

Chris says that after being out of work for approximately 1 month, he began feeling more lethargic and had difficulty pursuing activities that he normally enjoyed. "I simply get bored and don't know what to do with myself at times. I used to go out with friends from work, like lunch and weekend stuff, but now that I'm no longer employed and don't see them, it's like I've just been forgotten."

When you ask about solutions to this dilemma, he states, "I don't really have the energy to make plans with the guys. My daughter, Catherine, keeps trying to get me out of the house and tells me to go to a community center or get a volunteer job, but I just can't get going on anything these days."

"Do you feel that the ways you've been coping with all of this have worked for you?" you ask.

"No, but I don't know what else to do," he replies.

In addition to having headaches and losing his job, Chris states that he and his wife, Connie, divorced approximately 5 years ago and that he is still disturbed by the divorce. When you probe further, Chris states angrily, "My wife left me after 28 years of marriage. She was fed up with the whole thing. And Catherine has been caught in the middle between us, which is probably why she decided to go to school out of state. Because of the divorce, I had to move from a big suburban home to this little apartment I'm stuck in." Despite the manageable size of his present residence, he says he has difficulty taking care of the apartment and other tasks of daily living (e.g., laundry, cleaning, and self-care).

Chris reports weekly phone contact with his 24-year-old daughter, who is currently in graduate school. She is his only child. He no longer is in contact with his former wife except on rare occasions. His primary companion is his bloodhound, named Blue. Chris seems quite committed to his dog. He speaks at length about Blue's pedigree and his long walks with Blue late at night. He made reference to Blue throughout the conversation (e.g., "Blue and I had macaroni and cheese for dinner" and "Blue and I like to walk to the grocery store and get coffee in the mornings").

Chris notes, "In my day, I was an eloquent speaker, a member of a large social network (primarily through playing golf), and a good communicator. However, I no longer feel I'm part of a community like I was when I was working. Retirement is not all it's cracked up to be."

He also indicates that he used to play a lot of bridge when he was married, but since the divorce, he has had no one to be his bridge partner. "I'm embarrassed to go to bridge tournaments by myself. I feel like I've lost my job, my family, and all the important parts of my life."

He states that he had been married for so long that he didn't know how to function as a single person. "I go out for dinner with my friend Mack sometimes when he's available."

Throughout the interview, Chris appears sad when discussing his divorce and retirement. He seems engaged in the conversation and shows no signs of psychotic behavior. He does appear to have a slight trembling in both hands but makes no mention of this problem during the session.

When you ask about romantic interests, Chris laughs and responds, "Are you kidding? I haven't even looked at a woman since my wife left me."

Upon inquiry, Chris notes that although his first few years married to his wife were "romantic and fun," approximately 5 years prior to his wife's leaving, the couple began sleeping in separate rooms. He notes in a defensive tone, "I snore pretty loudly."

Chris is vague in response to questions about his sex life, but he does add, "I'm not what I used to be, if you know what I mean."

Chris consistently has a sad affect during the assessment. Even his sporadic laughter at his own jokes seems forced. He shows a tendency toward sarcasm and a pessimistic attitude, as evidenced by his statement, "Even though I want things to be different, I am what I am. Guess you can't expect me to change after all these years."

When you ask him if he has times when he feels good, he states, "There are times when I feel a bit better or worse, but I don't really ever feel like myself since my wife left." He adds that retirement is a challenge to a "workaholic like me."

"How do you think your mood has affected others?" you ask.

"Well, my daughter probably avoids coming to see me because I'm not exactly the life of the party," Chris replies. "I just don't want to continue living this way. Something's got to change in my life."

"Chris, do you have any goals that you can think of for the future?" you ask.

"It's all I can do to get through the day, and I don't think much beyond how to get from morning to night. But, I always used to set goals, and people said I was 'driven' to succeed."

"Can you imagine any ways that things could improve?" you ask.

Chris thinks for a few moments and replies, "I think I'm drinking more than usual, and it probably wouldn't hurt to cut down on my wine consumption, but I can do that anytime I want. I think it could be clouding my vision right now."

"Have you ever tried to cut down on your alcohol consumption?" you ask.

"One day I tell myself I'm going to stop drinking and start finding some healthy outlets for myself, and the next day, I can't get out of bed. Two days last week, I never got out of my pajamas, and Blue and I just spent the day watching videos and eating popcorn."

"What would you say is your purpose in life, Chris?" you ask.

"At this point, just getting through the day."

"Come on, think for a moment," you encourage.

"Okay, well, I'm really Blue's 'higher power,' I suppose. He needs me."

"Although I believe you're joking, I think you really care about your dog, don't you, Chris?" you ask.

"You bet. I don't think I would've made it this long without him."

16.11–1   What do you see as Chris' strengths?

16.11–2   What are the primary problems that Chris presents during this session?

16.11–3   What are some possible resources that might be helpful for Chris?

16.11–4   What is your preliminary diagnosis for Chris?
Axis I

Axis II

Axis III

Axis IV

Axis V

_____

Case 16.12

Identifying Information
Client Name: Jerome Parker
Age: 40 years old
Ethnicity: African American
Educational Level: High school diploma
Marital Status: Married
Children: Four children—Keesha, age 15; Delores, age 11; Martin, age 6; Jerome Jr., age 3

Background Information
You are a caseworker/counselor at a local AIDS organization. You work with men, women, and children who have been diagnosed as HIV positive. You provide both counseling and case-management services to individuals and families infected with and affected by AIDS.

Telephone Intake Worker Report
Jerome Parker was referred by his physician at the Metroplex Community Clinic where he is being treated for HIV/AIDS. Jerome stated that he, his wife, Mary, and his youngest child, Jerome Jr., are all HIV positive. Prior to becoming ill, Jerome worked as an operating room technician, and his wife worked as a nurse at the same hospital. Jerome told the intake worker that his older children from a prior marriage are not HIV positive, nor is Martin, age 6. He said that he has been on disability for the past 3 years following his diagnosis. The Parkers discovered their seropositive status at the birth of their youngest child, who was born with a positive status. Jerome stated that lately he's been feeling like he can't handle all the stress associated with his disabling condition and told his doctor he doesn't want to live anymore.

Initial Interview
Jerome Parker is sitting quietly in the waiting room where you meet him. He is dressed in blue jeans, a flannel shirt, and running shoes. He glances up at you when you say his name and smiles. Jerome stands, shakes your hand, and calmly says, "Nice to meet you." You notice that Jerome appears very thin for his height (over 6 feet tall). The bones beneath his eyes are quite obvious, and his cheeks appear sunken. He follows you back to your office.

"Please come in and have a seat," you offer Jerome as you approach your office. "The chair next to my desk is pretty comfortable," you suggest. Jerome slides into the chair and folds his hands over his lap. He looks at you expectantly, waiting for you to begin the conversation.

"The gentleman you talked to on the phone told me you've been experiencing a lot of stress lately," you begin.

Jerome shifts in his seat and shrugs, "Yeah, I guess you could say that. I'm just tired of all the doctors and medicine and all. Trying to get what I need to keep my family going. I can't seem to make ends meet anymore. My wife and I used to have good jobs at the hospital and didn't have all these financial troubles and bills. I just can't keep up anymore. I'm real tired."

"It can be exhausting trying to get what you need for your family, especially when you're not feeling real good. Can you tell me how you've been feeling physically lately?"

"Well, I've lost a lot of weight in the last, say, 6 months. My doctor put me on these nutritional supplements, which helped for a while, but they're pricey, and my wife and son needed medication and I just couldn't afford it all. So, I haven't gotten the supplements for about 3 months, and I've just dropped about 20 pounds since I quit. I'm taking the 'cocktail,' too, about 12 pills a day and that's real expensive. My insurance covers some of that cost, but not all of it. For three of us, it can cost about $800 a month. I just can't make ends meet anymore, and I'm too tired to figure it out. I'm thinking maybe I should just quit the meds so I can get my wife and son what they need. It's just getting too hard." Jerome hangs his head and twists his wedding ring back and forth. He pauses for several moments and looks as if he's trying to get his thoughts together.

"You're facing a very challenging and difficult situation," you respond. "Maybe I can help you figure some of this out. Have you been trying to do this all on your own?"

"Yeah, primarily. My mom takes the kids sometimes, but she's in her 70s and gets worn out quickly. Sometimes, she cooks supper for us when Mary, my wife, is too tired to do it. My daughters, Keesha and Delores, they help out, too, when they can. I want them to stay in school and get good grades, though. I keep telling them how important it is for them to graduate and go to college. They're going to need to be able to make it on their own sooner than most kids. I just want them to have the best shot at it."

"So, other than your mom and your daughters, who sound like they're busy with their own activities, you really haven't had much assistance with working out all these issues you're faced with. Is that correct?" you say.

"That's about it. I am just so tired of trying to jump through these hoops to get what my family needs," Jerome replies. "I just don't know what to do anymore."

"How long have you known about your HIV status, Jerome?" you ask.

"My wife and I found out when our last baby, Jerome Jr., was born—about 3 years ago. It was a real shock to us all. I feel so guilty every time I think about it." Jerome shakes his head. "I just didn't know I was positive; I just didn't know!"

"That must have been a very hard time for all of you. How did you handle it?" you ask.

"My wife and I spent a lot of time talking and holding each other and the baby. We just decided we were going to go through this together, no matter what. I just hope she goes before I do. I don't want her to have to manage all the kids and bills by herself. I can't even

think about it." Jerome looks down and wipes his eyes with the back of his hand. "It's just too much."

"You've been coping with some very challenging issues for a long period of time," you suggest. "More than most people deal with in a lifetime."

"Yeah, but I'm not doing so well now," Jerome states.

"You told me you were feeling really tired lately," you respond. "Can you tell me how you've been feeling emotionally?"

"Pretty down, I guess, like I just don't want to go on anymore," Jerome tells you.

"When you say 'down,' can you tell me more about that down feeling?" you ask.

"Angry, frustrated. I get irritated real easy these days. It all seems pretty hopeless to me. Some days I feel so tired I don't want to get out of bed. I can't handle these bills anymore. I have people calling about them all the time. I just take the phone off the hook. I can't stand to see Mary trying to be strong when she feels ill. And Jerome Jr. is getting sicker and sicker, and nothing seems to be working for him. I told Mary the other day that maybe it's just time for me to 'check out' of this world. She got real scared and told me to call you all and get an appointment for some counseling."

"Okay, so that 'down' feeling includes feeling angry sometimes, frustrated sometimes, irritated and tired sometimes, and I guess that hopeless feeling sometimes. How much of the time would you say you feel that hopeless feeling?" you ask.

"Well, lately, it's been about half the time," Jerome states.

"And the other half of the time?" you query.

"I guess I just feel frustrated and angry," Jerome states.

"Are there times when you feel okay? I mean not frustrated or angry?" you ask.

"Oh, yeah, I guess when I'm playing with the kids or holding Jerome Jr. I feel pretty happy," Jerome says. "When we're doing things together as a family, I'm pretty content. I just tell myself I've only got this moment I have to live, and it seems better for a while."

"It sounds like a lot of the time you're feeling pretty down, though. About what percentage of the time would you say you're feeling okay and content?" you ask.

Jerome stares at you for a minute and then shrugs his shoulders and says, "Maybe 5% of the time."

"Five percent isn't much of the time. And the rest of the time you're feeling pretty angry or frustrated or hopeless. Is that right?" you ask Jerome.

"Yeah, I guess that's about right. I just don't know what to do anymore. It's hard to walk around knowing you infected your wife and child with HIV."

"You think about that a lot. Has it affected your relationship with Mary?" you ask.

"It did at first. She was real angry. Cried for about 2 weeks straight. Then she just stopped crying and said we're going to fight this virus, and she didn't blame me or nothing. She just told me she loved me and that she would always be there for me. Made me feel real guilty. Mostly we argue when one of us doesn't feel good now."

"How is Mary's health now?" you ask.

"She's doing okay. She hasn't lost weight like I have. The medicine seems to be helping her more than me. Her viral load is real low right now. It's not helping the baby much at all, though. He's got full-blown AIDS, and developmentally, he's way behind his age group. He acts like a 9-month-old baby. He tries to walk but can't do it, and he's sick to his stomach a lot. But he doesn't act like he knows he's sick. He just crawls into our laps and goes to sleep. He's a wonderful boy." Jerome gets tears in his eyes again and looks wistfully out the window.

"Okay, I know that must be very hard for you to watch," you say empathically. "How are your other children coping with your and your wife's illness?"

"They're doing all right," Jerome says quietly. "Delores, she came home from school one day and said some of the kids were teasing her, telling her to get away because her parents had AIDS. I think that really affected her a lot. She's real quiet and doesn't talk about it much. She just wants to stay close to us all the time. Keesha is a little older, and she sometimes acts like the nurse in the family. She's always asking us if we're okay and if we need anything. She wants to get a job after school, but I told her she needs to stay in the chorus and other stuff she's doing if she wants to go to college. All my children, they're good kids."

"It sounds as if your children who aren't sick are handling things relatively well. And Mary and Jerome Jr. have their ups and downs with their illness. But, you've been feeling pretty down lately. Does that kind of summarize the situation at home?" you ask.

"Yeah, that about sums it up, I'd say. I just don't know what to do anymore," Jerome responds.

"You know, Jerome, you have every right to feel down and angry and frustrated at times. You're dealing with a whole lot. I have great respect for your ability to cope with all these issues you're confronted with right now. I'd like to talk for a few more minutes, though, about your angry and down feelings. Okay with you?"

"Sure, that'll be okay."

"Good. Tell me about how long you've been feeling down like this," you suggest.

"I'd say it's been at least a couple of months," Jerome responds.

"And, on a scale from 1 to 10, 1 being the best and 10 being the worst, how down would you say you've been this week?" you ask.

"Oh, probably a 10, I'd say."

"And have you had any suicidal thoughts?" you ask.

"Yeah, sort of off and on. One minute I think I'm just going to go ahead and 'check out,' and then I think about leaving my wife with Jerome Jr. and I think I can't do that."

"When you have those suicidal thoughts, do you think about how you might 'check out,' as you put it?" you query.

"Well, sometimes when I'm driving down the road, I think about just running the car into a light pole or something like that," Jerome responds. "Other times, I think I could just give up, quit taking meds, quit eating, and I probably wouldn't last too much longer."

"Have you ever found yourself beginning to run off the road?" you ask.

"No, it's never gone that far," Jerome replies. "And I haven't quit the medication or anything like that, just the supplements 'cause they cost so much."

"Okay, good, I'm glad you've never taken any action to harm yourself," you reply. You pause for a minute and then suggest to Jerome that counseling might be beneficial. "You know, I really think I might be able to assist you with some of the obstacles that are making your life really tough right now. I also think if we got together and talked on a weekly basis, I could help you with some of those really negative feelings you've been experiencing lately. Do you think you might be interested in doing that?" you ask.

"How could you help me?" Jerome replies.

"Well, for one thing, I could help you with some of those bills you're talking about by helping you apply for some programs that might take the financial burden off your shoulders. Would that be helpful to you?"

"Sure it would. I think I need all the help I can get right now," Jerome replies. He brightens and sits up in his chair a bit.

"Well, that's one area that I think we could work on together. The other area is in the emotional realm. I think I could help you feel less down and angry like you do sometimes. Although your feelings are understandable, it doesn't feel good to have the feelings you do. And it might be very helpful to have someone to talk to about all the feelings and issues you are experiencing during this time. Would that be of interest to you?"

Jerome sits back in his chair and breathes a sigh of relief. "It sure would. I knew Mary was right when she said I needed to go talk to somebody. I just don't think I wanted to admit it was all getting to me the way it has lately, if you know what I mean."

"I certainly do know what you mean, Jerome. It's very hard to open up to a stranger and talk about things that are bothering you. But you did very well today in explaining to me what the issues are in your life. I'm really glad you came in today. I'd like you to come back again in a few days, and we can talk more about how we're going to ease the stress in your life. I'd also like you to fill out some questionnaires before you leave today so that I can get a better idea of just where you are in terms of how you're feeling. Would that be all right with you?"

"Sure, I'll do anything if it will make me feel better," Jerome replies. "I'm glad you think there's some hope left in my life."

"I do feel there's hope, Jerome. Let's schedule another appointment in a few days."

16.12–1 What are some of Jerome's strengths?

16.12–2   Make a list of areas that need to be addressed in working with Jerome.

16.12–3   Why did you decide not to get more in-depth information about Jerome's psychosocial history?

16.12–4   What other information do you think is important to get from Jerome the next time he comes to a session with you?

16.12–5   Based on the information presented in this interview, what are some first steps you would plan on taking with Jerome?

16.12–6   What are some of the limitations that you perceive in working with Jerome?

16.12–7   Would you want other family members to come to a session with Jerome? Why or why not?

16.12–8   If other family members were to come to a session, whom would you want to see and in what sequence?

16.12–9   How long do you think you may need to work with Jerome?

16.12–10   Given all the information in this case, what would be your diagnosis for Jerome?
Axis I

Axis II

Axis III

Axis IV

Axis V

References

Achenbach, T. M., & Edelbrock, C. S. (1983). *Manual for the child behavior checklist and the revised child behavior profile.* Burlington, VT: University Associates in Psychiatry.

Ambrosini, P. J. (2000). Historical development and present status of the Schedule for Affective Disorders and Schizophrenia for School-Age Children (K-SADS): Statistical data included. *Journal of the American Academy of Child & Adolescent Psychiatry, 39,* 49–58.

American Psychiatric Association. (1980). *Diagnostic and statistical manual of mental disorders* (3rd ed.). Washington, DC: Author.

American Psychiatric Association (2000). *Diagnostic and statistical manual of mental disorders* (4th ed., text rev.). Washington, DC: Author.

Andra, M. L., & Thomas, A. M. (1998). The influence of parenting stress and socioeconomic disadvantage on therapy attendance among parents and their behavior disordered preschool children. *Education and Treatment of Children, 21,* 195–209.

Bauer, M. S., Crits-Cristoph, P., & Ball, W. A. (1991). Independent assessment of manic and depressive symptoms by self-rating. *Archives of General Psychiatry, 48,* 807–812.

Baum, A., & Andersen, B. L. (Eds.). (2001). *Psychosocial interventions for cancer.* Washington, DC: American Psychological Association.

Bayley, N. (1993). *Bayley Scales of Infant Development—Second Edition* (BSID-II). San Antonio, TX: Psychological Corporation.

Beals, J., Manson, S. M., Keane, E., & Dick, R. W. (1995). Factorial structure of the Center for Epidemiologic Studies Depression Scale among American Indian college students. *Psychological Assessment, 3,* 623–627.

Beck, A. T., Steer, R. A., & Brown, G. K. (1996). *Manual for the Beck Depression Inventory* (2nd ed.). San Antonio, TX: Psychological Corporation.

Beeson, R., Horton-Deutsch, S., Farran, C., & Neundorfer, M. (2000). Loneliness and depression in caregivers of persons with Alzheimer's disease or related disorders. *Issues in Mental Health Nursing, 21,* 779–806.

Bernhard, L. A., & Applegate, J. M. (1999). Comparison of stress and stress management strategies between lesbian and heterosexual women. *Health Care for Women International, 20,* 335–348.

Bernstein, E. M., & Putman, R. W. (1986). Development, reliability, and validity of a dissociation scale. *Journal of Nervous and Mental Disease, 174,* 727–735.

Black, D. W., Warrack, G., & Winokur, G. (1985). The Iowa record-linkage study, I-II. *Archives of General Psychiatry, 42,* 71–88.

Breitbart, W., Rosenfeld, B., Roth, A., Smith, M. J., Cohen, K., & Passik, S. (1997). The Memorial Delirium Assessment Scale. *Journal of Pain and Symptom Management, 13,* 128–137.

Briere, J., & Runtz, M. (1989). The Trauma Symptom Checklist (TSC-33): Early data on a new scale. *Journal of Interpersonal Violence, 4,* 151–163.

Brink, T. L., Yesavage, J. A., Lum, O., Heersema, P., Adley, M. B., & Rose, T. L. (1982). Screening tests for geriatric depression. *Clinical Gerontologist, 1,* 37–44.

Bryant, R. A., Moulds, M. L., & Guthrie, R. M. (2000). Acute Stress Disorder Scale: A self-report measure of acute stress disorder. *Psychological Assessment, 12,* 61–68.

Butcher, J. N. (Ed.). (2000). *Basic sources on the MMPI-2.* Minneapolis: University of Minnesota Press.

Butcher, J. N., & Williams, C. L. (2000). *Essentials of MMPI-2 and MMPI-A interpretation* (2nd ed). Minneapolis: University of Minnesota Press.

Caldwell, C. B., & Gottsman, I. I. (1990). Schizophrenics kill themselves too: A review of risk factors for suicide. *Schizophrenia Bulletin, 16,* 571–589.

Canivez, G., & Watkins, M. (1998). Long-term stability of the Wechsler Intelligence Scale for Children-III. *Psychology Assessment, 10,* 285–291.

Chambless, D. L., Caputo, G. D., Jasin, S. E., Gracely, E. J., & Williams, C. (1985). The Mobility Inventory for Agoraphobia. *Behavioral Research and Therapy, 23,* 35–44.

Clum, G. A., Broyles, S., Borden, J., & Watkins, P. L. (1990). Validity and reliability of the Panic Attack Symptoms and Cognition Questionnaire. *Journal of Psychopathology and Behavioral Assessment, 12,* 233–245.

Conners, C. K. (1990). *Conners' rating scales manual.* North Tonawanda, NY: Mental-Health Systems.

Cook, J. A., & Razzano, L. (2000). Vocational rehabilitation for persons with schizophrenia: Recent research and implications for practice. *Schizophrenia Bulletin, 26,* 87–103.

Coolidge, F. L., Burns, E. M., & Mooney, J. A. (1995). Reliability of observer ratings in the assessment of personality disorders: A preliminary study. *Journal of Clinical Psychology, 51*(1), 22–28.

Coolidge, F. L., & Merwin, M. M. (1992). Reliability and validity of the Coolidge Axis II Inventory: A new inventory for the assessment of personality disorders. *Journal of Personality Assessment, 59,* 223–238.

Coolidge, F. L., Philbrick, P. B., Wooley, M. J., Bunting, E. K., Hyman, J. N., & Stager, M. A. (1990). The KCATI: Development of an inventory for the assessment of personality disorders in children. *Journal of Personality and Clinical Studies, 6,* 225–232.

Costin, C. (1999). *The eating disorder sourcebook.* Los Angeles: Lowell House.

Cox, C. (1995). Comparing the experiences of black and white caregivers of dementia patients. *Social Work, 40,* 343–346.

D'Ath, P., Katona, P., Mullan, E., Evans, S., & Katona, C. (1994). Screening, detection and management of depression in elderly primary care attenders. I: The acceptability and performance of the 15-item Geriatric Depression Scale and the development of shorter versions. *Family Practice, 11,* 260–266.

Davis, R. D., Woodward, M., Goncalves, A., Meagher, S. E., & Millon, T. (1999). Studying outcome in adolescents: The Millon Adolescent Clinical Inventory and Millon Adolescent Personality Inventory. In M. E. Maruish (Ed.), *The use of psychological testing for treatment planning and outcomes assessment* (2nd ed., pp. 381–397). Mahwah, NJ: Lawrence Erlbaum Associates.

Derogatis, L. R., & Savitz, K. L. (1999). The SCL-90-R, Brief Symptom Inventory, and matching clinical rating scales. In M. E. Maruish (Ed.), *The use of psychological testing for treatment planning and outcomes assessment* (2nd ed., pp. 679–724). Mahwah, NJ: Lawrence Erlbaum Associates.

Dickinson, A. (2000). Measuring up: Obesity in young boys is on the rise and so are eating disorders. Whose fault is it? *Time, 156*(21), 154.

Dohrenwend, B. P., Levav, I., Shrout, P. E., Schwartz, S., Naveh, G., Link, B. G., Skodol, A. E., & Stueve, A. (1992). Socioeconomic status and psychiatric disorders: The causation-selection issue. *Science, 255,* 946–952.

First, M. B., Spitzer, R. L., Gibbon, M., & Williams, J. B. W. (1995). *Structured Clinical Interview for Axis I DSM-IV Disorders—Patient Edition* (SCID-IP, ver. 2.0). New York: New York State Psychiatric Institute, Biometrics Research Department.

First, M. B., Spitzer, R. L., Gibbon, M., Williams, J. B. W., & Benjamin, L. (1994). *Structured Clinical Interview for DSM-IV Axis II Personality Disorders* (SCID-II, ver. 2.0). New York: New York State Psychiatric Institute, Biometrics Research Department.

Fischer, J., & Corcoran, K. (1994). *Measures for clinical practice: A sourcebook* (2nd ed.). New York: Free Press.

Folstein, M. (1998). Mini-mental and son. *International Journal of Geriatric Psychiatry, 13,* 290–294.

Folstein, M. F., Folstein, S. E., & McHugh, P. R. (1975). Mini-Mental State: A practical method for grading the cognitive state of patients for the clinician. *Journal of Psychiatric Research, 12,* 189–198.

Froland, C., Brodsky, G., Olson, M., & Stewart, L. (2000). Social support and social adjustment: Implications for mental health professionals. *Community Mental Health Journal, 36,* 61–75.

Garber, J., van Slyke, D. A., & Walker, L. S. (1998). Concordance between mothers' and children's reports of somatic and emotional symptoms in patients with recurrent abdominal pain or emotional disorders. *Journal of Abnormal Child Psychology, 26,* 381–391.

Garner, D. M. (1991). *The Eating Disorders Inventory-2.* Odessa, FL: Psychological Assessment Resources.

Garner, D. M., Olmsted, M. P., Bohr, Y., & Garfinkel, P. E. (1982). The Eating Attitudes Test: Psychometric features and clinical correlates. *Psychological Medicine, 12,* 871–878.

George, L., & Gwyther, L. (1986). Caregiver well-being: A multi-dimensional examination of family caregivers of demented adults. *Gerontologist, 23,* 626–631.

Gibb, G. D., Bailey, J. R., Best, R. H., & Lambirth, T. T. (1983). The measurement of the obsessive compulsive personality. *Educational and Psychological Measurement, 43,* 1233–1237.

Gillham, J., Carter, A., Volkmar, F., & Sparrow, S. (2000). Toward a developmental operational definition of autism. *Journal of Autism and Developmental Disorders, 30,* 269–278.

Graham, J. R., & Lilly, R. S. (1984). *Psychological testing.* Englewood Cliffs, NJ: Prentice Hall.

Grant, B. F., Harford, T. C., Dawson, D. A., Chou, P., Dufour, M., & Pickering, R. (1994). Prevalence of DSM-IV alcohol abuse and dependence: United States, 1994. *Alcohol Health & Research World, 18,* 243–248.

Greenhill, L. L., Pine, D., March, J., Birmaher, B., & Riddle, M. (1998). Assessment measures in anxiety disorders research. *Psychopharmacology Bulletin, 34,* 155–164.

Hamilton, M. (1967). Development of a rating scale for primary depressive illness. *British Journal of Social and Clinical Psychology, 6,* 278–296.

Hecht, M., Trost, M. R., Bator, R., & MacKinnon, D. (1997). Ethnicity and sex similarities and differences in drug resistance. *Journal of Applied Communication Research, 25*(2), 75–90.

Henderson, J. N., Gutierrez-Mayka, M., Garcia, J., & Boyd, S. (1993). A model for Alzheimer's disease support group development in African-American and Hispanic populations. *The Gerontologist, 33,* 409–414.

Herzog, D. (1997). A congressional briefing: *Dying to be thin: The prevention of eating disorders and the role of federal policy* [Online]. Available: www.apa.org/ppo/david.html.

Hodgins, D. C., & El, G. N. (1992). More data on the Addiction Severity Index: Reliability and validity with the mentally ill substance abuser. *Journal of Nervous and Mental Disorders, 180,* 197–201.

Hogarty, G. E., Anderson, C. M., Reiss, D. J., Kornblith, S. J., Greenwald, D. P., Ulrich, R. F., & Carter, M. (1991). Family psychoeducation, social skills training, and maintenance chemotherapy in the aftercare treatment of schizophrenia: II. Two-year effects of a controlled study on relapse and adjustment. *Archives of General Psychiatry, 48,* 340–347.

Hogarty, G. E., McEvoy, J. P., Munetz, M., DiBarry, A. L., Bartone, P., Cather, R., Cooley, S. J., Ulneb, R. E., Carter, M., & Madonia, M. J. (1988). Dose of fluphenazine, familial expressed emotion, and outcome in schizophrenia: Results of a two-year controlled study. *Archives of General Psychiatry, 45,* 797–805.

Holmes, T. H., & Rahe, R. H. (1967). The social readjustment rating scale. *Journal of Psychosomatic Research, 11,* 213–218.

Horowitz, A., Wilner, N., & Alvarez, W. (1979). Impact of Event Scale 4: A measure of subjective stress. *Psychological Medicine, 41,* 209–218.

Hughes, C. P., Berg, L., Danziger, W. L., Coben, L. A., & Martin, R. L. (1982). A new clinical scale for the staging of dementia. *British Journal of Psychiatry, 140,* 566–572.

Kaetner, E., Rosen, L., & Appel, P. (1977). Patterns of drug abuse: Relationships with ethnicity, sensation-seeking and anxiety. *Journal of Consulting and Clinical Psychology, 45,* 462–468.

Kaminer, Y., Bukstein, O. G., & Tarter, R. E. (1991). The Teen Addiction Severity Index: Rationale and reliability. *International Journal of Addictions, 26,* 219–226.

Kaminer, Y., Wagner, E., Plummer, B., & Seifer, R. (1993). Validation of the Teen Addiction Severity Index (T-ASI). *American Journal of Addictions, 2,* 250–254.

Kanoy, R. C., Johnson, B. W., & Kanoy, K. W. (1980). Locus of control and self-concept in achieving and underachieving bright elementary students. *Psychology in Schools, 17,* 395–399.

Kaplan, K. J., & Harrow, M. (1996). Positive and negative symptoms as risk factors for late suicidal activity in schizophrenics versus depressives. *Suicide and Life-Threatening Behavior, 26,* 105–121.

Kaplan, K. J., & Harrow, M. (1999). Psychosis and functioning as risk factors for later suicidal activity among schizophrenic and schizoaffective patients: A disease-based interactive model. *Suicide and Life-Threatening Behavior, 29,* 10–24.

Kaufman, J., Birmaher, B., Brent, D., Rao, U., Flynn, C., Mareci, P., Williamson, D., & Ryan, N. (1997). Schedule for Affective Disorders and Schizophrenia for School-Age Children—Present and Lifetime Version (K-SADS-PL): Initial reliability and validity data. *Journal of the American Academy of Child & Adolescent Psychiatry, 36,* 980–988.

Kay, S. R., Fiszbein, A., & Opler, L. A. (1987). The Positive and Negative Syndrome Scale (PANSS) for schizophrenia. *Schizophrenia Bulletin, 13,* 261–276.

Kazdin, A. E., French, N. H., Esveldt-Dawson, K., & Sherick, R. B. (1983). Hopelessness, depression, and suicidal intent among psychiatrically disturbed inpatient children. *Journal of Consulting and Clinical Psychology, 51,* 504–510.

Keane, T. M., Caddell, J. M., & Taylor, K. L. (1988). Mississippi Scale for Combat-Related Posttraumatic Stress Disorder: Three studies in reliability and validity. *Journal of Consulting and Clinical Psychology, 56,* 85–90.

Kellner, R., Slocumb, J., Wiggins, R. N., Abbott, P. J., Winslow, W. W., & Pathak, D. (1985). Hostility, somatic symptoms, and hypochondriacal fears and beliefs. *Journal of Nervous and Mental Disease, 173,* 554–560.

Kerns, R. D., Turk, D. C., & Rudy, T. E. (1985). The West Haven–Yale Multidimensional Pain Inventory. *Pain, 23,* 345–356.

Kessler, R. C., McGonagle, K. A., Zhao, S., Nelson, C. B., Hughes, M., Eshleman, S., Whittchen, H. U., & Kendler, K. S. (1994). Lifetime and 12-month prevalence of DSM III-R psychiatric disorders in the United States. *Archives of General Psychiatry, 51,* 8–19.

Kopelowicz, A. (1998). Adapting social skills training for Latinos with schizophrenia. *International Review of Psychiatry, 10*(1), 47–51.

Lancon, C., Auquier, P., Nayt, G., & Reine, G. (2000). Stability of the five-factor structure of the Positive and Negative Syndrome Scale (PANSS). *Schizophrenia Research, 42,* 231–239.

Landale, N. S., & Oropesa, R. S. (1999). Does Americanization have adverse effects on health?: Stress, health habits, and infant health outcomes among Puerto Ricans. *Social Forces, 78,* 613–642.

Lawton, M. P., Rajagopal, D., Broday, E., & Kleban, M. H. (1992). The dynamics of caregiving for a demented elder among black and white families. *Journal of Gerontology, 47,* 156–164.

Lazarus, R. S., & Folkman, S. (1984). *Stress, appraisal, and coping.* New York: Springer.

Lazowski, L. E., Miller, F. G., Boye, M. W., & Miller, G. A. (1998). The efficacy of Substance Abuse Subtle Screening Inventory-3 (SASSI-3) in identifying substance dependence disorders in clinical settings. *Journal of Personality Assessment, 71,* 114–128.

Lesieur, H. R., & Blume, S. B. (1987). The South Oaks Gambling Screen (SOGS): A new instrument for the identification of pathological gamblers. *American Journal of Psychiatry, 144,* 1184–1188.

Lesieur, H. R., & Blume, S. B. (1992). Modifying the Addiction Severity Index for use with pathological gamblers. *American Journal on Addictions, 1,* 240–247.

Lesieur, H. R., & Blume, S. B. (1993). Revising the South Oaks Gambling Screen in different settings. *Journal of Gambling Studies, 9,* 213–233.

Liberman, R. P., Eckman, T. A., & Marder, S. R. (2001). Training in social problem solving among persons with schizophrenia. *Psychiatric Services, 52,* 31–33.

Malgady, R. G., & Zayas, L. H. (2001). Cultural and linguistic considerations in psychodiagnosis with Hispanics: The need for an empirically informed process model. *Social Work, 46,* 39–49.

Maloney, M. J., McGuire, J. B., & Daniels, S. R. (1988). Reliability testing of a children's version of the Eating Attitudes Test. *Journal of the American Academy of Child & Adolescent Psychiatry, 27,* 541–543.

Mangum, W. P., Garcia, J. L., Kosberg, J. I., Mullins, L. C., & Barresi, C. M. (1994). Racial/ethnic variations in informal caregiving. *Educational Gerontology, 20,* 715–731.

Mannarino, A. P. (1978). Friendship patterns and self-concept development in preadolescent males. *Journal of Genetic Psychology, 113,* 105–110.

Manwell, L. B., Fleming, M. F., Johnson, K., & Barry, K. L. (1998). Tobacco, alcohol, and drug use in a primary care sample: 90-day prevalence and associated factors. *Journal of Addictive Disorders, 17,* 67–81.

March, J. S., Conners, C. K., Arnold, G., Epstein, J., Parker, J., Hinshaw, S., et al. (1999). The Multidimensional Anxiety Scale for Children (MASC): Confirmatory factor analysis in a pediatric ADHD sample. *Journal of Attention Disorders, 3,* 85–89.

March, J. S., Parker, J., Sullivan, K., Stallings, P., & Conners, C. K. (1997). The Multidimensional Anxiety Scale for Children (MASC): Factor structure, reliability and validity. *Journal of the American Academy of Child & Adolescent Psychiatry, 36,* 554–565.

Mattick, R. P., & Clarke, J. C. (1998). Development and validation of measures of social phobia scrutiny fear and social interaction anxiety. *Behaviour Research & Therapy, 36,* 455–470.

Mayfield, D., McLeod, G., & Hall, P. (1994). The CAGE questionnaire: Validation of a new measure. *American Journal of Psychiatry, 131,* 1121–1123.

McCrady, B. S., & Miller, W. R., Eds. (1993). Research on Alcoholics Anonymous: Opportunities and alternatives. New Brunswick, NJ: Rutgers Center on Alcohol Studies.

McLellan, A. T., Kushner, H., Metzger, D., Peters, R., Smith, I., Grissom, G., et al. (1992). The fifth edition of the Addiction Severity Index. *Journal of Substance Abuse Treatment, 9,* 199–213.

Millon, T., & Davis, R. D. (1993). The Millon Adolescent Personality Inventory and the Millon Adolescent Clinical Inventory. *Journal of Counseling & Development, 71,* 570–574.

Millon, T., & Davis, R. D. (1997). The MCMI-III: Present and future directions. *Journal of Personality Assessment, 68,* 69–85.

Mino, Y., Tanaka, S., Inoue, S., Tsuda, T., Babazono, A., & Aoyama, H. (1995). Expressed emotion components in families of schizophrenic patients in Japan. *International Journal of Mental Health, 24*(2), 38–49.

Moore, S. M., & Ohtsuka, K. (1999). Beliefs about control over gambling among young people, and their relation to problem gambling. *Psychology of Addictive Behaviors, 13,* 339–347.

Morris, J. C. (1993). The Clinical Dementia Rating (CDR): Current version and scoring rules. *Neurology, 43,* 2412–2414.

National Association for Children of Alcoholics (NACoA). (2001). About NACoA [Online]. Available: www.nacoa.net.

Newcomb, M., & Bentler, P. (1986). Substance use and ethnicity: Differential impact of peer and adult models. *The Journal of Psychology, 120,* 83–95.

Overall, J. E., & Gorham, D. R. (1962). The Brief Psychiatric Rating Scale. *Psychological Reports, 10,* 799–812.

Peckman, C. (1999). Eating disorders: Anorexia and bulimia nervosa [Online]. Available: www.noah.cuny.edu/Weldon/eatdisorders.html.

Perrin, S., & Last, C. (1992). Do childhood anxiety measures measure anxiety? *Journal of Abnormal Child Psychology, 20,* 567–578.

Phelan, J. C., Bromet, E. J., & Link, B. G. (1998). Psychiatric illness and family stigma. *Schizophrenia Bulletin, 24,* 115–126.

Phillips, M. R., & Xiong, W. (1995). Expressed emotion in mainland China: Chinese families with schizophrenic patients. *International Journal of Mental Health, 24*(3), 54–75.

Piers, E. V. (1984). *Revised manual for the Piers-Harris Children's Self-Concept Scale.* Los Angeles: Western Psychological Services.

Pomeroy, E. C., & Holleran, L. K. (in press). Chapter 7: Adults. In C. Jordan & C. Franklin (Eds.), *Clinical assessment for social work: Quantitative and qualitative methods.* Chicago: Lyceum Books.

Putnam, F. W., Helmers, K., & Trickett, P. K. (1993). Development, reliability and validity of a child dissociation scale. *Child Abuse & Neglect, 6,* 731–741.

Rabins, P., Mace, N., & Lucas, M. (1982). The impact of dementia on the family. *Journal of the American Medical Association, 248,* 333–338.

Radloff, L. S. (1977). The CES-D Scale: A new self-report depression scale for research in the general population. *Applied Psychological Measurement, 1,* 385–401.

Rapp, C. A. (1998). *The strengths model: Case management with people suffering from severe and persistent mental illness.* New York: Oxford University Press.

Reich, W. (2000). Diagnostic Interview for Children and Adolescents (DICA). *Journal of the American Academy of Child & Adolescent Psychiatry, 39,* 59–66.

Reynolds, W. M., & Gould, J. W. (1981). A psychometric investigation of the standard and short form Beck Depression Inventory. *Journal of Consulting and Clinical Psychology, 49,* 306–307.

Robertsson, B. (1999). Assessment scales in delirium. *Dementia & Geriatric Cognitive Disorders, 10,* 368–379.

Rotheram-Borus, M. J., & Hunter, J. (1994). Suicidal behavior and gay-related stress among gay and bisexual male adolescents. *Journal of Adolescent Research, 9,* 498–509.

Roy, A., Mazonson, A., & Pickar, D. (1984). Attempted suicide in chronic schizophrenia. *British Journal of Psychiatry, 144,* 303–306.

Rubin, A., & Babbie, E. (2001). *Research methods for social work* (4th ed.). Belmont, CA: Wadsworth/Thomson Learning.

Rust, J., & Golombok, S. (1986). The GRISS: A psychometric instrument for the assessment of sexual dysfunction. *Archives of Sexual Behavior, 15,* 157–165.

Saldana, D. H. (1994). Acculturative stress: Minority status and distress. *Hispanic Journal of Behavioral Sciences, 16,* 117–125.

Sartorius, N., Jablensky, A., Korten, A., Ernberg, G., Anker, M., Cooper, J. E., et al. (1986). Early manifestations and first contact incidence of schizophrenia in different cultures: A preliminary report on the initial evaluation of the WHO Collaborative Study on Determinants of Outcome of Severe Mental Disorder. *Psychological Medicine, 16,* 900–928.

SASSI Institute. (1997). *Substance Abuse Subtle Screening Inventory—3 manual.* Springville, IN: Author.

SASSI Institute. (2001). *Substance Abuse Subtle Screening Inventory—Adolescent Version 2 manual.* Springville, IN: Author.

Schwartz, R. C., & Cohen, B. N. (2001). Risk factors for suicidality among clients with schizophrenia. *Journal of Counseling & Development, 79,* 314–320.

Scott, S. (1999). Fragmented selves in late modernity: Making sociological sense of multiple personalities. *The Sociological Review, 47,* 431–460.

Selzer, M. L. (1971). The Michigan Alcoholism Screening Test: The quest for a new diagnostic instrument. *American Journal of Psychiatry, 127,* 89–94.

Shaffer, D., Fisher, P., Lucas, C. P., Dulcan, M. K., & Schwab-Stone, M. E. (2000). NIMH Diagnostic Interview Schedule for Children—Version IV (NIMH DISC-IV): Description, differences from previous versions, and reliability of some common diagnoses. *Journal of the American Academy of Child & Adolescent Psychiatry, 39,* 28–38.

Shugar, G., Schertzer, S., Toner, B. B., & di Gasbarro, J. (1992). Development, use, and factor analysis of a self-report inventory for mania. *Comparative Psychiatry, 33,* 325–331.

Skinner, H. A. (1982). The Drug Abuse Screening Test. *Addictive Behaviors, 7,* 363–371.

Slavin, L. A., Ranier, K. L., McCreary, M. L., & Gowda, K. K. (1991). Toward a multicultural model of the stress process. *Journal of Counseling and Development, 70,* 156–163.

Sparrow, S., Balla, D., & Chicchetti, D. (1984). *Vineland Adaptive Behavior Scale: Interview edition, survey form.* Circle Pines, MN: American Guidance Service, Inc.

Speilberger, C. D. (1983). *Manual for the State-Trait Anxiety Inventory for Children.* Palo Alto, CA: Consulting Psychologists Press.

Speilberger, C. D., Gorsuch, R. L., Lushene, R. D., Vagg, P. R., & Jacobs, G. A. (1983). *Manual for the State-Trait Anxiety Inventory.* Palo Alto, CA: Consulting Psychologists Press.

Substance Abuse and Mental Health Services Administration (SAMHSA), Office of Applied Statistics (OAS). (2000). *Summary of findings from the 2000 National Household Survey on Drug Abuse* [Online]. Available: www.samhsa .gov/oas/NHSDA/2kNHSDA/cover.htm.

Sullivan, J. T., Sykora, K., Schneiderman, J., Naranjo, C. A., & Sellers, E. M. (1989). Assessment of alcohol withdrawal: The revised Clinical Institute Withdrawal Assessment for Alcohol scale (CIWA-AR). *British Journal of Addiction, 84,* 1353–1357.

Thata, R., & Srinivasan, T. N. (2000). How stigmatizing is schizophrenia in India? *International Journal of Social Psychiatry, 46*(2), 135–142.

Touliatos, J., Perlmutter, B. F., & Straus, M. A. (Eds.) (1990). *Handbook of family measurement techniques.* Newbury Park, CA: Sage.

Vanderlinden, J., Van Dyck, R., Vertommen, H., Vandereycken, W., & Verkes, R. J. (1993). The Dissociation Questionnaire (DIS-Q): Development and characteristics of a new self-report questionnaire. *Clinical Psychology & Psychotherapy, 1,* 21–27.

Walker, L. S., Garber, J., & Greene, J. W. (1991). Somatization symptoms in pediatric abdominal pain patients: Relation to chronicity of abdominal pain and parent somatization. *Journal of Abnormal Child Psychology, 19,* 379–394.

Walker, L. S., Garber, J., & Greene, J. W. (1993). Psychosocial correlates of recurrent childhood pain: A comparison of pediatric patients with recurrent abdominal pain, organic illness and psychiatric disorders. *Journal of Abnormal Psychology, 102,* 248–258.

Wallace, J. M., & Bachman, J. G. (1993). Validity of self-reports in student based studies on minority populations: Issues and concerns. In M. R. de la Rosa & J. R. Adrados (Eds.), *Drug abuse among minority youth: Advances in research and methodology* (NIDA Research Monograph 130, pp. 167–200). Rockville, MD: National Institute on Drug Abuse.

Watson, C. G. (1990). Psychometric posttraumatic stress disorder measurement techniques: A review. *Psychological Assessment, 2,* 460–469.

Wechsler, D. (1989). *Wechsler Preschool and Primary Scales of Intelligence—Revised.* San Antonio, TX: Psychological Corporation.

Wechsler, D. (1991). *Wechsler Intelligence Scale for Children—Third Edition.* San Antonio, TX: Psychological Corporation.

Wegscheider, S. (1981). *Another chance.* Palo Alto, CA: Science and Behavior Books.

Weller, E. B., Weller, R. A., Fristad, M. A., Rooney, J. T., & Schecter, J. (2000). Children's Interview for Psychiatric Syndromes (CHIPS). *Journal of the American Academy of Child & Adolescent Psychiatry, 39,* 76–84.

Woodrow Wilson International Center for Scholars. (2000). Eating disorders in children. *The Wilson Quarterly, 24*(3), 10.

Young, R., Biggs, J., & Myers, D. (1978). A rating scale for mania: Reliability, validity and sensitivity. *British Journal of Psychiatry, 133,* 429–435.